CANADIAN POLICE WORK

THIRD EDITION

CURT T. GRIFFITHS

SIMON FRASER UNIVERSITY

NELSON / EDUCATION

NELSON / EDUCATION

Canadian Police Work, Third Edition
by Curt T. Griffiths

Vice President, Editorial Higher Education:
Anne Williams

Executive Editor:
Lenore Taylor-Atkins

Marketing Manager:
Terry Fedorkiw

Developmental Editor:
Caroline Winter

Photo Researcher:
Natalie Russell

Permissions Coordinator:
Natalie Russell

Content Production Manager:
Lila Campbell

Production Service:
Cenveo Publisher Services

Copy Editor:
Matthew Kudelka

Proofreaders:
Erin Moore and Mariko Obokata

Indexer:
Robert Swanson

Manufacturing Manager:
Joanne McNeil

Design Director:
Ken Phipps

Managing Designer:
Franca Amore

Interior Design:
Andrew Adams

Chapter Opener and Box Feature Image:
HPCPHOTO/iStockphoto.com

Cover Design:
Dianna Little

Cover Image:
Vancouver Police Department

Compositor:
Cenveo Publisher Services

Library and Archives Canada Cataloguing in Publication Data

Griffiths, Curt T. (Curt Taylor), 1948–
    Canadian police work/
Curt T. Griffiths.—3rd ed.

Includes bibliographical references and index.
ISBN 978-0-17-650658-2

    1. Police—Canada. 2. Police administration—Canada. 3. Law enforcement—Canada. I. Title.

HV8157.G756 2012
363.2'30971   C2011-908697-2

ISBN-13: 978-0-17-650658-2
ISBN-10: 0-17-650658-6

Brief Contents

Contents

Chapter 4: The Police Occupation   80

Chapter 10: Case Investigation   246

Preface to the Third Edition

Policing is perhaps the most high-profile, dynamic, and, oftentimes, controversial component of the Canadian criminal justice system. It is police officers who respond to criminal offences, disorder, and conflict in the community. How police services and police officers respond to the multifaceted demands that are placed on them affects individual citizens and their neighbourhoods and communities, as well as officers and the police services within which they work. Police are the only agents of the criminal justice system with whom most Canadians ever have contact.

In contrast to personnel in other components of the justice system, police officers work in environments that are always changing. Among their criminal justice coworkers, police officers are the most likely to be shot at, assaulted, criticized, praised, and relied on in times of crisis. Furthermore, it is police officers who are most likely to find themselves caught in personal and social conflicts, civil disobedience, conflicting and often unrealistic community expectations, and the political agendas of senior police administrators, government leaders, and community interest groups. They must often make decisions in a split second, with little time for reflection and deliberation.

These unique attributes of police work explain the ongoing popularity of movies and TV series featuring police. These same attributes also are responsible for the myths and misunderstandings that surround police work. And geography, demographics, and cultural diversity combine to make the environments in which police work is carried out more diverse in Canada than anywhere else in the world.

The decisions of police officers are highly visible, and the consequences of those decisions can be significant. The power to use lethal force distinguishes the police from most other criminal justice personnel. Canadian police have traditionally enjoyed high levels of public support, yet there are ongoing tensions between the need for the police to have sufficient authority to maintain law and order, and the rights of citizens guaranteed by the Charter of Rights and Freedoms. It is at this knife edge that many of the flashpoints of policing in Canadian society develop.

This, the third edition of *Canadian Police Work*, updates and extends the materials contained in the second edition. An attempt has been made to make the text more comprehensive while at the same time expanding coverage of various policing issues. This edition of the text contains three new chapters: "Police Governance and Accountability," "Police Ethics and Professionalism," and "Police Work in a Diverse Society." The challenge has been to incorporate new materials while not significantly increasing the page count. In an introductory-level text, it is not possible to provide detailed coverage of all areas of Canadian police work.

The text attempts to strike a balance between being an academic treatise on the police and addressing the more applied aspects of policing. To this end, both current research findings and case examples from the field are presented. An attempt has been made to avoid the more sensational portrayals of policing so often encountered in the media and at the same time to avoid the sterility that is so often evident in academic studies. One objective of this edition is the same as in the first two editions: to close what is often a wide gap between scholarly writing on policing and the experiences of police officers.

Any examination of police work in Canada is hindered by a paucity of scholarly research. Canada lacks a robust program of research support that would facilitate field research into the many facets of police work.

A variety of techniques have been incorporated into the text in an effort to make it more "user friendly": academic and police jargon has been held to a minimum, as have notes and exhaustive citations; **Research Files** provide concise and up-to-date information on the latest research findings; **Police Files** present materials on actual incidents. Near the end of each chapter, there are **At Issue** scenarios that challenge the reader to consider key issues in Canadian police work.

Each chapter ends with a Key Points Review and Key Term Questions. These are designed to ensure that students understand the important materials presented in each chapter. The reader will also note that references are now placed at the end of each chapter. As befits an introductory-level text, there are extensive source references from the published literature on policing. These will facilitate a more in-depth exploration of the topics covered in the text.

The extent to which the text captures the essential dimensions of Canadian police work while also stimulating students will be determined largely by the instructors who adopt it and by the students who read it. I encourage instructors and students to provide feedback about the book and suggestions as to how it can be improved. Please send your comments, suggestions, and queries to griffith@sfu.ca.

Thanks.
Curt Taylor Griffiths
Vancouver, British Columbia
February, 2012

Acknowledgments

I would like to acknowledge the many people in the field of policing who have contributed information and ideas that have been incorporated into this text. Special thanks to Deputy Chief Constable Doug LePard, Deputy Chief Adam Palmer, Staff Sergeant Earl Andersen, and Special Constable Ryan Prox, all of the Vancouver Police Department; Staff Sgt. Baltej Dhillon, E Division RCMP (BC); Inspector Rick Grosul, K Division RCMP (Alberta); Superintendent Peter Clark, Commanding Officer M Division (Yukon); Vern White, Chief Constable, Ottawa Police Service; Aart Garssen, District Commander, Nijmegen, Netherlands. Also, special thanks to Dr. Rick Parent, my colleague in the School of Criminology at Simon Fraser University.

I would also like to thank the external reviewers for their insightful recommendations for improving the text, many of which have been incorporated into this edition:

> Dr. Ashley Carver, Department of Sociology and Criminology,
>   Saint Mary's University
> Leo de Jourdan, Canadore College
> Dr. Rick Parent, Simon Fraser University, School of Criminology
> John Oke, triOS College
> Mike Massine, Victoria, British Columbia
> Peter Maher, Georgian College

As always, it has been a pleasure to work with the professionals at Nelson, whose energy and enthusiasm helped make it happen. And a special thanks to the world's best manuscript editor, Matthew Kudelka, for his outstanding work.

About the Author

Curt T. Griffiths is a Professor and Coordinator of the Police Studies Program in the School of Criminology at Simon Fraser University.

CANADIAN POLICE WORK
THIRD EDITION

Chapter 1

The Origins and Evolution of Police Work

Learning Objectives

After reading this chapter, you should be able to:

- Discuss the origins, structure, and evolution of policing in England

- Discuss the controversy that surrounded the creation of the first police force in England

- Identify the policing principles of Sir Robert Peel

- Describe the evolution of police work in Canada

- Identify the roles of the early municipal and provincial police and the RCMP

- Describe the key developments in Canadian police work during the late twentieth and early twenty-first centuries

Key Terms

best practices   21
collaborative policing   23
environmental scan   21
frankpledge system   4
hue and cry   3
Justice of the Peace Act
    (1361)   5

Metropolitan Police Act
    (1829)   6
pluralization of policing   23
Sir Robert Peel   6
Statute of Winchester
    (1285)   5

The development of policing in Canada was strongly influenced by the system of policing that emerged in England in the early 1800s. Canadian policing, however, has a unique history and has evolved so that its structure today is quite distinct from those of its counterparts in England and the United States.

THE ORIGINS OF POLICING

Full-time police forces, operating under the state's authority and enforcing sets of codified laws, are a relatively recent phenomenon. Prior to the emergence of centralized states with codified laws, order within and among groups was maintained through systems of self-policing. Personal, group, or tribal retaliation was applied against those whose behaviour contravened established folkways and customs. In these rural, agrarian societies, which were primarily concerned with day-to-day survival, there were no individuals or organizations charged with the task of enforcing law.

As societies increased in complexity, however, the effectiveness of these self-policing arrangements diminished. Systems of codified laws were enacted— the Hammurabi Code in 1200 BC and similar codes of law during the Shang (1500 BC) and Chou (1000 BC) Dynasties. These codes of law, enforced by military authority, outlined prescribed rules of conduct as well as penalties for noncompliance. The enactment of these codes of law signalled a shift in the enforcement of conduct from the individual and group level to that of centralized authority.

Centuries later, in the Greek city-states and in the Roman Empire, similar developments occurred. In Greece there emerged a system of self-policing called "kin police." Roman law was codified in the Law of the Twelve Tablets (450 BC), and officials were assigned the task of enforcing laws. At the height of the Roman Empire there were distinct police forces. In both Greece and the Roman Empire it was the military who were charged with policing; later on, the Romans were the first to utilize a nonmilitary unit, the *vigiles*, whose task it was to fight fires and to help maintain order. The *vigiles* in the Roman Empire and the kin police in the Greek city-states were early examples of policing, but it was in England that policing was to evolve into an institution. Developments there would have a profound influence on Canadian policing.

The Development of Policing in England

Before the Industrial Revolution and the development of capitalism, England was a feudal, village society. Policing was a community responsibility (hold this thought until we return to a discussion of policing in the early twenty-first century). Order was maintained under the principle of **hue and cry**, according to which every able-bodied man was responsible for assisting in the pursuit and apprehension of law violators. Failure to respond to the hue and cry could result in punishment of the derelict citizen, often equal to that imposed on the lawbreaker.

Law enforcement in England can be traced back to the reign of Alfred the Great (872–901). Lacking a standing army to maintain order, and lacking the funds to create a force specifically for peacekeeping, Alfred instituted

hue and cry
in early England, the requirement that able-bodied men assist the police

the **frankpledge system**. This system was based on the principle that every individual was responsible to his neighbours. Under the frankpledge system, every free man between fifteen and sixty was required to enroll in a grouping of ten families, called a tything. In each tything, a tythingman was responsible for keeping order. The other members were required to report crimes to the tythingman and to respond to his hue and cry (most often, "Halt! Who goes there?"). The forerunner of the English police officer, then, was the tythingman.

The tythingman was an elected community spokesman and was responsible for all aspects of local government within his community.[1] He also had the authority to collect fines from those charged with breaching the peace, as well as to demand surety or bail. Each adult male in the community was required to accept a turn as tythingman.

As villages grew, tythings were formed into "hundreds" (groups of ten tyths), each headed by a "hundredman." Constables, generally considered to be the first real police officers, were appointed by local noblemen and placed in charge of the equipment and weapons of the hundred. Hundreds were combined to form shires (parishes or counties), which were administered by officials known as "shire-reeves" (sheriffs). These were appointed by the king to represent his interests and to uphold the Crown's authority. The shire-reeve was invested with considerable military, civil, and judicial powers and made periodic visits to each hundred to ensure that the system of local policing was operating properly.

	Shire-Reeve		
	Hundredman	Hundredman	
Tythingman	Tythingman	Tythingman	Tythingman

This localized system of crime control was based on the concept that all individuals were responsible for one another.

The frankpledge system invested the tythingmen and hundredmen with a certain amount of authority to maintain community order. Another important attribute of this system is that it was organized "from the ground up." The tythingmen and hundredmen were locally chosen, were responsible to the community, and could be removed for dereliction of duty. This system was in sharp contrast to the policing arrangements that existed in continental Europe, where the police were directly attached to centralized autocracies.

After the Normans invaded England in 1066, the frankpledge system was continued by William the Conqueror. Around this time, though, there was movement away from community responsibility for maintaining peace (as established by the tything system) toward a concept of "state" responsibility. To help implement Norman policing, the shire-reeves were invested with considerable powers, which were often used to collect unjust and oppressive fines and taxes from the community. Military officers were made responsible for maintaining order in specific districts.

By 1252, during the reign of Henry III, the title of constable was being given to the local law enforcement officers previously known as tythingmen, and a "watch and ward" system had been introduced in communities to maintain order. The watch-and-ward system provided for two watchmen to supplement the duties of the constable: "A watch of up to sixteen men...was to be stationed at every gate of a walled town between sunset and sunrise, and the watchmen were given the power to arrest strangers during the hours of darkness."[2] All able-bodied men in the town were required to serve a term on watch, which reinforced their responsibility to participate in policing.

By the time the Police Act was passed in 1829, two important statutes had been enacted. The **Statute of Winchester**, passed in 1285, made policing a community responsibility. It called for the formation of village night watches, which were to support the local constables in their duties and to arrest those who were disruptive or who violated the law. This statute assigned to the hundred responsibility for all offences committed within it, revived the hue and cry, and reinforced the watch-and-ward system. In 1361 the **Justice of the Peace Act** centralized peacekeeping duties under justices of the peace, who were appointed directly by the king and who enjoyed stronger authority and greater powers than the constables. The justice of the peace replaced the shire-reeve as peace officer and also acted in a judicial capacity. For the first time, then, the police had been subordinated to the judiciary. This arrangement resulted in considerable injustice and corruption.

By the 1500s the system of community-based policing was beginning to deteriorate, mainly because of the growth of cities such as London, the increased mobility of the population, and the beginnings of the shift from an agricultural economy to one based on industry. As communities were transformed by these events, individuals avoided serving as constables, paying others to assume their duties. This had disastrous consequences, as it was often only the unemployed and the uneducated who were willing to take on the constables' duties. The old system of community-based policing was thereby undermined.

As a consequence of the profound changes taking place in English society, the increasing corruption of the justices of the peace, and the reluctance of townspeople to serve as constables, by the 1800s many towns and cities, including London, were virtually unpoliced. Justices of the peace had corrupted the system of criminal justice, and it was obvious that the tything system, the hue and cry, and the office of constable were failing to manage the changes happening in English society. Merchants and industrialists increasingly feared the "dangerous classes" and the threat they posed to law and order. Businessmen began to employ private police to protect their establishments and to help maintain order. It is against this backdrop—the deterioration of community-based policing, and the widening gap between the propertied classes and the landless peasantry—that modern policing as we know it developed.

The Emergence of Modern Policing

England's first organized body of police was established in the mid-1700s by Henry Fielding, a justice of the peace who was also a novelist and playwright. To enforce the decisions of his court and to address the growing problem of disorder, Fielding created the Bow Street Runners, named after the street on which his court was located. These constables, who were adequately paid so that they would not take bribes, were equipped with batons, handcuffs, and uniforms. Although Fielding had recruited men of high calibre and paid them well, the force's efforts were not enough to stem the rising tide of social disorder and chaos generated by the emerging Industrial Revolution.

Statute of Winchester (1285)
a statute that made policing a community responsibility

Justice of the Peace Act (1361)
centralized peacekeeping duties under justices of the peace

Sir Robert Peel
founded the first organized police service

During the late 1700s and early 1800s, London faced a series of riots, many of which were started by labourers protesting rising prices and the displacement of workers by increased mechanization. Yet there continued to be strong resistance to the idea of forming an organized, twenty-four-hour police force. In 1822 the Home Secretary, **Sir Robert Peel**, set out to establish a full-time police force. His initial attempts to create a metropolitan police force were repeatedly voted down. Between 1822 and 1828, no fewer than seventeen parliamentary subcommittees studied the need to reform the system of law enforcement. One committee report stated: "In a free society, there should only be rational and humane laws, making a police force unnecessary."[3]

For all the widespread opposition to the formation of a police force, by the late 1820s—at least among the propertied classes—the fear of crime and disorder had overshadowed the potential threat to liberty inherent in organized police units. In 1829 the **Metropolitan Police Act** was enacted, establishing a full-time, unarmed police force of one thousand men in London. Among the largely skeptical public, Peel's new officers were known derisively as "Bobbies" or "Peelers."

Metropolitan Police Act (1829)
established a full-time, unarmed police force in London

The public and many politicians were concerned about the power that would be vested in a formal police force, and when Peel finally won acceptance of his police plan for London, he was denounced as a potential dictator. "Reform!...No Peel! No new police!...No Standing Armies!" So chanted the crowds in 1830 as Londoners expressed their opposition to the new Metropolitan Police Force.[4] When it came time to vote on a budget for Peel's new police force in the House of Lords, one member stated: "What I really don't want to see is an efficient police, for an efficient police is a power—a power which we should not have outside the Crown itself."[5] Similar concerns were expressed in opposition to the expansion of the RCMP in Canada in the early 1900s.

Peel attempted to legitimize the new police force by arguing that the police would serve the interests of all citizens; that the police would include the prevention of crime as part of their mandate; and that the force's officers would be recruited from the working class. In a determined effort to create a professional police force and to reduce public suspicion and distrust of the police, he established high standards of recruitment and training and selected constables from the community. He also introduced the concept of community police stations. In contrast to the local watchmen who preceded them, the new police were to be proactive rather than reactive and were to engage in crime prevention activities. As well, the "new" police wore uniforms, and these were blue, in contrast to the red worn by the military.[6] This can be viewed as the first attempt at community policing by an organized police service.

In addition, Peel formulated several principles for law enforcement, which even today are viewed as the basis for community policing. These principles were captured by Charles Reith (1956) in *A New Study of Police History* (see Box 1.1).[7] These principles will provide the basis for much of the discussion throughout the rest of this book.

Box 1.1

The Principles of Sir Robert Peel

1. The basic mission of the police is to prevent crime and disorder.
2. The ability of the police to perform their duties depends upon public approval of their actions.
3. Police must secure the cooperation of the public in voluntary observance of the law in order to secure and maintain the respect of the public.
4. The degree of public cooperation with police diminishes proportionately to the necessity of the use of physical force.
5. Police maintain public favour by constantly demonstrating absolute impartial service, not by catering to public opinion.
6. Police should use physical force only to the extent necessary to ensure compliance with the law or to restore order only after persuasion, advice, and warnings are insufficient.
7. Police should maintain a relationship with the public that is based on the fact that the police are the public and the public are the police.
8. Police should direct their actions toward their functions and not appear to usurp the powers of the judiciary.
9. The test of police efficiency is the absence of crime and disorder.

Peel's police force generally succeeded in reducing the amount of crime in London. In 1865, Parliament passed an act that required all towns in England to establish their own police forces. As these forces were established throughout the country, justices of the peace gave up their law enforcement duties and focused their efforts solely on judicial activities.

Policing in England, then, was based on community control. In contrast, European police forces tended to be centralized, nationalized, and militarized. As the Canadian police scholar Chris Murphy has written: "The public police model created in England rejected secretive and authoritarian continental policing, developing instead a police model compatible with past community policing practices and growing democratic values."[8]

Early Private Police

Private security services are hardly a modern invention. In fact, they played a major role in policing communities in these early days. Some even predated the London Metropolitan Police. For example, the Bow Street Runners were supported in part by private contracts, and one Patrick Colquhoun formed the Thames River Police, the main costs of which were borne by merchants. Because of its success, this private police force was later converted into a public police force.

THE EVOLUTION OF POLICE WORK IN CANADA

Early Municipal Police

A number of important events have shaped Canadian policing. In many respects, the emergence of Canadian policing during the nineteenth century closely mirrored the development of systems of punishment and corrections.

In the earliest days, law enforcement in communities was carried out informally by community residents. In Halifax, for example, tavern owners were charged with maintaining order. Later, Halifax and other eastern port cities such as St. John's relied on militias and the navy, while the emptier regions of the country remained largely unpoliced. These arrangements were ultimately insufficient to meet the problems of an increasingly urbanized and industrialized society.

Newfoundland's history highlights the types of problems with law and order that existed in early settlements, as well as the solutions applied to them. In St. John's in the 1600s, criminal bands were committing crimes with impunity. Complaints by fishermen resulted in the first Court of Justice in North America, at Trinity Bay. It was headed by Captain Richard Whitbourne under the authority of the English High Court of Admiralty. This early attempt to maintain order and combat crime was a failure, so in 1634 the English authorities appointed "fishing admirals," captains of fishing vessels who were empowered to settle disputes.

This effort also largely failed. These admirals were untrained and were often as disorderly as those they sought to control: "Being untrained men, they were ill-fitted to carry out the functions of the law properly, and they abused their power by a particularly corrupt administration of the laws. In their judicial character, they would decide cases, according to their caprice, over a bottle of rum; and frequently would inflict summary punishment by flogging the culprit with a rope's end."[9]

So in 1792 a Royal Proclamation was issued that authorized the Governor of Newfoundland to appoint justices of the peace and constables, although no regulations governing their supervision were set down until many years later.

Early police work in Canada was characterized by a considerable degree of diversity. Before Confederation in 1867, each region of the country had its own policing arrangements, which reflected the size of settlements, the characteristics of the population, and the needs of specific communities. In areas settled by the French, for example, major town centres were policed under the traditional French system of militia captains. In Upper Canada, in contrast, the British influence was clear; there, a system developed based on the common law and carried out by sheriffs, high constables, constables, and justices of the peace.

The first police constables were appointed in Quebec City around 1651;[10] in Upper Canada (now Ontario), they appeared in the early 1800s. A policing system was also introduced in Montreal in the mid-1600s, though its main purpose was to protect the settlement from attacks by the Iroquois. It is likely that the first constables in Quebec City served mainly as night watchmen. It was not until justices of the peace were appointed in 1673 that these constables assumed law enforcement responsibilities.

The conquest of New France by the British in 1759 radically altered the French-influenced system of policing that had been developing in Lower

Canada. In 1787 an ordinance was passed that authorized justices of the peace in Montreal and Quebec to appoint individuals to help carry out court orders and to maintain order. This legislation introduced the position of constable, and thus served as a model for policing throughout the province.

In Upper Canada, the British settlers implemented a legal system similar to that of England. In 1792 the English common law was made the law of Upper Canada, and in 1793 the Parish and Town Officers Act was passed by the local assembly. This act provided for the appointment of high constables for each district; these men in turn were to appoint citizens to serve as unpaid constables in each parish and township in that district. In 1858, legislation was passed in Upper Canada that authorized towns and cities to create boards of commissioners to oversee police forces.

The 1858 legislation was intended to expand the system of policing throughout Upper Canada. However, community officials and residents did not regard crime as a serious problem; nor did they view as a high priority the development of crime control structures such as police forces and jails.

In 1845 a bylaw in the newly incorporated town of St. Catharines provided for "poundkeepers and constables," citizen volunteers who would provide assistance when required. The activities of this "police force" were supervised by a police board, which also served as the town council. The volunteers were paid according to a fee schedule—for example, 5 shillings for issuing a summons, making an arrest under a warrant, or assisting in an arrest. Escorting a prisoner to jail paid 15 shillings. The town hired its first full-time police officers in 1856.

Townspeople were often reluctant to serve as constables. While many of the charters establishing towns required that policing systems be created, these communities were often reluctant to do so unless confronted with serious disorder. Historians have pointed out that communities and settlements created formal police forces only when they saw a clear need to do so. Precisely for this reason, early attempts to establish a formal system of justice, including police, met with failure in Upper Canada and Quebec.[11] This illustrates one of the key factors in the emergence of formal policing: a general hesitancy in both England and early Canada to create police forces that had authority and power over the populace. Furthermore, when such forces were created, a great deal of criticism was often directed toward them. Similar concerns were to be expressed about the expansion of the then North-West Mounted Police (NWMP) into provincial and municipal policing.

During the early 1800s, though, concerns about crime and the "criminal classes" were growing. Whether this shift in attitude was due to an actual increase in the amount and seriousness of crime or merely a function of townspeople's perceptions that crime was increasing has been the subject of considerable scholarly debate. What *is* clear is that governments took a much more proactive approach to creating systems for controlling crime—including police forces.

Again, Newfoundland provides a good illustration of the changes occurring around this time. In the early 1800s, the police force in St. John's consisted of tavern keepers, who performed policing duties in return for their business licences. In 1848 the first night watch system was established in the city, consisting of sixteen special constables and four constables under the supervision of a high constable. These officers were the predecessors of the Royal Newfoundland Constabulary, formed in 1872.

Similar developments were taking place in Upper Canada. By 1835, as noted earlier, Toronto had a full-time police force of six men to replace the night watch system. Given the vast distances and sparse populations, municipal police forces developed much later in the western parts of Canada. This country's first territorial police force was established in 1858 in what is now British Columbia.

The Functions and Effectiveness of Early Municipal Police

When municipalities did appoint police constables, they generally had other duties as well. In Sudbury, Ontario, for example, the first constable was also the jailer, as well as a tax collector, sanitary inspector, truant officer, fire department engineer, bailiff, chimney inspector, and animal pound caretaker.[12] 1826, Kingston appointed its first paid constable, one Henry Wilkinson, who also held the position of street surveyor.

The early municipal police forces generally had a three-part mandate: (1) to police conflicts between ethnic groups, and between labourers and their employers; (2) to maintain moral standards by enforcing laws against drunkenness, prostitution, and gambling; and (3) to apprehend criminals.[13] Records from the time indicate that the five-man Kingston police force (created in 1841) spent most of its time dealing with the drunken and the disorderly.

Constables in Calgary were responsible for inspecting buildings and roads, and fresh fruits, vegetables, and meat. It was also their duty to issue licences and maintain the animal pound. The first constable appointed in Regina, in 1892, was also required to serve as dogcatcher, sanitation inspector, and fireman.[14] Today, only police officers posted to remote northern communities continue to provide a wide variety of services in addition to policing.

The historical record indicates that early municipal police forces were heavily influenced by politics and patronage. Following its incorporation in 1834, for example, the power to hire police officers in Toronto was held by the city council and individual aldermen could appoint police constables for their ward. One historian has noted: "There were no standards of recruitment and no training, and even though uniforms were first issued in 1837, it was stated at the time by one observer that the Toronto police was 'without uniformity, except in one respect—they were uniformly slovenly.'"[15] The Canadian historian John Weaver describes an all-to-common feature of the Hamilton (Ontario) police department of the day:

> Constable Coulter began inauspiciously. Hired in March 1878, he was fined 10 days pay that November for being found in house of ill fame. After being released from beat duty at midnight, constables Coulter, Sutherland, and Moore paid a visit to Jennie Kennedy's whorehouse and dallied for an hour. A little over a year later, Coulter fell asleep while on duty. In 1882 he paid a fine for disobedience. But he must have had an ability and straightened up, for the commission awarded him a good conduct badge in 1891, appointed him detective in 1895, and in 1911 made him inspector of the detective division.[16]

In Toronto, there were no fewer than twenty-six riots between 1839 and 1860, almost all of them arising from conflicts between rival political factions. Politicians often used the police as a private army against opposition groups.[17] Between 1870 and 1920, the Toronto Police focused their efforts on controlling the "dangerous classes"—lower-class working people:

Control of all aspects of working class people's lives was the goal set before the police…The force strove to curb the more unruly aspects of popular culture, prohibiting bonfires, restraining weekend revels, banning firecrackers, and curbing the activities of "mischievous urchins" who sought to soil the crinoline dresses of ladies on national holidays. Arresting drunks and prosecuting prostitutes became a major focus of Toronto Police activity.[18]

This focus of the Toronto police on issues related more to morals suggests that the crime-fighting role of the police was to develop much later.

In early Canada, when police officers were hired, a high premium was placed on physical attributes. The following describes the approach taken by municipal authorities in Hamilton in 1881:

Applicants lined up and Judge Sinclair asked them to take off their coats. This being done, Sinclair felt "their thighs and sinews," poking them with a finger "in the manner practiced by the gentry from the rural districts when examining a prize bull." Next, the men had to walk about, turning left and right while the commissioners commented on the good and bad points about their backs and shoulders. To measure stamina, five were singled out and asked to jog around council chambers.…The commissioners preferred married men, claiming that they were "steadier." Married men were also less likely than single men to leave town in search of better work.[19]

This passage suggests that, in selecting police constables, a premium was placed on physique, with little thought to providing new recruits with training in conflict resolution (see Chapter 4 for a discussion of modern-day training and recruitment, which is vastly different).

Early municipal police forces were not very effective in maintaining high moral standards or catching criminals. Many departments were notoriously corrupt: "While police forces did have chiefs and men who were honest and bent on doing a good job, many were only interested in getting a share of the wealth that was floating around. Corruption became accepted as a more or less integral part of police work."[20] Police chiefs and police officers took bribes to look the other way, and as a consequence, prostitution, gambling, and crime flourished in cities such as Montreal.

Municipal police officers often carried out their tasks with considerable tolerance. Many looked the other way regarding alcohol use and prostitution. And many were reluctant to involve themselves in strikes either by helping managers force employees back to work or by protecting strikebreakers who were crossing picket lines. In later years, the close ties between municipal police forces and their communities would lead the federal government to suspect that local police could not be trusted to maintain order, especially in situations involving strikes and political demonstrations. For this reason, the federal government often sent in the RCMP as a federal police force, often with disastrous consequences. (This partly explains the long-standing transfer policy of the RCMP, under which officers are regularly moved from one posting to the next.)

It was the North-West Mounted Police (NWMP)—forerunners to the modern-day RCMP—who most often responded to labour unrest in the early

1900s: strikes by coal miners in Nova Scotia and British Columbia, by textile workers in Quebec, by the building trades in Vancouver, and by railway workers in Winnipeg (see Box 1.2 on page 17) and Brockville.

Policing in the West

Police forces did not emerge in western Canada until the mid to late 1800s. In 1858 the West's first organized police force was founded in what is now the province of British Columbia. Modelled on the Royal Irish Constabulary, it was established as a response to the increasing violence and disorder that followed the discovery of gold in the region. This force was the predecessor of the British Columbia Provincial Police (BCPP), which was formed in 1871 when the province joined Confederation. British authorities worried that the United States had territorial ambitions in the area. BCPP officers carried out policing duties, collected revenues and excise taxes, and provided emergency services in communities. Calgary hired its first constable in 1885; Lethbridge appointed its first in 1891. In the absence of police forces, most communities in the West policed themselves. Aboriginal peoples, of course, already had systems of social control as well as mechanisms for sanctioning violations of customary law. These systems were gradually displaced by British law.[21] As settlements grew, they appointed constables, who were paid a small sum for carrying out peacekeeping duties and for controlling disorder, which largely involved drinking, prostitution, and gambling.

A unique feature of policing in the Canadian West was the role played by agents of the Hudson's Bay Company. As late as 1861, the presiding judicial officer of the HBC served as coroner, jailer, sheriff, and chief medical officer. There is little doubt that it was in the best interests of the HBC to maintain peace and order in the West to ensure that there were no disruptions to trade and commerce.[22]

The absence of serious crime was another reason for the late development of policing systems in the West. Except for the disorder surrounding fortune seekers and the whisky traders, the West was less violent in Canada than in the United States. The landscape of the American West was littered with the victims of battles between Native people and the U.S. Cavalry, and the streets of frontier towns were often the scene of "high noon" shootouts. The Canadian West was subdued with considerably less bloodshed, although the outcome of this conflict was the same (the destruction of Aboriginal cultures and communities). However, as discussed below, there were a number of similarities between the NWMP officers who policed the West and the U.S. cavalrymen south of the border.

Early Provincial Police

The emergence of provincial police forces after Confederation was closely linked to the establishment and growth of the federal police force, now known as the RCMP. Under the Constitution Act, 1867, the federal government had the authority to enact criminal law and procedures, while the enforcement of laws and the administration of justice were delegated to the provinces. This meant that provincial governments needed to establish law enforcement agencies, courts, and correctional institutions.

On entry into Confederation, each province enacted legislation to create a provincial police force. This was done by Manitoba and Quebec (1870), British Columbia (1871), Ontario (1909), New Brunswick (1927), Nova Scotia (1928), and Prince Edward Island (1930). In Newfoundland, which did not join Confederation until 1949, the Royal Newfoundland Constabulary had been operating since 1872. A second police force, the Newfoundland Company of Rangers, was formed in 1935.

All of the regions that eventually joined Confederation had police forces. However, the provincial police forces in Alberta, Saskatchewan, and Manitoba experienced a number of difficulties, including poor leadership and a lack of qualified officers. The Saskatchewan Provincial Police (SPP) was beset with so many problems that it became a major embarrassment for the provincial authorities. One police historian has noted that, while many SPP recruits were capable and experienced, others were merely "filling the gap....Some barely understood the words of their oath, while others would have been stumped to spell some of them."[23]

Alberta and Saskatchewan negotiated agreements with the federal government for the services of the Royal North-West Mounted Police (RNWMP). Under contracts signed between Ottawa and the governments of each of those provinces, the RNWMP would serve as the provincial police force under a cost-sharing agreement. There is no evidence in the historical record that these actions by the two provincial governments were ever challenged, although it represented a significant departure from the intent of the Constitution Act. By the late 1920s the provincial forces on the Prairies had been replaced by the RCMP.

Between 1917 and 1950 the Mounties assumed provincial policing responsibilities in all provinces except Quebec and Ontario, which continued to operate the only independent provincial police forces in Canada, along with Newfoundland. On October 13, 1909, an Order-in-Council authorized the immediate formation of the Ontario Provincial Police. The intent was to bring that province's widely dispersed policing services under one administrative umbrella.

Although the Constitution Act clearly gave the provinces the authority to enforce criminal law, in 1868 the federal Parliament passed the Police Act of Canada, which authorized the federal government to establish the Dominion Police Force, with Canada-wide jurisdiction. This force's primary mandate was to protect federal buildings, including Parliament, although it later became involved in enforcing counterfeiting laws and providing security for naval shipyards and other government properties. The Dominion Police Force was absorbed by the RCMP in 1920; the point is, this was the first time a police authority had been created with jurisdiction beyond the municipal level—a precedent that was to provide the basis for today's RCMP.

Early Federal Policing: The Origins and Expansion of the RCMP

The North-West Mounted Police was founded in 1873 to police the vast area known as Rupert's Land, which Canada had purchased from the HBC in 1869. The NWMP were a military-style police force, modelled on the Royal Irish Constabulary rather than on the urban model of police developed by Sir Robert Peel. The allegiance of the force was to the federal government. Murphy and McKenna note that "the RCMP was there to police the locals as an extension of the central government and its officers were only accountable to their commanding officers and not to local public or political authority."[24]

In 1904, the force's name was changed to the Royal North-West Mounted Police; then, in 1920, its name was changed again to the Royal Canadian Mounted Police (RCMP). It was anticipated that as Canada became more urbanized, responsibility for policing would shift to local communities. However, this did not often happen.

The reasons for the founding of the RCMP have long been debated. Some have suggested that the force was established mainly to preserve peace in the West and to protect Aboriginal people from whisky traders and overaggressive settlers. In fact, the NWMP's efforts to establish relationships of trust with Aboriginal peoples were constantly being undermined by Ottawa, which ignored the commitments it had made in its treaties with them. As one historian has observed:

> Canadian dealings with the Indian, with treaties, land surrenders, annuities, agents and land reserves, bore a close resemblance to American methods....Pressed to reduce public spending, Ottawa officials found logical economics by reducing rations, substituting bacon for beef on the Blackfoot reserves and dismissing junior employees. The era of starvation more than the advent of white settlement cost the N.W.M.P. its former standing with the native people.[25]

For an insightful comparative analysis of the role of the RCMP in the Canadian Northwest and the Texas Rangers in the United States in the late nineteenth and early twentieth centuries, see Graybill (2007).[26]

A number of Canadian scholars contend that the NWMP played much the same role as the Canadian Pacific Railway—that is, it established political and economic sovereignty over the farthest reaches of the country. This included settling indigenous lands in an orderly manner (i.e., with white settlers) and guarding against perceived threats of American annexation. An in-depth study of the role of the RCMP during Canada's residential school system for Aboriginal children that operated from the 1870s to 1996, found that officers were generally unaware of the abuse that children were suffering. The residential schools functioned as closed systems involving the Department of Indian Affairs, the churches that operated the schools, and the school administrators. The historical record indicates that RCMP officers were not systematically involved in taking children to the schools, nor retrieving children who ran away from the schools.[27]

The RCMP: Image and Reality

While there may be disagreement over the role of the Mounted Police in early Canada, there is little doubt that the RCMP has become the most widely recognized symbol of Canada throughout the world, far outdistancing the beaver, Canada's official symbol. Perhaps no other police force in the world is so closely intertwined with a nation's culture as the Mounties are with Canada.

The exploits and daring of the Mounties were immortalized by Canadian, European, and American authors in the early twentieth century in books like *Morgan of the Mounted*,[28] *Tales of the Mounted*,[29] *Yukon Patrol*,[30] and *Arctic Patrols*.[31] With the advent of motion pictures, these exploits soon found their way to the silver screen; more than six hundred films have been made with a Mountie as the hero. The image of the square-jawed, stoic, strong (yet polite) Mountie has been imprinted on Canadians and others around the world. A CBC film, *Scarlet Guardians*, produced in 1958 and available for viewing online, exemplifies this image.[32] This close association between the RCMP and Canada's national identity has, historically, helped mitigate criticisms of the sort that are generally directed toward police forces. In recent years, however, a number of high-profile incidents have undermined public trust in the RCMP. These are discussed throughout the text. Change and transformation of the RCMP is one of the challenges of Canadian police work.

It is not generally known that in its early days, the RCMP faced many internal difficulties. The historical record indicates that the Mounties faced high rates of desertion, resignation, and improper conduct, including drunkenness and illicit sexual alliances with women.[33] These difficulties were ascribed to the isolation and harsh conditions on the frontier, inadequate housing and medical attention, and the failure of officers to be paid, often for months at a time. One historian has noted that there were, in fact, a number of similarities between American cavalrymen and their Mounted Police counterparts: "Pay was meager and often in arrears. Traders at military and police posts were equally rapacious. Barracks were often temporary shacks, ill-constructed, frigid in winter and sometimes unsanitary. Arms and equipment were sometimes obsolete and often inappropriate for western conditions. Political interference in both countries pervaded every sphere of administration, from forage contracts to promotions."[34]

Also, considerable hostility was directed toward the Mounties by both settlers and federal members of Parliament (MPs). Many Canadians disliked the Mounties. In 1920, the federal government's decision to found the RCMP by merging the NWMP with the Dominion Police (Canada's first federal police force) met considerable opposition, especially from Atlantic MPs. For example, Robert H. Butts, representing Cape Breton South, declared:

> I have been a magistrate, sometimes I have been called a judge, of a town of between 9,000 and 10,000 people. We never had need of Mounted Police down there and we have no need of them now....Do not send hayseeds from away across the plains to Nova Scotia....I say that it is dangerous to send them here. I speak for 73,000 people in Cape Breton, and I can say that they will not appreciate any such intrusion.[35]

A Nova Scotia MP, J.H. Sinclair, echoed these views:

> The Federal Government are assuming a duty that they do not require to assume, that the provinces are not asking them to assume, and that the provinces themselves are well able to take care of.[36]

It is also likely that criticism of the Mounties was, at least in part, politically motivated, an outgrowth of conflicts that often arose between the Mounties and municipal police forces. These conflicts often led to situations where members of different forces arrested each other. To illustrate one community's attitude toward the Mounties, an editorial in the *Regina Leader* charged that "many a scalawag and scoundrel, many an idle loafer, many a brainless young blood, has worn its uniform and fed at its trough."[37]

But Ottawa's concern over growing labour unrest, subversive activities, and the ineptitude of provincial police forces had provided the Mounties with an opportunity to greatly expand their "market share" and, ultimately, to become heavily involved in provincial and municipal policing. MPs failed several times to abolish the RCMP in 1922 and 1923. Needless to say, had the RCMP been phased out, the landscape of Canadian policing would be far different than it is today. To summarize, the RCMP's emergence as Canada's national police force was more by historical accident than by master plan.

The RCMP and Political Dissent: The Historical Record

On a number of occasions in the early 1900s, the federal government used the Mounted Police to quell labour unrest and to counter what it perceived as the growing influence of left-wing activists.[38] On some occasions, this was due to the reluctance of municipal police forces to involve themselves in political demonstrations. In 1886 the Commissioner of the Mounted Police wrote, in reference to a railway strike the previous year: "I sent a detachment of police to points threatened....I instructed the men in charge of the detachment to use the very severest measures to prevent cessation of the work of construction."[39] This involvement continued into the 1900s.

A notable example is the Winnipeg General Strike of May and June 1919. When the Winnipeg police refused to break it, the Mounted Police were called in, assisted by specially sworn agents (see Box 1.2).

In 1935, over the objections of the Attorney General of Saskatchewan, the federal government used the RCMP to stop the "On to Ottawa" trek, which involved more than four hundred men who jumped aboard boxcars in Vancouver, heading for Ottawa to confront Prime Minister R.B. Bennett about the poor economy and the lack of jobs. The trekkers made it as far as Regina, where the RCMP confronted them with tear gas and clubs. The men were then sent back to B.C.[40]

Throughout the twentieth century, the RCMP carried out extensive surveillance of politicians, university students, and faculty. It also maintained confidential files on hundreds of thousands of Canadians. Covert surveillance on university campuses began during the First World War and continued into the late 1990s.[41] The Mounties were especially interested in left-wing student organizations and faculty in during the 1960s, and they used student informants as well as undercover police to gather information. "Subversive" groups targeted for surveillance by the RCMP included those involved in the "counterculture"; this included "hippies," who were identified by their long hair, facial hair (on men), conformist clothing, and drug use. In a report prepared in 1969, an RCMP undercover officer wrote: "My experience and conclusion of the drug user is that he is slowly destroying [the] society that we have tried to develop and perfect."[42] The reports of the undercover officers during these times were designed to bolster the case against the legalization of marijuana: "In the case of hippies, RCMP officers wanted to undermine their social appeal, particularly by revealing what the police considered the disturbing implications of the cultural changes that hippies wanted to introduce."[43] Similarly, the historical record indicates that the RCMP conducted surveillance on the "Abortion Caravan" sponsored by the Vancouver Women's Caucus. The caravan travelled from Vancouver to Ottawa to protest Canada's restrictive abortion laws. The police were concerned about the group's ties to left-wing organizations.[44]

Box 1.2

Bloody Saturday: The RCMP and the Winnipeg General Strike, June 21, 1919

The Winnipeg General Strike of 1919 is perhaps Canada's most famous work stoppage. The strike was part of the labour unrest that arose after the First World War and was fuelled by mass unemployment, as well as by the success of the Russian Revolution in 1917. The strike was called after negotiations broke down between labour and management in the building and metal trades. Workers were demanding the right to bargain collectively as well as improved wages and working conditions. The strike spread across the city until nearly 30,000 workers had left their jobs. Factories closed, the retail trade was severely affected, and public transit came to a halt. Other public sector employees, including police officers, firefighters, and utilities workers, soon joined the strike in support of the workers and coordinated the provision of essential services. Anxious to prevent the spread of labour unrest to other cities,

the federal government intervened. The federal Minister of Labour and the acting Minister of Justice travelled to Winnipeg and declared the government's support for the employers.

On June 17 the government arrested ten leaders of the Central Strike Committee and two propagandists from the newly formed One Big Union for conspiracy to overthrow the government. Seven of the leaders were subsequently convicted and received jail sentences ranging from six months to two years. On June 21, in what came to be known as "Bloody Saturday," Mounted Police officers charged into a crowd of protesters, injuring thirty and killing one. Federal troops later occupied the city. Faced with the combined forces of the government and the employers, the strikers returned to work on June 25. It would take another three decades for Canadian workers to gain the right to union recognition and collective bargaining.

http://www.canadianheritage.ca

RCMP on horseback charge striking workers in downtown Winnipeg.

Sources: http://www.thecanadianencyclopedia.com; http://www.manitoba.ca/cocoon/launch/en/themes/strike; http://canadaonline.about.com/od/canadianhistory.a.winnipegstrike.htm

Another example of the use of the RCMP by the federal government was during the Cold War (the struggle between the democratic West and the Communist Soviet Bloc) of the 1950s and early 1960s. The federal government worried that Soviet spies were infiltrating the federal government, and it perceived homosexuals to be a threat to national security. It was reasoned that spies could blackmail homosexuals into giving up government secrets. People who were assumed to be gay were fired from their government positions.

To help detect gays in government, the RCMP and a psychology professor from Carleton University developed a "homosexual detector" (more commonly referred to as "the fruit machine"). This involved showing applicants to the civil service images of nude and semi-nude men and women and filming how the pupils of their eyes responded. The assumption was that homosexuals' pupils would respond in a certain way to the male images. The machine was developed but never used. In 2005, the CBC produced a short film documenting this endeavour. It is available for viewing online.[45]

The McDonald Commission, which completed its report in 1980–81, documented a broad range of illegal activities and deceptions on the part of the RCMP during and after the October Crisis in Quebec between 1970 and 1972. These activities included surreptitious entry, the use of electronic surveillance, and illegal opening of mail. Furthermore, the RCMP was maintaining files on more than 800,000 individual Canadians. The findings of the McDonald Commission provided the catalyst for the passage of Bill C-9, which created the Canadian Security Intelligence Service (CSIS). This civilian agency, which is separate from the RCMP, is responsible for all foreign and domestic intelligence and security.

The RCMP in the Remote North

A unique feature of Canadian police work is that RCMP officers are posted to small Aboriginal and Inuit communities in Yukon, the Northwest Territories, and Nunavut. The role of the police in these regions, both today and in the past, remains largely unexplored by Canadian police scholars. This topic is examined in Chapter 11. An example is the role the RCMP played during the Klondike Gold Rush of the late 1800s.

Prior to 1894, except for the occasional surveyor, there were no government or law officials in Yukon (at the time known as "*the* Yukon"). Order was maintained by the miners themselves through what were called "miner's meetings": "Criminal cases were swiftly and, in the beginning, fairly dealt with."[46] With the discovery of gold in 1896, which led to the

MacBride Museum of Yukon History, 1989-2-1A-157.

NWMP posing in front of their tent detachment on the Chilkoot Pass, Yukon Territory, c. 1899–1900.

Gold Rush of 1897, the large trading companies grew concerned that the Americans (who had purchased Alaska in 1867) intended to occupy the area. Besides this, liquor traffic was increasing, and the federal government wanted to collect "levies" from the miners. All of this prompted the federal government to send a small force of NWMP officers to the region. Soon after, detachments were established at points on the Yukon River where gold was being mined, as well as at entry points into the territory. In the words of one historian, the NWMP "became the chief means by which the federal government eventually established its law, its economic and cultural policies, and its welfare system over the North."[47] The police officers spent a considerable portion of their time on civil tasks; for example, they acted as magistrates and justices of the peace, postal workers, land agents, coroners, and election officers.[48]

In the 1920s and 1930s, when RCMP officers were first posted to eastern Arctic communities (in what is now Nunavut), most Inuit in the region were living on the land, moving camp with the seasons and with the wild game that were their sustenance. RCMP officers sent there carried out little "real" police work; many had no occasion to arrest anyone during their entire tour of duty. Instead, they played a multifaceted role in the communities.

Even in later years, most RCMP officers were poorly equipped to live and work in the eastern Arctic and relied heavily on the Inuit for their survival. One member recalled: "There was nothing in the manual about how to use a dog sled. I learned from the [Inuit] Special Constable. He did all the travelling with me." Another officer recalled a time when the Inuit Special Constable guided him through a blinding whiteout: "I went along like a puppy dog. He ran the show. And it was the same thing when we got to the camps." RCMP officers were outsiders and were closely scrutinized by the community. Officers spent much of their time visiting the hunting and fishing camps of Inuit who were living on the land. The challenges of policing in the Canadian North in contemporary times are explored in Chapter 11.

POLICE WORK IN THE LATE TWENTIETH/EARLY TWENTY-FIRST CENTURY

The late twentieth century was a time of growth, and change, for Canadian police services. There were many developments that altered the policing landscape. Concurrent with this was the emergence of increasingly sophisticated forms of criminality, including cybercrime, human trafficking, organized gangs, and various terrorist threats and acts. It was also a time of amalgamation and regionalization of police services in the province of Ontario, which resulted in the regional police services that exist today.

Specific trends in policing that emerged during this time included the following.

The Increasing Costs of Policing

Policing is an expensive proposition. During the decade 1999 to 2009, overall spending on police services in Canada increased 40 percent. Policing eats up a substantial portion of municipal budgets: Vancouver (22.4 percent), Peel Region

(28.7 percent), and Calgary (23.8 percent) head the list in terms of budget percentage. Many cities, though, spend much less (Toronto, only 9.7 percent). A major contributor to these costs is police salaries, which have risen steadily, often more quickly than the cost of living.[49] Police officer strength (authorized positions) is at the highest point since 1981; total spending on police (in 2009 $12 billion, or $365 per Canadian) is at record highs. The factors driving police costs include wages, technology, and the considerable resources required to investigate more sophisticated types of criminal activity. Police services have developed specialized units to address new forms of criminality. In the words of one police superintendent: "The public police are pricing themselves out of the market" (personal communication).

At the same time, many municipal councils are under pressure to hold the line on budgets and tax levies. In contrast to previous decades, police services often find themselves competing with other public sector agencies and services for their share of the budget pie. A municipal council, for example, may find itself having to choose between cutting hours at public libraries and community centres, and providing funding increases for the police service. As a result, police services are under growing pressure to develop strategic plans and to measure and evaluate the performance of patrol officers, investigative units, and support services. Police services have also been experimenting with new types of police officers, including community constables (see Chapter 8), and with "offloading" officers' activities to other police agencies and to private security services.

The Increasing Visibility of the Police

The police are unique in the criminal justice system in that most of their activities take place on the street and away from the confines of office buildings. Police officers have more contact with the community than other criminal justice professionals (such as judges, probation officers, and correctional officers), who operate in relative obscurity. Except for occasional high-profile cases and incidents (e.g., the sentencing of a violent offender or a prison riot), criminal justice practitioners are relatively immune from the scrutiny that police officers receive in carrying out their day-to-day tasks. Technological developments—most notably the explosion in mobile phone cameras and Internet platforms such as YouTube and Facebook—have significantly increased the visibility of police actions.[50] In the words of one Chief Constable, "there is an incident outside a bar in the entertainment district, and it's on YouTube before my officers complete their report."

For example, an airline passenger's cell phone camera recorded the incident at the Vancouver International Airport involving four RCMP officers that resulted in the death of a newly arrived immigrant, Robert Dziekanski (see Chapters 6 and 7). Also, more and more patrol cars have in-car video cameras that record interactions with the public, particularly during traffic stops. These cameras have the capacity to record all interactions between a police officer and the public. Many officers wear microphones that record all of the audio during an encounter. A number of police services have installed minicams on Tasers; others are considering placing minicams on the officer that would record his or her activities and interactions. These technologies protect both the officer and the general public by providing visual evidence of encounters and actions. In the words of one Toronto police sergeant: "You are the director of your own destiny. Both our officers and the public make the choices of how they will be viewed and perceived."[51]

TABLE 1.1	Estimated Time to Complete All Steps for Selected Occurrences (in hours)			
Year	1975	1985	1995	2005
Occurrence Type				
Break & enter	Up to 1 hour	5 to 7 hours	6 to 10 hours	5 to 10 hours
Domestic assault	Up to 1 hour	1 to 2 hours	3 to 4 hours	10 to 12 hours
Driving under the influence	1 hour	2 hours	3 hours	5 hours

Source: Rethinking Police Governance, Culture & Management, "Estimated Time to Complete All Steps for Selected Occurrences (in hours)" p. 20, Christopher Murphy, PhD; Paul McKenna, MA, MLS, Public Safety Canada, 2007. Reproduced with the permission of the Minister of Public Works and Government Services, 2011.

The Impact of Legal and Regulatory Changes

There has been an increase in the legal regulation and accountability of police (see Chapter 3). Also, court decisions have placed additional responsibilities on the police and have increased the time they require to process criminal case files. An analysis of RCMP data found a dramatic increase between 1975 and 2005 in the time required to complete all the procedural elements for three offences: Break & Enter; Domestic Assault; and Driving Under the Influence (see Table 1.1).[52] We can assume that these times have increased still more since these data were published.

The Adoption of Private Sector Practices

Police services are increasingly adopting practices found in the private sector, including strategic planning, environmental scans, and the use of best practices. This has been driven in large measure by governments that are responding to fiscal crises by pressuring police services to become accountable, effective, and efficient.

Strategic planning involves identifying priorities with regard to how existing police resources will be allocated, as well as establishing the objectives to be achieved on an annual and/or multiyear time frame. **Environmental scans** are studies designed to identify community, legislative, policy, and other forces in the community (here referred to as "the environment") that will result in demands on the police. A typical environmental scan involves gathering information on a number of factors external to the police service, including demographic, social, and economic trends, calls for police service and crime trends, and the impact of legislative and policy changes. Many police services conduct scans annually to ensure a constant flow of information, on the basis of which changes in policies and operational practice can be made. The 2009 Toronto Police Service environmental scan, for example, examined demographic trends, crime trends, youth crime, victimization, traffic, calls for service, urban trends, technology and policing, police resources, public perceptions of the police, and the impact of legislation on the police.

Best practices are organizational, administrative, and operational strategies that have succeeded in preventing and responding to crime. Many of these

environmental scan
a study designed to identify trends that may impact demands on the police

best practices
organizational, administrative, and operational strategies that are effective in preventing and responding to crime

practices were first developed in the corporate sector before being adapted by police services. An example of a best practice is the community survey, which provides police services with information about citizen satisfaction with the police, problems in the community that may require police attention, and the extent of criminal victimization (including the fear of crime). The extent to which Canadian police services have adopted best practices is considered throughout this text. The focus on best practices is closely tied to the concept of evidence-based policing, wherein police services strive to ensure that their policies and practice are informed by research studies.

Police services also conduct risk management studies that are designed to identify organizational factors that may affect the ability of the police service to respond to demands placed on it. Similarly, audits are used to assess the effectiveness and efficiency of police policies and practice.

Concurrent with these developments has been the depiction of the police service as a "learning organization" that constantly seeks to improve itself. This requires the police service to develop the capacity to gather, analyze, and learn from information that is available from external sources as well as within the police service itself.

The Changing, Challenging Nature of Crime

The complexity of crime has continued to increase. Many forms of criminal activity are highly sophisticated and involve international criminal syndicates that require costly and time-consuming investigations. These syndicates engage in transnational criminal activities such as human trafficking, money laundering, and drug smuggling.[53]

Much of this criminal activity can be categorized as organized crime, which is found everywhere in the country. There has been exponential growth in new forms of crime related to technology (e.g., identity theft), and many criminal investigations involve collecting digital evidence from computers and smartphones.

The Evolution of Community Policing

The philosophy of community policing re-emerged in the 1980s and continues to have a strong impact on the structure and delivery of police services across Canada (see Chapter 8). Community policing emphasizes the development of police–community partnerships as well as specific strategies that focus on crime prevention and problem solving. In recent years, community policing has come to encompass both crime prevention and crime response strategies (see Chapter 9).

The Rise of Private Security Services

Beginning in the early twenty-first century, police work became increasingly "decoupled" from governments and more closely associated with the private sector.[54] This was reflected in the increasing breadth of activities of private security guards, who began to be involved in surveillance, arrests, and searches of individuals found on private premises, including shopping malls. Private security firms have been growing exponentially and are now providing services once performed solely by provincial and municipal police services. The public police no longer have a monopoly on the provision of police services, and there is growing concern that the line between private and public policing is becoming blurred. Private security officers now outnumber police officers in Canada by a ratio of at least three to one. Recall from our earlier discussion that private police forces existed even before the first organized police service was founded, in London in the early 1800s.

Police scholars have referred to the new reality as the **pluralization of policing**. This transformation of policing is, perhaps, as significant as the creation of the first organized police forces in England in the 1800s.

This trend has been fuelled by a number of factors, including increased public concern about security and safety, the rising costs of public policing, and gaps in police service delivery. As well, there has been a growth in the number of private property spaces where people actually live (condominiums, gated communities, and the like). There is a concern that policing has become increasingly "decoupled" from governments and more closely associated with the private sector and that there has been an increased focus on security.

There has also been the emergence of **collaborative policing** arrangements, which involve public police and private security officers working together in venues such as sporting arenas. The public police are contracted by the company that operates the venue. The result is a network of surveillance comprising public and private police (see Box 1.3).

Also, the line is being blurred between the powers and duties of private security officers and those of the public police. This confusion is often heightened by the fact that the uniforms of private police often look very similar to those of the public police, especially to a citizen who is in distress or under suspicion.

> **pluralization of policing**
> the expansion of policing beyond the public police to include parapolice and private security

> **collaborative policing**
> the cooperation between public and private police

Increasing Civilianization of Positions in Police Services and Increasing Civilian Personnel

Historically, civilians in police services were confined primarily to support roles, the largest of which was clerical. In recent years, police services have begun to civilianize many core positions previously held by sworn members. In 2010, 29 percent of civilians in police services were employed as management professionals.[55] Police services have come to recognize that civilians can provide expertise that is not often available in the ranks of sworn officers. Civilians also provide a thread of continuity in police services, within which sworn personnel are frequently moved between positions. In the Vancouver Police Department, for example, civilians head the research, policy, and planning section and the audit section.

New Technologies

Three technological innovations in the twentieth century radically altered the delivery of policing services: the telephone, the patrol car, and the two-way radio. These led to fundamental changes in how police services were delivered and were the basis for the professional model of police work (see Chapter 8). Policing became reactive: that is, when a citizen telephoned with a complaint,

Box 1.3

Networks of Surveillance: Policing at Pearson International Airport

As one enters…[the airport]…one notices the newness of the structures, the cleanliness of the walls and ceilings, and the brightness and bustle of the building. Passengers move along various queues for airline tickets, baggage checks, and car rentals. Perhaps less noticeable are two of Canada's federal police talking to a pair of constables from the Peel Regional Police Service. After the discussion ends, the RCMP officers begin to patrol, nodding hello to two security officers from Excalibur Security making similar rounds. Farther along, they watch two armed Brinks guards carry money satchels from a nearby current exchange kiosk. They wind by Commissionaires issuing parking tickets and Group 4 Securitas security guards checking the luggage of passengers. On the lower level, Canadian Customs agents spot a suspicious traveller and call the RCMP and an immigration officer. In a processing centre just off the tarmac, security guards from Metropol Security meet with the immigration officials while the detainee is handed over to the security firm for transport to the privately run Mississauga Immigration Detention Centre.…The detainee is handcuffed, placed in the caged rear of an unmarked van, and driven to the centre, which from the outside looks just like another inconspicuous motel. As one gets closer, however, a 12-foot chain link fence topped with barbed wire encircling the rear of the building comes into view.…On this short imaginary stroll you have come under the gaze of three federal policing agencies, one municipal police service, a quasi-public security force, four private contracted security companies, and an unknown number of in-house airline security agencies, all of them working alongside one another in a generally unproblematical chain of surveillance.

Source: Rigakos, G.: "The Networks of Surveillance," pp. 37–38, from *The New Parapolice: Risk Markets and Commodified Social Control*, © University of Toronto Press, 2002. Reprinted by permission of the publisher.

officers in patrol cars were dispatched to the scene by two-way radio. While this allowed officers to cover a large area, officers became more isolated from the communities they served. The patrol car, rather than the neighbourhood beat, became the "office" of the police officer, and this led to the centralization of police command and control. Other new technologies, such as centralized dispatch systems and computer terminals in patrol cars, further distanced officers from the community. The computer screen, rather than community residents, often became the primary source of information for officers. No longer could "civilians" interact with and communicate their concerns to local police constables. Instead, all calls were to be made to a centralized telephone number. Calls for assistance were prioritized by dispatchers who were far removed from the neighbourhood and unfamiliar with residents and their concerns.[56]

An ongoing question is whether police services have come to rely too heavily on technology to the exclusion of the human dimension of police work. An example is the introduction of Mobile Data Terminals in patrol cars in the 1980s.

A 1940s police patrol car.

These are computers that provide patrol officers with instant access to a variety of data files, including those of persons and vehicles. The fear is that officers have become so wedded to accessing information from the in-car computer that they no longer spend time out of the patrol car on a proactive basis, becoming familiar with the communities they police and developing alternative sources of information, including informants. In one First Nations community in Ontario, the Ojibwa word used to describe the police translates roughly into "men with no legs," referring to the fact that officers who patrol the reserve rarely leave their cars.

Among the high-tech innovations that were introduced during the late twentieth century were new weapons, including conducted energy devices (CEDs) such as the Taser (see Chapter 6). Other recent innovations include global positioning systems (GPSs) for patrol cars, sophisticated computer programs for crime analysis and criminal intelligence analysis (see Chapter 9), and DNA analysis for crime investigation (see Chapter 10).

The Globalization of Police Work

The emergence of the global village, the increasing interdependence of the world's nations, and the rapid development and spread of technology have created opportunities for new and more sophisticated forms of criminal activity as well as new channels for more traditional types of crime. Police services must now consider the world beyond their immediate jurisdictions and collaborate with other police organizations, both national and international. Today, working groups of cybercops are patrolling the Internet, and officers are involved as peacekeepers in a number of countries. In 2011, Canada and the U.S. signed a perimeter and security agreement designed to increase information-sharing and to integrate cross-border criminal and intelligence investigations. Among the concerns raised by critics is the need to safeguard information on Canadian citizens and the provision that U.S. police officers may be present in Canada.

At Issue 1.1

Canadian Police History

In reading the history of Canadian police work, what surprised (or concerned) you the most?

Key Points Review

1. Prior to the Industrial Revolution and the development of capitalism, policing in England was a community responsibility.
2. There was widespread opposition to the creation of the first organized police service in London in the early 1800s.
3. Sir Robert Peel sought to legitimize the new metropolitan police in London by setting out a number of principles for policing—principles that guide police work to this day.
4. Policing in Canada was strongly influenced by the evolution of policing in England. However, a number of major events have shaped the course of Canadian policing from the days of the early settlers to the present.
5. The early municipal and provincial police and the RCMP had very distinct roles.
6. There was often tension between municipal police forces and the RCMP.
7. There have been a number of important developments in Canadian police work during the late twentieth and early twenty-first centuries. These include the increasing visibility of the police, the rise of collaborative policing, the increasing use of technology, and the rising costs of policing.

Key Term Questions

1. What was the **hue and cry**, and how did this reflect the arrangements for policing in England prior to the Industrial Revolution and the development of capitalism?
2. Describe the principle underlying the **frankpledge system** and how it operated.
3. What was the importance of the **Statute of Winchester**, passed in England in 1285?
4. What was the importance of the **Justice of the Peace Act**, passed in 1361?
5. Who was **Sir Robert Peel,** and what was his contribution to the field of policing?
6. What did the **Metropolitan Police Act**, passed in 1829, do, and why is this act important in any study of policing?
7. What are the factors that have given rise to the **pluralization of policing** and **collaborative policing**?
8. What roles do **environmental scan** and **best practices** play in Canadian police work?

Notes

1. P.C. Stenning, *Status of the Police* (Ottawa: Law Reform Commission of Canada, 1981).
2. T.A. Critchley, *A History of the Police in England and Wales* (London: Constable, 1978), 6.
3. G. Berkley, *The Democratic Policeman* (Boston: Beacon, 1969), 5.
4. M. Ignatieff, "Police and People: The Birth of Mr. Peel's 'Blue Locusts,'" in *Policing: Key Readings*, ed. T. Newburn (Portland: Willan, 2005), 25–29 at 25.
5. Berkley, *The Democratic Policeman*, 5.
6. J. Styles, "The Emergence of the Police—Explaining Police Reform in Eighteenth and Nineteenth Century England," in *Policing: Key Issues*, ed. T. Newburn (Portland: Willan, 2005), 80–87.
7. C. Reith, *A New Study of Police History* (London: Oliver and Boyd, 1956).
8. C. Murphy, "Securitizing Community Policing: Towards a Canadian Public Policing Model," *Canadian Review of Policing Research* 2 (2005): 25–31 at 26.
9. J.A. Fox, *The Newfoundland Constabulary* (St. John's: Robinson Blackmore, 1971), 4.
10. J.A. Dickson, "Reflexions sur la police en Nouvelle-France," *McGill Law Journal* 32, no. 3 (1987): 497–522.
11. T.J. Juliani, C.K Talbot, and C.H.S. Jayewardene, "Municipal Policing in Canada: A Developmental Perspective," *Canadian Police College Journal* 8, no. 3 (1984): 315–85 at 326.
12. Ibid.
13. Ibid.
14. Juliani et al., "Municipal Policing in Canada," 326.
15. P. Vronsky, "History of the Toronto Police, 1834–1860, Part 1: 'Formidable Engines of Oppression'" (2003–4), 2, http://www.russianbooks.org/crime/cph3.htm
16. J.C. Weaver, *Crimes, Constables, and Courts* (Montreal and Kingston: McGill–Queen's University Press, 1995), 101.
17. P. Vronsky, "History of the Toronto Police, 1834–1860."
18. P. Vronsky, "History of the Toronto Police, 1870–1920, Part 4: 'Constables as Urban Missionaries,'" (2003–4), 2, http://www.russianbooks.org/crime/cph6.htm
19. Weaver, *Crimes, Constables, and Courts*, 89.
20. Ibid., 337.
21. M. Jenkins, *Bloody Falls of the Coppermine: Madness, Murder, and the Collision of Cultures in the Arctic, 1913* (New York: Random House, 2005).
22. R. Smandych and R. Linden, "Administering Justice Without the State: A Study of the Private Justice System of the Hudson's Bay Company to 1800," *Canadian Journal of Law and Society* 11, no. 1 (1996): 21–61.
23. F.W. Anderson, *Saskatchewan's Provincial Police* (Calgary: Frontier, 1972), 18.
24. C. Murphy and P. McKenna, "Rethinking Police Governance, Culture, and Management" (Ottawa: Public Safety Canada, 2007), 11, http://publicsafety.gc.ca/rcmp-grc/_fl/eng/rthnk-plc-eng.pdf
25. D. Morton, "Cavalry or Police: Keeping the Peace on Two Adjacent Frontiers, 1870–1900," *Journal of Canadian Studies* 12, no. 1 (1977): 27–37 at 32.

26. A.R. Graybill, *Policing the Great Plains: Rangers, Mounties, and the North American Frontier, 1875–1920* (Lincoln: University of Nebraska Press, 2007).

27. M.E. LeBeuf, *The Role of the Royal Canadian Mounted Police During the Residential School System* (Ottawa: Royal Canadian Mounted Police, 2011), http://www.cbc.ca/news/pdf/RCMP-role-in-residential-school-system-Oct-4-2011.pdf

28. S.A. White, *Morgan of the Mounted* (New York: Phoenix Press, 1939).

29. W. Brockie, *Tales of the Mounted* (Toronto: Ryerson, 1949).

30. L.C. Douthwaite, *Yukon Patrol* (London: Blackie, 1936).

31. W. Campbell, *Arctic Patrols* (Milwaukee: Bruce, 1936).

32. CBC Digital Archives, "Scarlet Guardians" (1958), http://archives.cbc.ca

33. E. Morgan, "The North-West Mounted Police: Internal Problems and Public Criticism, 1874–1883," *Saskatchewan History* 26, no. 2 (1973): 41–62.

34. Morton, "Cavalry or Police," 31.

35. R.C. MacLeod, "The RCMP and the Evolution of Provincial Policing," in *Police Powers in Canada: The Evolution and Practice of Authority*, ed. R.C. MacLeod and D. Schneiderman (Toronto: University of Toronto Press, 1994), 44–56 at 45.

36. MacLeod, "The RCMP and the Evolution of Provincial Policing," 46.

37. Morgan, "The North-West Mounted Police," 60.

38. W.M. Baker, "Superintendent Deane of the Mounted Police," *Alberta History* 4, no. 4 (1993): 20–26; C. Betke, "The Mounted Police and the Doukhobors in Saskatchewan, 1899–1909," *Saskatchewan History* 28, no. 1 (1974): 1–14.

39. C.K. Talbot, C.H.S. Jayewardene, and T.J. Juliani, *The Thin Blue Line: A Historical Perspective of Policing in Canada* (Ottawa: Crimcare, 1983), 22.

40. S. Hewitt, *Riding to the Rescue: The Transformation of the RCMP in Alberta and Saskatchewan, 1914–1939* (Toronto: University of Toronto Press, 2006).

41. S. Hewitt, "'Information Believed True': RCMP Security Intelligence Activities on Canadian University Campuses and the Controversy Surrounding Them, 1961–1971," *Canadian Historical Review* 81, no. 2 (2000): 191–228; Hewitt, *Spying 101: The RCMP's Secret Activities at Canadian Universities, 1917–1997* (Toronto: University of Toronto Press, 2000).

42. M. Martel, "'They Smell Bad, Have Diseases, and Are Lazy': RCMP Officers Reporting on Hippies in the Late Sixties," *Canadian Historical Review* 90, no. 2 (2009): 215–45 at 215–16.

43. Ibid., 229.

44. C. Sethna and S. Hewitt, "Clandestine Operations: The Vancouver Women's Caucus, the Abortion Caravan, and the RCMP," *Canadian Historical Review* 90, no. 3 (2009): 463–95.

45. CBC Digital Archives, "RCMP Uses 'Fruit Machine' To Detect Gays" (2005), http://archives.cbc.ca

46. W.R. Morrison, *Showing the Flag: The Mounted Police and Canadian Sovereignty in the North, 1894–1925* (Vancouver: UBC Press, 1985), 13.

47. J. Roberts-Moore, "Review of *Showing the Flag: The Mounted Police and Canadian Sovereignty in the North, 1894-1925*," *Archivaria* 25 (1987): 138–40 at 138.

48. W.R. Morrison, "The North-West Mounted Police and the Klondike Gold Rush," *Journal of Contemporary History* 9, no. 2 (1974): 93–105 at 102.

49. A. Morrow, "What Price for Law and Order?" *Globe and Mail*, January 8, 2011, A4.

50. A.J. Goldsmith, "Policing's New Visibility," *British Journal of Criminology* 50, no. 5 (2010): 914–34.

51. Toronto Police Service, "Cameras' Role in Cars," in *Annual Report* (Toronto: Toronto Police Service Public Information Unit, 2009), 18.

52. Murphy and McKenna, "Rethinking Police Governance, Culture, and Management," 20.

53. Ontario Provincial Police, "Environmental Scan 2010" (Orillia: Strategic Initiatives Office, 2010), http://www.policecouncil.ca/reports/OPP_Env_Scan_2010.pdf

54. C. Murphy and C. Clarke, "Policing Communities and Communities of Policing: A Comparative Study of Policing and Security in Two Canadian Communities," in *Reimagining Policing in Canada*, ed. D. Cooley (Toronto: University of Toronto Press, 2005), 209–59 at 221.

55. M. Burczycka, *Police Resources in Canada, 2010* (Ottawa: Minister of Industry, 2010), 6.

56. A.J. Reiss, "Police Organization in the Twentieth Century," in *Modern Policing: Crime and Justice*, vol. 15, ed. M. Tonry and N. Morris (Chicago: University of Chicago Press, 1992), 51–95.

Chapter

2

The Structure of Police Work

Learning Objectives

After reading this chapter, you should be able to:

- Provide a definition of policing

- Discuss the dynamics that surround police work in a democratic society

- Discuss the legislative framework in which the police carry out their mandate

- Discuss the basis for the exercise of authority and discretion by police officers

- Describe what is meant by the "political" role of the police

- Describe the structure of contemporary policing in Canada

- Describe provincial and municipal police services

- Identify and discuss the unique organizational and operational attributes of the RCMP

- Identify the distinctions between public police and private police

- Identify and discuss the contexts of police work

Key Terms

The police occupy a unique and important place in the criminal justice system and in Canadian society. With a few notable exceptions, police officers are the only personnel in the justice system with the authority to arrest and detain people and to use lethal force while carrying out their legally mandated duties. Policing issues are discussed and debated every day by politicians, the media, and the community—as well as within police forces themselves.

DEFINING POLICE WORK

A definition of policing must include public *and* private police. Here is one: policing is the "activities of any individual or organization acting legally on behalf of public or private organizations or persons to maintain security or social order while empowered by either public or private contract, regulations or policies, written or verbal."[1]

Police Work in a Democratic Society

Among all the institutions and organizations in society, it is the police that can have a direct impact on the rights and freedoms of individual citizens. This is due to the powers that police officers are given under the law. The Law Reform Commission of Canada identified four key values that form the framework for understanding police work in Canadian society:

- *Justice.* The police are to maintain peace and security in the community while ensuring that individuals are treated fairly and that human rights are respected.
- *Equality.* All citizens are entitled to policing services that contribute to their feelings of safety and security.
- *Accountability.* The actions of police services, and police officers, are subject to review.
- *Efficiency.* Policing services must be cost-effective.[2]

The police mandate is at heart contradictory: they are expected to protect both public order *and* individual rights. There are natural tensions between the power and authority of the police and their legal mandate to maintain order, on the one hand, and the values and processes that exist in a democratic society, on the other. This tension is inevitable and, generally, irreconcilable. The governments and the public rely on the police to prevent and respond to crime and to apprehend offenders; yet at the same time, these governments are committed to the principles of democracy and due process. It is not surprising, then, that police officers often experience conflict in carrying out their duties.

What Do Police Do?

The police role has traditionally been viewed as having three components: crime control (catching criminals), order maintenance (keeping the peace), and service (providing assistance). These components, however, may no longer accurately capture the diversity and complexity of the police role in a highly technological, global society. More and more, police officers are knowledge workers who spend much of their time gathering and processing information.

Many of the difficulties experienced by the police in fulfilling their mandate are the result of having staked out a "vast and unmanageable social domain." This has led to unrealistic expectations on the part of the general public regarding what the police can realistically accomplish in terms of crime prevention and response. And it has challenged police services to document the effectiveness and efficiency of their operations.[3]

Most police officers view themselves primarily as peacekeepers rather than law enforcers: depending on the specific area being policed, many officers spend most of their time attending to order maintenance activities and less than 10 percent of their time actually enforcing laws. A large portion of police work involves officers restoring order in situations of conflict without resorting to the criminal law.[4]

The Legislative Framework of Police Work

Police officers carry out their tasks within a number of legislative frameworks that define their roles, powers, and responsibilities. These are generally set out in provincial legislation and—in the case of the RCMP—in the federal RCMP Act. When new legislation is enacted, it may result in increased demands on the police and extend the role and activities of the police. Among the more significant pieces of legislation are these:

Canadian Charter of Rights and Freedoms
a component of the Constitution Act that guarantees basic rights and freedoms

Constitution Act, 1867
legislation that includes provisions that define the responsibilities of the federal and provincial governments in the area of criminal justice

- **Canadian Charter of Rights and Freedoms.** This is the primary law of the land in Canada and guarantees basic rights and freedoms for citizens. The Charter contains specific sections on fundamental freedoms, legal rights, equality rights, and enforcement. The courts may use the Charter to strike down legislation and criminal laws as unconstitutional. No other piece of legislation has had as strong an impact on the powers and activities of the police as the Charter, specifically Sections 7 to 14, the "Legal Rights" section. This topic is discussed in Chapter 6.

- **Constitution Act, 1867.** This sets out the responsibilities of the federal and provincial governments in the area of criminal justice. The federal government has the sole authority to enact criminal laws and to establish the procedures to be followed in criminal cases (s. 91(14)), while the provinces are assigned responsibility for actually administering justice (s. 92(27)). If the Constitution Act were followed to the letter, the federal government would be limited to passing laws, with the provinces and territories given the task of policing and justice administration. In reality, it's much more complex than that. The RCMP is a national police force involved in federal, provincial, and municipal policing. The federal government operates a corrections system for individuals who receive sentences of two years or more. Also, provincial and municipal governments enact their own laws; however, provincial laws and municipal bylaws are generally for less serious types of offences and are most often punished by fines. Even though bylaws are relatively minor in the overall scheme of laws, they can generate considerable controversy. This was illustrated when municipalities began passing bylaws that severely restricted where people could smoke.

- **Criminal Code.** This sets out the criminal laws as well as the procedures for administering justice.

- *Other federal statutes.* These include the Anti-Terrorism Act, the Controlled Drugs and Substances Act, the Canadian Youth Justice Act, the Canada Evidence Act (which pertains to evidentiary matters in the courts), the Freedom of Information Act, and various privacy acts.

- *Provincial and municipal legislation.* This includes a wide range of statutes such as motor vehicle administration acts, highway traffic acts, liquor acts, and provincial/municipal police acts. All of these provide the framework within which police services are structured and delivered. As well, the various police acts set out the principles of policing, processes for filing complaints against police officers, and disciplinary procedures for police officers, besides providing for and defining the activities of police commissions and municipal police boards.

- **Royal Canadian Mounted Police Act.** This provides the legislative framework for the operations of the RCMP. It also contains provisions relating to the operations of the External Review Committee and the Public Complaints Commission; as well as to officer grievances, discipline, discharge, and demotion.

> **Criminal Code**
> federal legislation that sets out criminal law, procedures for prosecuting federal offences, and sentences and procedures for the administration of justice

> **Royal Canadian Mounted Police Act**
> federal legislation that provides the framework for the operations of the RCMP

The Authority of Police Officers

A key element of the police role in society relates to their use of authority.[5] This authority includes depriving citizens of their freedom, as well as the application of physical force—in extreme circumstances, lethal force. Police observers have pointed out, however, that police officers are generally quite subtle in their exercise of authority. They often project it merely by being a uniformed presence in public settings and by soliciting information from citizens. Canadian police officers derive their authority from the Criminal Code and various provincial statutes. The legal authority of police officers, however, does not automatically translate into *moral* authority. The latter requires officers to establish their legitimacy in the community.[6] This issue is discussed in Chapter 8.

The Unique Role of the Police in the Criminal Justice System

The police are only one component of the criminal justice system. While police officers have much in common with their professional counterparts in that system (e.g., they exercise considerable discretion in making decisions), they are also unique in many ways, including these:

- Police work is carried out in diverse environments.

- Police officers have the authority to detain people and to use force, including lethal force.

- Police work—especially community police work—involves extensive personal contact with the general public and (increasingly) the development of partnerships with communities, nongovernmental organizations (NGOs), the private sector, and international partners.

- Police work takes place in a wide variety of situations and circumstances, many of which may involve personal conflict, crises and chaos, biohazards, blood, and sometimes death.
- Police work involves much more than law enforcement; it includes order maintenance, service, prevention, conflict mediation and dispute resolution, and public relations.
- Police work presents officers with situations in which they must make split-second decisions or decisions based on a limited amount of information.

The Exercise of Discretion

A predominant feature of the police role is the exercise of **discretion.** Discretion permeates all aspects of police work. Although there is no specific legislation that addresses the use of discretion by police officers, the Criminal Code apparently encourages officers to exercise it in the course of their duties. The Code states, for example, that a police officer *may* make an arrest in circumstances where there are reasonable and probable grounds to believe that an offence has been committed.

The policing literature reflects considerable diversity of opinion regarding the exercise of discretion by police officers and the extent to which such powers should be structured and controlled. Opinions vary as to how much discretion police officers actually have and whether they are exercising their discretion in a fair and equitable manner.

In his classic treatise on police discretion, written decades ago, Kenneth Culp Davis argued that, while police discretion should not (and cannot) be eliminated, it needs to be structured, confined, and controlled. As well, the police should acknowledge that it is impossible to enforce the law in full at all times.[7] The reality is that the police engage in selective enforcement, which necessarily involves the exercise of discretion. Police officers must have the discretion to tailor their decision making to the requirements of a given encounter or case. This raises a question: How are we as a community to define the parameters within which discretion is to be exercised? It may well be that police officers are most effective when they do not exercise their full enforcement powers, but instead use discretion to mediate situations and to resolve conflicts at hand in an informal manner.

Properly applied, discretion enables police officers to be effective in their work, although it is important that officers be held accountable for the misuse of their discretion. There is often a fine line between discretion and discrimination. The effective use of discretion often develops as the officer gains on-the-job experience. Many of the landmark decisions of the Supreme Court of Canada concern decisions and actions taken by police officers in carrying out their tasks.

The discretion exercised by police officers will be discussed in greater detail in Chapter 5.

The Authority to Use Force

Another defining attribute of the police role is the authority to use force. Except for correctional officers, no other personnel in the criminal justice

discretion
the freedom to choose between different options when confronted with the need to make a decision

system are invested with this authority. This authority is integral to all facets of the police role, from selection and training to operational patrol and high-risk policing situations. And while most incidents are resolved without the use of force, the potential for its use is always present. In recent years there have been several high-profile cases involving police officers who used force in encounter situations. The police use of force and its consequences for police services, officers, suspects, and the community is considered in Chapter 6.

The Political Role of the Police

Although in theory, the police are apolitical and are to direct their attention toward ensuring the safety and security of the community, all police services operate in a political environment. In the discussion of police history in Chapter 1, it was noted that police forces have been used by the federal government to break strikes, monitor the activities of Canadians, and "pacify" the Canadian West so that it could be settled and developed by Europeans.

Except for the RCMP, police services are under the control of local and provincial political authorities. City councils control the budgets of municipal police services. The Chief Constable and the senior executive of the police service must be aware of, and sensitive to, the political dynamics that may affect their ability to secure resources. As well, the police are mandated to enforce the criminal law, which reflects political values and political ends. Police services often find themselves caught between government and persons involved in civil disobedience. Among the more recent high-profile incidents were the actions taken by the Toronto Police during the G8 summit in 2010 and the role of the Ontario Provincial Police (OPP) during the land dispute in Ipperwash, Ontario, in 1995. These incidents are profiled later in this book.

Given these circumstances, it is impossible for the police to avoid becoming involved in and affected by politics and other outside influences. A key issue is the extent to which this involvement, or influence, affects the ability of the police to carry out their mandate in a fair and impartial manner. This issue is examined in Chapter 7.

Police Work: Common Misconceptions

To understand the roles of the police in contemporary society, we must separate fact from fiction. Some of the more common myths of police work are presented in Box 2.1.

There is in our culture a fascination with the police that portrays the world of police officers in a highly seductive fashion: at times extremely dangerous, at other times isolated and lonely.

Popular police dramas such as the *CSI* series whet what appears to be an endless appetite for the danger, intrigue, and excitement of police work. That these shows only distort the realities of police work is of little concern to either the producers or the viewing audience. Yet these images may have a strong impact on the perceptions of police, on their activities, and on their ability to respond to crime. After all, on-screen police officers almost always solve the crime and

Box 2.1

Common Misconceptions of Modern Police Work

Myth	Fact
Police work in itself prevents crime.	The specific causes of criminal behaviour and disorder in a community are generally beyond the capacity of the police to address on their own. However, adoption of the principles and practices of community policing, with its emphasis on partnerships with neighbourhoods, the private sector, not-for-profit organizations, and other government ministries and agencies, may increase the preventive capacity of the police. Also, there is evidence that the use of statistically-driven approaches such as Compstat and "target-hardening" can impact specific types of crime in a defined area.
The Mounties always get their man.	It's not only the Mounties that don't always get their man (or woman): police services generally struggle to solve the myriad of crimes they are presented with. For many categories of offences, especially those involving transnational crime and white-collar crime, the chances of being detected and apprehended by the police are relatively small. This is due in part to a lack of police resources and in part to the fact that in the past, police resources were not allocated effectively.
Police work involves the frequent use of force.	If TV shows and films about the police were to be believed, police officers are involved in shootouts on a daily basis. Even in the United States, where guns are far more prevalent than in Canada, officers are generally reluctant to use deadly force or physical force. In 97 percent of all police incidents, mere presence and communication skills are used to defuse and resolve crises. Many police officers go their entire careers without drawing or discharging their weapons except in training. However, the possibility that force will be used is present in every encounter situation.
Police work is dangerous.	Statistically, police work is a less hazardous occupation than underground mining and garbage collection. Police officers do have a high rate of risk of on-the-job homicide, second only to that of taxi drivers (for whom it is two times the rates for police officers). Police work has often been described as long hours of boredom punctuated by brief periods of sheer terror. Officer complacency is one of the biggest dangers in police work.
Police work primarily involves pursuing criminals.	Contrary to popular images and most fictional accounts, most of a police officer's time is spent on order maintenance and service-type activities, including attending traffic accidents and mediating disputes between citizens and among family members. While the specific breakdown of service to order maintenance to crime control varies across task environments, pursuing and apprehending criminals generally accounts for less than 10 percent of an officer's time.
When you call the police, they come.	Except in smaller communities, which may receive "Cadillac service" under a "no call too small" policy, police patrol units may not be dispatched. Even 911 calls may be screened out (with, in some instances, tragic consequences).

arrest the suspects, and crime scene investigators are able to complete complex case investigations in the span of a one-hour time slot. These programs may have an impact on the expectations of jurors in criminal trails—an issue discussed in Chapter 10.

THE STRUCTURE OF CONTEMPORARY CANADIAN POLICING

Public policing in Canada is carried out at four levels: federal, provincial, municipal, and First Nations. In addition, there are private security services and parapolice services. The latter are generally staffed by officers with Special Constable status. These include the Canadian Pacific Railway Police Service and the Canadian National Railway Police Service, as well as transit police forces, which provide security and protection for property and passengers in major urban centres such as Montréal, Toronto, and Vancouver. The members of the South Coast British Columbia Transportation Authority Police Service (Transit Police Services) have full peace officer powers and are the only armed transit police in the country.

Five Canadian police services—the RCMP, the Toronto Police Service, the Ontario Provincial Police (OPP), the Sûreté du Québec (SQ), and the Service de police de la Ville de Montréal (SPVM)—account for just over 60 percent of all police officers in Canada.

Canadian police services vary greatly in size and in terms of the areas for which they are responsible. At one end of the scale, there are three-officer RCMP detachments in many remote northern communities; at the other, there are thousands of officers in the urban centres of Toronto and Montréal.

The major urban police services have similar divisions, or sections. These include the following:

- *Operational patrol.* Patrol division, dog or canine unit, identification squad, traffic, reserve/auxiliary.
- *Investigative.* General investigation, major crimes, special crimes (e.g., sexual offences).
- *Support services.* Information, report, or filing; communications centre; victim services; community services/crime prevention.
- *Administrative.* Finance and payroll, property office.
- *Human resources.* Staff development, recruiting, training.
- *Research and planning.* Strategic planning, crime analysis, audit.

Canadian police services, like their counterparts worldwide, have a rank structure that reflects their paramilitary organization. Most police services have a chief constable, one or more deputy chief constables, superintendents, inspectors (often referred to as *commissioned officers*, although they are not actually commissioned), and *noncommissioned officers*, including staff sergeants, sergeants, corporals, detectives, and constables.

The Arrangements for Policing

To a foreigner (and to many Canadians), the arrangements for the delivery of police services in Canada can be quite confusing. For example, the London (Ontario) Police Service, an independent municipal police service, has responsibility for policing within the city boundaries, while the London detachment of the OPP has jurisdiction in the rural areas outside the city. In addition, the RCMP has its provincial headquarters in London and operates as a federal police force in the areas policed by the London Police and the OPP.

The picture is especially complex in Greater Vancouver, which is the last urban region in the country without one dominant police force (see Figure 2.1).

Driving around the Lower Mainland–Vancouver area of B.C., for example, you would cross a number of police jurisdictions, several of which are policed by independent municipal police forces and others by the RCMP under contract. Run a stoplight in Vancouver and you'd be stopped and perhaps ticketed by a constable from the Vancouver Police Department. Run a red light in one of the surrounding municipalities, and here's who you'd get to talk to: the RCMP in Surrey, Richmond, and North Vancouver; the Delta Police Department in Delta; and the West Vancouver Police Department in West Vancouver. Speed across the province and you'd be stopped by the RCMP. Speed in one of the seven communities of the Stl'atl'imx Nation and you'd speak with a tribal police officer. Jump the turnstile at the Skytrain station

FIGURE 2.1   Policing in the Greater Vancouver Region

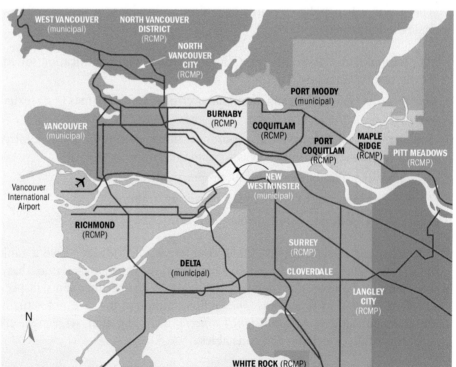

in Vancouver and you could be arrested by an officer from the Transit Police Service. There has been considerable debate as to whether a regional police service should be developed in the Greater Vancouver Region. (See At Issue 2.1 at the end of the chapter.) While the arrangements for police services are less complex in other provinces, this delineation of services illustrates the uniqueness of policing in Canada.

In Ontario and Québec, there are provincial police forces and municipal police forces, although in Québec, the Sûreté du Québec (SQ), the provincial police force, is not involved in policing municipalities under contract. The RCMP in these provinces functions only as a federal police force enforcing federal statutes. In contrast to the western regions of the country, the RCMP is not highly visible in Ontario and Québec. And, in a unique twist, the Royal Newfoundland Constabulary—a provincial police force—provides policing services to three areas of Newfoundland and Labrador: St. John's, Mount Pearl, and the surrounding communities referred to as the Northeast Avalon; Corner Brook; and Labrador West, which includes Labrador City, Wabush, and Churchill Falls. The rest of the province is policed under contract by the RCMP.

If the Constitution Act had been followed to the letter, Ontario and Québec would not be the only two provinces with independent provincial police forces, RCMP officers would not be involved in municipal policing, and there would be no independent municipal police services. Historical events, however, have led to unique arrangements for the delivery of police services in Canada.

FEDERAL POLICE: THE ROYAL CANADIAN MOUNTED POLICE

The RCMP is unique among the world's police forces and is organized into sixteen divisions, fourteen of which are operational divisions. The RCMP divisions are organized into the following four regions: Pacific, Northwest, Central, and Atlantic. The headquarters of these divisions are generally located in the provincial and territorial capitals and are under the supervision of a commanding officer. The regions are overseen by a Deputy Commissioner West and East. The divisions, in turn, are organized into subdivisions, which are themselves organized into detachments. It is at the detachment level that uniformed officers deliver most police services. Specialized services and operational support units are available at the subdivision to support officers at the detachment level.

The RCMP Act provides the framework for the operations of the RCMP. As the federal police force in all provinces and territories, the RCMP enforces most federal statutes, the Controlled Drugs and Substances Act, the Securities Act, and lesser-known statutes such as the Canada Shipping Act and the Student Loans Act. Under the RCMP Act, RCMP officers have the powers of peace officers as well as the powers of customs and excise officers for the entire country. This makes RCMP members unique among Canada's police officers. The federal government covers the costs of the RCMP when it serves as a federal police force. When the RCMP functions as a provincial or municipal police force, policing costs are shared between the federal and provincial/territorial or municipal governments. The split in cost sharing varies among jurisdictions.

The RCMP, through its Aboriginal Policing Branch, also operates a number of Aboriginal policing programs, including the RCMP First Nations Community Policing Service. This service, which is the main Aboriginal policing initiative of the RCMP, recruits, trains, and posts Aboriginal police officers to First Nations communities. These officers are full-status members of the RCMP with all of the attendant powers and responsibilities. First Nations communities have the right to request the services of Aboriginal members of the RCMP.

Policing Provinces and Municipalities under Contract

contract policing
an arrangement whereby the RCMP and the Ontario Provincial Police provide provincial and municipal policing services

Although the RCMP is a federal police force, roughly 60 percent of RCMP personnel are involved in **contract policing**, serving as provincial and municipal police officers under agreements between the RCMP and the provinces/territories (except in Ontario and Québec, which have their own provincial police forces, and a portion of Newfoundland and Labrador). To provide policing services under contract, the RCMP, through the Government of Canada, negotiates municipal policing agreements with individual municipalities. The sole exception is in British Columbia, where there is a general policing agreement between the federal and provincial governments for the delivery of contract policing services to specific municipalities. RCMP members employed under these agreements also conduct federal enforcement investigations.

The RCMP's reach extends to the international level: there are RCMP liaison officers in a number of countries in the Asia–Pacific Region, in Europe, and in the Americas. RCMP liaison officers provide a bridge between foreign police forces and their Canadian counterparts; they also assist in cross-national investigations.

Peacekeeping

The international profile of the RCMP has been greatly enhanced by its involvement in a number of peacekeeping missions under the auspices of the United Nations. RCMP officers (as well as provincial and municipal police officers) have served in, or are currently serving in, Sierra Leone, Afghanistan, Haiti, Iraq, Ivory Coast, Democratic Republic of Congo, and Sudan. The primary role of these peacekeeper officers is as technical advisers; they also instruct police forces in new policing strategies. The effectiveness of these deployments is debated. There have been few evaluations of the impact these officers have in the areas to which they are deployed. The difficulties with these peacekeeping efforts are several: pre-deployment training is often limited for officers being sent on peacekeeping missions; Canadian officers are often folded into multinational forces of police officers whose members vary widely in their skills and professionalism; and the net benefit to the officer's home detachment and department upon their return has been questioned.[8] This suggests that "showing the flag" may be as important a component of peacekeeping as ensuring effective police practice.

Organizational Features of the RCMP

As a national police force, the RCMP has several distinctive organizational characteristics, including these:

A broad mandate. The RCMP is involved in a broad range of policing activities, including federal policing, contract policing at the provincial and municipal levels, and international peacekeeping. One result is that the resources and capacities of the Mounties have been overextended. This has led many observers to question whether the RCMP can effectively carry out all of its current mandates. Most Western countries have created different organizations to carry out specialized policing functions. Figure 2.2 illustrates the range and complexity of the RCMP's policing responsibilities.

Policing diverse environments. RCMP members carry out their duties in a variety of environments across the country, from small coastal villages in Newfoundland and British Columbia, to Aboriginal and Inuit communities in the North, to large suburban communities. The three largest RCMP detachments—each with several hundred officers—are all in British Columbia (Surrey, Burnaby, Coquitlam). At the other extreme are three-officer detachments, such as the one in the Inuit community of Resolute Bay (population 150), in Nunavut. The challenges of policing in remote northern communities are discussed in Chapter 11.

FIGURE 2.2   The Broad Mandate of the RCMP

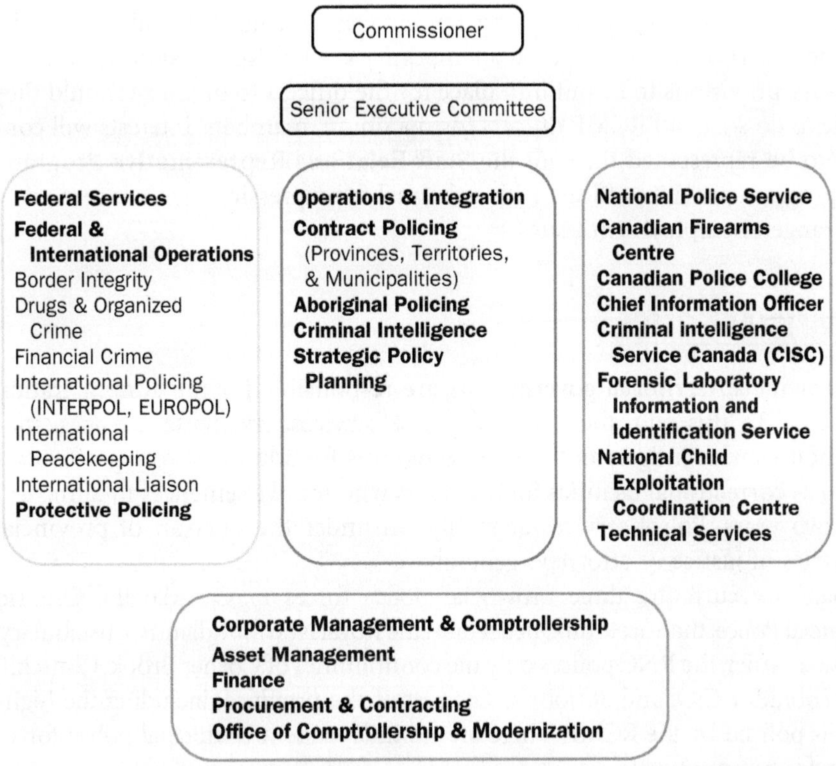

Source: C. Murphy and P. McKenna, "Rethinking Police Governance, Culture, and Management" (Ottawa: Public Safety Canada, 2007), 33, http://publicsafety.gc.ca/rcmp-grc/_fl/eng/rthnk-plc-eng.pdf. Reproduced with the permission of the Minister of Public Works and Government Services, 2011.

The absence of structures of accountability to local municipalities and to provincial governments. The RCMP is primarily a federal police force, and this has a significant impact on the structure and delivery of policing services. In municipalities that are policed under contract by the RCMP, there is no police board, and the mayor and council have no mandated oversight of the police. RCMP officers engaged in provincial and municipal policing, are accountable only to the RCMP Act and to other directives issued by RCMP headquarters in Ottawa. Many of the new twenty-year contracts that were negotiated in 2011–12 include provisions to increase the accountability of the RCMP as the contracted provincial police service.

Nationwide recruiting and centralized training. As a national police force, the RCMP recruits officers from across the country and trains them at a central facility in Regina, Saskatchewan, known as the Training Academy.

Transfer policy. Traditionally, and quite unlike their municipal counterparts, RCMP officers were rotated among detachments every two years or so. The transfer policy provides members with the opportunity to police in a number of different environments in the course of their career, thereby enhancing their skills and expertise. The drawbacks of this policy may include the disruptive impact on the officer's family, officers' lack of familiarity with the communities they are policing, and lack of continuity in program initiatives and police–community partnerships.

Non-union. Unlike their provincial and municipal counterparts, RCMP officers have historically been prohibited by legislation from forming a union. In 2009 an Ontario Superior Court judge ruled that the sections of the RCMP Act that prohibited officers from forming a union were unconstitutional. In 2010 the Ontario Court of Appeal imposed a temporary stay of this decision to allow the necessary provisions to be put into place for the officers to unionize should they decide to do so. Until RCMP officers form a union, members' interests will continue to be represented through the **Staff Relations Representative Program**. This program provides officers with a channel for expressing their concerns on a wide range of employment issues.

Staff Relations Representative Program in lieu of a union, a program that provides RCMP officers with a way to express their concerns to management

PROVINCIAL POLICE

The provincial/territorial governments are responsible for the administration of justice. To this end, they oversee police services, prosecute offences, staff courthouses with judges, and operate programs for adult and young offenders as well as correctional facilities for offenders who receive sentences totalling less than two years. Police services generally fall under the purview of provincial ministries of justice or attorneys general.

There are currently three provincial police forces in Canada: the Ontario Provincial Police, the Sûreté du Québec, and the Royal Newfoundland Constabulary. As noted earlier, the RNC polices only the communities of Corner Brook, Churchill Falls, Labrador City, and St. John's. The rest of the province, including the highways, is policed by the RCMP. There are no independent municipal police forces in Newfoundland.

Provincial police forces police rural areas and areas outside municipalities. They enforce provincial laws as well as the Criminal Code. Some municipalities in Ontario are policed under contract by the OPP. Except in Ontario and

Québec and certain parts of Newfoundland and Labrador, the RCMP provides provincial policing under contract with provincial governments. When the RCMP acts as a provincial police force, it has full jurisdiction over the Criminal Code as well as provincial laws. Similar to the RCMP, provincial police officers may be rotated between detachments.

In Ontario, the OPP provides policing services to communities that do not have municipal police services. It also polices waterways, trails, and roadways; maintains the province's ViCLAS (Violent Crime Linkages Analysis System) and the provincial Sex Offender Registry; and provides policing services to a number of First Nations communities that have not exercised the option to have a First Nations police service.

REGIONAL POLICE SERVICES

Especially in eastern Canada, regional police services are a prominent feature of Canadian policing. Most of these services have been formed through the amalgamation of several independent police departments into one large organization. Regional police services have been a feature of policing in Ontario for many years. Today a number of regional police services, including the Peel Regional Police (the largest regional police force in Canada) and the Halton Regional Police, provide policing services to more than half of Ontarians. In Québec, the Service de police de la Ville de Montréal (SPVM) provides policing services to the city of Montréal and several surrounding municipalities.

MUNICIPAL POLICE

As the name suggests, municipal police services have jurisdiction within a city's boundaries. Municipal police officers constitute two-thirds of the police personnel in the country and enforce the Criminal Code, provincial statutes, municipal bylaws, and certain federal statutes such as the Controlled Drugs and Substances Act. Most police work is carried out by services operating at this level.

Municipalities can provide police services in one of three ways: (1) by creating their own independent police service; (2) by joining with another municipality's existing police force, which often means becoming involved in a regional police force; or (3) by contracting with a provincial police force—the OPP in Ontario, and the RCMP in the rest of Canada except Québec, where there is no provision under provincial law for the Sûreté du Québec to contract out municipal policing services.

Municipalities with their own policing services generally assume most of the policing costs, sometimes with assistance from the provincial government. A notable trend in Ontario has been the decline in the number of independent municipal police services due to regionalization and an increase in contracting with the OPP.

FIRST NATIONS POLICE

Aboriginal peoples have become increasingly involved in the administration of justice, especially in the area of policing. This is perhaps appropriate, given the conflicts that have arisen between the police and Aboriginal peoples both today and in the past. Autonomous Aboriginal police forces build on a history of Aboriginal peacekeeping that preceded European settlement.

Within the framework of the federal **First Nations Policing Program**, the federal government, provincial and territorial governments, and First Nations communities can negotiate agreements for police services that best meet the needs of First Nations communities. These communities can choose to develop an autonomous reserve-based police force or to use First Nations officers from the RCMP (the OPP in Ontario). Funding for Aboriginal police forces is split between the province and the federal government.

Today there are autonomous Aboriginal police services in all of the provinces except Prince Edward Island and Newfoundland and Labrador, although there are none in the territories. Among the larger Aboriginal police forces that are involved in policing multiple reserve communities are the Ontario First Nations Constable Program, the Six Nations Tribal Police, the Nishnawbe-Aski Police Service in Ontario, the Amerindian Police in Québec, and the Dakota–Ojibway Police Service in Manitoba. There are smaller Aboriginal police forces in Alberta and B.C.

Aboriginal police officers generally have full powers to enforce the Criminal Code, federal and provincial statutes, and band bylaws on reserve lands—and in some circumstances, off reserve as well. There are also band constables, appointed under provisions of the Indian Act, who are responsible for enforcing band bylaws. Band constables are not fully sworn police officers, and their powers are limited. A survey of Aboriginal community representations found general satisfaction with the quality of policing services delivered under the Aboriginal Policing Program.[9]

First Nations police services experience challenges in a number of areas, including recruitment and training and meeting the demands for service in communities, many of which are afflicted with poverty and high levels of violent crime. There is a shortage of qualified on-reserve police candidates and of pre-employment training and upgrading programs to prepare potential First Nations recruits for careers in policing. In recent years, the number of Aboriginal officers both in RCMP detachments and in First Nations self-administered police services has declined, although the number of female officers and the level of education of officers have both increased. And, officers working in Aboriginal communities report high levels of job satisfaction.[10]

SPECIAL CONSTABLES

Provincial police acts generally provide for the appointment of special constables, who are granted powers similar to those of a police officer, to be used in special settings and circumstances, including campus police services. In Ontario, the duties of OPP special constables have been expanded to include providing assistance for security in courtrooms, collecting DNA samples, and serving as prison guards. This expansion of duties is part of the trend toward tiered policing.

In addition to public police officers and private security officers, there are officers who are most appropriately categorized as **parapolice**. These officers are not fully accredited peace officers. Generally, though, they are sworn as special constables, which gives them the power to make arrests if there are reasonable and probable grounds to do so.

> **First Nations Policing Program**
> a framework that allows First Nations to negotiate a policing arrangement suitable to their needs

> **parapolice**
> unarmed officers who generally have special constable status

Parapolice officers are involved in policing airports, university campuses, and national and provincial parks and in protecting railway property. These officers are generally not armed, but they may carry handcuffs and pepper spray and wear body armour. Most larger police services, including the RCMP, also have auxiliary officers who perform a wide range of functions. Box 2.2 highlights one initiative of the RCMP. Box 2.3 outlines the police services by jurisdiction.

UNIVERSITY AND CAMPUS POLICE SERVICES

Another type of police force are university police services. In Ontario, these services are commonly referred to as "campus community police," as in the University of Windsor Campus Community Police and the University of Toronto Campus Community Police. These police services are staffed by special constables appointed under the Ontario Police Act, and their officers have full police officer powers on university property. The University of Alberta Campus Security Service is also staffed by officers with special constable status. Other

Box 2.2

The RCMP Community Safety Officer Program

To help meet increasing demands for service, several RCMP detachments in B.C. have launched pilot programs that involve hiring community safety officers (CSOs). The intent of these programs is to have persons *from* the community working *in* the community. CSOs, who are designated as "Special Constables," make an eighteen-month commitment to the detachment in which they work, a period that is extended when performance is satisfactory. The CSOs have the same benefits and pension plans as regular members and carry handcuffs, pepper spray, and a baton. CSOs are not police officers and do not have the same powers and authority as sworn police.

The CSOs work in five primary areas: community safety, crime prevention, traffic support, community policing, and investigation support. CSOs also participate in foot patrols and various crime prevention and crime reduction activities,

and they ride along with regular members. The RCMP's CSO program has (as of mid-2012) not been evaluated; however, CSO programs in the United Kingdom have been found to reduce some types of crime and disorder. This has contributed to high levels of public support for the program, increased feelings of safety among community residents, and improvements in police–community relationships.

Sources: Northumbria Police Authority, "Police Community Support Officers—Final Evaluation Report from Northumbria University" (Newcastle upon Tyne: 2006), http://online.gateshead.gov.uk/docushare/dsweb/Get/Document-16100; C. Cooper, "A National Evaluation of Community Support Officers," (London: Research, Development, and Statistics Directorate, Home Office, 2006); C. Paskell, "'Plastic Police' or 'Community Support'? The Role of Police Community Support Officers within Low-Income Neighbourhoods," *European Urban and Regional Studies* 14, no. 4 (2007): 349–61.

Box 2.3

Police Services by Jurisdiction

	Provincial	Municipal	Aboriginal
Alberta	RCMP contract	municipal police services; RCMP contract	yes
British Columbia	RCMP contract	municipal police services; RCMP contract	yes
Manitoba	RCMP contract	municipal police services; RCMP contract	yes
Newfoundland	RCMP contract	Royal Newfoundland Constabulary polices several communities, including St. John's; no independent municipal police services	no
New Brunswick	RCMP contract	municipal police services; RCMP contract	yes
Northwest Territories	RCMP contract	RCMP contract	no
Nova Scotia	RCMP contract	municipal police services; RCMP contract	yes
Nunavut	RCMP contract	RCMP contract	no
Ontario	Ontario Police	provincial municipal police services; OPP contract	yes
Prince Edward Island	RCMP contract	municipal police services; RCMP contract	no
Québec	Sûreté du Québec	municipal police services	yes
Saskatchewan	RCMP contract	municipal police services; RCMP contract	yes
Yukon	RCMP contract	RCMP contract	no

universities are patrolled by contract security officers under the supervision of campus-based supervisors.

A number of factors influence the effectiveness of university police services, even where the officers have special constable status. These include the view commonly held by local police that university officers are glorified security guards; and the reluctance of local police to respond in support of university police, owing to the perception that university-related issues and incidents are mundane and not a priority. This may result in a "gap" between the expectations of the university community and the level of interest and response from local police services.

TIERED PUBLIC POLICING IN ALBERTA

In Chapter 1 it was noted that the late twentieth and early twenty-first centuries have witnessed a rise in the costs of policing and the search for alternative models of public policing. The development of tiered public policing is most notable in the Province of Alberta. There, RCMP officers serve as federal, provincial, and (in many communities) municipal police officers under contract. There are also eight independent municipal police services, the largest of which are in Calgary and Edmonton. In addition, the province has created the Public Security Peace Officer Program, which operates under the provincial Peace Officer Act. These officers enforce provincial statutes. Community Peace Officers, Level 1, respond to nonurgent calls, including theft under $5,000 and mischief under $5,000. They have the authority to arrest and release and to investigate and submit reports on non-injury motor vehicle collisions. Level 2 Community Peace Officers are primarily involved in administrative roles.

Alberta has also expanded the activities of sheriffs beyond their traditional role of ensuring order in the courts and transporting prisoners. Sheriffs in Alberta manage counter-terrorism security information, provide protection to provincial executives (including the premier), staff the Fugitive Apprehension Sheriff Support Team (FASST), and conduct traffic enforcement. Also, the Sheriffs Investigative Support Unit (SISU) provides investigative support to police services. Whether the tiered model of policing in Alberta will serve as a model for other jurisdictions remains to be seen.

PRIVATE SECURITY SERVICES

The rapid expansion of private security services during the late twentieth and early twenty-first centuries was noted in Chapter 1. There are two main forms of private security: (1) private security firms contracted to provide services to businesses, industry, private residences, and neighbourhoods; and (2) in-house company security officers. Some private security firms specialize in forensic accounting and other investigative activities. These firms are often staffed by ex-police officers and have an international clientele. Some private firms have been expanding into the case investigations area. White-collar crimes—which include credit card fraud, extortion, bid rigging, and price fixing—are highly resource intensive, and the costs to investigate these types of offences are often prohibitive for police services.

In-house security officers engage in a wide range of activities, such as crowd control, protecting businesses and property (including neighbourhoods, shopping malls, and college and university campuses), and conducting investigations for individuals and businesses.

The activities of private security officers include mobile and foot patrol, property protection, medical/emergency response, arrest (using citizen's arrest powers), criminal investigations, crime prevention consulting, security surveillance, and personal protection.

There are also "hybrid" police—that is, police employed by organizations that are private yet have some features of public police services in terms of accountability. These include the previously mentioned university-based officers (who have special constable status), bylaw enforcement officers, members of Corps of Commissionaires, and individuals employed by the Canadian Air Transport Security Authority (CATSA), who are in charge of security screening at airports.

There are a number of important distinctions to be made between public police and private security officers:

- Private security officers work for private companies whose raison d'être is profit. Public police officers, in contrast, work for the public and are generally not involved in issues related to economic profit.
- Public police are controlled and held accountable through various public, government-sponsored agencies and organizations.
- Private security services are not required to adhere to provincial police acts or to the policing standards that supplement police act legislation.
- There is no onus on private security services to engage in community-based policing. Private security forces are, in essence, an extension of company management and are concerned primarily with protecting the owner's investment.
- Public police are armed and have the authority to use deadly force, enforce the law, maintain order, and provide a wide range of non-enforcement services to the general public.

Generally, private security personnel have no more legal authority than ordinary citizens to enforce the law or protect property, although they can arrest and detain people who have committed a crime on private property. Recent court rulings have established that private security personnel must adhere to the Charter of Rights and Freedoms only when making an arrest.

THE CONTEXTS OF POLICE WORK

Canadian police officers carry out their mandate and tasks in a variety of "environments." The environment in which a police service operates and in which police officers carry out their tasks has a strong impact on what police do and what is expected of them, as well as on the administrative, operational, and investigative activities of the service as a whole. This environment includes the various internal and external contexts in which police services go about their work.

The internal environment includes the organizational features of the police service, including its size and structure and the activities and attitudes of its leaders, middle managers, civilian members, patrol officers, and investigative officers. It also includes the strategic planning and research capacities of the police service—that is, the organization's ability to develop strategic plans, evaluate its own performance, and implement reforms when required.

The external environment of a police service includes a multitude of factors. These are certainly not limited to the following: the patterns of crime in the area; relations between the police service and other components of the justice system;

the requirements imposed on the police by legislation, government policies, and court decisions; the demographics of the community; the forms of oversight and accountability faced by the service; the types of criminal activities that are present; the fiscal decisions of governments and municipal councils; the media; and the specific incidents to which officers respond and what happens during those encounters. The environment for policing can be hostile or friendly, depending on a variety of political, economic, and socio-demographic factors and on the demands that are made on the police service. Much more research must be done on how the context of policing affects policies and practices.

The Crime Context

Official crime data from 2010 reveal the following:

- The volume and severity of police-reported crime continues to decline, as does the crime rate. Severity and volume of the police-reported crime rate continues its decade-long decline.
- Violent crime has declined, although there were increases in attempted murders, extortion, firearms offences, and criminal harassment. Violent crime remains high in the Northwest Territories, Nunavut, and Newfoundland/Labrador.
- The severity of non-violent crime continues to decline.
- Police-reported crime severity and rates of crime are generally highest in the West and in the Northwest Territories and Nunavut.
- The rate of police-reported break-ins continues to decline as does the number of vehicle thefts, due in large measure to targeted initiatives such as the "Bait Car" program (discussed in Chapter 9).
- The number of crimes committed by youth continue to decrease.
- Aboriginal people are more likely to report being victimized than non-Aboriginal people and have a higher rate of sexual assault victimization than non-Aboriginal people.
- Overall, Canada has a lower crime rate than the United States, although the crime rates in Yukon, the Northwest Territories, and Nunavut are higher than in the American South, which has the highest rates in that country.[11]

Any discussion of police work in Canada must bear in mind that, in general, the rates and severity of crime are decreasing. Police officers across the country carry out their tasks in environments that vary in terms of the amount and types of criminal activity. These patterns also indicate that an RCMP officer posted to a remote village in the territories may encounter a much higher incidence of violent behaviour than his or her counterpart in an urban area in the south. (These challenges are discussed in Chapter 11). Similarly, in larger urban areas, neighbourhoods will vary regarding the nature and types of criminal activity. And besides the more traditional types of crime (i.e., robberies, assaults, property crimes), police services are now being confronted with increasingly sophisticated criminal activities that are often international in scope.

A number of factors may influence police-reported crime statistics, including legislative changes, the policies and procedures of individual police services, and public reporting rates. There is also the **dark figure of crime**—that is, the

dark figure of crime
the difference between how much crime occurs and how much crime is reported to or discovered by the police

amount of crime that for whatever reasons is not reported to the police. Even homicides may be underreported, especially in cases involving organized crime or the deaths of individuals who live and/or work on the street. (Conversely, in cases of theft or damage when the victim has insurance, report rates are higher.) This dark figure is a result of many factors, including the unwillingness of crime victims to report to the police, the fact that some crimes have no direct victim (e.g., pollution), and the fact that many of the conflicts to which police officers respond are resolved informally without any charges being laid.

The Criminal Justice System

Clearly, the police are at the front end of the system: along with the general public who call the police, it is their activities and decisions that largely determine which individuals and cases will become involved further in the justice system.

A number of factors can prevent the criminal justice system and its personnel from operating as a "system" and hinder the efforts of the police. These include the multiple mandates of justice agencies and the difficulties of sharing information between agencies.[12] A major issue for the police is **interoperability**—that is, how to share intelligence and case information and coordinate data from multiple databases from multiple agencies, including other police services, so that all parts of the system communicate and cooperate with one another. For the police, this is especially important in case investigations; see Chapter 10.

> **interoperability**
> the sharing of case file and database information among police services and criminal justice agencies

The Police Organization

Police services engage in a wide variety of activities, including these: establishing policies and procedures that officers must follow; strategic planning; statistical analysis; resource allocation; and setting standards for assessing officers' performance and career advancement.

Police officers in Canada work in departments and detachments that vary greatly in terms of size, structure, and activities. For example, although an RCMP officer may be posted to a three-officer detachment in a remote area, the officer is still accountable to an organizational hierarchy that stretches many kilometres from the detachment to the subdivision, to the division headquarters, to RCMP headquarters in Ottawa. RCMP policies and procedures are formulated in Ottawa and then transmitted regularly to the detachments through the divisional headquarters.

The discussion throughout this text will highlight the importance of the police organization for understanding the occupational experience of police officers (Chapter 5); police use of force (Chapter 6), police ethics and professionalism (Chapter 7); and the degree of success in meeting the challenges of policing in a diverse society (Chapter 11).

The Community Context

The community in which the police service operates greatly affects the demands made on police officers, the role that the police assume in the community, and the patterns of relationships that exist between the community and the police (which, in turn, will determine the potential for police–community partnerships; see Chapter 8).

Communities vary on a number of important dimensions, including these: their size; their socioeconomic, ethnic, cultural, and religious composition; the types and levels of crime and disorder; the attitudes toward and expectations of the police; the demands citizens make on the police; and the level of citizens' interest in becoming involved in police–community partnerships. Residents in neighbourhoods with higher levels of crime and social disorder generally place heavier demands on the police than those in quieter neighbourhoods. Police services have to tailor their crime prevention and response strategies to the needs of specific neighbourhoods.

Residents often have unrealistic and conflicting expectations of the police. Community residents often assign equal importance to crime prevention, crime control, order maintenance, and service functions and rarely provide any input into how police resources are to be allocated. Similarly, many individuals who phone the police expect an immediate response by a patrol car, no matter how minor the incident. Put simply, community residents often want the police to be all things to all people, which is an impossible goal. See At Issue 2.2 at the end of this chapter.

At Issue 2.1

Should Policing Services in the Greater Vancouver Region and in the Greater Victoria Region Be Regionalized?

British Columbia is one of the last jurisdictions where major metropolitan areas are not policed by a single police service. In the Greater Vancouver Region, 15 RCMP and municipal police services provide policing services to a population of just over 2 million, while in the Greater Victoria Region, seven RCMP and municipal police departments serve a population of 350,000 (see *Blue Line NewsWeek*, September 23, 2010, 2–3). There has been ongoing debate about whether regional police services should be developed for Greater Vancouver and Greater Victoria. Proponents make the following case for regional policing:

- It is more effective at providing a full range of policing services to communities, especially small communities whose police services have limited capacities. All areas of the region would have access to specialized resources, including major crime investigators and forensic and emergency response teams.

- It is more effective than establishing a myriad of integrated specialized units composed of RCMP and municipal police officers, especially given that not all departments and detachments participate in the units that are created. The Vancouver Police Department, for example, does not participate in the provincial Integrated Homicide Investigation Team (IHIT).

- It is more cost-effective than having a number of independent municipal departments—a key factor in times of fiscal restraint and the escalating costs of policing.

- B.C. is the only jurisdiction in Canada that has not embraced regionalization. In Ontario, for example, regionalization began in the 1970s and continued into the 1990s with the merger of three police services into the Ottawa Police Service. In the United Kingdom there are forty-three police services, and future reforms could reduce that number to ten.

(Continued)

- Problems of crime and social disorder, and issues related to quality of life, are regional, not local. Criminals and offenders acknowledge no boundaries, and B.C.'s various municipal services and RCMP detachments have serious difficulty working together.
- If community residents served by smaller municipal police services knew the true costs of "no call too small" policing, there would be widespread support for a regional police service.
- Surveys reveal that most residents in the Greater Vancouver Region support the formation of a regional police service.

Opponents of regional policing counter with these points:

- Most municipal mayors in the Greater Vancouver Region oppose a regional police service.
- The presence of several large (350+ officers) RCMP detachments in a number of municipalities surrounding Vancouver and several RCMP detachments in the Greater Victoria area preclude a regional police service.
- The Halifax Regional Police joined with the RCMP to police outlying municipalities. This "blended" model has experienced difficulties.
- A regional police service would be too centralized and would not enable effective community policing.
- Regional policing is "anonymous"; that is, officers know little about the communities they are policing, and this hampers their effectiveness.

- Regional policing would concentrate power with police personnel in the Vancouver Police Department and the Victoria Police Department.
- Smaller municipalities with less crime and disorder would see a decrease in patrol car presence, since police resources would be directed toward major crime areas.
- The policing needs of Greater Vancouver are being adequately met by "integrated" teams and task forces composed of RCMP and municipal officers.

The Research Evidence

Little research has been done on the effectiveness of regional police services, as measured by cost and other performance outcomes. There is, however, a general consensus among police leaders and mayors and councils in Ontario that regional police services are efficient and effective. An evaluation of the blended policing model in Halifax recommended that it be abandoned and that the RCMP be removed from policing in the region, noting that this would save $28 million in policing costs over three years. (The City Council rejected this recommendation and continued with the blended model.)

The absence of a regional police service was a factor in the disappearance of many women from Vancouver's Downtown East Side. This refers, of course, to the notorious Pickton Case, discussed in Chapter 10. Lack of cooperation and communication between the Vancouver Police Department and the RCMP has been cited as enabling Robert Pickton to keep murdering women for so many years.

You Make the Call!

Which of the above arguments do you find most persuasive? Least persuasive?

Sources: R.M. Gordon and B. Stewart, "The Case for the Creation of a Metro Vancouver Police Service" (Burnaby: School of Criminology, Simon Fraser University, 2009), http://www.sfu.ca/criminology/newsevents/documents/metrovanpolicepositionpaper.pdf; Perivale + Taylor Consulting, "Partners in Policing—the Halifax Regional Police Service, the Royal Canadian Mounted Police, and the Community, 'Taking Care of Business' Together'" (Halifax: City Council, 2002), http://www.halifax.ca/council/documents/021126cai03.pdf; Vancouver Police Board, "Options for Service Delivery in the Greater Vancouver Region: A Discussion Paper of the Issues Surrounding the Regionalization of Police Services" (Vancouver: 2008), http://www.curtgriffiths.com/pdfs/RegionalPolicingIssuesPaper.pdf

At Issue 2.2

The Priorities of the Police

Given the finite resources available for policing, it is important that the objectives and activities of a police service be prioritized.

Exercise

Rank the following activities of the police on a scale of 0 to 10, with 0 being not important at all and 10 being extremely important. You may assign the same numerical value to multiple activities.

____ Reduce property crime

____ Reduce violence against seniors

____ Reduce violence against sex trade workers

____ Reduce domestic violence

____ Reduce violence against children

____ Reduce violence caused by gangs

____ Reduce violence caused by guns

____ Improve traffic safety by targeting speeders

____ Improve traffic safety by targeting impaired drivers

____ Improve traffic safety by increasing police presence on the street

____ Reduce street disorder

____ Arrest more violent criminals

____ Arrest more drug dealers

____ Generate more criminal charges

____ Solve more violent crimes

____ Solve more property crimes

____ Respond faster to emergencies

____ Respond faster to calls for service that are not emergencies

____ Spend more time on each call for service

____ Ensure that victims of crime have adequate assistance

____ Investigate criminal incidents in a timely manner

____ More visible vehicle patrols

____ More visible foot patrols

You Make the Call!

- Explain the rankings you assigned to each of the activities.
- What do your rankings say about how you view the role of police in Canadian society?
- Who should decide what the priorities of a police service will be? The police? Politicians? Community residents? All of the above working together?
- What would be the best way to determine the community's priorities?

Key Points Review

1. Policing can be defined as the "activities of any individual or organization acting legally on behalf of public or private organizations or persons to maintain security or social order while empowered by either public or private contract, regulations or policies, written or verbal."

2. There are natural tensions between the power and authority of the police and their legal mandate to maintain order, and the values and processes that exist in a democratic society.
3. Police officers carry out their tasks within a number of legislative frameworks that define their roles, powers, and responsibilities.
4. Canadian police officers derive their authority from the Criminal Code and various provincial statutes.
5. Discretion permeates all facets of police work.
6. Although in theory, the police are apolitical and are to direct their attention toward ensuring the safety and security of the community, all police services operate in a political environment.
7. Public policing in Canada is carried out at four levels: federal, provincial, municipal, and First Nations.
8. The RCMP has a number of organizational and operational features that make it unique among the world's police services.
9. There are key distinctions between public police and private police.
10. Police work is carried out in a variety of contexts, including the the crime context, the criminal justice system, the context of the police organization, and the community context.

Key Term Questions

1. Why are the **Canadian Charter of Rights and Freedoms**, the **Constitution Act**, and the **Criminal Code** important in any discussion of Canadian police work?
2. What is the **RCMP Act**?
3. What role does **discretion** play in police work, and what are some of the features of police discretion?
4. What is **contract policing**, and where does it occur in Canada?
5. What is the RCMP's **Staff Relations Representative Program**?
6. What is the federal **First Nations Policing Program**, and what options are provided to First Nations communities by this policy?
7. Who are the **parapolice**?
8. What is the **dark figure of crime**?
9. Why is **interoperability** important in police work?

Notes

1. C. Clarke and C. Murphy, "In Search of Security: The Roles of Public Police and Private Agencies," discussion paper (Ottawa: Law Reform Commission of Canada, 2002).
2. Law Reform Commission of Canada, "In Search of Security: The Future of Policing in Canada" (Ottawa: Minister of Public Works and Government Services, 2006), 120–21, http://www.policecouncil.ca/reports/LCC2006.pdf
3. P.K. Manning, "The Police: Mandate, Strategies, and Appearances," in *Policing: Key Readings*, ed. T. Newburn (Portland: Willan, 2005), 191–214.
4. D.H. Bayley, "What Do the Police Do?" in *Policing: Key Readings*, ed. T. Newburn (Portland: Willan, 2005), 141–49.

5. E. Bittner, *The Functions of the Police in Modern Society* (Washington: U.S. Government Printing Office, 1971).

6. S. Miller and J. Blackler, *Ethical Issues in Policing* (Aldershot: Ashgate, 2005).

7. K.C. Davis, *Police Discretion* (Minneapolis: West, 1975).

8. B. Dupont, "Not Always a Happy Ending: The Organizational Challenges of Deploying and Reintegrating Civilian Peacekeepers (A Canadian Perspective)," *Policing and Society* 19, no. 2 (2009): 134–46

9. Public Safety Canada, "2009–2010 Evaluation of the First Nations Policing Program," (Ottawa: Evaluation Directorate, 2010), http://www.publicsafety.gc.ca/abt/dpr/eval/_fl/fnpp-psppn-eng.pdf

10. R. Gill, D. Clairmont, D. Redmond, and J. Legault, "Socio-Demographic Survey of Police Officers Serving in Aboriginal Communities." (Ottawa: Public Safety Canada, 2008), http://sociologyandsocialanthropology.dal.ca/Files/Socio_Demo_Survey_Police_Aboriginal_Comm_2008.pdf

11. S. Brennan and M. Dauvergne, "Police-Reported Crime Statistics in Canada, 2010," in *Juristat* (Ottawa; Minster of Industry, 2011), http://www.statcan.gc.ca/pub/85-002-x/2011001/article/11523-eng.pdf; S. Perreault, "Violent Victimization of Aboriginal People in the Canadian Provinces, 2009," *Juristat,* March 11 (Ottawa: Minister of Industry, 2011), http://www.statcan.gc.ca/pub/85-002-x/20100110/article/11415-eng.pdf

12. C.T. Griffiths, *Canadian Criminal Justice,* 4th ed. (Toronto: Nelson, 2011), 30–32.

Chapter 3

Police Governance and Accountability

Learning Objectives

After reading this chapter, you should be able to:

- Describe the various ways in which the police are held accountable

- Discuss the role of police acts and policing standards in ensuring police accountability

- Describe the role of police boards and police commissions in ensuring police accountability

- Describe the provisions for the oversight of the RCMP

- Discuss the models of police oversight in Canada and the advantages and disadvantages of each model and their subtypes

- Describe the role of the Special Investigations Unit (SIU) in Ontario and the findings of an inquiry into the operations of the SIU

- Discuss how the case of an off-duty police officer led to reform in police oversight in Manitoba

- Briefly describe the issues surrounding the adequacy of the complaints process, including for First Nations people

Key Terms

Commission for Public Complaints Against the RCMP (CPC)   60

dependent model (of investigation)   63

independent model (of investigation)   68

interdependent model (of investigation)   67

Office of the Independent Police Review Director (OIPRD)   61

Ontario Civilian Police Commission (OCPC)   61

No other criminal justice professional comes under as much constant and public scrutiny—but no other criminal justice professional wields so much discretion in so many circumstances. The scrutiny is understandable when one realizes that the police are power personified.[1]

Chapter 2 highlighted the tensions that exist in democratic societies between the need to maintain order and the simultaneous need to ensure that citizens' rights are protected. Accountability of the police to the public relates to, among other things, the conduct of police officers and how those officers treat citizens. This, in turn, affects the level of trust that the public has in the police as well as public perceptions of fairness and the extent to which the public views the police as legitimate. Chapter 6 will examine what happens when the legitimacy of the police is undermined by perceptions that officers have abused their authority with respect to the use of force.

Given the unique powers that police officers have, which include the power to use lethal force and the power to deprive a citizen of freedom, it is essential that there be structures of governance and accountability. It is also important that those structures be, to the greatest possible extent, transparent and accessible to citizens. Should the citizenry come to perceive that police officers are not being held accountable for their actions, and that the structures of governance are distant and impersonal, community confidence and trust in the police will be compromised.

A key trend in Canadian police work is the increasing focus on governance and accountability. This has happened in tandem with the increasing visibility of the police (see Chapter 1). It has also been driven in part by a number of high-profile incidents that have focused media and public scrutiny on the police. Concurrent with this has been a critique of traditional structures of police accountability that is based on the inherent drawbacks of police investigating themselves. The result has been a rise in civilian oversight and the emergence of models of accountability that include civilian involvement in investigations and (in several jurisdictions) independent civilian investigations and oversight.[2] This chapter explores the various models of police oversight that have developed in Canada.

GOVERNANCE OF THE POLICE

Police work in Canada today is carried out in the context of legislative and administrative frameworks that are designed to provide governance and accountability of police services and their officers.

There are differences in how federal, provincial, regional, and municipal police services are governed. The federal Minister of Public Safety and Emergency Preparedness is responsible for overseeing the RCMP within the framework of the RCMP Act; the Ontario Provincial Police, the Sûreté du Québec, and the Royal Newfoundland Constabulary are governed by their provincial ministries. Municipal and regional police services, on the other hand, are governed by police commissions or police services boards, which are composed of elected or appointed citizens.[3]

Governance models are designed to achieve a number of goals. These include maximizing use of available resources, achieving performance targets, maintaining specific standards of service, maintaining client (citizen) confidence, and ensuring that complaints about officers—and the service as a whole—are considered fairly and responded to expeditiously.[4]

The growing complexity of police work has led to an increased emphasis on public approval, transparency, and service, and this in turn has required new accountability structures.[5] In recent years the trend has been toward civilian or independent review bodies replacing the traditional "police investigating police" models.[6] A concern is that structures of accountability have not kept pace with the pluralistic nature of police work in the twenty-first century. Another concern is that those structures tend to view the public and private police as separate entities when in fact there is considerable overlap and collaboration in their activities. The regulation of private policing "tends to reflect a business regulation model rather than a model of public service goverance."[7]

A key objective of the oversight of the police is to ensure accountability. Canadian police services are held accountable through several means:

- Political accountability to governing authorities
- Legal accountability to the law through the courts and judiciary
- Accountability to administrative agencies, including complaints commissions, human rights commissions, provincial police commissions, auditor generals, and ombudsmen
- Direct public accountability through mechanisms such as freedom of information legislation
- Accountability to the community, often through community policing committees that play an advisory role
- Special ad hoc accountability through processes such as Royal Commissions, commissions of inquiry, task forces, and inquests.[8]

Police officers can be held accountable for their actions under the Criminal Code, as well as under civil law, provincial statutes, and freedom of information acts. As well, various police boards, complaint commissions, and investigative units both within and outside police services have the authority to oversee and review the actions and decisions of police officers. Governments may also call commissions of inquiry or appoint task forces to inquire into specific incidents involving the police. A number of these inquiries are discussed throughout the text.

The arrangements for police oversight in Ontario and for the RCMP illustrate one way in which governments have attempted to ensure accountability.

One perennial issue is that RCMP officers who police under provincial or municipal contract are not accountable to the provincial jurisdiction in which they are policing, but rather to a federal structure. Several jurisdictions have addressed this by writing agreements that provide for RCMP officers to be subjected to provincial investigative bodies. For example, serious incidents involving RCMP officers in Yukon are investigated by the Alberta Serious Incident Team, an independent civilian body.

Police Acts

Police acts provide the legislative framework within which police services are structured and delivered. They also set out the principles of policing, the processes for filing complaints against police officers, and disciplinary procedures, and they define the activities of police commissions and police boards. All of the provinces have police acts. None of the territories do, although Yukon was developing one in 2012. The federal RCMP Act contains provisions relating to the operations of that force's External Review Committee and Public Complaints Commission.

> **police acts**
> the legislative framework for police services

Policing Standards

A number of provinces have **policing standards** that supplement the provisions of the provincial police act. The Alberta Policing Standards Manual, for example, contains a number of sections, including these:

> **policing standards**
> provisions that set out how police services are to be maintained and delivered

- *roles and responsibilities of the police:* the legislative framework and accountability
- *organizational management:* community policing, planning, and financial management
- *personnel administration:* recruitment, selection, and training, professional standards, performance evaluations
- *operations:* traffic, patrol, investigations, the use of force
- *support services:* including crime analysis, victim and witness assistance, media relations.[9]

Police Boards and Police Commissions

In many jurisdictions, municipal **police boards** and provincial **police commissions** play a major role in overseeing the activities of police services. The authority of police boards flows from provincial police acts. Municipal police boards, however, do not operate in all provinces (they have never existed in Québec or Newfoundland) or in all municipalities (in Manitoba, only Brandon and Winnipeg have boards). A municipal police board is composed of community members and city councillors and is usually chaired by the mayor. The board's activities may include hiring the chief constable, preparing and overseeing the police budget, and authorizing increases in police personnel. Where they exist, provincial police commissions are involved in developing policing standards, promoting research, and providing training programs for municipal and provincial officers.

> **police boards** (*also,* **police commissions**)
> bodies that provide oversight of police

Section 31(1) of the Ontario Police Services Act identifies the duties of the police services boards in that province. Those duties include appointing the members of the municipal police force; establishing, in consultation with the chief of police, the priorities and objectives of the police service; recruiting and hiring the chief of police; and allocating and administering police service budgets. The activities of First Nations police forces are overseen by reserve-based police commissions or by the local band council.

There is evidence that some police boards are ineffective in their efforts to provide governance of the police. Also, that benchmarks are lacking that can be used to evaluate the governance provided by boards. Some boards suffer from poor leadership, a lack of direction, high turnover, and members who are political appointees. To be effective, the members of the police board must have a good understanding of governance; they also need to involve themselves in issues related to police policies and strategies.[10] Chiefs of police sometimes perceive political pressure or interference from board members; such interference can undermine the role of police boards as a mechanism for ensuring police accountability while protecting police independence.[11]

Oversight of the RCMP

RCMP External Review Committee

an oversight body of the RCMP that hears appeals from RCMP officers who have been disciplined

Two bodies oversee the conduct of RCMP officers: the **RCMP External Review Committee** and the **Commission for Public Complaints Against the RCMP (CPC)**. The former hears appeals from RCMP members who have been disciplined for an infraction of force regulations. The CPC, on the other hand, is an independent federal agency that receives and reviews complaints made by citizens about the conduct of RCMP officers who are policing under contract (i.e., who are serving as provincial or municipal police officers; see www.cpc-cpp.gc.ca). These complaints are initially referred to the RCMP for investigation and disposition. If the complainant is not satisfied with the outcome of the RCMP investigation, the commission may conduct an independent review and recommend appropriate actions to the RCMP Commissioner.

Commission for Public Complaints Against the RCMP (CPC)

an independent civilian body that receives complaints made by citizens against sworn and civilian members of the RCMP

Roughly one-tenth of the 2,500 or so complaints that are made against the RCMP each year are reviewed by the commission at the request of complainants. In most cases, the commission's findings support the RCMP's disposition of the complaint. In many cases the commission uses alternative dispute resolution (ADR), which brings together the complainant and the RCMP member(s) as soon as possible after the incident in an attempt to resolve the outstanding issues informally.

The RCMP also has an Independent Observer Program, which as of 2012 was operating in British Columbia and Yukon. This involves a civilian working with a sworn RCMP member to investigate incidents involving RCMP members that involved serious injury or death. The program's objectives are to ensure that investigations into these incidents are conducted impartially and to increase public confidence in RCMP-led investigations, although the independent observers have no legal standing and cannot address RCMP policy. An evaluation of the Observer Program found that RCMP officers, the Commission for Public Complaints Against the RCMP, and the observers themselves all perceived that the program had a positive impact on RCMP investigations and that the program had been effective in assessing the impartiality of internal investigations.[12]

Police Oversight in Ontario

Ontario is the most advanced jurisdiction in Canada in terms of police oversight and the "civilianizing" of accountability. The **Office of the Independent Police Review Director (OIPRD)** is a civilian agency that is responsible for receiving all complaints about municipal, regional, and provincial police services and their officers in Ontario. This does not include RCMP officers who work only in a federal capacity in Ontario. The OIPRD was created in 2009 "to provide an independent, transparent, accessible and effective oversight system that will build confidence and trust in the public complaints process."[13]

When a complaint is received by the OIPRD, it is generally forwarded to the police service in question for investigation. The OIRPD then oversees the investigation. If it feels that this is not proceeding appropriately, it may take over the investigation. The OIRPD has the authority to launch investigations into police services if evidence emerges that systemic organizational issues need to be addressed. Note that individual police services retain the authority to discipline members and to hold disciplinary hearings.

The **Ontario Civilian Police Commission (OCPC)** is a quasi-judicial civilian agency located in the provincial Ministry of Community Safety and Correctional Services. It has the authority to investigate police services and how policing services are being delivered and to inquire into the performance of police officers at all levels of a police service. The OCPC also hears appeals from police officers who dispute the decisions of disciplinary hearings in their police service (www.ocpc.ca).

The **Special Investigations Unit (SIU)**, which operates under the province's attorney general, investigates cases involving serious injury, allegations of sexual assault, or death that may have been the result of criminal offences committed by municipal, regional, or provincial officers in the province. Established under provisions of the Police Services Act, the SIU is a civilian agency that operates at arm's length to the provincial Attorney General. It is independent of any police service in Ontario, and the investigators cannot be from the subject officer's police service.

Unlike police complaints commissions, the SIU works proactively—that is, it does not have to wait for a citizen's complaint before launching an investigation. It tries to complete case investigations within thirty days, although in more complex cases, this is not often possible. The SIU's director has the authority to lay criminal charges against police officers as the result of an investigation and reports any decision to do so directly to the provincial Attorney General.[14] One case that the SIU investigated is presented in At Issue 3.2.

Every jurisdiction in Canada has review and investigative structures, although none as sophisticated as those in Ontario. These are set forth in the following section, in the discussion of models of public complaints and investigations.

Office of the Independent Police Review Director (OIPRD)
a civilian agency in Ontario responsible for receiving complaints about the police

Ontario Civilian Police Commission (OCPC)
oversees police services in Ontario and hears appeals of officers who have been disciplined

Special Investigations Unit (SIU)
a civilian agency that investigates serious police incidents in Ontario

HOLDING POLICE SERVICES AND OFFICERS ACCOUNTABLE: THE COMPLAINT PROCESS

Key to police work in a democratic society is that there be an open and transparent process whereby citizens can complain about the police and whereby serious incidents involving the police can be investigated. Structures of police accountability and procedures for receiving and investigating complaints are vital to police governance.

In the past, people in the community who had complaints about the behaviour of police officers were required to file their grievances with the officer's department, which then conducted an investigation. This was an intimidating process that undoubtedly discouraged many complainants and that resulted in biased investigations even when complainants went ahead. Traditionally, police services resisted attempts to establish external review processes, although this has diminished in recent years. Recently, increasing attention has been paid to the investigation of complaints against the police. As well, existing systems for responding to complaints have come under increasing scrutiny.

In general terms, a citizen anywhere in Canada can file a complaint about the conduct of a police officer or the policies or services of a police department. B.C.'s Police Act, for example, provides for three types of complaints: (1) service or policy complaints, which relate to the policies, procedures, and services of a police service; (2) public trust complaints, which relate to alleged misconduct by one or more police officers; and (3) internal discipline complaints, relating to an officer's conduct in the police service.

The most frequent complaints against police officers involve their conduct. Most often this involves allegations of disreputable behaviour, abuse of authority, or poor attitude.

A complaint can also be filed against the conduct of an off-duty police officer if that conduct compromised the officer's duties or the reputation of the police service (see Chapter 7). There is a time limit (generally six months) for filing a complaint, and complaints are usually restricted to the person who was directly affected by the actions of the officer or of the police service.

Informal Resolution of Complaints

All jurisdictions and the RCMP provide for the informal resolution of complaints and most of the complaints filed against police officers are resolved informally, often through some form of mediation. The subject officer and the complainant must agree beforehand to participate in a session guided by a facilitator. For example, the Commission for Public Complaints Against the RCMP (CPC) operates an informal dispute resolution program. Complainants who participate do not relinquish their right to file a formal complaint later on. A representative from the CPC serves as the facilitator; the complainant and the RCMP member(s) explore ways to informally resolve the complaint.

A case in which a complaint was resolved informally is presented in Box 3.1. In this instance, the officers were alleged to have violated public trust and abused their authority. Additional cases are presented in the discussion of police ethics and professionalism in Chapter 7.

Box 3.1

A Night Out Gone Bad

A woman was at a bar with some friends. The bartender had a confrontation with the woman's friends. The woman calmed the situation down and the bartender indicated that they could remain at the bar. The woman and her friends were playing pool when the police showed up and asked everyone to leave. The woman asked the police why they were being kicked out. The officer repeated that they had to leave. The woman went to get her belongings and the officer yelled at her to put her drink down and leave. She indicated that the she was just getting her things. The officer grabbed her by the arm and dragged her out of the bar. She was not allowed to get her jacket and she ended up losing a shoe on the way to the police car.

The officers took her to the drunk tank. They would not tell her why she was hauled out of the bar and would not answer any of her questions. The woman said she was arrested without grounds and the officers were abusive and rude to her.

The complaint was resolved informally with a meeting between the woman and the officers involved.

Source: "Manitoba Justice: Annual Report, 2008," Officer of the Commissioner, Law Enforcement Review Agency (LERA) (Winnipeg: 2008), 22–23, http://www.gov.mb.ca/justice.lera/annual_report/pdf/2008/2008-annual_report.pdf

AN OVERVIEW OF MODELS OF PUBLIC COMPLAINTS AGAINST THE POLICE AND INVESTIGATIONS OF POLICE OFFICER MISCONDUCT

There is considerable variation across the country in the models used for ensuring police accountability. These include the *dependent* model (with two subtypes), in which the police essentially investigate themselves; the *interdependent* model (again, with two subtypes), which incorporates civilians into the process to varying degrees; and the *independent* model, in which investigations are controlled by civilians.[15] See Figure 3.1 and Table 3.1.

The following discussion provides an overview of the various models and the advantages and disadvantages of each approach.

The Dependent Model

In the **dependent model,** complaints filed against the police and serious incidents are investigated by the police themselves. The police service undertakes investigations—including criminal investigations—into cases involving other police officers. There are two subtypes to this model: in one, the police service investigates its own officers (internal); in the other, the investigation is conducted by officers from another police service, which may be within or outside the particular jurisdiction (external).

dependent model (of investigation)
the practice of police investigating themselves

FIGURE 3.1   Models of Public Complaints and Investigations of Police Officer Misconduct

Source: C. Murphy and P.F. McKenna, Commission for Public Complaints Against the RCMP, "Police Investigating Police: Final Public Report," August 25, 2010, 17, http://www.cpc-cpp.gc.ca/prr/rep/chair-pre/pipR/pip-finR-eng.pdf; Reproduced with the permission of the Minister of Public Works and Government Services, 2011.

All police services have internal policies to which police officers are accountable, internal units to investigate alleged misconduct by officers, and a disciplinary process that includes a variety of sanctions that can be imposed on officers found guilty of misconduct.

Police services will sometimes request that officers from another police service conduct the investigation. The goal here is to ensure that the officer's peers and/or colleagues do not conduct the investigation. It is common practice, for example, for the RCMP and other police services to call on officers from other police agencies (and other RCMP detachments) to conduct investigations, especially in more serious cases.[16] The main benefit of the dependent model is that expert and legally empowered police officers do the investigation.

This model of police accountability has come under increasing scrutiny in recent years. There is a widespread perception among the public and politicians that the police should not investigate themselves. This is due to the poor optics of police-on-police investigations; it is widely doubted that the police can conduct thorough and unbiased investigations of their colleagues. One concern is the influence of the police culture on investigations. As one police scholar noted: "One of the reasons that the police cannot be trusted to investigate themselves is the way they are socialized. Policemen and women have been shown to spend much of their time socializing with other policemen and

TABLE 3.1   Models of Investigations of Police

1. Dependent Model		2. Interdependent Model		3. Independent Model
1.1 **Police Investigating Police**	**1.2** **Police Investigating Another Police Force**	**2.1** **Police Investigation and Civilian Review/ Monitoring**	**2.2** **Police/Civilian Investigation and Civilian Review**	**3.** **Civilian Investigation and Review**
Represents police investigating police criminal investigations • Police fully responsible for the investigation and administration of public complaints • No civilian involvement in a criminal investigation • Oversight body recognizes complaints regarding service, internal discipline or public trust • Oversight body may be an appellate authority	Represents police investigating another police force Involves formal arrangements (memoranda of agreement) in place with another police force to handle investigation of police officers in cases of death or serious bodily harm • Unlegislated process • In place only in select provinces in Canada	Introduces civilian observation to investigation Civilian observer responsible to monitor criminal investigation (not direct or oversee investigation) • Regular reporting on status of investigation required • Police responsible for investigation, adjudication and administration of public complaints	Oversight body may choose from various options which include: a) may supervise/ manage parts of police criminal investigation (beyond monitor/ oversee) conducted by police b) may assume control over police investigation c) may undertake independent criminal investigation • Oversight body can refer investigation to police force • Police can be involved in some form of collaboration, cooperation or coordination of the actual investigation of public complaints with oversight body	Oversight body undertakes independent criminal investigation for cases within its mandate • Police are excluded or removed from process of investigating public complaints • Hallmark of this system is that civilian personnel are fully responsible for investigation • Nil ability to refer investigation to police

Source: Commission for Public Complaints Against the RCMP, "Police Investigating Police: Final Public Report" (Ottawa: 2009), 74, http://www.cpc-cpp.gc.ca/prr/rep/chair-pre/pipR/pip-finR-eng.pdf; Reproduced with the permission of the Minister of Public Works and Government Services Canada, 2012.

women. As a result, they may be insensitive to prevailing social norms and public expectations."[17]

This may in turn lead to cover-ups, the purposeful mishandling of investigations, and public perception that the police are protecting their own. These concerns may or may not have a basis in any particular case. The point is that

TABLE 3.2 The Dependent Model: Advantages and Disadvantages	
Internal Type	All public complaints managed internally by officers within the police department
Advantages	• Investigative expertise • Knowledge of the police organization • Greater police cooperation (legitimacy) • Legal authority established
Disadvantages	• May not take complaints seriously • Overly sympathetic to police culture—undermines investigation • Pressure by other officers, "blue wall" of silence • No evidence of actual higher cooperation • Disciplinary process may not reflect public standards/ expectations • Low level of substantiated complaints
External Type	All public complaints managed internally by officers outside the police department
Advantages	• Investigative expertise • Knowledge of the police organization • Greater police cooperation (legitimacy) • Legal authority established • Measure of independence and objectivity • Enhanced public legitimacy • Limits internal responsibility for negative feelings • Avoids civilian review while maintaining independent investigation
Disadvantages	• Only the appearance of an independent investigation • Objectivity often criticized by those outside policing • Overly sympathetic to police culture—undermines investigation • Pressure by other officers, "blue wall" of silence • No evidence of actual higher cooperation • Low level of substantiated complaints • Diminished public confidence in the legitimacy for meeting adequate standards of accountability

Source: Compiled from Commission for Public Complaints Against the RCMP, "Police Investigating Police: Final Public Report" (Ottawa: 2009), http://www.cpc-cpp.gc.ca/prr/rep/chair-pre/pipR/ pip-finR-eng.pdf; Murphy and McKenna (2010).

perceptions of bias and favouritism provide the strongest support for movement toward more independent, civilian-led models.

An in-depth examination by the Commission for Public Complaints Against the Police found serious flaws in the practice of the RCMP investigating its own officers for alleged misconduct.[18] Specifically, it was found that in 25 percent of cases, the investigator knew the officer being investigated; that in one-third of the cases, the primary investigator was at either the same rank as the officer being investigated or at a lower one; and that in 60 percent of the cases, only one investigator was assigned. The report also found that there were no uniform standards for conducting investigations and that there was considerable variation in the qualifications of the officers conducting them.

The advantages and disadvantages of the dependent model are presented in Table 3.2.

The Interdependent Model

In the **interdependent model** of investigation, there are varying degrees of civilian involvement. The two subtypes of this model are (1) police investigation and civilian review/monitoring, and (2) police/civilian investigation and civilian review (see Table 3.3).

The first subtype of the interdependent model limits civilian involvement in the investigation phases of a complaint, which are conducted solely by police officers. Civilians oversee the investigation after it has been completed in order to ensure that the investigation adhered to policy. In the hybrid subtype, there is considerably more civilian involvement. Typically, civilians work closely with police officers to investigate a complaint. The hybrid model thus extends civilian involvement beyond an oversight role to one of active participation in the investigation.[19]

> **interdependent model (of investigation)**
> a procedure for complaint investigation with varying degrees of civilian involvement

TABLE 3.3   Interdependent Models

Oversight Body (Location)	Jurisdiction	Reports to
Police Investigating Police + Civilian Review/Observation		
Commission for Public Complaints Against the RCMP (Canada)	All RCMP officers	Public Safety Minister
Office of the Police Complaint Commissioner (British Columbia)	All British Columbia police*	British Columbia Legislature
Law Enforcement Review Agency (LERA) (Manitoba) Independent Investigation Unit (Manitoba)	All Manitoba police officers *	Annual report to the Minister of Justice; administratively to the ADM, Criminal Justice
Ontario Civilian Police Commission	All Ontario police*	Ontario Minister of Public Safety and Correctional Services
Police/Civilian Investigation Hybrid + Civilian Review		
Serious Incident Response Team (ASIRT) (Alberta)	All municipal police*	Alberta Solicitor General and Public Security Minister
Public Complaints Commission (PCC) (Saskatchewan)	All municipal police in the province*	Saskatchewan Deputy Minister of Justice
Serious Incident Response Team (Nova Scotia)	All municipal police in the province	Ministry of Justice

*Indicates jurisdictions where the public complaints authority has no jurisdiction over RCMP officers.

Sources: Commission for Public Complaints Against the RCMP, "Police Investigating Police"; Murphy and McKenna (2010).

TABLE 3.4	The Interdependent Model: Advantages and Disadvantages

Police Investigation and Civilian Review/Monitoring

	A civilian observer is assigned to the police investigation to ensure that it is conducted with impartiality
Advantages	• Enhances public accountability and transparency • Provides opportunity to monitor effectiveness of investigations • Provides opportunities to make recommendations regarding outcomes • Provides opportunity for independent assessment and review of management and operational practices
Disadvantages	• Does not fully address public concerns about independence of investigations • Limited authority, resources, or powers to meet public standards for accountability • Cannot conduct investigations, so are reliant on police investigations • Insufficient and limited understanding of police operations • Viewed as illegitimate and inappropriate by some police • Viewed as costly, ineffective, and time consuming • Critics argue it has not increased satisfactory outcomes

Police/Civilian Hybrid Investigation and Civilian Review

Advantage	• Civilians involved in the investigation; goes beyond the role of mere overseer; may include retired officers
Disadvantages	• Hybrid model still fails the public test of full accountability and independence • Police involvement may undermine the independence of civilian oversight—may make it less effective • Involvement of retired or seconded police may inhibit the development of a new civilian organizational culture • Difficult to attract experienced police investigators when they do not have control or command

Source: Commission for Public Complaints Against the RCMP, "Police Investigating Police"; Murphy and McKenna (2010).

A number of criticisms have been directed at the interdependent model, chief among them being that there is no true "independent" review of the police.[20] Generally, the investigation is conducted by police officers, and in most cases, the civilian reviewers cannot conduct independent investigations or hearings, subpoena witnesses, or retrieve documents.[21] The advantages and disadvantages of the two interdependent approaches are set out in Table 3.4.

independent model (of investigation)

a complaint procedure in which civilians conduct all phases of the investigation

The Independent Model

The **independent model** relies exclusively on civilians to conduct all phases of the investigation, including investigating complaints and incidents and making recommendations (see Table 3.5).

TABLE 3.5 The Independent Model

Oversight Body (Location)	Jurisdiction	Reports to
Special Investigations Unit (SIU) (Ontario) Office of the Independent Police Review Director (Ontario)	All Ontario police officers*	Attorney General of Ontario
Independent Investigations Office (British Columbia)	RCMP and municipal police officers*	Attorney General of British Columbia

*Indicates jurisdictions where the public complaints authority has no jurisdiction over RCMP officers.

Sources: Commission for Public Complaints Against the RCMP, "Police Investigating Police"; Murphy and McKenna (2010).

This model often uses the services of retired police officers, who are well versed and experienced in such investigations, but these people no longer possess their original police powers. Conversely, the model may operate exclusively with civilians who have no prior connections to or experience with policing. This model is seen as highly objective and impartial, for the police play no role in the investigation. Table 3.6 sets out the advantages and disadvantages of the independent model.

TABLE 3.6 The Independent Model: Advantages and Disadvantages

Civilian Investigation/Review	
	Exclusive reliance on civilians to conduct all phases of the complaints process, including investigations and outcome recommendations
Advantages	• Regarded by the public as the most independent model • Greater accountability within the civilian organizational culture • Complainants have more confidence with nonpolice investigators • Stronger public validation of police positions
Disadvantages	• Lacks police experience and expertise • Perceived by police as being inadequate and unsympathetic • Lack of police inclusion may diminish police cooperation and lead to unsuccessful investigations • If investigations fail from lack of cooperation, public may lose confidence • Arguably the most expensive model—lack of internal resources (forensics, etc.) • Higher training costs for civilians • Requires special legal and investigative powers for civilians • Undermines the authority and responsibility of police management

Source: Commission for Public Complaints Against the RCMP, "Police Investigating Police"; Murphy and McKenna (2010).

MECHANISMS FOR ENSURING COMMUNITY INPUT INTO POLICING

In recent years there have been a number of initiatives across Canada to provide community input to and oversight of the police. In Alberta, for example, communities policed by the RCMP under contract have the option to establish a policing committee. The activities of policing committees in Alberta include the following: overseeing the agreement between the city and the Government of Canada for the employment of the RCMP; providing key feedback to the RCMP concerning policing and city bylaw enforcement strategies and activities; cooperating and liaising with key groups in creating programs and pursuing initiatives to improve public safety; reviewing and advising the City Council on goals and priorities; and helping resolve public complaints.[22] Similar provisions for policing committees exist in Ontario. Community policing committees are not mandatory and there is no legal requirement that the police consult with these committees.

INCREASING POLICE ACCOUNTABILITY IN MANITOBA: THE LEGACY OF A TRAGEDY

At 7 a.m. on a February morning in 2005, Crystal Taman was driving to work. While stopped at a red light, her vehicle was rear-ended by a pickup truck driven by an off-duty police officer, Derek Harvey-Zenk, who was returning home from an all-night party with his colleagues from the Winnipeg Police Service.

The provincial government appointed a special prosecutor for the case. Harvey-Zenk was charged with impaired driving causing death, refusing a breathalyzer test, dangerous operation of a motor vehicle causing death, and criminal negligence causing death. Two years later, however, the charges were pled down to dangerous driving causing death (a lesser charge than criminal negligence causing death) and the other charges were dropped. At sentencing, Harvey-Zenk received a conditional sentence of two years less a day, to be served at his home. He also resigned his position in the Winnipeg Police Service.

The controversy surrounding the case—specifically, concerns that Harvey-Zenk had received preferential treatment as a police officer—prompted the Manitoba government to appoint a commission of inquiry. That inquiry, headed by a retired Ontario Provincial Court judge, examined the response, and decisions, of the Chief of the East St. Paul Police Service and several of his officers. Also investigated was the investigation conducted by the Winnipeg Police Service Professional Standards Unit, which had been requested by the St. Paul Police Service to conduct an investigation.

The inquiry found that the then Chief of the East St. Paul Police Service, who had previously worked with Harvey-Zenk in the Winnipeg Police Service, had botched the investigation, falsified his field notes, and given false evidence at the inquiry. In late 2010, after an external investigation by the RCMP, the former chief was charged with perjury, criminal breach of trust, and obstruction of justice.

The inquiry also found that the status of Harvey-Zenk as a police officer had had a profound effect on the investigation by the police and on the actions of the special prosecutor. The commissioner's final report stated that the findings of the inquiry "showed the perils of having police officers investigate, or even interview, other police officers from their own force in criminal cases.…It is graphically demonstrated that internal police investigations are ill-advised in criminal cases."[23]

A key recommendation of the inquiry was that the provincial government create an independent oversight agency to investigate alleged criminal acts of police officers. After the inquiry the provincial government enacted a new Police Services Act, which established the Manitoba Police Commission and civilian-led boards with the power to hire and fire police chiefs for major municipal police services. The same act directed the police commission to establish an Independent Investigation Unit to investigate serious incidents involving the police, including police use of lethal force. The provincial government also settled a civil suit that had been filed by the Taman family. The East St. Paul Police Service was disbanded and replaced by an RCMP detachment.

Another tragedy, this one in Yukon and involving the death of an Aboriginal man, served as the catalyst for reform in that jurisdiction. The case is examined in Chapter 11.

THE ADEQUACY OF POLICE COMPLAINT/INVESTIGATION PROCESSES

There are a number of ongoing concerns about the adequacy of police complaint and investigation processes. Some that have been raised about the RCMP's practices were mentioned earlier in this chapter in the section on the dependent model.

Concerns have also been expressed about lengthy delays that often arise in resolving complaints about police officers. A former Commissioner of the RCMP noted that internal discipline often moved at a "glacial pace," with officers waiting as long as six years for their disciplinary hearings to be held.[24] In contrast, in 2009, Manitoba's Law Enforcement Review Agency took an average of four months to conclude an investigation.[25]

The final report on the tasering death of Robert Dziekanski at Vancouver International Airport (see Chapter 6), released in 2010, recommended the creation of an Independent Investigation Office (IIO) to investigate police incidents involving serious harm or any alleged Criminal Code violation by a police officer. The IIO, created in 2012, reports directly to the provincial Attorney General.

Aboriginals and the Complaint Process

A number of inquiries have questioned whether existing police complaint processes meet the needs of First Nations people. A related concern is that First Nations may not be aware of processes for filing complaints against the police and/or may not have faith in complaint processes.[26] The Commission for Public Complaints Against the RCMP receives almost no complaints from First Nations and Métis people. This means either that no difficulties arise between the police and Aboriginal people, or that for a variety of reasons, Aboriginal people do not exercise their right to complain about the police (which is the more likely scenario).

A review of policing in Yukon found that many residents had little understanding of or faith in the complaints process. Some residents expressed the fear that there would be retaliation if they filed a complaint. Said one resident: "I wouldn't make a complaint even if I knew how to do it. I would fear what they would do to me when they found out I made a complaint and they would find out. This is a small town and there is no way to keep it from them."[27]

Among the recommendations of the review, completed in 2010, were that the territorial government establish an independent civilian complaint coordinator and that initiatives be undertaken to educate community residents about the complaint process.[28]

To better serve the interests of First Nations and Métis people in Saskatchewan, the Federation of Saskatchewan Indian Nations operates a SIU composed of First Nations staff with policing and justice-related experience. The issues surrounding the police and Aboriginal peoples are discussed in Chapter 11.

The Effectiveness of Oversight and Investigations

Despite increased attention to the need to provide oversight of the police and to ensure that investigations of the police are transparent, thorough, and unbiased, there has been little research on the effectiveness of the structures for governance and the various models for responding to complaints against the police and investigating police officer misconduct. See At Issue 3.1.

In 2008, a report of the Ontario Ombudsman found significant difficulties with the operations of the SIU in that province, including lengthy delays in investigating incidents and a pattern of accommodative relationships between the police and the SIU that often created the perception that the SIU was not independent. In its report, the Ontario Ombudsman concluded that the SIU had to change its image as a "toothless tiger and muzzled watchdog" in order to function effectively.[29] The issues surrounding the operation of the SIU reflect the larger issue as to whether police officers may be "above the law." See the CTV *W5* program "Above the Law, Part One," available online (www.ctv.ca). In a subsequent report (2011), the Ombudsman criticized the provincial government for undermining the efforts of the SIU to address the issues that had been identified and for failing to act on recommendations for legislative reform.[30]

The Commission for Public Complaints Against the RCMP has also been called a "toothless wonder," since it must rely on input from the RCMP for its investigations into public complaints.[31] In recent years the commission's chair has criticized the RCMP for being less than forthcoming with documents and information required to investigate citizens' complaints.[32] This has led some observers and politicians to call for increased powers for the commission, including legislation that would force the RCMP to respond to requests made by the chair.

In mid-2010, Bill C-38, An Act to Amend the RCMP Act and to Make Consequential Amendments to Other Acts, was tabled by the federal government.

The act creates an arm's-length public complaints commission for the RCMP, named the RCMP Review and Complaints Commission. This will replace the current CPC. (To check on the status of this bill, and others in Parliament, visit http://www2.parl.gc.ca/Sites/LOP/LEGISINFO/index.asp)

Serious reservations have been expressed about the new commission. Although it will have the power of a Superior Court to summon persons to appear before it and compel them to provide evidence, the commission's recommendations will not be binding on the RCMP. Also, the commission will have to secure ministerial approval for self-initiated investigations, and its recommendations will not be binding on the RCMP.

At Issue 3.1

How Effective Are Police Oversight Agencies?

An independent and effective complaints system is of fundamental importance for the operation of a democratic and accountable police service....Independent and effective determination of complaints enhances public trust and confidence in the police and ensures that there is no impunity for misconduct or ill-treatment.[a]

The discussion in this chapter has identified a number of models for police oversight, each of which has advantages and disadvantages. A challenge that has been identified by police scholars is how to measure the effectiveness of police oversight agencies and the extent to which these agencies have developed best practices based on their performance outcomes. One measure of effectiveness might be a decrease in the number of complaints filed against the police in a particular jurisdiction, indicating a reduction in police misconduct. However, a decrease could, alternatively, be interpreted as a lack of trust on the part of citizens in the oversight agency, resulting in fewer complaints being filed. Similarly, there are often no procedures in place to monitor the impact of an intervention by a police complaints agency on the subsequent attitudes and behaviours of the subject officer.

Among the suggestions that have been offered by police scholars for assessing the effectiveness of police oversight agencies are these:

1. The quantity and quality of received complaints: a higher level of relevant complaints indicates improved process performance.
2. Complaints completion process and time: complaints are handled in a professional and timely manner.
3. Conviction rate from complaints charges: more convictions relative to prosecutions indicates improved results performance.
4. Learning and advice for police agencies: the oversight agency communicates information back to the police service on the cases handled; the agency then uses this information.
5. Confidence in the police oversight agency: a higher level of confidence among the public and the police indicates improved process and result performance.

---

[a]Source: C. Filsted and P. Gottschalk, "Performance Evaluation of Police Oversight Agencies," *Policing and Society* 21, no. 1 (2011): 96–109, Taylor and Francis Journals, 2011.

(Continued)

You Make the Call!

1. In your opinion, which of the measures (if any) set out above could be used to evaluate the effectiveness of police oversight agencies?
2. What are the strengths and weaknesses of the proposed measures?

3. What criteria would you use to assess the effectiveness of police oversight agencies? And what are the strengths and weaknesses of each of the criteria that you have identified?

At Issue 3.2

A Case Investigation by the Special Investigations Unit (SIU), Ontario

On April 6, 2007, the SIU was notified that two Hamilton Police Service (HPS) officers had fatally shot a man outside a building. Ten investigators were sent to Hamilton to probe the circumstances.

As part of the investigation, two HPS officers were defined as having discharged their firearms during the incident and were designated as subject officers. Investigators interviewed a total of 18 police and civilian witnesses. The police communication tape was reviewed and the involved officers' uniforms and firearms were examined. Six cartridge cases, a large knife, and a hatchet were retrieved from the scene and also analyzed. A second knife, slingshot, and small rocks were found on the man; a handcrafted copper badge was also affixed to his shirt.

The SIU investigation revealed that on April 6, 2007, at approximately 2:05 a.m., the owner of M&J Billiards and Video on Parkdale Ave. North called 911 to report that a man had entered his store and struck him on the head with a hatchet. While the owner was on the phone with the 911 operator, the man fled.

Two HPS officers arrived at about 2:09 a.m. and found the man at the front door of Taps Tavern. They exited their cruiser and started walking toward him, but stopped when he turned around holding a hatchet.

The officers ordered the man to drop the hatchet and pointed their guns at him. He stared at the officers while reaching inside his jacket and pulling out a knife. He held a hatchet in one hand and a knife in the other. Both officers repeatedly ordered him to stop and put his weapons down. He ignored their commands and started walking toward them. One officer retreated backwards around the rear of a parked police cruiser, while the second officer retreated toward the front of a cruiser to put some distance between himself and the advancing man. The man was about 8–10 feet away from the first officer when he suddenly turned and ran towards the second officer, who was in front of the cruiser. Both officers fired several shots. The man was struck and fell to the ground. The officers removed the weapons, handcuffed him, and administered first aid until the paramedics arrived. At approximately 2:18 a.m. the man was transported to hospital, where he was pronounced dead. A post-mortem examination determined that he died as a result of two gunshot wounds to his torso. The SIU Director concluded that the officers reasonably interpreted the man's actions as a clear and immediate threat to their lives and that the use of deadly force was regrettably necessary in this incident. He said: "The evidence indicates that less than 30 seconds elapsed from the time the subject officers arrived at the scene to the time they fired their weapons.

Once the police arrived, the man's actions escalated and they did so quite quickly. Nothing that the officers did or said was successful in de-escalating the situation. They did not shoot until the man had significantly closed the gap between himself and them."

You Make the Call!

1. From this brief description of the incident, what factors might have influenced the behaviour of the suspect?
2. From the materials presented in this selection, do you agree with the findings of the commission?

Source: © Queen's Printer for Ontario, 2007. Reproduced with permission.

At Issue 3.3

An Investigation by the Commission for Public Complaints Against the RCMP (CPC)

Mr. A was a passenger in a vehicle in Alberta. RCMP Constable C attempted to stop the vehicle and the driver initially refused and, when the vehicle did come to a stop, the driver exited the vehicle and ran. Mr. A was eventually tackled to the ground by Constable C, who punched Mr. A while subduing him. Constable B arrived on the scene and delivered several strikes to Mr. A. Mr. A was arrested and then taken to hospital with multiple injuries. Mr. A subsequently filed a complaint with the RCMP, alleging that the constables had used excessive force in the incident.

The RCMP conducted an investigation and determined that the allegations made by Mr. A were not substantiated. The CPC received a request to review the findings of the RCMP investigation and, in an interim report, concluded that Constable C had used force appropriately, but that Constable B had used excessive force on Mr. A. The Acting RCMP Commissioner responded to

the findings of the CPC's interim report, agreeing with the finding with respect to Constable C, but disagreeing with the finding that Constable B had used excessive force: "[A] more forceful intervention than simply restraining Mr. A's legs was reasonable, justifiable, and necessary" (p. 2). In response to this, the CPC reaffirmed its findings that the level of force used by Constable C was reasonable and proportionate, while the level of force used by Constable B was not reasonable. The CPC recommended: "That a senior officer review with Constable B the need to constantly assess all situations in light of the RCMP's Incident Management/Intervention Model" (p. 2).

Source: Commission for Public Complaints Against the RCMP, "Chair's Final Report After Commissioner's Notice—Incident Related to Excessive Use of Force," February 8, 2010, http://www.cpc-cpp.gc.ca/prr/rep/rev/chair-pre/finR-090716-eng.aspx

(Continued)

You Make the Call!

How does this incident, and the way in which it was reviewed by the CPC, illustrate the positive and less positive features of the RCMP complaint process?

Key Points Review

1. There has been increasing scrutiny of the structures for police governance and accountability.
2. Canadian police services and their officers are held accountable through several means.
3. Police acts, policing standards, and police boards and commissions are designed to provide governance and accountability of the police.
4. The process by which a person may file a complaint against the police is similar across the country, although there is considerable variation in the structures that are in place to receive and investigate the complaints.
5. Most complaints against the police are resolved informally.
6. With the Office of the Independent Police Review Director (OIPRD), the Ontario Civilian Police Commission (OCPC), and the Special Investigations Unit (SIU), Ontario has the most advanced structures for police governance and accountability.
7. There are several models of police complaints and investigations across the country.
8. There have been a number of initiatives across the country to increase community input into and oversight of the police.
9. The death of Crystal Taman in Manitoba was the catalyst for significant reforms in police oversight and accountability in that province.
10. There are concerns surrounding the adequacy of the complaints process for Aboriginal people.
11. There has been little research on the effectiveness of the various structures of police governance and accountability.

Key Term Questions

1. What role do *police acts, policing standards, police boards,* and *police commissions* play in the governance of the police?
2. Describe the role and activities of the *Special Investigations Unit (SIU)* in Ontario.
3. Describe the role of the *RCMP External Review Committee* and the *Commission for Public Complaints Against the RCMP (CPC)* in the oversight of the RCMP.
4. Discuss the role of the *OIPRD* and the *OCPC* in the province of Ontario.
5. Describe the *dependent, interdependent,* and *independent models* of police complaints and investigation, the subtypes that exist within each model, and the advantages and disadvantages of each model and subtype.

Notes

1. J.M. Pollock, *Ethical Dilemmas and Decisions in Criminal Justice* (Belmont: Wadsworth/Cengage, 2010), 182.
2. C. Murphy and P.F. McKenna, "Police Investigating Police: A Critical Analysis of the Literature" (Ottawa: Commission for Public Complaints Against the RCMP, 2010), http://www.cpc-cpp.gc.ca/prr/inv/police/projet-pip-pep-eng.aspx
3. Law Reform Commission of Canada, "In Search of Security: The Future of Policing in Canada" (Ottawa: Minister of Public Works and Government Services, 2006), 88–89, http://www.policingsecurity.ca/Final.pdf; Reproduced with the permission of the Minister of Public Works and Government Services Canada, 2011.
4. P. Stenning, "Governance and Accountability in a Plural Policing Environment—The Story So Far," *Policing* 3, no. 1 (2009): 22–33.
5. Police Foundation, "Police Governance and Accountability," Oxford Policing Policy Forum (Oxford: Oxford University, 2006), http://www.police-foundation.org.uk/files/POLICE0001/OxfordForum/OPPF%202%20Report.final%20version.pdf
6. G. Smith, "Citizen Oversight of Independent Police Services: Bifurcated Accountability, Regulation Creep, and Lesson Learning," *Regulation and Governance* 3, no. 4 (2009): 421–41.
7. Stenning, "Governance and Accountability."
8. Law Reform Commission of Canada, "In Search of Security."
9. Alberta Solicitor General and Public Security, "Provincial Policing Standards Manual" (Edmonton: 2006), 2–4, http://www.assembly.ab.ca/lao/library/egovdocs/2006/alsg/158320.pdf
10. S. Synyshyn, "Civilian Oversight of Police in Canada: Governance, Accountability, and Transparency" (Winnipeg: Manitoba Association for Rights and Liberties, 2008), http://www.marl.mb.ca/sites/default/files/CIVOVER%20Executive%20Summary%2006-06-2008_0.pdf
11. D.R. Caul, "Municipal Police Governance in Canada: An Examination of the Relationship Between Board Structure and Police Independence," MA thesis, University of the Fraser Valley, Abbotsford, 2009.
12. Commission for Public Complaints Against the RCMP, "Final Report—Review of the Independent Observer Pilot Project" (Ottawa: 2009), http://www.cpc-cpp.gc.ca/prr/rep/opp/review-examen08-eng.aspx
13. Ontario Office of the Independent Police Review Director (OIPRD), 2011, http://www.oiprd.on.ca; Ombudsman Ontario, "Oversight Unseen: Investigation into the Special Investigation Unit's Operational Effectiveness and Credibility" (Toronto: 2008), 3, http://www.ombudsman.on.ca/media/30776/suireporteng.pdf
14. Law Reform Commission of Canada, "In Search of Security," 92.
15. Commission for Public Complaints Against the RCMP, "2009–2010 Annual Report" (Ottawa: Minister of Public Works and Government Services, 2010), http://www.cpc-cpp.gc.ca
16. Commission for Public Complaints Against the RCMP (2010).
17. C. Leuprecht, "Reforming Security Management: Prospects for the RCMP," *Policy Options* 28, no. 8 (2007): 67–72 at 69.

18. Commission for Public Complaints Against the RCMP, "Police Investigating Police: Final Public Report" (Ottawa: 2009), http://www.cpc-cpp.gc.ca/prr/rep/chair-pre/pipR/pip-finR-eng.pdf

19. Ibid.

20. S. Walker and B.W. Kreisel, "Varieties of Citizen Review: The Implications of Organizational Features of Complaint Review Procedures for Accountability of Police," *American Journal of Police* 15, no. 3 (1996): 65–88.

21. M. Bobb, "Internal and External Police Oversight in the United States," in *Police Accountability and the Quality of Oversight* (Conference Proceedings), ed. C. Stone (The Hague: Ministry of Foreign Affairs, 2005).

22. Alberta Urban Municipalities Association, "Policing in Alberta" (Edmonton: 2009), http:///www.auma.ca/live/digitalAssests/26/26798_Task_Force_Policy_Paper_on_Policing_06102009.pdf

23. Hon. R. Salhany (Commissioner), "Taman Inquiry into the Investigation and Prosecution of Derek Harvey-Zink" (Winnipeg: Ministry of Attorney General, 2008), 8, 13, http://www.tamaninquiry.ca

24. G. Dimmock, "Pace of RCMP Discipline 'Glacial,'" *Vancouver Sun*, September 18, 2010, B2.

25. Manitoba, Law Enforcement Review Agency, "Annual Report 2009," Law Enforcement Review Agency (Winnipeg: Attorney General, 2009), 38, http://www.gov.mb.ca/justice/lera/annual_report.pdf/2009/2009-annual_report.pdf

26. Commission on First Nations and Métis Peoples and Justice Reform, "Legacy of Hope: An Agenda for Change," vol. 1: Final Report (Regina: Department of Justice, 2004), http://www.justicereformcomm.sk.ca

27. R. MacDonald, "Review of Yukon's Police Force: The Views of Clients of the Salvation Army in Whitehorse, Yukon," unpublished report prepared for the Review of Yukon's Police Force (Whitehorse: 2010), 29.

28. S. Arnold, P. Clark, and D. Cooley, "Sharing Common Ground: Review of Yukon's Police Force. Final Report" (Whitehorse: Government of Yukon, 2010), http://www.policereview2010.gov.yk.ca

29. Ombudsman Ontario, "Oversight Unseen," 74.

30. Ombudsman Ontario, "Oversight Undermined: Investigation into the Ministry of the Attorney General's Implementation of Recommendations Concerning Reform of the Special Investigations Unit" (Toronto: 2011), http://www.ombudsman.on.ca

31. T. Banks, J. Day, C. Kenny, G. Mitchell, W. Moore, and R. Zimmer (Senators), "Toward a Red Serge Revival: A Position Paper" (Ottawa: 2010), http://colinkenny.ca/en/resources/media/PDF/RedSergeFinal_Web2.pdf

32. RCMP Watch, "RCMP Watchdog Adopts Snail as Symbol" (2009), http://www.rcmpwatch.com/rcmp-watchdog-adopts-snail-as-symbol/.

Chapter

4

The Police Occupation

Learning Objectives

After reading this chapter, you should be able to:

- Identify and discuss the basic and preferred qualifications for police officers

- Describe the recruit selection process

- Discuss the competition for previously experienced officers (PEOs)

- Discuss the models of recruit training

- Describe the socialization of police recruits into the role of police officer

- Discuss operational field training

- Discuss the issues surrounding being a police officer, including the working personality of police, the police culture, and the types of police officers

Key Terms

basic qualifications   81

blue-light syndrome   95

careerism   100

code of silence   94

competency-based
   training   89

hypervigilance   95

in-service training   92

operational field
   training   93

preferred qualifications   81

previously experienced
   officers (PEOs)   92

tired cop syndrome   101

working personality of police
   officers   94

Police work presents challenges, risks, and rewards and requires special knowledge, skills, and abilities. Policing as an occupation is often characterized by considerable role ambiguity. The daily tasks of police officers are often difficult and at times unappealing. Officers must often search people who are dirty, neglected, or carriers of communicable diseases such as hepatitis or HIV/AIDS. Many of the people they deal with are impaired by alcohol, drugs, and/or mental illness.

BECOMING A POLICE OFFICER

The basic reasons why people choose to become a police officer—most commonly, the opportunity to help people, job security, and the prestige of the profession—have remained fairly constant over the years.[1] However, there has been a continued decline in the number of youth who are interested in a career in policing, as well as in the perceived levels of support from their family and friends for becoming a police officer. In 2010, only 3 percent of youth surveyed nationwide indicated that policing was their primary choice for a career. Also, 10 percent of those surveyed felt that a person's race could affect their chances of becoming a police officer.[2] This has required police services to become more proactive in their recruiting efforts. The RCMP, for example, has special units of recruiting officers who target specific populations, including women and visible minorities.

Competition among applicants to police services is highly competitive at every stage of recruiting. Many of those accepted have completed some postsecondary education, and many have an undergraduate degree. Most police recruits are mature individuals with a variety of life skills and have had a variety of life experiences that include travel, volunteer work, and/or full-time employment. An applicant must be prepared to have every aspect of his or her life examined (good, bad, and ugly). In future, this may include providing one's Facebook password (see At Issue 4.1 at the end of the chapter).

Basic Qualifications

Those who are considering a career in policing must have certain **basic qualifications,** often referred to as "core competencies." These include Canadian citizenship (some police services will accept landed immigrants), being able to complete a rigorous physical abilities test, at least a grade twelve education, integrity and honesty, and good judgment. It is on the issue of integrity that many applicants to police services "wash out." This includes providing incomplete and/or inaccurate information to police recruiting officers.

> **basic qualifications**
> the minimum requirements for candidates applying for employment in policing

Preferred Qualifications

Police agencies also seek out candidates with **preferred qualifications.** These include knowledge of a second language or culture, an important skill set in policing a diverse society; as well as volunteer experience, which may include volunteering at a community police station, serving as an auxiliary or reserve in a police service, and coaching youth sports. Some postsecondary work is also important. Perhaps a key attribute for a prospective candidate is work/life experience, which may include international travel and/or living abroad, work involving extensive contact with the public, and positive references from past employers.

> **preferred qualifications**
> requirements that increase the competitiveness of applicants seeking employment in policing

Arguably, those with broader life experience are more likely to cope well with the stresses inherent in police work. They are also more likely to empathize with the troubled individuals they encounter. Applicants who are still living at home with meals and laundry service provided will generally be at a competitive disadvantage, and their applications may be put on hold until they have gained life experience in the "outside" world. In 2011, the average age of RCMP cadets at the Training Depot in Regina was 28.9 years. This reflects the emphasis that is placed by police services on maturity and life experience.

The extent to which preferred qualifications may be a deciding factor in an applicant being hired by a police service will depend on a variety of factors, including the overall applicant pool, the number of positions to be filled, and the specific police service. Police services attempt to hire applicants who are a good "fit" with the organization, and this may result in some applicants being successful with one police service and not in another. Note well that persons interested in a career in policing may have to be flexible in terms of which police services they apply to: owing to fiscal restraints, police services in one province may not have many positions, while in another province police services may be hiring. Candidates who are willing to travel may have a greater likelihood of securing a position.

The Ontario Constable Selection System (OCSS) sets out a number of competencies that applicants for police services in that province must possess. *Essential* competencies are those which a recruit must possess before becoming a police officer; they include self-confidence, communication skills, adaptability and flexibility, the ability to think analytically, and the ability to exercise self-control. *Developmental* competencies are those which can be acquired through training; they include assertiveness, a community orientation, and the ability to network and collaborate in gathering information and solving problems.

Pre-Employment Education Programs

Québec's provincial police act requires that all applicants first complete a three-year college program and obtain a diploma awarded by the École nationale *de police du Québec,* or meet standards of equivalence to this program. This program of study includes general academic courses as well as instruction in criminology, policing, and law. After this, candidates must complete the basic Patrol Officer Training Program.

In Ontario, the Police Foundations Program is a pre-employment training program offered by a number of community colleges. It includes courses in criminology and psychology as well as in more specific areas of police work, such as criminal law, rules of evidence, forensic investigation, case investigation, and conflict resolution. On completing the two-year course, students receive a Foundations Training Certificate and write a provincial exam. Applicants who pass the exam are eligible for employment by any police service in Ontario, although graduation from the program is not a requirement for applicants to police services in Ontario, nor does it guarantee employment with a police service. Over the past thirty years, 30 percent of the graduates of the Police Foundations program have found employment in policing.

PROMOTING DIVERSITY

Recall from Chapter 1 that one of Sir Robert Peel's principles was that "police should maintain a relationship with the public that is based on the fact that the police are the public and the public are the police."

Besides seeking applicants with preferred qualifications, police services seek to attract qualified applicants who reflect the diversity of the communities they will be serving. Police services are making efforts to increase their numbers of female, visible minority, Aboriginal, and gay/lesbian/bisexual/transgendered (GLBT) officers. This often involves targeting specific communities and holding "outreach" recruiting sessions.

This wasn't always the case. As recently as 1990, RCMP policy did not allow officers to wear the Sikh turban. There was considerable controversy surrounding the decision of the RCMP Commissioner at the time to support a change in policy—a change that the federal government did finally make. Opponents of the change had argued that the new policy would forever alter a national icon: the Stetson-wearing Mountie. A CBC news clip, produced in 1990 and available online, presents the story.[3]

Police services have made considerable progress in attracting visible and cultural minorities to police work. However, there is still much work to be done. The City of Toronto, for example, is approximately 46.9 percent visible minority, 0.5 percent Aboriginal, and nearly 51.8 percent female. In 2009, 18 percent of the city's police officers were visible minorities, 0.9 percent were Aboriginal, and 28.2 percent were female.[4] These same groups, however, are severely underrepresented among staff sergeants, sergeants, and senior officers, not only in Toronto, but other police services as well (see Figure 4.1).

Of the just over 1,400 sworn officers in the Edmonton Police Service, 176 (about 12 percent) identified themselves as a visible minority or Aboriginal.[5] In 2010 the RCMP revised its hiring benchmarks for new classes of recruits: 30 percent women, 20 percent visible minorities, and 10 percent Aboriginal.

FIGURE 4.1 **Composition Profile of Police Officers in the Toronto Police Service by Uniform Rank, 2008.**

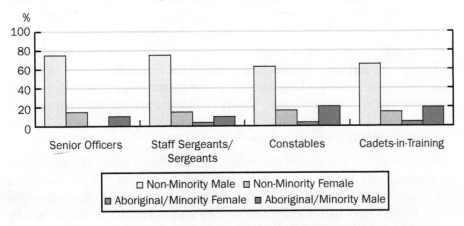

Source: Toronto Police Service, "2009 Update to the Environmental Scan" (Toronto: 2009), 97, http://www.torontopolice.on.ca/publications/files/reports/2009envscan.pdf

At the time these benchmarks were set, the RCMP was 20 percent female, 7 percent visible minority, and 7 percent Aboriginal.[6]

Female officers now represent about one in five officers (compared to one in fifteen in 1990). There has also been an increase in the number of women in senior police positions: about 9 percent of senior officers and 15 percent of noncommissioned officers were women in 2010.[7] Observers have noted that women have broken through the "glass ceiling" in Canadian policing, although it is still important to identify the factors that limit opportunities for women to achieve promotions.[8]

Recruiting Programs to Increase Diversity

Many police services have developed initiatives to attract qualified visible minority and Aboriginal recruits. The OPP operate a number of programs, including these:

- *PEACE* (Police Ethnic and Cultural Exchange), which encourages students from visible and cultural minorities to participate in a police-sponsored summer employment program.
- *Asian Experience,* a program in which potential recruits of Asian background spend several days interacting with in-service members.
- *OPPBound,* a multiday program in which potential minority recruits and women participate in a variety of activities with in-service members.

For its part, the OPP has produced recruiting brochures and pamphlets in a variety of languages, including Cree, Farsi, Hindi, and Pashto (www.opp.ca/ecms/index.php?id=132).

Owing to a long history of mutual suspicion and distrust, police services have faced challenges in attracting Aboriginal recruits. The RCMP has perhaps been the most successful at doing so, having developed and expanded its Aboriginal Policing Program, which is designed to recruit Aboriginal members, who then become involved in policing Aboriginal communities. Two programs are of note:

- *Aboriginal Cadet Development Program (ACDP).* This is directed at Aboriginal people who are interested in a policing career with the RCMP but who do not meet the basic entry requirements. It is designed to help them overcome identified deficiencies. Those who enroll in the program are assessed at the Training Academy in Regina and then returned to a detachment in their home area. They are provided with financial support and given two years to meet the RCMP's basic entry requirements. If they do so, they enter the RCMP Training Depot in Regina.
- *Aboriginal Youth Training Program (AYTP).* This is a summer program for Aboriginal youth that includes three weeks at the Training Academy in Regina and fourteen weeks working under the supervision of an RCMP member in a detachment near their home. The AYTP is not a pre-employment training program, but it does provide an opportunity for Aboriginal youth to become familiar with the role and activities of the RCMP.

It is increasingly recognized that police services should reflect the diversity of the communities they serve, but this is easier said than done. The official record reveals some encouraging developments, but it also reflects the difficulties police services have had in recruiting women and minorities. The reasons why are complex, but they surely include the following: the failure of police services to devote the necessary resources to attracting women and minorities, and the negative perceptions of the police held by many visible minorities, based on experiences with the police in their country of origin and in Canada and the view that policing is not an honourable profession.

GLBT Recruiting

There was long an extreme reluctance on the part of GLBT persons to apply to join the police, due to mistrust of the police, caution about revealing their sexual orientation, and concern that some police officers would refuse to work with them. The acceptance of GLBT by police services has been facilitated by human rights legislation and by the increasing number of outreach initiatives to the GLBT community taken by police services (see Chapter 11). Police services often place recruiting ads in gay lifestyle publications and appear at GLBT events.

GLBT officers may indeed view their sexual orientation as an occupational asset, and they can be an asset in helping the police service develop stronger relationships with the community.[9] In Canada, the presence of openly GLBT officers in police services is becoming normalized and is a non-issue. This reflects a general trend in Western police services.

THE SELECTION PROCESS

Those applicants who have the basic qualifications as well as some preferred qualifications must still complete a number of further steps before being accepted as recruits. Selection processes vary somewhat among police services, but most involve some or all of the following steps:

- *Initial application.* Interested applicants submit a résumé and complete an application form that includes sections on education, employment history, key life events, and volunteer experience.
- *Entrance examination.* Typically, applicants must complete a written, timed examination. Most examinations include a variety of questions covering spelling, grammar, reading comprehension, and general arithmetic. They may also include a number of scenarios for which the applicant is required to select a course of action and/or recall specific items of information. These exercises are designed to provide the police agency with preliminary insights into the character, personality, and judgment of the candidate.
- *Psychological testing.*
- *Polygraph.* In some provinces, candidates are subjected to a polygraph test. Such tests are not used in Ontario. As of 2011, they were being used on a trial basis in Québec. Polygraphy has not been without controversy. See At Issue 4.2 at the end of the chapter.
- *Intake interview.* Most police agencies require that the applicant be interviewed early on by a recruiting officer. The questions range from general queries about personal history, attitudes, and behaviour to specific questions about drug use and personal integrity.
- *Pre-entry physical testing.* Depending on the agency, the applicant will be required to pass a test of physical abilities (see the previous section on basic qualifications). If they excel, so much the better for the applicant.

- *Peer interview.* Some police agencies require the applicant to participate in a peer interview. Typically, several officers from the police service question the applicant on his or her suitability for policing.

If all of these stages are successfully completed, the applicant's documentation is forwarded to an execuvr or review committee. All of the selection process results and documents are then reviewed to determine whether the applicant should be hired. At this crucial stage, the applicant is compared against other suitable candidates.

In Ontario, the Constable Selection System (OCSS) is used by most police services to assess applicants. Although the Government of Ontario does not mandate that all police services use the OCSS, it is managed by the Ministry

Box 4.1

The Ontario Constable Selection System

The OCSS is composed of 2 stages (the process is also illustrated in Figure 4.2).

Stage 1: Testing

The applicant completes registration paperwork and a number of tests, including these: (1) the Police Analytical Thinking Inventory (PATI), which measures deductive, inductive, and quantitative reasoning; (2) the Written Communication Test (WCT), which evaluates the candidate's ability to organize information and draw conclusions in a coherent and comprehensive manner; and (3) the Physical Readiness Evaluation for Police (PREP) Test, a pursuit/restraint circuit. Candidates who successfully pass these tests then take the Behavioural Personnel Assessment Device for Police (B-PAD). This is an interactive video simulation in which candidates view a number of scenarios and are required to respond as if speaking to the people at the scene. Candidates must also pass technician-administered vision and hearing tests. Successful completion of all of these components produces a Certificate of Results.

Stage 2: Interview and Post-Interview Assessments

Once a candidate receives a Certificate of Results, he or she can apply to any of the OCSS-licensed police services. If called for an interview by a police service, the candidate enters the second stage of the system. This stage involves the completion of a Pre-Background Questionnaire, an Essential Competencies Interview, and other background checks. The focus is on how the candidate behaved in various situations in school, at work, or in the community. The candidate must also respond to a number of questions relating to personal character and habits (criminal record, drug use, credit record, etc.). Applicants who progress beyond the interview stage will be required to complete a psychological test. Upon completion of this stage, the candidate may be offered conditional employment by the police service. Successful completion of the tests does not guarantee employment.

Beyond the Constable Selection System

A conditional offer of employment by a police service will require the candidate to pass a full medical clearance. Individual services may also have additional tests or questionnaires, beyond what is required in the OCSS, specific to their own jurisdiction.

Source: © 2011. Reprinted by permission of the Ontario Association of Chiefs of Police.

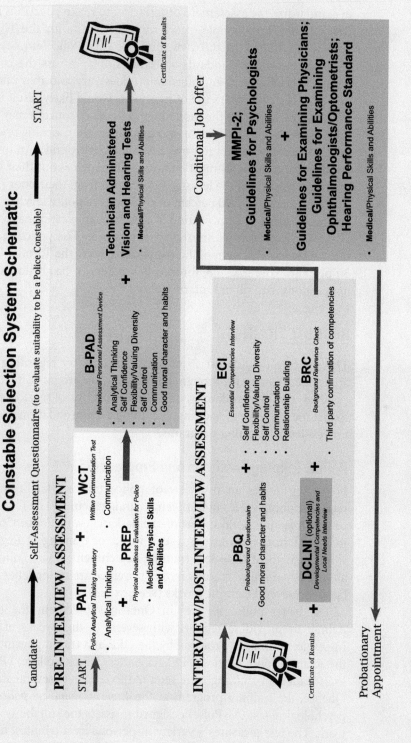

FIGURE 4.2   Schematic Flowchart of the Ontario Constable Selection System

Constable Selection System Schematic

Candidate ➤ Self-Assessment Questionnaire (to evaluate suitability to be a Police Constable) ➤ START

PRE-INTERVIEW ASSESSMENT

START

PATI + **WCT** · Communication
Police Analytical Thinking Inventory   *Written Communication Test*
· Analytical Thinking

+

PREP
Physical Readiness Evaluation for Police
· Medical/Physical Skills and Abilities

B-PAD
Behavioural Personnel Assessment Device
· Analytical Thinking
· Self Confidence
· Flexibility/Valuing Diversity
· Self Control
· Communication
· Good moral character and habits

+

Technician Administered Vision and Hearing Tests
· Medical/Physical Skills and Abilities

Certificate of Results

START

INTERVIEW/POST-INTERVIEW ASSESSMENT

PBQ
Prebackground Questionnaire
· Good moral character and habits

+

DCLNI (optional)
Developmental Competencies and Local Needs Interview

+

ECI
Essential Competencies Interview
· Self Confidence
· Flexibility/Valuing Diversity
· Self Control
· Communication
· Relationship Building

+

BRC
Background Reference Check
· Third party confirmation of competencies

Certificate of Results

Conditional Job Offer

**MMPI-2;
Guidelines for Psychologists**
· Medical/Physical Skills and Abilities

+

**Guidelines for Examining Physicians;
Guidelines for Examining Ophthalmologists/Optometrists;
Hearing Performance Standard**
· Medical/Physical Skills and Abilities

Probationary Appointment

Source: Adapted from Applicant Testing Services Inc., 2011.

of Community Safety and Correctional Services and is licensed for use by the Ontario Association of Chiefs of Police. This system was designed to eliminate multiple testing of applicants by police services across the province, which typically resulted in multiple assessments of the same applicant. It is also meant to standardize the assessment criteria and to make selections less arbitrary (see Box 4.1). For an example, check out the website for the Thunder Bay Police Service in Ontario (http://www.thunderbay.ca/Police/employment.htm).

While recruiting standards are quite similar across the country, the weight given to specific items of information does vary and may change over time. A decade ago, a candidate's use of marijuana would likely result in disqualification. This may no longer be the case; rather, a primary concern may be how recent the drug use was (e.g., a candidate who used drugs the morning prior to the interview to calm their nerves will not make it to the next round). An important consideration is that candidates must be honest and open about their lives, the decisions they have made, and the lessons they learned from their poor decisions.

It is estimated that 90 percent of applicants to police services across the country are unsuccessful. The proportion of successful applications appears to vary among police services, even within the same province. The police in London, Ontario, hire on average 7 percent of their applicants, while the Toronto Police Service hires 30 percent. Note that the Toronto Police Service has historically received fewer applications than other Ontario police services.[10]

RECRUIT TRAINING

There is considerable variation across the country regarding how new recruits are trained. Generally, though, recruit training programs focus on three things: physical training, academics, and skills. Most police services require the trainee to assume the costs of training, including accommodation and room and board for residential training programs.

Police Training Facilities and Programs

Box 4.2 provides an overview of police training facilities in Canada. Basic recruit training varies in both length and structure. The Ontario Police College program is eight weeks; that of the Saskatchewan Police College is seventeen. RCMP recruits receive twenty-two weeks of training in Regina, followed by a similar length of time at a training detachment. B.C.'s Police Academy, where all municipal police recruits in that province are trained, has a unique program based on several training blocks (see Box 4.3).

The larger police services in Ontario supplement the training offered at Aylmer by providing recruits with several further weeks of in-house training. In-service training is provided by the OPP at a training facility in Orillia and by the Toronto Police Service (TPS) at Charles O. Bick College. TPS recruits (referred to as "cadets-in-training") are required to complete several stages of training. In Québec, the training program at the École national de police has introduced a psychological test (M-Pulse) designed to assess the suitability of cadets for police work. The test measures a variety of personality attributes, from poor interpersonal skills, to racist or sexist attitudes, to the likelihood that the cadet will use excessive force. Speaking in support of the M-Pulse test, one police observer in the

Box 4.2

Police Training Facilities in Canada

Province	Training Facility
British Columbia	Justice Institute of British Columbia, Police Academy
Alberta	Edmonton Police Service and Chief Crowfoot Learning Centre, Calgary Police Service
Saskatchewan	Saskatchewan Police College, University of Regina
Manitoba	Winnipeg Police Service Training
Ontario	Ontario Police College, Aylmer; Ontario Provincial Police Academy, Orillia; Charles O. Bick Police College (Toronto Police Service)
Québec	École nationale de police du Québec, Nicolet
Nova Scotia	Atlantic Police Academy, Holland College, Charlottetown, P.E.I.
Prince Edward Island	Atlantic Police Academy, Holland College, Charlottetown, P.E.I.
New Brunswick	Atlantic Police Academy, Holland College, Charlottetown, P.E.I.
Newfoundland and Labrador	Police Officers Training Program, Memorial University
Yukon, Northwest Territories, Nunavut	RCMP Training Academy, Regina

province stated: "You can have a very bright wacko who can run 8 km in nothing flat—but there's no assessment of his suitability [to become an officer]."[11]

An underlying theme throughout training and promotion processes in police services is **competency-based training**, which focuses on the acquisition of specific, measurable skills and knowledge that can be transferred to the operational level. This sort of training includes legal studies, the use of force, and various skill sets.

At all training centres in Canada, police officers are instructed in the law, investigation and patrol, community relations, use of force (firearms), and traffic control (including driving). They also receive physical training.

Training programs are designed to introduce recruits to "real life" situations they may encounter on the street. The Ontario Police College, for example, has a replica drug lab, which it uses to train both recruits and in-service officers in how to identify, investigate, and safely dismantle illegal drug operations. In Regina, the RCMP has two modern houses and a "detachment" on the grounds of the academy. The houses are used for various scenarios, including those involving domestic violence; the detachment is used to train recruits in the various tasks and activities that arise at the operational level. Similarly, the Québec Police Institute has a "virtual police station."

competency-based training
recruit training that focuses on the acquisition of specific skills and knowledge

Box 4.3

Recruitment and Training in British Columbia: A Unique Approach

The recruitment and training of municipal police officers in British Columbia has several unique features. All prospective recruits are required to pass a review at the Assessment Centre located at the Justice Institute Police Academy. Candidates are tested in five exercises: (1) a group discussion, (2) an oral communication situation, (3) a fact-finding, decision-making scenario, (4) a writing exercise, and (5) a background interview. Among the attributes measured in each of these exercises are decision making, decisiveness, flexibility, initiative, integrity, interpersonal tolerance and sensitivity, observation skills, oral and written communication skills, personal impact, practical intelligence, problem confrontation, stress tolerance, and the ability to learn. Recruits are assessed by a team of officers from the various independent municipal police services.

Once hired by a municipal police service, recruits are trained at the Justice Institute of British Columbia Police Academy. The training consists of three blocks, during which classroom learning alternates with field experience.

- *Block I* (13 weeks) at the Police Academy. Emphasis on police skills, including driver training, firearms, arrest and control, investigation and patrol techniques, legal studies, and physical fitness.
- *Block II* (13–17 weeks) at the recruit's home police department. Field training under the guidance of a field trainer provides an opportunity for the recruit to apply Block I knowledge in an operational setting.
- *Block III* (8 weeks) at the Police Academy. Additional knowledge and skills development.

After completion of Block III, the recruit graduates as a qualified municipal constable and returns to his or her home police service.

Source: Courtesy Justice Institute of British Columbia.

The RCMP Pre-Employment Training Model

In contrast to their provincial and municipal counterparts, RCMP cadets are not employees of the RCMP. Rather, a cadet is classified as a *potential* member of the RCMP, on a temporary contract while at the Training Academy in Regina. This makes it far easier for the academy to release trainees who do not meet the Mounties' requirements. Only a cadet who completes the entire cadet training program, and who achieves all of its standards, will be offered an employment contract with the RCMP. The training that RCMP recruits receive at "Depot" is generic and is meant to provide them with a core foundation of policing knowledge and skills. On graduation, recruits are officially hired by the RCMP and sent to a field training detachment. Having completed six months of field training, they may be posted anywhere in Canada as a federal officer or as a provincial or municipal police officer working under an RCMP contract. In contrast, police officers in independent municipal and provincial police services across Canada

Police recruits in physical training.

are often trained at a location in the community or within the province, are hired by their respective departments before entering the training academy, and know which municipality they will be policing after they graduate—probably for their entire policing career.

Because cadets are not considered members of the RCMP, they are not governed by the RCMP Act, nor are they represented by the Staff Relations Representative Program (see Chapter 2). The academy has focus groups to ensure that cadets are able to voice their concerns to senior management when a conflict arises. Cadets may also appeal any decision made regarding their evaluation or their dismissal from the academy. This appeal can go all the way to the Federal Court of Canada, as occurred in a case presented in Box 11.2.

Cross-Cultural Training

Training is essential to addressing racism and cultural insensitivity among police officers. Police services generally include cross-cultural training as part of the curriculum for new recruits. However, it is questionable whether this training is sufficient to prepare officers for the diversity in the communities they will be policing. Cultural awareness training often comprises only a small portion of the overall training program, and there is often no time to consider specific groups. For example, course materials on First Nations, Métis, and Inuit are often combined with course materials on visible and cultural minorities.

Despite the need for police recruits (and in-service officers) to receive cross-cultural training, officers continue to be posted to First Nations, Métis, and Inuit communities with minimal knowledge of the culture and history of the people they serve and who often do not have the language skills to communicate with elderly residents, who may not speak English or French. The challenges of policing in these regions are discussed in Chapter 11.

Competition for Previously Experienced Officers (PEOs)

The need for qualified recruits has spawned increased competition among municipal and provincial police forces and the RCMP for **previously experienced officers (PEOs),** who, for a variety of personal and/or professional reasons, may be amenable to leaving their current police service. A number of police services have special recruiting teams that target PEOs, and it is not unusual for police services to "raid" officers from one another. Most of the larger police services have a specific section on their websites devoted to attracting in-service officers.

The increasing mobility of PEOs presents a number of challenges. Police services must find ways not only to attract but also to retain personnel. It can no longer be assumed that a police officer will spend an entire career with the same department, and there is today an unprecedented movement of officers among police services, including the RCMP. In Ontario, officers may move between municipal police services as well as between the OPP and municipal police services.

Police services must carefully examine the performance records of PEOs to ensure that they are not "problem" officers who are being pushed out of their existing police service.[12] This task is made more difficult by the reluctance of police personnel to provide negative references for a colleague applying to another police service.

> **previously experienced officers (PEOs)**
> in-service police officers who are interested in leaving their current police service

IN-SERVICE TRAINING

The training provided to police officers as their careers progress is variously referred to as **in-service training,** refresher training, requalification training, advanced training, or career development training. Usually, it is conducted by individual police agencies or by provincial training centres. A key issue regarding this type of training is whether it should be mandatory or optional. Some police services require officers to complete a specified number of training hours or an in-service training course; others offer in-service training as an option. As well, police services require officers to qualify on an ongoing basis in the use of firearms, control techniques, batons, Tasers, and oleoresin capsicum (OC, or "pepper spray"). The trend in Canadian police services is toward integrating in-service training with career development; in other words, officers are required to achieve certain educational and training competencies in order to apply for advancement.

The Canadian Police College (CPC), in Ottawa, is funded by the federal government and administered by the RCMP. The education and training programs it offers are national in scope and are designed to provide municipal and provincial police officers, as well as RCMP officers, with upgrading and development programs, research and information, and advice.

The specialized training courses at the CPC are typically two to three weeks in duration and cover a variety of subject areas: advanced collision analysis, clandestine laboratories investigation, electronic search and seizure, senior police administration, strategic intelligence analysis, and so on.

> **in-service training**
> training courses for serving police officers

FROM THE ACADEMY TO THE STREET: SOCIALIZATION INTO THE ROLE OF POLICE OFFICER

Becoming a police officer involves two distinct socialization processes: formal and informal. Formal socialization is accomplished through the selection process and police training programs. These programs provide new recruits with a vast amount of information on a myriad of subjects related to policing. Informal socialization occurs when recruits interact with older, more experienced officers and with their peers on the job.

Impact of the Police Academy

Besides providing knowledge and skills, training academies provide a mechanism for socializing new recruits into the occupation of policing. Far too little attention has been paid by police scholars to the experiences of police recruits in training programs as they are transformed into police constables. This process of "socialization" into the police occupation may have an impact on the recruit's self-image, values, perceptions, and behaviour. A challenge is to develop ways to assess the validity of the criteria used for selecting and training police recruits, and to measure the effectiveness of police officers during their careers.[13]

Most police recruits are motivated, at least initially, by a desire to help people and serve the community. The training experience can have a strong impact on this, however. Research studies have found that, for many recruits, the police academy experience makes them more cynical, more suspicious of people, and generally more vigilant.[14] The recruit's level of education has been found to have no effect on success in the academy or as a police officer, which raises a number of questions relating to the issue of how to predict the performance of recruits. The extent to which recruits exhibit these attitudinal and behavioural traits, however, depends on the personalities and values of the individual. There are attributes of the police academy that do not fit well with the principles of community policing, including a hierarchical, paramilitary structure that encourages an "us versus them" mentality, deference to authority, and the development of strong bonds and in-group loyalty among recruits. The extent to which these features of the police academy experience have hindered the implementation of community policing has yet to be researched in Canada.[15]

Despite the critical role that recruit training plays in policing careers, very little is known about how new recruits feel about the training they receive. As well, little is known about the relevance and impact of academy training once recruits are assigned to operational patrol. It does appear that the occupational culture of front line policing exerts an equal if not greater influence on the attitudes and behaviour of the new police officer than does the formal instruction received at the police academy.[16]

The Field Training Experience

During this second component of the training/learning process, known as **operational field training,** the recruit learns to apply the basic principles taught at the training centre. Under the guidance and assistance of a senior officer, the

operational field training
instructing the recruit on how to apply principles from the training academy in the community

recruit is exposed to a wide variety of general police work. During this critical phase, the specially trained senior officer (often referred to as the field trainer or mentor) makes sure that the recruit is able to meet the demands and challenges of police work.

The length, and structure, of field training varies among police services. For example, Vancouver police recruits spend up to seventeen weeks under the supervision of a field training officer (FTO), whereas new RCMP officers work with a Field Coach for twenty-four weeks after graduating from the RCMP Training Academy and being sworn in as peace officers. And while municipal police recruits in B.C. complete their field training during Block II, prior to returning to the police academy for Block III, new RCMP officers receive their field training *after* completing the program at the training academy.

Police services are paying increasing attention to ensuring continuity between the training a recruit receives in the academy and the supervision provided once the new recruit is involved in operational policing. FTOs play a significant role in the training process and have a strong influence on the attitude and policing style that the new recruit develops. A key objective of the FTO is to enhance the skills and knowledge the recruit has gained at the academy in a way that lessens the "disconnect" between the training academy and the street. This will reduce the likelihood that the new officer will become cynical and discard the skill sets and attitudes learned in recruit training.

There is some evidence, though, that field training may negate the recruit's positive attitudes toward various aspects of policing, including community policing and problem solving.[17] Given the importance of FTOs in moulding the attitudes and perceptions of new recruits, it is important for police services to select FTOs carefully and to monitor their approach to that role.[18] New recruits need to be matched with competent and motivated trainers who represent the best skill sets the organization has to offer.

BEING A POLICE OFFICER

Having completed academy and field training, the new officer becomes a full member of the police service and begins adopting and adjusting to the attitudes and behaviours that distinguish the occupation of police work. Research on the police occupation has generated a list of key attitudes, perceptions, and behaviours of police officers. Many of these are components of what Jerome Skolnick (1966) labelled the **working personality of police officers**—a set of attitudes and behaviours that develop out of the unique role police officers play and the duties they are asked to perform.[19]

working personality of police officers
a set of attitudinal and behavioural attributes of police officers

The Working Personality of Police Officers

Components of the working personality include:

- a preoccupation with danger, an excessive suspicion of people and activities, and a protective cynicism;
- the practice of a **code of silence** to protect fellow officers;

code of silence
officers protecting one another from outside scrutiny and criticism

- strong in-group solidarity (the "blue wall") with other police officers;
- attitudes that emphasize the high-risk/action component of police work, often referred to as the **blue-light syndrome**; and
- **hypervigilance**, which includes physiological arousal, elevated levels of alertness, attentiveness to details of the environment, and interpretation of seemingly neutral aspects of the environment as potentially dangerous.

In reality, police officers consistently face a lower fatality rate than those employed in mining, construction, commercial fishing, and forestry. Police officers, however, may face a higher risk of being assaulted and of having nonlethal violence used against them. This includes being bitten by people with infectious diseases and being exposed to toxic environments. And it is important to remember that the *potential* for violence and death is always present in police work. Officers become preoccupied with danger largely because of the unpredictability of the people and events they encounter. Even routine activities, such as traffic stops, hold the potential for violence.

Reconsidering the Working Personality of Police Officers

It has been forty-plus years since Skolnick proposed the existence of an occupational culture of police and identified the components of the working personality of police officers. Throughout that time, the validity of his arguments has been strongly debated. One question is whether the police personality is a result of nature or nurture. Put another way, do people who apply to become police officers already have many of the above-noted personality traits, or do these traits develop as a result of police work? A possible answer is that "it depends": on the personality of the individual officer, that person's response to training, and the police service itself.

A second question revolves around the extent to which police officers' isolation, in-group solidarity, and traditional distrust and suspicion of the general public are being undermined by emerging trends in policing. These trends include community-focused policing, the decentralization of traditional command-and-control structures, the empowerment of patrol officers, the development of partnerships between police and communities, and the increasing diversity of police services.

A third issue that Skolnick did not address is the impact of the specific operational environment on the police personality. As previously noted, police officers carry out their tasks in a variety of environments, ranging from small towns and rural areas to large cities. Police officers assigned to community stations or posted in small detachments in remote areas have little choice but to interact with community residents; those who work in large cities *can* choose not to do so. The size of the community does not guarantee positive police–community interactions: relations between the police and Aboriginal persons in rural and remote areas of the country have often been afflicted by mutual suspicion and distrust (see Chapter 11).

Fourth, there may well be at least two distinct cultures within police services: one is occupied by senior managers, who are focused on a much broader range

blue-light syndrome
an attitudinal set that emphasizes the high-risk/action component of police work

hypervigilance
elevated alertness about potential dangers in the environment

of issues and street-level police and case investigators. Police managers are often judged according to their success at convincing patrol officers to support the organization's goals and incorporate the objectives of senior managers into daily patrol practice.

Police scholars generally agree that the traditional police culture has been transformed in recent decades although researchers continue to find elements of a police culture characterized by an "us versus them" mentality, suspicion and distrust of certain segments of the community, and strong in-group loyalties.[20]

There are remnants of the traditional police culture, especially in terms of the view that police officers are "different" from other people. Also, police services are still structured on a paramilitary model wherein the primary mission is "to serve and protect" the community from society's less desirable elements. There does appear to be an overarching identity among police officers, one that states: "A cop is a cop is a cop. Some are better than others, some are worse. But we are all made out of the same stuff."[21]

That said, every patrol officer has his or her own style of policing, and not every officer exhibits the characteristics of the working personality. There is variation in the extent to which the attitudes and behaviours of officers reflect the tenets of the police culture.

The Occupational Outlook and Career Aspirations of Police Officers

Not all police officers share the same orientation and career aspirations.[22] Many attempts have been made to develop typologies of police officers in order to determine the differences in how they view their careers. Most classifications are based on officers' occupational outlook and career aspirations. At least five "types" of police officers have been identified, based on their key interests and career orientations:

- *Self-Investors.* Family life, job stability, security.
- *Careerists.* Promotion, prestige, achieving a management position.
- *Specialists.* Professional growth, acquisition of new skills, challenging positions.
- *Social Activists.* Social and institutional change, helping others.
- *Enforcers.* Gathering evidence, apprehending criminals, solving crimes, obtaining convictions.[23]

Attached to each type are a number of assumptions relating to how officers exercise discretion and carry out police work. It is generally thought that an officer's operational style remains constant across policing environments and encounter incidents. Research into police activities and decision making, however, suggests that this assumption may be simplistic and that typologies may in fact obscure many factors that influence the behaviour of police officers. There is some evidence that attitudes, behaviours, and career orientations may change in the course of an officer's training and career. A police recruit may enter the training academy with a certain set of attitudes and exit it with modified views (see Box 4.4). Similarly, a rookie officer may begin his career viewing himself as a social activist or enforcer but have a different orientation in later years, having developed more realistic expectations of what he can accomplish or having experienced a certain level of "burnout."

Moreover, the attitudes of patrol officers may vary with the particular area being policed and the types of encounters in which they become involved. For example, increasing levels of crime and disorder in patrol districts may heighten the cynicism of patrol officers if they see few results from their efforts and become pessimistic about improving the community's quality of life. Officers patrolling districts where there is less crime and disorder may experience less frustration and cynicism.

Positive and Negative Features of the Police Culture

The police culture has many positive features. Given the unpredictability of the encounter situations in which officers become involved and the potential for violence, it is crucial for officers to trust one another and develop camaraderie. Also, in-group solidarity is a source of support and helps individual officers cope with the more stressful aspects of police work.

There are a number of potentially negative consequences of the police culture, however, including police alienation from the general public and other agencies and organizations; police alienation from management; resistance to organizational and operational change; unethical and unprofessional behaviour (see Chapter 7); and biased policing and racial profiling (see Chapter 11).

To summarize, while it may not be possible to quantify the existence of a distinct police personality, and while a considerable mythology surrounds police work, many police officers believe there *is* a working personality of police that sets them apart as an occupational group. Ironically, this belief may in itself make the working personality of police a reality. The occupational perspectives of police officers and their working personality may have a significant impact on operational patrol work and decision making in encounter situations on the street and in case investigations.

THE CHALLENGES OF POLICE WORK

Although police work can be satisfying and challenging, it can also be stressful. The effects of stress experienced by police officers range from minor annoyances (which can be managed) to alcohol or drug addiction, and suicide.[24] There is research to suggest that high stress levels may make officers more susceptible to misconduct. As well, constant exposure to stressors may lead to "burnout," a general term used to describe physical, emotional, and mental exhaustion.[25] Police officers who have been assigned to small detachments in remote areas may experience high stress levels because of the challenging environments in which they work. Remote and rural communities often have much higher rates of crime—especially violent crime—than urban centres. Policing in these high-demand environments, where backup may not be readily available, can take a toll on officers. In recognition of this, officers are generally posted to these isolated locations for no more than two or three years (see Chapter 11).

Box 4.4

Perceptions, Attitudes, and Career Orientations of Police Recruit Officers in B.C.

To study how the perceptions, attitudes, and career orientations of police recruit officers are affected by the training academy experience, one researcher surveyed three classes of police recruits during the first and final weeks of the eight-month training process at the Justice Institute of British Columbia Police Academy. Among the findings of that study:

- Most of the recruits began their careers with similar perceptions and expectations about the nature and functions of police work. Pre-training perceptions included the view that policing is more challenging than other occupations; that the police are there mainly to serve the public; and that police work is more dangerous than other occupations.

- Cynicism scores increased significantly in the course of recruit training, and more negative views of the criminal justice system were expressed.

- Greater importance was assigned to apprehending criminals.

- There was a significant lessening of the view that the principal function of policing is to serve the public.

- Most recruits indicated that the training academy had changed them in some way; they reported increased confidence and assertiveness as well as greater open-mindedness, and they were more aware of their surroundings.

As indicated in Box 4.3, police recruits in B.C. complete a three-block sequence of training. Blocks I and III are in the training academy, and Block II is in their home department with an FTO. It is likely that the findings of the study were affected by the recruits' experiences with their FTOs in an actual policing environment.

Source: E.L. Andersen, "Perceptions, Attitudes, and Career Orientations of Police Recruit Officers," MA thesis, 2006, School of Criminology, Simon Fraser University, Burnaby.

The potential sources of stress for officers are discussed in the following subsections.

The Police Role and Mandate

Police officers may experience role conflict as they try to carry out their enforcement duties while at the same time exercising their discretion and authority so as not to infringe on the Charter rights of those with whom they come into contact. This stress may be especially acute when politicians and the general public have unrealistic expectations based on misperceptions of crime rates. As well, strikes, protests, and other disturbances (such as those associated with Aboriginal land claims) can place police officers in the midst of chaos and indecision by politicians and may result in actions by the police that are later found to have been racist and discriminatory. The police are also often required to enforce unpopular laws; and when they do, as the most visible and accessible component of the criminal justice system, they find themselves targets of public wrath.

The Criminal Justice System

Police work is strongly affected by the decisions of Crown counsel, judges, probation officers, and parole boards, as well as by court decisions (especially in Charter cases) and changes in the criminal law. Police recruits may develop cynicism toward the justice system during training. Experienced officers may mitigate these frustrations by focusing on their own sphere of influence rather than becoming frustrated by the decision making of Crown counsel and the judiciary.

The Demands of Police Work

Police personnel are often required to inject themselves into situations that others are fleeing. They are exposed to extreme violence, individual suffering, and death. Because of the realities that surround police work, officers may become desensitized to life in general. Much of police work involves long periods of monotony punctuated with bursts of extreme excitement, often referred to as the "startle effect." Many situations demand a quick response by officers, and this jolts them both mentally and physically. For example, an officer may be sitting peacefully in a restaurant having coffee at 3 a.m. only to be dispatched suddenly to a man-with-a-gun call. The officer goes from a calm, relaxed situation to a life-and-death situation within seconds. Officers who are assigned to high-intensity special units, such as emergency response teams and strike forces, may find themselves in high-stress situations for hours or days at a time.

Traumatic events such as homicides, suicides, the deaths of children, and multivictim accidents can also take a toll on officers.

Another source of trauma is involvement in a shooting incident (see Chapter 6). Exposure to incidents like these may lead officers to develop post-traumatic stress syndrome, which is characterized by flashbacks, depression, and loss of sleep.

Another source of stress for police officers is paperwork. Officers often spend hours recording events that took only a few minutes to transpire. For example, an officer who detains an impaired driver after a failed breathalyzer test may spend many hours processing the individual and completing the necessary paperwork, even though it took only a few minutes to detect and arrest the offender. Legislation and Supreme Court decisions have placed a greater onus on police officers to provide extensive documentation on cases.

The Community

The community may be a source of stress for police officers. Officers assigned to environments with high levels of crime and social disorder may encounter interpersonal conflicts and threats of violence on a daily basis. Patrol officers may find themselves working in communities where residents neither trust nor support the police.

Communities often have unrealistic, and conflicting, expectations of what the police can accomplish with respect to preventing and responding to crime and social disorder. These expectations may also be a source of stress for police officers. In some communities there may be tense relations between the media and the police, and between the police and advocacy groups. Many Canadian communities are multicultural, and most police officers assigned to strongly ethnic patrol areas do not speak the language or know the culture of the local residents. Also, officers who police rural and remote communities may experience higher levels of stress than their urban colleagues (see Chapter 11).[26]

The Police Service

A variety of stressors arise from the police service itself. Departmental policies, a lack of resources, conflict with peers, and unsupportive or ineffective management may increase the stress levels of officers. This has led some observers to contend that the police organization is a greater source of stress than police operations themselves.[27] One factor that may affect interactions among officers in a police service as well as the extent to which the police service is effective in achieving its objectives, is **careerism.** This occurs when individual officers place their professional interests above those of the police service.

> **careerism**
> individual police officers putting their professional interests above those of the police service

Among the findings of an annual RCMP employee survey were that 50 percent of the officers surveyed indicated they did not feel that their senior leaders were competent to carry out their responsibilities, although just over 70 percent indicated that there were clear goals and objectives for their job and just over 60 percent responded that they would strongly recommend their job to someone who was interested in a career with the RCMP. Of concern is that nearly 50 percent of the respondents stated that they did not feel that action would be taken on the results of the survey. This suggests that, with respect to this survey and the RCMP, there is considerable work to be done in improving the force's organizational climate and dynamics.[28] A perceived lack of career opportunities has been associated with officers leaving police work. Also, officers may find the traditional paramilitary structure of their police service a source of frustration.

Female officers in a police service may experience higher levels of stress than their male counterparts.[29] This is due to experiences of sexual harassment as well as (along with minority officers) more subtle forms of discrimination. Research studies have shown that women who work in male-dominated professions, such as policing, the military, and firefighting, are more likely than women in other professions to be harassed.[30]

Harassment, especially of female police officers, is an issue that has received increasing attention. A national survey of RCMP officers found that 19 percent of the respondents indicated that they had been harassed on the job by a superior, supervisor, or co-worker during the previous year (although no gender breakdown was indicated).[31] Research has found that female police officers believe that less serious forms of police sexual misconduct are quite prevalent, owing in large measure to the police culture and the difficulties of changing this culture. This includes making vehicle stops in order to meet the driver or occupants and flirting with female citizens. Efforts to address harassment in the police service may have limited effectiveness. As one female officer stated:

> Things haven't changed much. It's business as usual. We have a sexual harassment policy, everybody got training, the chief did a big song-and-dance about how this stuff [sexual harassment] was a thing of the past, but it didn't change things much. The same guys who acted like jerks before are still jerks today.[32]

The issue of harassment is examined in Chapter 7.

Female officers may experience stress in trying to combine being a police officer with being a mother. A study of female officers who were also mothers found that they perceived a need to prove themselves *again* in the force. One officer stated: "And I always feel like I'm having to prove myself all over again to that person, or to that group of people, or to that team. Even though my work and my past should speak for itself, like everybody else."[33] This study also found that motherhood isolated these officers from their co-workers and led to changes in their career and personal priorities; at the same time, these women sensed that their career choices and opportunities had become more restricted.

Another source of stress for officers is inadequate resources to respond to the community's demands for service. This may result in patrol shifts being short-staffed and investigative units being backlogged. Whether senior managers are able to secure the necessary officers, as well as equipment for those officers, and how they deploy the available resources (i.e., efficiently or not), has an impact on the stress levels of rank-and-file officers. Officers who begin their shift with a lengthy list of "calls waiting" and who spend their entire shift responding to calls with little time for proactive policing may become frustrated and disillusioned.

Shift Work and Tired Cop Syndrome

Concern is growing about **tired cop syndrome,** a jet-lag state that may place officers at greater risk of accidents and poor decision making. Shift work is a major contributor to officer fatigue and is often identified by officers as a major impediment to high-level performance.[34]

> **tired cop syndrome**
> a jet-lag state of police officers, primarily due to shift work

The impact of shift work on the health and well-being of workers is well documented. Prolonged exposure to night shifts results in an individual who is sleep deprived and prone to poor performance, accidents, and health problems. Research studies indicate that shift workers suffer accumulating sleep deficits. Furthermore, night-shift workers in general perform at a lower level than their day-shift counterparts, are involved in more on-the-job accidents, and are less alert. Shift work increases the risk of cardiovascular disease, gastrointestinal disorders, miscarriage, preterm birth, and menstrual problems. It also increases feelings of irritation and strain, and can result in a general feeling of malaise.[35] A research study of approximately 5,000 Canadian and U.S. police officers found that sleep disorders were common. These officers reported higher levels of physical and mental health conditions and were at a greater risk of falling asleep while driving and making errors on the job due to fatigue.[36]

Despite this, many police services continue to shift officers in a two-days/two-nights/four-off pattern. Officers must also make court appearances, which may result in an officer being at the court all day and then working a night shift. While administratively convenient, there is concern that this type of shift schedule takes a toll on officers. Many officers seek "day job" and specialty unit positions in the police service in an attempt to escape from uniform patrol shifts. Promotions often allow officers to move out of uniformed patrol.

It has been suggested that police services modify shift schedules so as to have longer shift intervals, and/or that they keep officers in the same shift for several weeks or months at a time. In Toronto, for example, officers work seven "day" shifts, followed by six days off; six "evening" shifts, then five days off; and seven "night" shifts, then three days off.

Police officers posted in rural and remote communities may be at particular risk of tired cop syndrome. In the absence of systems of support and in communities with high rates of crime and disorder, officers may find themselves working long hours without relief and are never really "off shift" (see Chapter 11).

Police Work and the Police Family

Police work has often been referred to as anti-family. It has the potential to generate family stress and crises, yet little research has been done on this topic. Sources of stress on the police family include the following:

- *Being always on duty.* It is not uncommon for a police officer's friends or neighbours to contact the off-duty officer for advice or involvement in a situation. At other times, the officer while off duty may observe a situation and feel compelled to take action. The pressure is especially severe for officers in rural and remote areas, who must be available twenty-four hours a day, even during their days off.

- *The ever-present potential for call-outs.* The police officer may have to cancel holidays or a family outing due to an unscheduled call-out—that is, a sudden request relating to a court appearance, or a critical event in the community such as a natural disaster or public disturbance.

- *The RCMP transfer policy.* The Mounties' practice of rotating officers to new detachments every two or three years has slowed because of the financial costs. Even so, many RCMP officers and their families are still moved every few years. These moves can disrupt family life and may interfere with the spouse's employment, the children's education, and relationships with extended family.

- *Policing in the North:* Families of RCMP members who are posted to remote detachments may face hardships associated with living in a geographically isolated area as well as cultural adjustments (when the member is posted to an Aboriginal or Inuit community) (see Chapter 11).

A national survey of RCMP officers found that nearly 30 percent of the respondents did not feel that they were able to balance their personal, family, and work needs.[37]

Most police services have employee assistance plans, and some have wellness coordinators who provide support and assistance to officers who are experiencing difficulties on the job or in their personal and family lives.

On Second Thought: Is Police Work *That* Stressful?

In recent years, research findings have challenged the conventional wisdom that being a police officer is more stressful than other occupations and that police officers drink more, have higher rates of suicide and divorce than the general population. Note that most of the research is on U.S. police officers. In the absence of Canadian studies, it is difficult to determine the circumstances of Canadian police officers.

Compared to employees in other federal departments, RCMP officers take considerably fewer days off. The average number of days off taken in 2008–9 by RCMP officers (15.6) was lower than for federal employees in Fisheries (16.4), Public Works (16.8), and Human Resources (19.4). As well, in percentage terms, the biggest increases in days off per year per employee between 2000–1 and 2008–9 were in Fisheries (+74%), Agriculture (+67%), and Environment (+53%), compared to the RCMP (+38%).[38]

Research studies in the United States suggest that, generally speaking, the suicide rates of police officers are not significantly different from those of the general population. Nor do police officers seem to consume alcohol in greater amounts than the general population.[39] Studies have also found that the divorce rate for police officers is lower than for the general population.[40]

Research on Canadian police services is needed to determine whether these findings hold true in this country and whether certain officers (e.g., women, visible minorities, officers posted to northern communities, and Aboriginals) are more susceptible to high levels of stress and negative experiences. As well, it is important to determine the incidence of post-traumatic stress disorder among officers, much of which may go undiagnosed and untreated.[41]

Of course, it may be that the police occupation is more stressful and that officers have developed more effective coping mechanisms than their counterparts in other federal agencies. The nature and impact of specific stressors on police officers varies among individual officers as well as across police services. Most officers develop strategies for coping with the stressors they encounter on the job. One Indo-Canadian officer stated to your author: "I meditate every day, do yoga, and go to the gym."

At Issue 4.1

Should Police Services Have the Right to Ask Applicants for Their Facebook Password?

Across North America, more and more employers are requesting that potential employees provide their Facebook password as part of the application process. A news item in early 2011 reported that the police department in Norman, Oklahoma, was asking applicants for their Facebook passwords, and a number of other police services in the United States have followed suit (Cacho 2011). It can be anticipated that the trend will follow to Canada. Proponents of this strategy argue that applicants should be open and transparent about their activities; critics argue that it constitutes an invasion of privacy.

You Make the Call!

1. What is your position on this issue?
2. If you applied to a police service and your Facebook password was requested as part of the application process, would you provide it?
3. Is there anything currently on your Facebook that might affect your application to a police service?

Source: M. Cacho, "Employers Asking Job Applicants for Facebook Passwords," *Geektown Tech and Gadgets*, March 1, 2011, http://www.geektown.ca/2011/03/employers-asking-job-applicants-for-facebook-passwords.html

At Issue 4.2

Should the Polygraph Be Used as Part of the Selection Process for Police Recruits?

Police services use a variety of assessment instruments in recruiting. Among the more controversial are the polygraph and psychological tests, both of which are designed to assess the suitability of applicants for a career in policing and to screen for drug use and other illegal behaviour. While the RCMP and police services in western Canada have long used the polygraph, doing so is illegal in Ontario. In 2011 the Québec City police service became the first police service in that province to use the polygraph. This stirred controversy. Critics argue that the tests are not 100 percent reliable; that polygraph evidence is not admissible in court; and that a good interview and thorough background check are more effective.

Supporters of the polygraph counter that the polygraph is just one instrument and that the results are corroborated with information gathered in the background check and interviews. The most common reason, other than medical, that candidates are washed out of the recruiting process is dishonesty and failing to disclose all information about their background.

You Make the Call!

1. Should police services use the polygraph as part of the selection process for police recruits?

2. Would having to take a polygraph test discourage you from applying to become a police officer?

Key Points Review

1. There are both basic qualifications (core competencies) and preferred qualifications for individuals considering a career in a Canadian police service.
2. Canadian police services are making efforts to increase their diversity.
3. The recruit selection process has many stages and includes interviews, a medical examination, various tests, a background investigation, a polygraph examination (except in Ontario and most of Québec), and other assessments.
4. There are a number of models of police recruit training in Canada.
5. There is competition among police services for previously experienced officers (PEOs).
6. Police recruits undergo a process of socialization into the role of police officer as they move from the academy to the street.
7. During operational field training, the recruit learns to apply the basic principles taught at the police training academy under the guidance of a field training officer (FTO).
8. Facets of the police occupation include the working personality of the police, the culture of the police, and the various occupational outlooks and career orientations of individual police officers.

9. The challenges of police work include role conflict, the decisions of other components of the criminal justice system, the demands of police work, the often unrealistic and conflicting demands of the community, conflicts with peers and supervisors, and shift work.
10. Police work can place stress on the officer's family.

Key Term Questions

1. Identify and describe the **basic qualifications (core competencies)** required of prospective police recruits and the **preferred qualifications** that may be advantageous in applying to a police service.
2. What is meant by **competency-based training**?
3. Why are **previously experienced officers (PEOs)** important in any discussion of police recruiting, and what are the issues surrounding the efforts of police services to attract these officers?
4. What types of **in-service training** are available to police officers?
5. Discuss the importance of **operational field training** and the role of field training officers (FTOs).
6. What is the **working personality of police officers**? Why is this concept important in any study of police work, and what does the research say about the extent to which it exists in police work today?
7. Define and discuss the importance of the following for discussions about police culture: (a) the **code of silence,** (b) the **blue-light syndrome**, and (c) **hypervigilance**.
8. What is **careerism** and how might it affect the environment in which police officers work?
9. What is **tired cop syndrome** and how might it affect police work?

Notes

1. P.F. Foley, C. Guarneri, and M.E. Kelly, "Reasons for Choosing a Police Career: Changes over Two Decades," *International Journal of Police Science and Management* 10, no. 1 (2007): 2–8.
2. Ipsos Public Affairs, "Trends in Youth Perceptions of the Police and Police Recruitment (2007, 2009, 2010)" (Ottawa: Police Sector Council, 2010), http://www.policecouncil.ca/reports/PSC%20Youth%20Attitudes%2010.pdf
3. CBC Digital Archives, "Sikh Mounties Permitted to Wear Turbans" (1998), http://archives.cbc.ca
4. Toronto Police Service, "2009 Update to the Environmental Scan" (Toronto: 2009), 95, http://www.torontopolice.on.ca/publications/files/reports/2009envscan.pdf
5. Edmonton Police Service and Edmonton Police Commission, "Annual Report to the Community" (Edmonton: 2009), http://www.edmontonpolice.ca
6. C. Freeze, "Mounties to Recruit Women and Minorities," *Globe and Mail,* September 24, 2010, http://www.globeandmail.com
7. M. Burczycka, "Police Resources in Canada, 2010" (Ottawa: Statistics Canada, 2010), 8, http://www.statcan.gc.ca/pub/85-225-x/2010000/part-partie1-eng.htm
8. C.A. Archbold, K.D. Hassell, and A.J. Stichman, "Comparing Promotion Aspirations Among Female and Male Police Officers," *International Journal of Police Science and Management* 12, no. 2 (2010): 287–303; T.B. Shea, "Female

Participation in the Police Promotion Process: Are Women Competing for Promotion in Numbers Proportionate to Their Statistical Representation in Policing?" (London: University of Western Ontario, 2008), http://www .policecouncil.ca/Shea_Gender_Promotions09.pdf

9. R. Colvin, "Shared Perceptions Among Lesbian and Gay Police Officers: Barriers and Opportunities in the Law Enforcement Work Environment," *Police Quarterly* 12, no. 1 (2009): 86–101.

10. G. Hadley, "The Identification of Participation Barriers Associated with Employment Testing in the Ontario Constable Selection System," (Toronto: Police Sector Council, 2009), http://www.policecouncil.ca/reports/LPS_ GHadley_2009.pdf

11. I. Peritz, "Fitness Tests, Intelligence Tests, and, Now, 'Suitability' Tests," *Globe and Mail*, September 16, 2010, A1, A9.

12. J. Middleton-Hope, "Misconduct Among Previously Experienced Officers: Issues in the Recruitment and Hiring of 'Gypsy Cops,'" *Canadian Review of Policing Research* 1, (2004): 178–88.

13. B. Henson, B.W. Reyns, C.F. Klahm, and J. Frank, "Do Good Recruits Make Good Cops? Problems Predicting and Measuring Academy and Street-Level Success," *Police Quarterly* 13, no. 1 (2010): 5–26.

14. J.B.L. Chan, *Fair Cop: Learning the Art of Policing* (Toronto: University of Toronto Press, 2003).

15. A.T. Chappell and L. Lanza-Kaduce, "Police Academy Socialization: Understanding the Lessons Learned in a Paramilitary–Bureaucratic Organization," *Journal of Contemporary Ethnography* 39, no. 2 (2009): 131–58.

16. S. Mastrofski and R.R. Ritti, "Police Training and the Effects of Organization on Drunk Driving Enforcement," *Justice Quarterly* 13, no. 2 (1996): 290–320.

17. R.N. Haarr, "The Making of a Community Policing Officer: The Impact of Basic Training and Occupational Socialization on Police Recruits," *Police Quarterly* 4, no. 4 (2001): 402–33.

18. M. Novakowski, "Police Field Training Officers: It's the Singer, Not the Song," *Canadian Review of Policing Research* 1, (2004): 220–30.

19. J. Skolnick, *Justice Without Trial: Law Enforcement in a Democratic Society* (New York: John Wiley, 1966).

20. C. Murphy and P. McKenna, "Rethinking Police Governance, Culture, and Management" (Ottawa: Public Safety Canada, 2007), http://publicsafety .gc.ca/rcmp-grc/_fl/eng/rthnk-plc-eng.pdf; E.A. Paoline, "Shedding Light on Police Culture: An Examination of Officers' Occupational Attitudes," *Police Quarterly* 7, no. 2 (2004): 205–36.

21. R.L. Wood, M. Davis, and A. Rouse, "Diving into Quicksand: Program Implementation and Police Subcultures," in *Community Policing: Can It Work?* ed. W.G. Skogan (Belmont: Wadsworth/Thomson, 2004), 136–61 at 139.

22. Paoline, "Shedding Light on Police Culture."

23. R.J. Burke, "Career Stages, Satisfaction, and Well-Being Among Police Officers," *Psychological Reports* 65, (1989): 3–12.

24. M. Morash, R. Haarr, and D.-H. Kwak, "Multilevel Influences on Police Stress," *Journal of Contemporary Criminal Justice* 22, no. 1 (2006): 26–43; J.R.L. Parsons, "Occupational Health and Safety Issue of Police Officers in Canada, the United States, and Europe: A Review Essay," (2004), http://www .safetynet.mun.ca/pdfs/Occupational%20H&S.pdf

25. M.L. Arter, "Stress and Deviance in Policing," *Deviant Behavior* 29, no. 1 (2008): 43–69; C. Regehr, D. Johanis, G. Dimitropoulos, C. Bartram, and G. Hope, "The Police Officer and the Public Inquiry: A Qualitative Inquiry into the Aftermath of Workplace Trauma," *Brief Treatment and Crisis Intervention* 3, no. 4 (2003): 383–96.

26. J. Buttle, C. Fowler, and M.W. Williams, "The Impact of Rural Policing on the Private Lives of New Zealand Police Officers," *International Journal of Police Science and Management* 12, no. 4 (2010): 596–606.

27. J.M. Shane, "Organizational Stressors and Police Performance," *Journal of Criminal Justice* 38, no. 4 (2010): 807–18.

28. RCMP, "Results—RCMP Employee Opinion Survey 2009" (Ottawa: 2009), http://www.rcmp-grc.gc.ca/surveys-sondages/2009/emp/empl2009_result-eng.htm

29. K. Dowler and B. Arai, "Stress, Gender, and Policing: The Impact of Perceived Gender Discrimination on Symptoms of Stress," *International Journal of Police Science and Management* 10, no. 2 (2008): 123–35.

30. K.D. Hassell and S.G. Brandl, "An Examination of the Workplace Experiences of Police Patrol Officers: The Role of Race, Sex, and Sexual Orientation," *Police Quarterly* 12, no. 4 (2009): 408–30; T.M. Maher, "Police Sexual Misconduct: Female Police Officers' Views Regarding Its Nature and Extent," *Women and Criminal Justice* 20, no. 3 (2010): 263–82.

31. RCMP, "Results."

32. Maher, "Police Sexual Misconduct," 276.

33. S. Goodwin, "The Experience of Combining Motherhood with Career for Members of the Royal Canadian Mounted Police," MA thesis, Department of Educational and Counselling Psychology, University of British Columbia, Vancouver, (1999), 65.

34. J.M. McDonald, *Gold Medal Policing: Mental Readiness and Performance Excellence* (New York: Sloan Associates, 2006); B. Vila, "Sleep Deprivation: What Does It Mean for Public Safety Officers?" (Washington: U.S. Department of Justice, Office of Justice Programs, 2009), http://www.ncjrs.gov/pdffiles1/nij/225762.pdf

35. S.R. Senjo and K. Dhungana, "A Field Data Examination of Policy Constructs Related to Fatigue Conditions in Law Enforcement Personnel," *Police Quarterly* 12, no. 2 (2009): 123–36.

36. S.M.W. Rajaratnam, et al. "Sleep Disorders, Health, and Safety in Police Officers," *Journal of the American Medical Association,* 306, no. 23 (2011): 2567–578.

37. RCMP "Results."

38. A. Mayeda, "Federal Employees Taking More Sick Days," *National Post*, November 13, 2010, A10.

39. V. Lindsay, W.B. Taylor, and K. Shelley, "Alcohol and the Police: An Empirical Examination of a Widely Held Assumption," *Policing: An International Journal of Police Strategies and Management* 31, no. 4 (2008): 596–609; R. Loo, "A Meta-Analysis of Police Suicide Rates: Findings and Issues," *Suicide and Life-Threatening Behavior* 33, no. 3 (2003): 313–25.

40. S.P. McCoy and M.G. Aamodt, "A Comparison of Law Enforcement Divorce Rates with Those of Other Occupations," *Journal of Police and Criminal Psychology* 25, no. 1 (2010): 1–16.

41. D. McGinn, "The Untold Perils of Policing: Post-Traumatic Stress Disorder Quietly Affects Many Officers," *Globe and Mail*, February 27, 2010, M4.

Chapter

5

Patrol and General Duty Policing

Learning Objectives

After reading this chapter, you should be able to:

- Understand the nature of patrol and the areas of patrol work

- Discuss the role of dispatchers and communications officers in managing calls for service

- Discuss the issues surrounding the deployment of mobile patrol units

- Identify and discuss the key concepts that are useful in understanding the decision making of patrol officers

- Discuss the use of mediation and conflict resolution skills by patrol officers

- Describe the issues surrounding policing the mentally ill and multineed populations

Key Terms

allocated patrol time   116
call shedding   114
call stacking   114
Canadian Police Information Centre (CPIC)   112
differential police response (DPR)   115
recipes for action   122
selective (or situational) enforcement   121

soft skills (of police work)   119
symbolic assailants   123
task (or policing) environment   124
typifications   122
unallocated patrol time   117
"W" system   112

Early in this text it was noted that a key attribute of police work (and one that distinguishes it from the work of other criminal justice personnel) is that it is carried out in the community rather than in the safe confines of an office. The street is the domain of patrol officers, and there is no way for them to avoid the weather, the long nights, or people and their problems. These realities force officers to become intimately familiar with their working environment and to develop skill in assessing situations, exercising discretion, and making effective decisions. Uniformed patrol officers are often referred to as the "eyes, ears, arms, and legs" of police services.

It is patrol officers who respond to the primary calls for service that the public makes to police, and it is citizen requests that generate most police contacts with the public. As the most visible representatives of the criminal justice system, they are—more than most other criminal justice personnel—subject to attacks on their judgment and decision making. It is they who are most often blamed for the failings of the criminal justice system generally. And they are often the first to be held accountable by politicians, the public, the courts, and even their own supervisors when difficulties arise.

PATROL WORK

Five duties of police officers are recognized under common law and are at the core of police work: (1) to prevent crime, (2) to protect life and property, (3) to preserve the peace, (4) to apprehend offenders, and (5) to enforce laws. Patrol officers are involved in a wide range of situations, including responding to incidents involving law enforcement, order maintenance, and service; conducting investigations; making arrests; executing warrants; and attending court.

In actuality, patrol officers are not equally involved in all of these activities. Much depends on the specific environment in which officers are carrying out

Patrol officer.

their duties—for example, whether it is a high-crime inner-city neighbourhood or an affluent wealthy suburban community. Other factors include the resources the police service has at its disposal and the amount of time officers have to engage in proactive, preventive policing (as opposed to responding to calls for service). Generally speaking, the prevention and apprehension components of the officer's duties are secondary to maintaining order and providing service.

Depending on the level of calls for service, patrol officers may have an opportunity to engage in problem-solving policing, address problem premises, and engage in a wide range of proactive policing activities, including conducting street checks of individuals of interest. Note that not all of the activities of patrol officers are captured in "dispatched" calls for service. On a daily basis, patrol officers are involved in many interactions and situations with community residents that do not result in any formal action being taken. This includes situations in which officers use their discretion to defuse conflicts and resolve disputes. It also includes cultivating "sources" (informants)—that is, people in the patrol area who can provide them with information on crimes that have been committed, or are going to be committed, and the names of people involved in criminal activities. It also includes participating in various community policing initiatives.

Patrol work can be highly diversified, though much depends on the size of the department. Officers in smaller police services tend to be responsible for a broader spectrum of duties. This is especially the case in policing remote northern communities (see Chapter 11). Larger police services provide a buffer and a "safety in numbers" environment for patrol officers; they also have more extensive support services for patrol officers, including victim services, traffic sections, canine units, and so on. Also, patrol work takes place in a wide variety of task environments, and this determines the volumes and types of calls to which officers are asked to respond.

The types of activities that patrol officers are involved in are determined largely by calls to the police from the general public. One of the more persistent myths surrounding police work is that officers spend most of their time racing from one high-action call to the next, red lights flashing and siren wailing. In fact, as noted, officers spend most of their time responding to order maintenance or service calls, gathering information, and writing reports.

The Waterloo police serve around 500,000 residents in seven communities (Cambridge, Kitchener, Waterloo, North Dumfries, Wellesley, Wilmot, and Woolich). In 2009 the service received nearly 95,000 citizen-generated calls for service—an average or 260 calls per day. Table 5.1 indicates the ten most frequent calls for service for the Waterloo Regional Police Service during 2009 as well as the total number of calls for each type and the average frequency for each type. The majority of incidents to which officers respond are quality-of-life concerns and disorder.

In Calgary, suspicious persons, unwanted guests, and disturbance calls account for a high percentage of the dispatched calls. See Figure 5.1. In Toronto, the number of Criminal Code offences reported per constable was at its lowest ratio in twenty-five years—a 10 percent decrease from 1999. This reflects the overall decline in crime rates that has occurred across the country.[1]

The new recruit soon learns that a large part of police work is routine and administrative—in van Maanen's words, "the proverbial clerk in a patrol car."[2]

TABLE 5.1	Top Ten Citizen-Generated Calls for Service, Waterloo Regional Police, 2009	
Top 10 citizen-generated calls	**Frequency**	**New call every . . .**
1. Bylaw complaint*	10,944	48 minutes
2. Injured/sick person	5,907	1 hour, 29 minutes
3. Domestic dispute	5,783	1 hour, 31 minutes
4. Theft under $5,000	5,201	1 hour, 41 minutes
5. Alarm	4,257	2 hours, 3 minutes
6. Check well-being	4,127	2 hours, 7 minutes
7. Driving complaint	3,532	2 hours, 29 minutes
8. Unwanted person	3,304	2 hours, 39 minutes
9. Disturbance	2,669	3 hours, 17 minutes
10. Break and enter	2,604	3 hours, 22 minutes

*For bylaw complaint calls, a bylaw officer is dispatched.

Source: Courtesy Waterloo Regional Police.

FIGURE 5.1   Dispatched Calls by Event Type, Calgary Police Service, 2009

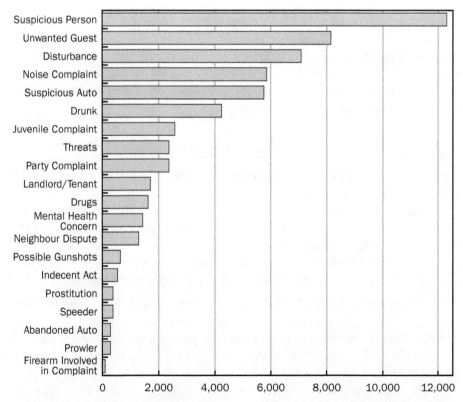

Source: "Annual Statistical Report 2005–2009," p. 12, Calgary Police Service Centralized Analysis Section, Strategic Services Division, 2010. Reprinted with permission.

For most patrol officers, this work is not enough to hold their interest and maintain their enthusiasm. In the view of one police officer: "It's monotonous at times. Pushing a police car is pretty boring, until something happens. You can make it as exciting as you want to—you can stop every car that ever drove through your area. Or you can choose to do nothing. For the most part, it's fairly monotonous."[3]

The modern patrol vehicle is virtually an office on wheels. Police services have equipped their vehicles with laptop computers, cell phones, and radios. Mobile display terminals (MDTs) allow police officers to communicate with other patrol officers, to access drivers' records, and to run criminal information checks on people through the **Canadian Police Information Centre (CPIC).** This is a computerized information system that contains information on vehicles, individuals, marine equipment, criminal records, dental characteristics, prison inmates, and wandering persons.

Some observers have expressed concern that police services are becoming too dependent on technology. Officers may come to rely too heavily on computer-generated information, to the exclusion of "human" intelligence gathered by developing contacts in the community. Patrol officers may not have—or take—the opportunity to engage in proactive activities outside their patrol vehicles. In one Ojibway community in Ontario, the Aboriginal word for the police translates to "men with no legs," the subtext being that the officers who patrol the community never leave their patrol cars.

> **Canadian Police Information Centre (CPIC)**
> the centralized, computer-based information system used by police services

STRATEGIES FOR MANAGING CALLS FOR SERVICE

As the only public safety agency open "24/7," police services receive hundreds or—in some locales—even thousands of requests for service every day. The public's requests for service and the policing tasks mandated by the law and government policy far outstrip available police resources.

Dispatchers and Communications Officers: The Gatekeepers

The greater part of police work is assigned to patrol officers by dispatchers or communications officers.

Dispatchers and communications officers (COs) receive the initial request for service, gather basic information from the caller (including name, address, and type of situation), prioritize the call, and allocate available patrol resources. To ensure that they are gathering the information necessary to properly interpret and prioritize calls, they apply the **"W" system,** which includes the following types of questions:

> **"W" system**
> the approach used by police dispatchers to determine key facts about a call

> WHERE: Where did this happen? Where are you now? Where is the suspect?
> WHAT: What is happening? What is the problem? What do you need?
> WHEN: Is this happening now? How long ago? When did he/she leave?
> WHO: Who is calling? Who is the suspect? Who else is involved? Who told you this?
> WHY: Why did you wait to call? Why is he/she threatening you? Why do you think that?
> WEAPONS: Are there any weapons? What are they? Does he/she carry weapons?

The dispatcher uses all this information to determine the call's priority (see below) and then forwards it to the patrol officers. It is important that officers obtain as much information as they can about the situation. Much of this information is provided by the dispatcher while the officers are en route to the scene. An increasing number of calls to police are made from cell phones, which causes some problems, for unlike with land lines, the exact location of the caller cannot be pinpointed.

Dispatchers must "get it right." Failure to do so has sometimes resulted in serious injury and even death. A tragic case is described in Police File 5.1.

Police File 5.1

The Winnipeg 911 Murders: A Failure of Dispatch

On the night of February 16, 2000, two Aboriginal sisters—Corrine McKeown and Doreen Leclair—were murdered by McKeown's ex-boyfriend, William Dunlop. At the time of the murders, McKeown had a restraining order against Dunlop. Before their deaths, the two women had telephoned the Winnipeg Police Service 911 number five times over an eight-hour period.

First 911 call. The first call from the women is disconnected. When the operator phones back, one of the women states that someone has been shot. A patrol car is dispatched, but at the scene, Dunlop gives the police a false name and McKeown does not complain.

Second 911 call. The 911 operator instructs the women to phone the police directly.

Third 911 call. The women tell the 911 operator that McKeown has been stabbed by a man violating a restraining order. The operator responds: "Both of you are at fault right now," and then asks whether "Everybody's had a few to drink there."

Fourth 911 call. The tape of this call is difficult to decipher. However, one of the women can be heard saying, "Please help me." The operator promises to send a patrol car, but one is not dispatched.

Fifth (and final) 911 call. Faint sounds from one or both of the sisters are drowned out by barking dogs. The 911 operator hangs up and calls the house. Dunlop answers the telephone and says there "is no problem at all." Increasingly suspicious, the operator dispatches a patrol car to the residence. The officers find the two sisters dead in the home.

Dunlop was subsequently found guilty of second degree murder and given a life sentence with no eligibility for parole for seventeen years. Aboriginal groups were outraged, arguing that, had the women not been Aboriginal, the police would have responded and interceded following the first 911 call.

A coroner's inquest recommended that Winnipeg 911 operators receive more training in dealing with domestic disputes and that the operators be more closely monitored. An independent review ordered by the Manitoba Justice Department, conducted by a provincial court judge, made sixty-two recommendations, including that staffing levels and morale among dispatchers be improved.

Source: CBC News, "The Winnipeg 911 Murders" (2003), http://www.cbc.ca/news/background/aboriginals/winnipeg911.html

Call Priority Categories

Police services prioritize calls for service in basically the same way across the country. Priority 1 are emergency calls that require immediate police attention. These include life-threatening situations that can lead to death or grievous bodily harm. Priority 2 calls are serious but are not life threatening; they include break and enters in progress. Priority 3 and Priority 4 calls are routine and less serious, such as "cold" B&Es. Most calls to the police are for order maintenance or service.

Police File 5.2 presents an incident to which patrol units responded that would be classified as "assist general public."

Calls for service to police organizations are managed both at the organizational level and at the street level. Police services have developed response strategies aimed at reducing organizational costs, ensuring operational effectiveness and efficiency, and providing an adequate level of service. **Call shedding** is a practice that acknowledges that the police can no longer respond to all calls for service and that other organizations and community agencies must help them.

When the volume of calls to the dispatch centre exceeds the number of available patrol units, **call stacking** occurs. In other words, the calls are placed in a queue until a unit becomes available. Most calls in the queue at any given point in time are in the Priority 3 and Priority 4 categories; during heavy demand times, though, Priority 2 calls may be awaiting dispatch as well. An excessive volume of calls can have a negative impact on response times to Priority 1, 911 calls for service.

> **call shedding**
> a strategy to discard or divert calls for service to match available police resources

> **call stacking**
> prioritizing calls for service

Police File 5.2

A Call for Assistance

Patrol officers in a major urban centre are dispatched to an apartment occupied by a man, a woman, and a newborn. A call had been made to the police by the midwife of the woman, who had been called by the husband, who felt that his wife was depressed and possibly suicidal. A supervising sergeant, two male constables, and one female constable respond to the call. The husband admits the sergeant and the female constable to the premises, wherein a lengthy discussion ensues about the situation. A key issue that emerges from the discussion is that the mother is emotionally exhausted and, as well, is experiencing stress due to an inability to breast-feed her baby. Her usual source of breast milk in such situations is closed for the weekend and she is opposed to feeding the baby commercially sold formula. The sergeant places a call to a patrol unit staffed by a police constable and a social worker, who attend the scene. The sergeant and the three constables depart the premises. After a long discussion with the social worker, the woman agrees to feed her baby formula until breast milk can be obtained. The social worker speaks further with the couple about the other issues in their life and relationship.

Differential police response (DPR) strategies attempt to differentiate among requests for police service in terms of the optimal forms of police response. DPR strategies are an important way for police services to allocate their resources so as not to be overwhelmed by less serious calls for service. Calls are scanned by police personnel, who determine whether the call is a request for information, or a referral, or requires police attendance. Guidelines mandate whether police attendance at the scene is necessary. It may surprise some to learn that patrol units are not always dispatched.

DPR strategies enable a broader range of response options than traditional practice, which is to dispatch a patrol officer as quickly as possible. Response alternatives include delayed response by patrol officers to some types of calls; dispatch of civilian personnel instead of sworn officers; taking reports of some crimes by telephone; or asking complainants to walk in or mail in their reports. Many police services have Telephone Response Teams that handle many complaints and follow-ups over the telephone, including cases involving minor property damage complaints.

> **differential police response (DPR)** categorizing calls for service based on the response required; e.g., patrol car/no patrol car

The Computer-Aided Dispatch (CAD) System

The CAD system is used by communications personnel in emergency services and policing to record calls for service and to monitor the responses of units in the field. This system contains a variety of information on the incident, including the identity of the caller, the location of the incident, the time at which the call was received and dispatched, and the identity of the officers and how long they were at the scene. The CAD system provides an important database for police services when they analyze demands for and responses to service.

THE DEPLOYMENT OF PATROL UNITS

Police services are paying increasing attention to patrol deployment, with particular emphasis on officer workloads (time spent on reactive and proactive activities), responses to calls for service, including response times, and number of arrests.

The challenge for police services is to link patrol resources with call workloads and to maintain consistent levels of service that will allow for proactive policing activities as well as responses to calls for service. In most jurisdictions, demands for police service are not spread equally throughout the week; there are "peak" periods, most often Friday and Saturday nights.

Patrol Shifts

How a police service allocates its patrol resources can have a strong impact on the effectiveness and efficiency of police work. A key factor here is how patrol officers' shifts are arranged. Any shifting model must consider service delivery issues and issues relating to the quality of life of patrol officers. In an ideal world, the shift system used by a police service would match as closely as possible the demands for service, thus ensuring an adequate number of available patrol units. This ideal is tempered, however, by the provisions of labour agreements as well as by the importance of considering quality-of-life issues for patrol officers. Recall from Chapter 4 that shift work is a key source of stress for police officers.

Patrol officers across Canada work a variety of shift lengths, ranging from eight to twelve hours. Shifts typically last ten or twelve hours. With the exception of the RCMP, which is not unionized, shift hours are generally established through collective bargaining between the police union and the municipality. Note that police officers who work in remote and rural areas are on call twenty-four hours a day, a challenge that is discussed in Chapter 11.

One- and Two-Officer Patrol Units

In some police services, patrol car staffing falls under the collective agreement between management and the police officers' association or union. In Vancouver, for example, the collective agreement stipulates that 60 percent of patrol units will have two officers and 40 percent will have one officer; in Toronto, the collective agreement requires that after dark, police must work in two-officer cars. In other police services, such as the Durham Regional Police, patrol car staffing is not part of the collective agreement and is decided by management.

There is a debate in academic and policing circles as to whether patrol officers are most efficiently deployed in one- or two-officer patrol units. Many front line patrol officers contend that one-officer units compromise officer safety. Also, many officers prefer to work in pairs and believe that doing so improves both performance and morale. Many police managers, on the other hand, contend that officers who work in single-patrol units are more efficient, make more arrests, complete more reports, and receive fewer citizen complaints. There is also the issue, not researched, as to how the personalities of officers who work in two-officer units may affect their performance. Distractions, misunderstandings, and disagreements may occur during long shifts in the patrol car. It is also possible that mixed-gender patrol cars may generate dynamics that affect officer performance, although this topic has not been researched.

Studies attempting to correlate the size of patrol units with officer efficiency, productivity, attitudes, perceptions, and safety have produced few conclusive results. American studies suggest that one-officer patrol units are safer and more efficient than two-officer units; figures from Statistics Canada indicate that more officers in two-officer patrol cars were killed than in one-officer cars.[4] An exhaustive study of patrol deployment in the Vancouver Police Department found that response times to Priority 1 calls were longer for one-officer units than for two-officer units during both the day (21 percent longer) and the night (35 percent longer); furthermore, two-officer units were more likely to proactively enforce warrants and court orders, conduct street checks (routine checks where officers speak with known criminals or suspicious persons), generate intelligence information, arrest individuals, locate stolen vehicles, conduct licensed premise checks, and investigate suspicious circumstances (including suspicious persons and vehicles).[5]

Patrol Unit Utilization

allocated patrol time
the amount of time that patrol officers spend responding to calls from the general public

A key issue in police services is how patrol units are utilized. **Allocated patrol time** (also referred to as reactive policing) is the amount of time that uniformed patrol officers spend responding to calls for service from the general public. In many police services, patrol officers have little time for non-reactive policing, and it is not unusual for them to begin their shifts with twenty or thirty calls for service in the queue. **Unallocated patrol time** (also referred to as proactive patrol) is the amount of time uniformed officers have that is not committed to responding to calls for service. The best-practice standard is for patrol officers to have 40 or 50 percent of their time "unallocated" so that they can engage in proactive and problem-solving activities. Most police services do not come close to the 40–50 percent standard.

Figure 5.2 provides a breakdown of proactive/reactive/administrative duties for police officers in the Waterloo Regional Police Service. The figure indicates that Waterloo officers have 20% unallocated (proactive/problem solcing) time. This compares to 6.67% for officers in the RCMP Municipal Detachment in Kelowna, B.C.[6]

The specific breakdown of officer time and tasks will vary across the environments in which police officers work, as will the types of calls to which they respond. Police services vary greatly in terms of the amount of reactive and proactive time that uniformed patrol officers have. Key factors include the level of demand for policing services, how efficiently patrol resources are deployed, and the availability of patrol resources.

Patrol officers who spend more than half their time responding to calls for service may experience higher levels of stress. Also, they are unable to engage in crime prevention initiatives and problem solving, and they may not conduct proper on-scene investigations. In the words of one patrol officer: "I feel like I don't have time to fully address the complainant's issues; there is pressure to wrap up the incident as soon as possible and move on to the next call" (personal communication). In a community policing model, it is important that officers have time to engage in problem solving; to develop relationships with agencies, community groups, and residents; to utilize proactive enforcement strategies, including problem-solving policing; and to participate in various crime prevention and response initiatives (see Chapter 9). Such initiatives include hotspot

FIGURE 5.2   **Duties of Patrol Officers in the Waterloo Regional Police Service, 2009**

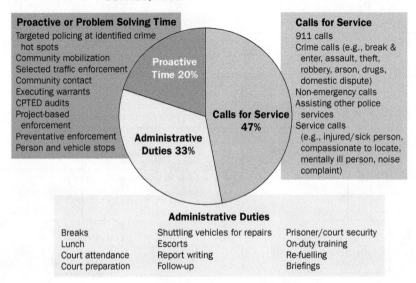

Source: Courtesy Waterloo Regional Police

policing, problem-oriented policing, conducting street checks, cultivating informants, and addressing issues of street disorder.

When patrol units spend most of their time doing reactive policing, a question needs to be asked: Is the police service underresourced, or is it deploying its patrol resources inefficiently? This question has been studied in an effort to ensure that patrol units are deployed as effectively as possible. When that is the case, police services have a strong argument to take to municipal councils when lobbying for additional patrol positions.

Patrol Car Response Times

A key element in the police response to calls for service is the amount of time that elapses between when the call is received at the communications centre and when a dispatched unit arrives at the scene (see Figure 5.3).

Response time is generally broken down into dispatch delay and travel time; service time refers to the travel time and the time the units remain at the scene. There is some evidence that the time that officers remain on scene for Priority 1 calls has increased in recent years. Factors here include the seriousness and complexity of the call, legislated procedures that must be followed, and the training and experience of officers.

The "best practice" response time for Priority 1 calls is generally considered to be seven minutes: on average, two minutes for dispatch and five minutes' travel time. In most urban police services, however, the response time to Priority 1 calls is much longer. In Toronto in 2009, for example, the average response time for Priority 1 calls was just over ten minutes.

There is no conclusive evidence that crime levels are affected by the response times of police patrol units to Priority 1 calls. However, rapid response to Priority 1 calls does strengthen the ability of the police to protect victims and complainants, to arrest offenders, and to preserve and gather evidence. As well, a short response time to a Priority 1 call may increase the likelihood that suspects, victims,

FIGURE 5.3   Response Timelines

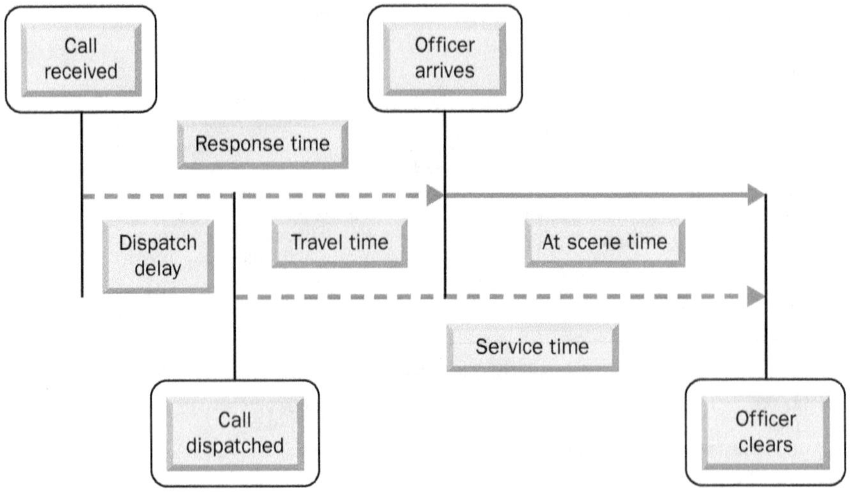

Source: Shreveport Police Department. Reprinted with permission.

witnesses, and complainants will still be at the scene. Also, community residents *expect* the police to respond promptly to calls for service, especially those involving life-threatening situations. A failure of the police to do so may reduce levels of public support for the police and undermine their legitimacy in the community.

PATROL OFFICER SKILL SETS

Given the highly interactive nature of patrol work, officers must develop skills that facilitate information gathering, conflict resolution, and the provision of service to community residents. This requires that officers be good listeners, be able to process large amounts of information quickly, and make definitive decisions. These are the so-called **soft skills of police work.**

Years of service and the age of uniformed officers are important factors in any discussion of patrol officer skill sets. Canadian police services in the early twenty-first century are "junior" police services, with large numbers of officers having fewer than five years on the job. Figures 5.4 and 5.5 present the average age and years of service of primary response (PR) officers in the Toronto Police Service (TPS). Nearly 32 percent of the PR officers were under the age of 30, as compared to 19 percent of all constables in the TPS. The median years of service for primary response constables was 3.7 (as compared to an average of 8.1 years of service for all constables in the TPS). Nearly six in ten PR constables (58 percent) had less than five years' experience.

The junior police officer corps in Toronto is hardly unique; the same profile is found in police services across the country. This has challenged police services to ensure effective supervision of these officers on the road; it has also confronted officers with a steep and fast learning curve.

An important skill for patrol officers is good judgment. Officers must be firm and authoritative, yet they must also be able to show empathy and compassion. Officers must also avoid becoming cynical. Recall from Chapter 4 that a core element of the working personality of the police is cynicism. In the words of one officer: "You become cynical and develop this sick sense of humour. You have to watch out, because it grows around you. You need to be able to

> **soft skills (of police work)**
> patrol officer skills sets centred on information collection, communication, and conflict resolution

FIGURE 5.4   Age of Primary Response Officers, Toronto Police Service, 2008

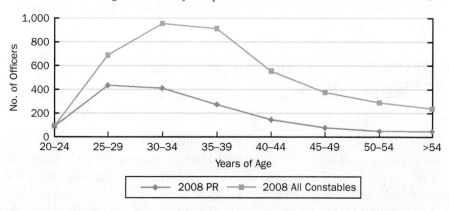

Source: "2009 Update to the Environmental Scan," p. 91. Toronto Police Service 2009. Reprinted with permission.

FIGURE 5.5   Years of Service, Primary Response Officers, Toronto Police Service 2008

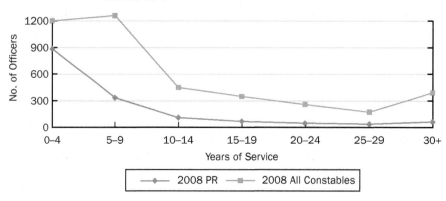

Source: "2009 Update to the Environmental Scan," p. 92. Toronto Police Service 2009. Reprinted with permission.

identify it and step away."[7] Patrol officers must not become so jaded that they lose the capacity to empathize. This is reflected in the comments of a school resource officer:

> I thought, "You know what? Screw it. I don't pull numbers at bingo. You broke the law and I'm gonna charge you." I came down on this kid. Then this hard-ass kid (who had been telling me to "f–off," "f–k the school") says, "I just don't care anymore." All of a sudden, my spider senses kicked in and I thought, "Whoops! He doesn't care about whether there are charges. He doesn't care about getting kicked out of school. What else doesn't he care about?" I poured on the caring and he just lost it—just started bawling. I had turned it around.[8]

In contrast to what one might expect given the police culture, research studies indicate that officers with more experience tend to have *lower* levels of cynicism than their younger counterparts. As noted in Chapter 4, levels of officer cynicism may also be more prevalent in high-crime communities.[9] Nor do experienced officers tend to be more authoritarian than less experienced officers.[10] Both cynicism and authoritarianism may affect the use of force by officers (see Chapter 6).

STREET WORK: PATROL OFFICER DISCRETION AND DECISION MAKING

Police Discretion

A unique feature of police work is that patrol officers, who occupy the lowest level in the organizational hierarchy of the police service, exercise the most discretion on a day-to-day basis. The exercise of discretion comes into play long before the officer actually arrives at the scene. How does a citizen decide to report an incident to the police? How is the call prioritized by the dispatcher? How much latitude do individual patrol officers have in determining the order in which they attend calls?

Officers may decide whether or not to make to make an arrest where, by law, an arrest may be warranted. In encounter situations, police officers are more likely *not* to arrest than they are to arrest. Among the non-arrest options are threats, warnings, mediation, separating the parties, or simply doing nothing. An important part of the patrol officer's job is problem solving.

Research suggests that a variety of considerations come into play: whether making an arrest will make a difference in the long run; the organizational priorities of the police service; and practical issues, such as the amount of time and paperwork that an arrest would require. An example is an officer issuing a twenty-four-hour roadside suspension for an impaired driver rather than undertaking the multihour process required to formally arrest a person for DUI.[11] This is why caution must be exercised in measuring the success of anti–drinking and driving initiatives by the police: the rates of arrest for DUI may drop, but there may be a corresponding increase in the number of twenty-four-hour roadside suspensions, which involve less paperwork.

In many incidents, particularly those of a minor nature, the officer may encounter ethical dilemmas owing to the situation. These might include having to decide whether to arrest an alleged shoplifter who is poor and/or elderly. In such situations, the officer may have to weigh the demands of the business owner that the person be arrested, with the moral conundrum of arresting a person who is no threat to the community and who stole out of need or because of a mental disability.

Other dilemmas surround incidents where there is no clear violation of the law. This requires the officer to find a solution and to solve a problem. Family and interpersonal disputes present these types of dilemmas: "Typically boyfriends want girlfriends removed, girlfriends want boyfriends removed, parents want children removed, and husbands want wives removed, or vice versa, and the police officers called to the scene must apply the law to what is essentially a family dispute."[12]

Because it is impossible for officers to enforce all laws all the time, they practise **selective** or **situational enforcement,** which in turn requires them to exercise discretion. They base their actions on a number of factors, including safety and the seriousness of the incident/offence. The call load of the officer(s) may also affect how much time the officers at the scene have to consider various options in an encounter situation. Obviously, as the level of seriousness of the call increases, the amount of police discretion decreases.

selective (or situational) enforcement discretionary enforcement due to the inability of police officers to enforce all of the laws at all times

Officers should also be aware of factors that may influence their decisions. They must take pains to remain objective and free of bias. They should make every attempt to de-escalate situations and to avoid conflict or a physical confrontation. Verbal skills rather than force should be used to encourage the subject to comply with the officer's request.

It is important to emphasize that every action a police officer may be reviewed by a supervisor and, ultimately, by the courts or the public, or both. Controversies that erupt over decisions made by police officers are often a consequence of how officers exercised discretion in specific encounters and whether they abused their discretionary power or violated the rights of suspects (see Chapter 6).

For example, a police officer who lets an impaired driver park his car instead of arresting him may be responsible for any subsequent behaviour on the part of that driver. If the impaired individual returns to his vehicle, drives away, and causes an accident in which an innocent person is killed, that officer will likely be called to justify the decision not to arrest the driver. In other instances, the public may have been watching the officer's actions—and in more and more incidents, photographing or recording them with a smartphone.

Patrol officers sometimes deliberately avoid involving themselves in problem situations. This has been referred to as FIDO, an acronym for "F*** it, drive on." Perhaps the officer concludes that, instead of becoming involved in an incident that may lead to a citizen complaint (or one that often recurs), it is best to pass on by, pretend not to have witnessed it, and let someone else deal with it. But this (lack of) response isolates officers from the communities they police; furthermore, abdicating police authority can be as inappropriate as abusing that authority. The FIDO phenomenon may have become more prevalent with the increased visibility of the police (see Chapter 1).

Controlling Police Discretion

Court decisions, legislation, and the operational policies of police services have constrained the discretion exercised by patrol officers. One example is the zero tolerance policies toward domestic violence and spousal assault that have been adopted by provincial governments across Canada. Check out At Issue 5.2 at the end of the chapter.

In the case of *R. v. Beaudry* (2007, 1 S.C.R. 190), the SCC held that a police officer's discretion is not absolute and its use must be justified on both subjective and objective grounds. Officer Beaudry was convicted of obstruction of justice for having failed to gather evidence in an incident involving another police officer who was suspected of impaired driving.

Police Perceptions of Persons and Events

Patrol officers bring to their work a cognitive lens through which they determine the levels of trouble and danger (or the potential for these) that people and situations present. This lens affects how officers exercise discretion as well as the specific actions they take in encounter situations. To respond to incidents efficiently, they use a conceptual shorthand consisting of typifications and recipes for action.

Typifications are constructs or formulations of events based on the officer's experience; they denote what is typical or common about people and events they routinely encounter. **Recipes for action** are the decisions normally made and the actions normally taken by police in certain situations. As we'll see, the action taken and the way discretion is exercised can depend, at least in part, on the individual officer.

Most officers divide situations into those requiring "real" police work and those that are "bulls***."[13] Real police work includes situations where officers may need to "use the tools of the trade."[14] In the view of more traditional officers, most requests from the public are not real police work. "Not real" includes neighbourhood disputes, minor traffic accidents, and noisy parties. Note here that community policing, by definition, involves many "not real" service and order maintenance activities.

Police officers, using typifications and recipes for action, tailor their decision making to the particular neighbourhood and population being policed.

typifications
how patrol officers depict or categorize the people and situations they encounter

recipes for action
the actions taken and decisions made by patrol officers in various types of encounter situations

While on patrol, they use a variety of visual *cues* to determine whether a person is out of place or an activity is unusual for the area. A poorly dressed individual or an older vehicle in an upscale neighbourhood, for example, would attract the attention of patrol officers; so would a well-dressed individual loitering on skid row. Also, police may ignore deviant (even illegal) behaviour in one neighbourhood where it is common, yet respond to it aggressively in a neighbourhood where it is rare. Many officers try to learn as much as possible about the area they are policing, and much of their information comes from community residents rather than patrol car computer databases. These officers understand the importance of face-to-face contact in police work.

It is often said that police officers have a "sixth sense" about people and situations that helps them in their work (see Box 5.1).

Patrol officers are especially wary of **symbolic assailants:** "persons who use gestures, language and attire that the policeman has come to recognize as a prelude to violence."[15] A primary cue that officers use in determining the potential for violence is the demeanour of the subject.

> **symbolic assailants**
> individuals encountered by patrol officers who display mannerisms and behaviours that suggest the potential for violence

Box 5.1

An Officer's "Sixth Sense"

Question: You have mentioned a "sixth sense" that you use in your police work. What do you mean?

Officer: I remember making a case once where a guy was driving a stolen car. They asked me in court to describe the guy. I could not describe him, but I knew it was a stolen car. They said, "Why did you know it was a stolen car?" Because the car was sitting at the intersection and I drove past the car and the light was such on Bladensburg Road at that particular time that I could see the guy's eyes follow my patrol car as I went by without his turning his head. His eyes just followed my car as it went by. I saw that. And I also saw that he had on a skullcap and I knew what color the skullcap was, but to describe the individual, I couldn't.

Question: So the fact that his eyes followed you was sufficient to clue you in that the car was stolen?

Officer: Well, that clued me in to taking a second look at this car. So I made a U-turn as he pulled away from the stop sign. As I made the U-turn, he sped away and we got into this chase and, of course, he abandoned the car, jumped out, and ran up the street. I immediately stopped the car and chased him on foot.

He was 17 years old; I was 42, 43. I mean, let's face it, as good a shape as I am in, a foot chase here is not my forte. But that sixth sense I told you about: I remembered something else about that car. After he ran and after I went around to try to head him off in my patrol car at the other end of the alley, I remembered something about his car at that point, and that is that I heard the engine of his car roar as it was pulling away from the curb.

So what did I do? My sixth sense acted: I went back to the curb he pulled away from, and lo and behold, that's where the guy lived. He had run home. So there he was, coming around the corner. I arrested him there. This is all an example of that sixth sense I told you about.

Source: Maggs, G.E., "Flexibility and Discretion in Police Work," *The World and I* 7, no. (1992): 525.

Assessments of people and situations and the subsequent risk assessments are important elements of street-level police work. When officers err in their assessments, they risk exercising discretion inappropriately and placing themselves or others present at risk. Furthermore, all police encounters—even those that officers typify as routine—are potentially violent. Risk is always present, and officers must be prepared at all times to use lethal force. As one patrol officer commented: "My thought process is that if you're prepared for the worst, then everything is going to be so much easier to handle."[16]

A major challenge for patrol officers is to avoid complacency. One officer stated: "In policing, complacency is dangerous. It also depends upon the people you are dealing with. If you're dealing with a drug addicted person, for example, repetition will happen. But even if you deal with them on a daily basis, never assume everything's going to be fine. You never know."[17]

A defining attribute of police (and patrol work) is the uncertainty that surrounds many encounters and the *potential* for serious injury and death. One police scholar has described this uncertainty and its impact on patrol officers as follows:

> Although patrol work is mostly trivial and non-criminal, it is nonetheless fraught with uncertainty. Officers can never forget that at any moment the boredom of a long shift can be shattered by a call that can be harrowing, traumatic, dangerous or life-threatening. The dilemma for patrol officers is that they must prepare for war even though they are rarely called upon to fight. To relax invites risk; to be constantly on guard invites over-reaction.[18]

That patrol officers can find themselves thrust into traumatic and life-threatening situations is illustrated by an incident that occurred in the early morning hours of March 25, 2006, in Seattle, Washington. The 911 dispatch tapes recorded the response of patrol officer Steve Leonard—and, subsequently, several other patrol officers—to shots fired at a Seattle house. Leonard arrived on the scene forty-five seconds after the first 911 call and saw the perpetrator stalking victims. He had already killed seven people at a post-rave house party. When ordered to drop his weapon, the suspect shot and killed himself. The 911 tapes (which are quite graphic) can be accessed at http://seattletimes.nwsource.com/html/localnews/2002901121_911tapes31m.html.

In 2005, four RCMP officers were murdered in the rural Alberta community of Rochfort Bridge, near Mayerthorpe, northwest of Edmonton. The officers had gone to the property to execute a search warrant for stolen property. The perpetrator died of a self-inflicted gunshot wound prior to police backup arriving.

Statistics on the deaths of Canadian police officers indicate that, over a nearly fifty-year period, officers were most often murdered while investigating robberies or during domestic disputes. In recent years, however, more officer homicides have occurred during traffic stops of suspicious vehicles/persons and during traffic violation stops.[19]

The Task (or Policing) Environment

task (or policing) environment

the organizational context and the community or areas in which patrol officers carry out their activities

The **task (or policing) environment** includes the organizational context in which police officers work (the internal environment) as well as the community setting in which police services are delivered (the external environment). The use of lethal force, the number of arrests, citation rates, and success in solving cases all vary greatly among police organizations; this reflects differences in policies, performance standards, and the area being policed.[20] Research studies have also found that patrol practice may vary from district to district and even between precincts within the same police service. Similar situations may be handled differently, depending on the officers who are assigned to the area, the style and orientation of supervising officers, cultural and community expectations, and so on.[21]

With respect to the settings in which police officers carry out their tasks, the attributes of a given neighbourhood or community—including its socioeconomic features and the composition of its population (i.e., age, diversity)—determine in large measure the types of incidents that occur there, the demands that are made on the police, the types of encounter situations that arise, the relationships that develop between the police and the community, and the ability of the police to respond to the community's needs. Observers have pointed out, for example, that the "greying (aging)" of the Canadian population will mean that the police will be required to give more attention to the needs of the elderly, not just as victims of crime, but as consumers of police services.[22] An emerging challenge for police services, particularly the RCMP, is policing "boomtowns." These are primarily northern communities that have experienced rapid population growth centered around resource-based development. (Recall from Chapter 1 that the RCMP was called upon to police the chaos that often surrounded the Klondike gold rush in the late 1800s.) The influx of young men and women, transient workers, and young families places strains on community infrastructure and services, including policing. Police services may struggle to respond to escalating rates of crime, including drug trafficking and to develop effective crime prevention and crime reduction initiatives.[23]

Police services and officers need to develop operational strategies that are appropriate to the environment at hand. These strategies may be especially difficult to devise for cultural and ethnic communities because of language and cultural barriers.

The types of activities in a particular police district may also affect the number and types of complaints filed against police officers. In District 1 in Vancouver, for example, which includes the entertainment district (with 6,000 bar seats), there are more complaints filed against officers, generally resulting from incidents between police and bar patrons on the street near or after bar closing times. And in District 2, which encompasses the area known as the Downtown East Side, there is a multineeds population, a high percentage of whom are homeless, addicted, and/or mentally ill (see page 129).

From the perspective of many officers, a "busy" area is one with a relatively high diversity of calls; they view these areas as the most interesting to work in. In busy areas the police are exposed to a greater number of calls involving violence, high-risk incidents, and serious crimes. Skills such as conducting interrogations, preparing search warrants, cultivating informants, and carrying out surveillance are more likely to be used in busy districts. In Vancouver, many rookies, fresh from graduation at the Justice Institute Police Academy, are assigned to the troubled Downtown Eastside, which provides them with the opportunity to develop skills that will serve them throughout their careers.

Patrol officers develop an intimate knowledge of the "flora and fauna" of the areas they police: "Like tour guides in the museum of human frailty, they can point to houses where they are repeatedly called to mediate family disputes, up-market apartment complexes where young swingers frequently hold noisy parties, troublesome 'biker' bars where drugs are sold, business premises patrolled by a vicious dog, street corners where drug dealers collect, car parks often hit by thieves, warehouses with poor alarm systems and places where police officers have been shot and wounded."[24] Part of the skill set of patrol officers is knowing not only what is going on in their territory, but also who may be involved in criminal activity and who may be vulnerable to victimization.

The Encounter

While carrying out their duties, patrol officers find themselves in a variety of encounters. Some arise as the result of a call for police service that has been relayed to the officer; others result from actions taken by the officer. Researchers have attempted to identify the factors that create the dynamic of the encounter as well as its outcome. Attention has focused on the following: the officer; the suspect, if one is present; the complainant/victim; and the occurrence itself.

The Officer

Chapter 4 examined the career orientations of police officers. The particular background and orientation a police officer brings to his or her work may influence how discretion is exercised as well as the decisions made in encounter situations. In addition, the behaviour of officers can sometimes escalate an incident and place them at risk of assault.

Research studies have found that the behaviour of police officers in encounter situations is the primary determinant of attitudes toward the police and of public confidence in the police (see Chapter 8). Citizens who felt they were treated with respect by the officer report higher levels of trust and confidence in the police.[25] Conversely, citizens who are not happy about their contacts with the police may hold less favourable opinions of the police.[26] In the United States, the ethnicity and/or gender of the officer seems to have no direct influence on outcomes in routine police–citizen encounters. Female officers do not appear to have differential views of community policing or community residents and neighbourhoods.[27] American researchers have found no relationship between the levels of education of police officers and the probability of arrest or a search of the suspect.[28] The absence of field studies precludes a determination of whether the same is true in Canada. It is not known, for example, whether First Nations police officers make decisions differently than their non-Aboriginal colleagues when policing First Nations communities.

The Suspect

Officers tend to distinguish between the general public, who are to be protected, and (in police parlance) "scroats" or "scum," who are to receive police attention. Police researchers have tried to find links between police action and a suspect's alleged offence and his or her attributes (e.g., ethnicity, age, relationship to the victim, demeanour). It may be that suspects who are young, a member of a visible minority, and from a lower socioeconomic background are more likely to be typified as requiring police intervention. The demeanour of both the officer and the suspect may also influence the outcome of an encounter.[29] Some research suggests that the less respectful police officers are toward suspects and community residents, the less likely these people are to comply with the law and with any requests the officers make.[30]

There is no conclusive evidence that, in their actions and arrest practices, Canadian police systematically discriminate on the basis of a person's ethnicity. However, the high arrest rates of Aboriginal people in many parts of the country and the ongoing conflicts between visible minorities and the police in some urban areas warrant close examination. Of particular concern is whether police officers engage in racial profiling. This issue is examined in greater detail in Chapter 11.

Conflicts between patrol officers and citizens often involve traffic stops. In recent years, more and more police services have equipped patrol cars with digital cameras to record encounters between the police and the public. The Ottawa Police Service was the first in Canada to install minicams on Tasers, and several police services are experimenting with placing minicams on police officers. This is being done to protect both the officer and the public.

The Complainant/Victim

Complainants themselves do much to determine the actions that officers take during encounters. The extent to which officers provide assistance and act on the complainant's wishes may depend on the attributes and actions of the complainant and on the officer's assessment of the his or her credibility. Complainants who are uncooperative, aggressive, and known to the police from past encounters may receive less assistance than those deemed sincere and "respectable." Also, officers may be less likely to consider the preferences of complainants who are perceived as having contributed to their own victimization. Of course, in certain encounters—for example, those involving domestic assault—the officers must act even if it means going against the preferences of the complainant/victim.

Chapter 11 examines efforts by police services to encourage people in the G/L/B/T communities to overcome their traditional hesitation and report victimization to the police.

The Occurrence

The seriousness of the alleged offence, the presence of weapons or violence, the circumstances surrounding the event, the individuals involved—all of these may affect officers' actions. Also, the task environment in which the occurrence takes place may affect the actions taken by police. For example, two individuals fighting in a skid row area may merely be separated and sent on their respective ways, while a similar incident in a higher income neighbourhood, where such an occurrence is rare and out of character, may result in a more formal police response, especially if one of the combatants is not from the area.

Patrol Officer Use of Mediation and Conflict Resolution

Patrol officers make an arrest in only a small percentage of encounters.[31] What, then, do they do the rest of the time? Police scholars have paid surprisingly little attention to how patrol officers mediate and resolve conflicts, although officers may utilize a number of methods other than making an arrest:

- *Avoidance.* Taking no action, doing nothing, or telling the disputants to "take a walk" and clear out of the area.
- *Referring the conflict to other agencies for resolution.* Accessing agencies or services with the expertise to address the problem at hand, including neighbourhood

dispute resolution groups, landlord–tenant dispute resolution boards, and other community or government services.

- *Intimidation and coercion.* Threatening to arrest the disputants if hostilities do not cease.

- *Mediation.* Acting as a neutral third party in an attempt to address the interests of the disputing parties. This requires the disputants (minimum of two) to cooperate in the process and is most appropriate for one-time disputes that do not have a history of underlying issues (see Police File 5.3).[32]

- *Restorative justice approaches.* Conducting or participating as a member of a sentencing circle, family or community conference, or other restorative justice program designed to resolve conflict or to respond to criminal behaviour or youth offending (see Chapter 9).

During an encounter, patrol officers often employ subtle techniques to defuse the conflict. These include taking a period of time to check identification and record information on the incident; providing an opportunity for the disputants to calm down and de-escalate the conflict; and speaking individually with each party.

As patrol officers become more experienced, they develop strategies for resolving conflicts and disputes informally. These strategies are influenced by the officer's personal style of policing, including the way he or she exercises discretion, and by their "verbal judo" skills. When community policing is adopted, patrol officers are more likely to become involved in identifying solutions to problems instead of merely reacting to them with formal interventions.

An incident that could have resulted in an arrest but was informally resolved through mediation is presented in Police File 5.3.

Police File 5.3

Private Restitution: Washroom Mayhem in Yaletown, 12:40 a.m.

A Vancouver Police Department Sergeant and two patrol officers are dispatched to a bar–restaurant in the trendy Yaletown section of the city. The manager has summoned the police to deal with an unruly patron who has gone on a rampage in the men's washroom and caused several hundred dollars' worth of damage. The manager identifies the culprit, and the officers discreetly handcuff him and remove him from the premises. Outside, the officers discuss the situation with the slightly impaired patron, all the while being constantly interrupted by the patron's girlfriend, who promises to take him home if they release him. The restaurant manager joins the discussion and indicates that, while he does not wish to press charges, he does want the damages covered. The patron produces a credit card, which is given over to the manager, who adds the damage to the patron's bar bill. The charge slip is signed by the patron, who is released and departs with his girlfriend.

Police Officers and the Victims of Crime

In carrying out their mandate, police officers must consider the needs of crime victims. This includes providing information on how to access resources such as counselling, as well as providing feedback on the progress of the case investigation. Many police services operate victim services units; others have entered into collaborative arrangements with community agencies and organizations to provide victim assistance. Victim assistance programs are staffed mainly by volunteers, who provide information to crime victims on the progress of case investigations, facilitate the return of property to victims, and refer victims to other services in the community.

A key objective of these programs is to ensure that "secondary victimization" does not occur—that is, that the crime victim has his or her needs addressed by the police and other criminal justice personnel. Special challenges are presented by incidents involving G/L/B/T victims (see Chapter 11).

Police Encounters with Persons with Mental Illness (PwMI)

Patrol officers are encountering more and more persons with mental illness although as one police officer with extensive experience in this area stated: "The police are not the appropriate resources for dealing with the mentally ill" (personal communication). Whatever the common image of police activities, officers are as likely to be called to a mental illness crisis as to a robbery. The number of incidents involving mentally ill persons increased significantly after provincial governments failed to provide enough community-based treatment programs and facilities following the massive deinstitutionalization of the mentally ill during the 1960s and 1970s. Police officers have become de facto community mental health workers and are the first responders to the mentally ill on the streets and in neighbourhoods. In Vancouver, a study found that 31 percent of calls for service received by the department had some mental health component. Some individuals in that city had almost daily contact with the police.[33] A follow-up report, completed by the Vancouver Police Department two years later in 2010, found that many of the issues identified in the first study had not been addressed by the provincial government and mental health agencies. PwMI continue to have high levels of contact with the police and to not have access to appropriate mental health services.[34]

It is often patrol officers who determine whether PwMI will be put into the criminal justice system or diverted to the mental health system. Officers face many difficulties in dealing with mentally ill people on the street, including a lack of referral resources and the fact that many persons with mental illness cannot be apprehended under mental health acts, as they do not meet the criterion of being a danger to themselves or others. The efforts of officers to divert PwMI from the justice system are often hindered by a lack of resources. This is illustrated by the individual in Vancouver profiled in Police File 5.4.

Concerns have been raised that the police inappropriately use arrest to resolve encounters with mentally disordered people; this is most commonly referred to as the "criminalization" of the mentally ill. Research studies, however,

Police File 5.4

A High-Needs PwMI

There is a well known, regular occupant of the VPD jail who typically gets arrested for minor offences on a weekly basis. He is diagnosed with schizophrenia, often fails to take his medication, and subsequently presents as a very ill individual. Once in jail, it is not uncommon for him to smear feces all over himself and the cell that he is in. He then masturbates to the camera, yells profanities, and bangs his head against the walls. Jail guards wash him down, move him to a new cell, and bleach the old one clean. Once relocated, he repeats this behaviour, often requiring several moves. This male has had 112 documented contacts with the police in 2007 alone. He was taken to hospital under the provisions of the Mental Health Act nine times during this same time period.

Source: Wilson-Bates, F., "Lost in Transition: How a Lack of Capacity in the Mental Health System is Failing Vancouver's Mentally Ill and Draining Police Resources," p. 32, © 2008 Vancouver Police Department. Reprinted by permission.

have not supported this assertion.[35] Rather, Canadian police officers demonstrate high levels of benevolence and empathy toward mentally ill people, as well as a strong interest in linking them with appropriate services.[36] Nor does it appear that PwMI are subject to any higher levels of use of force than mentally stable suspects.[37]

Over the past decade, police agencies have been developing specialized approaches for managing encounters with mentally ill people.[38] Most major police services ensure that officers receive Crisis Intervention Training (CIT), where they learn about mental illness and various strategies for managing encounters with PwMI. Positive outcomes have been reported by police services that have adopted the CIT model, including lower rates of arrest of PwMI.[39]

All of Canada's police colleges and training academies provide recruits with information on dealing with mentally ill persons.[40] Most of the large urban police services have specific initiatives to better manage encounters with PwMI. These include mobile patrol units staffed by a police officer and a mental health worker. Studies have shown that in those jurisdictions with a specialized response, there are lower rates of inappropriate arrest of mentally ill people.[41] A study of an integrated mobile crisis service in Halifax, involving clinicians and police officers, found improved response times despite an increase in the use of this service by patients, families, and service partners; it also found an increase in the use of follow-up services by patients, as compared to a control group.[42]

There are limits to what the police can accomplish without effective partnerships with other agencies and organizations in this field. A key challenge is the lack of interoperability between the police and other agencies and nongovernmental organizations. This has hindered the development of multifaceted interventions that may be effective in addressing the needs of this population. One officer who has policed Vancouver's troubled Downtown Eastside stated: "The police are not the appropriate resource for dealing with the mentally ill" (personal communication).

Policing Multineeds Populations: The Vancouver Downtown Eastside (DTES)

The Downtown Eastside (DTES) in Vancouver provides an example of the challenges that police services encounter in policing a multineeds population. The DTES is often referred to as "Canada's poorest postal code" (although redevelopment is rapidly changing the area). Estimates are that one-quarter of its 16,000 residents suffer from some form of mental illness and that 5,000 are users of IV drugs. Forty percent of Vancouver's violent crime occurs in District 2, which encompasses the DTES. It is estimated that 30 percent of the calls attended by Vancouver police officers involve a person with a mental illness. Many residents of the DTES are not only mentally ill but also homeless and addicted.

A number of residents of the DTES are "frequent flyers." One of them, Bill, has ongoing contact with the justice and medical systems (see Figure 5.6). Bill is a crack cocaine addict diagnosed with both schizophrenia and bipolar disorder. He is too violent to qualify for a residence for mentally ill people and so is left to his own devices on the street.

FIGURE 5.6   A Calendar Showing Bill's Contacts with the Police, the Time He Has Spent in a Psychiatric Facility, and the Time He Has Spent in Jail, January 2007 to October 2007

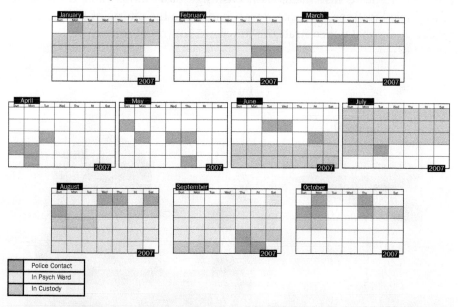

Source: Wilson-Bates, F., "Lost in Transition: How a Lack of Capacity in the Mental Health System is Failing Vancouver's Mentally Ill and Draining Police Resources," p. 37, © 2008 Vancouver Police Department. Reprinted by permission.

The efforts of the Vancouver Police Department in the DTES have been documented in a series of films, produced by a group of patrol officers called "The Odd Squad." Check out the website at http://www.oddsquad.com.

Policing Social Disorder and Political Protests

As the front line of the criminal justice system, the police have always been drawn into situations involving social disorder and public protest. Recall from Chapter 1 the RCMP's response to the Winnipeg General Strike of 1919 and the use of the Toronto police for political purposes.

Police officers often find themselves involved in political demonstrations; labour strikes; public protests and blockades over resource development issues; and blockades and occupations by Aboriginal people asserting their land rights. This occurred in Ontario in 2006, when the Six Nations launched a campaign against a housing development in Caledonia, Ontario. They argued that the development was being built on land that had been wrongfully taken from them more than a century earlier. The dispute pitted townspeople against Aboriginal people and the provincial government and also raised tensions between the federal and provincial governments. After months of protests by Six Nations, counter-protests by non-Aboriginal residents of the area, and destruction of property and occasional violence, the provincial government purchased the land and compensated the developer. In 2011, the Ontario government agreed to pay $20 million in compensation to residents and small businesses in Caledonia. One perspective of the events that occurred in Caledonia is provided in *Helpless: Caledonia's Nightmare of Fear and Anarchy and How the Law Failed All of Us*.[43] Policing crowds involved in social protests and riots has become more challenging with the advent of personal technologies, including laptops, smartphones, and various apps. Protestors and rioters can communicate instantaneously, creating "flash mobs" and disturbances in multiple locations. This can thwart and elude the efforts of the police and render traditional police strategies for crowd control obsolete.

Protestors at the land dispute in Caledonia, Ontario, 2006.

THE CANADIAN PRESS/Hamilton

At Issue 5.1

Exercising Discretion

You are a member of a police service with two years' service. It is 4:30 a.m. on a quiet morning. There is little traffic. From your patrol car, you notice that the car ahead of you has just failed to stop for a red light and is exceeding the posted speed limit. You accelerate to match the speed of the motorist and notice that the vehicle is travelling at a constant speed of 80 km/h in a posted 50 km/h zone.

You activate the emergency equipment of your police vehicle and the motorist pulls over.

As you approach the driver you contemplate whether to issue the motorist a citation for failing to stop for a red light or for excessive speed, or both.

When you arrive at the driver's side of the vehicle, you recognize the driver as a friend you went through college with and haven't seen for years. There is no sign that the driver has been drinking or that he is otherwise impaired.

You Make the Call!

1. What options do you have? What are the consequences of each?
2. Would the options and the factors you weigh be different if the driver was:
   - a stranger?
   - an attractive member of the opposite gender?
   - an off-duty police officer from your department?
   - an off-duty police officer from a neighbouring department?
   - a firefighter from your municipality?
   - a firefighter from another municipality?
   - a known criminal?
   - an individual from a cultural or ethnic group unlike your own?
   - travelling at 100 km/h rather than 80 km/h?

At Issue 5.2

Policing Domestic Violence: Discretion Versus Zero Tolerance

For decades, considerable criticism has been directed toward police services for their response to situations in which women are abused by a spouse, partner, or boyfriend. To ensure the protection of women, the police are directed by provincial/territorial governments to adhere to

(Continued)

a zero tolerance policy for spousal assault and abuse.

In recent years, concerns have been expressed that without meaning to, zero tolerance policies may have reduced the likelihood that victims of spousal assault will call the police for help. Knowing that an arrest will probably be made if the police attend the scene, some women may be choosing not to call for help (including visible minority and immigrant women, who may feel especially vulnerable to family and community recriminations or to possible deportation if their spouse is incarcerated).

This concern has led some community groups, including women's groups, in many areas of the country to call for a review of zero tolerance policies. Among other things, they suggest that zero tolerance should not apply to all situations and that police should consider the specific circumstances of the victim on a case-by-case basis. Other groups, though, are hesitant to alter a policy that took years to implement; they fear that many police officers will revert to their previous lackadaisical attitudes toward spousal abuse and assault.

You Make the Call!

1. Considering the arguments on either side of the issue, would you support modification of zero tolerance enforcement policies for spousal abuse and assault? Explain.

2. Can you think of other areas where zero-tolerance policies might be effective?
3. Identify some ways in which zero tolerance policies might affect police work.

Key Points Review

1. The five duties of patrol officers recognized under common law are to prevent crime, protect life and property, preserve the peace, apprehend offenders, and enforce laws.
2. The types of activities that patrol officers are involved in are determined largely by calls to the police from the general public.
3. Police services utilize a variety of strategies for managing calls for service, including call shedding, prioritizing calls, and differential response strategies.
4. Police services are paying increasing attention to patrol deployment, including officer workloads and the performance of patrol units.
5. In most police services, a large number of officers have less than five years on the job.
6. Patrol officers have considerable discretion in carrying out their tasks.
7. Police officers bring to their work a cognitive lens through which they determine levels of trouble and danger, or the potential for trouble and danger, that people and situations present.
8. It is often said that police officers have a "sixth sense" about people and situations.
9. Police officers carry out their tasks in a variety of task (or policing) environments.
10. Police officers are experiencing more and more encounters with the mentally ill, and police services have developed initiatives to more effectively respond to this population.

Key Term Questions

1. What is the *Canadian Police Information System (CPIC)*?
2. Describe the *"W" system* as used by police dispatchers and communication officers.
3. What is *call shedding,* and what does it signify in police work?
4. Describe the phenomenon of *call stacking.*
5. What is *differential police response (DPR),* and what are some of the strategies used by police to allocate patrol resources?
6. Define *allocated patrol time* and *unallocated patrol time,* and note why these two concepts are important in any discussion of police mobile unit utilization.
7. What is meant by the *soft skills of police work?*
8. What is *selective* (or *situational*) *enforcement,* and how is this practice related to the police exercise of discretion?
9. What are *typifications* and *recipes for action,* and how do these two concepts help us understand the decision making of patrol officers?
10. What is a *symbolic assailant,* and how does this concept help us understand police decision making?
11. What is the *task* (or *policing) environment,* and how does it affect the decision making of police patrol officers?

Notes

1. Toronto Police Service, "2009 Update to the Environmental Scan" (Toronto: 2009), http://www.torontopolice.on.ca/publications/files/reports/2009envscan.pdf
2. J. Van Maanen, "Observations on the Making of Policemen," *Human Organization* 32, no. 4 (1973): 407–18.
3. J.M. McDonald, *Gold Medal Policing: Mental Readiness and Performance Excellence* (New York: Sloan Associates, 2006), 82.
4. S. Dunn, "Police Officers Murdered in the Line of Duty, 1961 to 2009" (Ottawa: Statistics Canada, 2010), http://www.statcan.gc.ca/pub/85-002-x/2010003/article/11354-eng.htm
5. S. Demers, R. Prox, A. Palmer, and C.T. Griffiths, "Vancouver Police Department Patrol Deployment Study" (Vancouver: Vancouver Police Department, 2007), http://www.city.vancouver.bc.ca/police/assets/pdf/studies/vpd-study-patrol-deployment.pdf
6. City of Kelowna (2010), "Policing Services," http://www.kelowna.ca
7. McDonald, *Gold Medal Policing,* 83.
8. McDonald, *Gold Medal Policing,* 57.
9. J.J. Sobol, "The Social Ecology of Police Attitudes," *Policing: An International Journal of Police Strategies and Management* 33, no. 2 (2010): 253–69.
10. L. Laguna, A. Linn, K. Ward, and R. Rupslaukyte, "An Examination of Authoritarian Personality Traits Among Police Officers: The Role of Experience," *Journal of Police and Criminal Psychology* 25, no. 2 (2009): 99–104.
11. W. Terrill and E.A. Paoline, "Nonarrest Decision Making in Police–Citizen Encounters," *Police Quarterly* 10, no. 3 (2007): 308–31.

12. J.M. Pollock and H.W. Williams, "Using Ethical Dilemmas in Training Police," in *Justice, Crime, and Ethics,* ed. M.C. Braswell, B.R. McCarthy, and B.J. McCarthy (Cincinnati: Anderson, 2012), 91–109 at 97.

13. R.J. Lundman, *Police and Policing—An Introduction* (New York: Holt, Rinehart, and Winston, 1980), 110.

14. Van Maanen, "Observations on the Making of Policemen," 413.

15. J. Skolnick, *Justice Without Trial: Law Enforcement in a Democratic Society* (New York: John Wiley, 1966), 45.

16. McDonald, *Gold Medal Policing,* 98.

17. Dunn, "Police Officers Murdered in the Line of Duty, 1961–2009," 98–99.

18. D.H. Bayley, "What Do the Police Do?," in *Policing: Key Readings,* ed. T. Newman (Portland: Willan, 2005), 141–49 at 144.

19. Dunn, "Police Officers Murdered in the Line of Duty, 1961–2009."

20. W. Skogan and K. Frydl, "Fairness and Effectiveness in Policing: The Evidence" (Washington: National Academies Press, 2005).

21. K.D. Hassell, "Variation in Police Patrol Practices: The Precinct as a Sub-Organizational Level of Analysis," *Policing: An International Journal of Police Strategies and Management* 30, no. 2 (2007): 257–76.

22. J. Liederbach and C.D. Stelle, "Policing a Graying Population: A Study of Police Contacts with Older Adults," *Journal of Crime and Justice* 33, no. 1 (2010): 37–69.

23. R. Ruddell, "Boomtown Policing: Responding to the Dark Side of Resource Development," *Policing* 5, no. 4 (2011): 328–42.

24. Bayley, "What Do the Police Do?" 144.

25. J.M. Gau, "A Longitudinal Analysis of Citizens' Attitudes About Police," *Policing: An International Journal of Police Strategies and Management* 33, no. 2 (2010): 236–52; L. Hinds, "Public Satisfaction with the Police: The Influence of General Attitudes and Police–Citizen Encounters," *International Journal of Police Science and Management* 11, no. 1 (2009): 54–66.

26. B. Bradford, J. Jackson, and E.A. Stanko, "Contact and Confidence: Revisiting the Impact of Public Encounters with the Police," *Policing and Society: An International Journal of Research and Policy* 19, no. 1 (2009): 20–46.

27. M. Poteyeva and I.Y. Sun, "Gender Differences in Police Officers' Attitudes: Assessing Current Empirical Evidence," *Journal of Criminal Justice* 37, no. 5 (2009): 512–22.

28. J. Rydberg and W. Terrill, "The Effect of Higher Education on Police Behavior," *Police Quarterly* 13, no. 1 (2010): 92–120.

29. R.G. Dunham and G.P. Alpert, "Officer and Suspect Demeanor: A Qualitative Analysis of Change," *Police Quarterly* 12, no. 1 (2009): 6–21.

30. L.W. Sherman, D. Gottfredson, D. MacKenzie, J. Eck, P. Reuter, and S. Bushway, *Preventing Crime: What Works, What Doesn't, What's Promising* (Washington: Justice Department of Justice, Office of Justice Programs, 1997), 8.1, http://www.ncjrs.gov/works

31. Terrill and Paoline, "Nonarrest Decision Making in Police–Citizen Encounters."

32. C. Cooper, "Patrol Police Officer Conflict Resolution Processes," *Journal of Criminal Justice* 25, no. 2 (1997): 87–101.

33. F. Wilson-Bates, "Lost in Transition: How a Lack of Capacity in the Mental Health System Is Failing Vancouver's Mentally Ill and Draining Police

Resources," (Vancouver: Vancouver Police Department, 2008), http://www.cbc.ca/bc/news/bc-080204-Vpd-mental-health-report.pdf

34. S. Thompson, "Policing Vancouver's Mentally Ill: The Disturbing Truth. Beyond Lost in Transition," (Vancouver: Vancouver Police Department, 2010), http://vancouver.ca/police/assets/pdf/reports-policies/vpd-lost-in-transition-part-2-draft.pdf

35. R.S. Engel and E. Silver, "Policing Mentally Disordered Suspects: A Re-examination of the Criminalization Hypothesis," *Criminology* 39, no. 2 (2001): 225–52.

36. D. Cotton and T.G. Coleman, "The Attitudes of Canadian Police Officers Toward the Mentally Ill," *International Journal of Law and Psychiatry* 27, no. 2 (2004): 135–46.

37. R.R. Johnson, "Suspect Mental Disorder and Police Use of Force," *Criminal Justice and Behavior* 38, no. 2 (2011): 127–45.

38. D. Cotton and T.G. Coleman, "Canadian Police Agencies and Their Interactions with Persons with a Mental Illness: A Systems Approach," *Police Practice and Research* 11, no. 4 (2010): 301–14; J.D. Livingston, C. Weaver, N. Hall, and S. Verdun-Jones, "Criminal Justice Diversion for Persons for Mental Disorders: A Review of Best Practices" (Vancouver: Law Foundation of British Columbia, B.C. Mental Health and Addiction Services, and Canadian Mental Health Association, B.C. Division, 2008), http://www.cmha.bc.ca/files/DiversionBestPractices.pdf

39. S. Franz and R. Borum, "Crisis Intervention Teams May Prevent Arrests of People with Mental Illness," *Police Practice and Research* 12, no. 3 (2010): 265–72.

40. Cotton and Coleman, "Canadian Police Agencies and Their Interactions."

41. H.J. Steadman, J.P. Morrissey, M.W. Deane, and R. Borum, "Police Response to Emotionally Disturbed Persons: Analyzing New Models of Police Interactions with the Mental Health System" (Washington: U.S. Department of Justice, 1999), http://www.ncjrs.gov/pdffiles1/nij/grants/179984.pdf

42. S. Kisely, L.A. Campbell, S. Peddle, S. Hare, M. Psyche, D. Spicer, and B. Moore, "A Controlled Before-and-After Evaluation of a Mobile Crisis Partnership Between Mental Health and Police Services in Nova Scotia," *Canadian Journal of Psychiatry* 55, no. 10 (2010): 662–68.

43. C. Blatchford, *Helpless: Caledonia's Nightmare of Fear and Anarchy, and How the Law Failed All of Us* (Toronto: Doubleday, 2010).

Chapter

6

Police Powers and the Use of Force

Learning Objectives

After reading this chapter, you should be able to:

- Discuss the impact of the Charter of Rights and Freedoms on police powers
- Describe the powers of the police with respect to arrest and detention, search and seizure, entrapment, and interrogation
- Discuss the legal provisions for the police use of force
- Describe the National Force Options Framework and Ontario's Use of Force Model
- Identify and discuss the correlates of the police use of force
- Identify the five levels of resistance that individuals may present to a police officer
- Identify and discuss the levels of force intervention and the associated progressive use-of-force response levels available to police officers
- Discuss the issues surrounding the use of less lethal force options
- Define and discuss the phenomenon of victim-precipitated homicide ("suicide by cop")

Key Terms

In the opening pages of the text, it was noted that there will always be tension between the need to maintain order and the rights of citizens. This tension is evident in the discussion of the powers of the police. A key question is this: How can Canadian society balance the rights of citizens with the police authority to ensure order and to pursue criminal offenders? One of the difficulties is that persons who have contact with the police may not know what powers the police have and their individual rights. This may be especially problematic for persons newly arrived in Canada, but it may also be the case for many Canadian citizens, including the elderly and the mentally disabled.

Historically, Canadians have been willing to trust the police to "do the right thing" in exercising their powers and have been prepared to give the police more powers to detect and arrest criminals even if this means that the civil rights of some individuals will be violated. In recent years, however, owing to a number of high-profile incidents and the increased visibility of the police, these views seem to be shifting.

The following discussion does not present a detailed examination of police powers. Space limitations aside, it is assumed that students have access to more in-depth materials in other courses. Readers with an interest in police powers are encouraged to monitor Supreme Court of Canada decisions, which can be accessed at http://scc.lexum.org. The cases presented in this chapter should be considered only as illustrative of the types of issues that arise surrounding police powers.

An equally important feature of the police role is the authority to use force, including lethal force. This is also considered in the following discussion.

THE CHARTER AND POLICE POWERS

As noted in Chapter 2, Canadian police officers derive their authority from the Criminal Code and various provincial statutes. The Criminal Code provides the authority to arrest (Section 495); to use force (Section 25), to search (with a warrant, Section 487); and to obtain DNA samples (Section 487.05), among others.

The Canadian Charter of Rights and Freedoms has had a significant impact in defining the powers of the police. Section 7 of the Charter states: "Everyone has the right to life, liberty and security of the person and the right not to be deprived thereof except in accordance with the principles of fundamental justice." The Charter has entrenched the constitutional rights of those accused of crimes, who have the right to challenge the actions of the police if those rights have been violated. Charter rights, combined with pre-existing legal rules, provide legal safeguards against the unlimited use of police power.

The police cannot use certain investigative techniques (e.g., electronic surveillance) without prior judicial authorization, and if the police gather evidence illegally, it may be excluded from a trial if its use would bring the administration of justice into disrepute. All relevant information gathered during a case investigation must be disclosed to the defence attorney. In addition, severe restrictions have been placed on the investigative strategy of placing an undercover officer in a jail cell to elicit evidence from a criminal suspect.

On the flipside, as a result of judicial decisions, police officers now have the authority to use a warrant to obtain DNA from a suspect, by force if necessary;

to obtain a variety of warrants to intercept private audio and video communications; to run "reverse stings" (e.g., sell drugs as part of an undercover operation and then seize both the money and the drugs); and to obtain foot, palm, and teeth impressions from a suspect.

The specific powers of Canadian police are constantly evolving as a result of court decisions and changes in law. There is the view that, in its decisions, the Supreme Court of Canada has tipped the balance of individual liberties/police powers toward the police.[1] More specifically, the SCC has:

- ruled in favour of the police practice of using thermal-imaging technology deployed from aircraft to detect high levels of "heat" from homes, a key indicator of marijuana grow-ops (*R. v. Tessling*, 2004, 3 S.C.R. 432);
- established the legality of "Mr. Big" stings, wherein suspects are placed in a position where they "confess" to having committed one or more crimes. (*R. v. Grandinetti*, 2005, 1 S.C.R. 27). This controversial technique is discussed in Chapter 10;
- reaffirmed the principle that the police can continue to question a suspect at length, even if the suspect repeatedly tries to invoke his right to silence (*R. v. Singh*, 2007, 3 S.C.R. 405); and
- held that the Charter does not require the presence, upon request, of defence counsel during a custodial interrogation (*R. v. McCrimmon*, 2010, 2 S.C.R. 402; *R v. Sinclair*, 2010, 2 S.C.R. 310).

Canadian courts are increasingly presented with cases involving the right of privacy and electronic evidence. Recent cases have considered whether e-mail messages on a cell phone used as part of a criminal conspiracy could be admitted into evidence. A B.C. court ruled that this evidence could be admitted, while an Ontario court rejected cell phone evidence in a murder trial.

The Power to Detain and Arrest

The authority of the police to arrest is provided by the Criminal Code and other federal statutes as well as by provincial laws such as motor vehicle statutes. Police can make an arrest to prevent a crime from being committed, to terminate a breach of the peace, or to compel an accused person to attend trial.

In most cases, persons who are alleged to have committed an offence are issued an appearance notice by the police officer or are summoned to court by a justice of the peace (JP). A suspect who is arrested will generally be released from custody as soon as possible, on the authority of the arresting officer, the officer in charge of the police lockup, or a JP.

If an arrest is justified, and there is time to do so, a police officer may seek an **arrest warrant** by swearing an **information** in front of a JP. If the JP agrees that there are "reasonable grounds to believe that it is necessary in the public interest," a warrant will be issued directing the local police to arrest the person. Accessing a JP can pose difficulties in rural areas. Several provinces have developed "telewarrant" programs that provide twenty-four–hour access to JPs. Police officers can apply for and receive warrants by fax or telephone instead of having to appear in person before a JP.

arrest warrant

a document that permits a police officer to arrest a specific person for a specific reason

information

a written statement sworn by a police officer alleging that a person has committed a specific criminal offence

Sometimes the police must act quickly and have no time secure a warrant from a JP. Police officers can arrest a suspect *without* an arrest warrant in the following circumstances:

- The person has committed an indictable offence, or the officer believes, on reasonable grounds, that he or she has committed or is about to commit an indictable offence.
- The officer finds the person actually committing any criminal offence, be it an indictable or a summary conviction offence.
- The officer has reasonable grounds to believe that a warrant of arrest or criminal committal is in force within the jurisdiction in which the person is found.

Two further conditions apply when making an arrest. First, the officer must not make an arrest if he or she has "no reasonable grounds" to believe that the person will fail to appear in court. Second, the officer must believe on "reasonable grounds" that an arrest is "necessary in the public interest." This is defined specifically as the need to

- establish the identity of the person;
- secure or preserve evidence of or relating to the offence; *and/or*
- prevent the continuation or repetition of the offence or the commission of another offence.

To make a *lawful* arrest, a "police officer should identify himself or herself, tell the suspect that he or she is being arrested, inform the suspect of the reason for the arrest or show the suspect the warrant if there is one, and, where feasible, touch the suspect on the shoulder as a physical indication of the confinement."

In practice, arrests are usually made only for indictable offences. For minor crimes, called summary conviction offences, arrest is legal only if the police find someone actually committing the offence or if there is an outstanding arrest warrant or *warrant of committal* (a document issued by a judge directing prison authorities to accept a person into custody on his or her sentencing, or a document issued by a parole board to revoke an offender's conditional release). An officer who makes an arrest without reasonable grounds risks being sued for assault or false imprisonment. Note that a person who resists an unlawful arrest is not guilty of resisting a police officer in the execution of his or her duty.

In all cases of arrest, with or without a warrant, the Criminal Code requires that the suspect be brought before a justice of the peace "without unreasonable delay"—in practice, within twenty-four hours unless a JP is not available, in which case it must be as soon as possible. Failure on the part of the police to ensure that the suspect appears before a JP in a timely fashion may result in a breach of the Criminal Code and the suspect's Charter rights.

Arrest versus Detention

An officer can detain a person without arrest for purposes of investigation, although the courts have generally held that "the standard for an investigation should be one of 'reasonable suspicion' as distinguished from reasonable cause."[2]

The police cannot be said to "detain," within the meaning of Sections 9 and 10 of the Charter, every suspect they stop for purposes of identification or even interview. A person who is stopped is always "detained" in the sense of "delayed" or "kept waiting." But the constitutional rights recognized by Sections 9 and 10 of the Charter are not engaged by delays that involve no significant physical or psychological restraint (*R. v. Mann*, 2004, SCC 52). A police officer, however, cannot detain a person for the sole purpose of interrogation, nor can the officer compel that person to answer questions.

The Supreme Court of Canada has held that a detention occurs when a police officer "assumes control over the movement of a person by a demand or direction that may have significant legal consequence and that prevents or impedes access to [legal] counsel" (*R. v. Schmautz*, [1990] 1 S.C.R. 398). The Supreme Court has also held that detention under the Charter can be physical or psychological. A psychological detention occurs when a citizen feels compelled to comply with the directives of a police officer, even though there is no legal authority for the officer's demand. In such cases, the failure to comply is not an offence.

Whether the person is arrested or detained, an important threshold in the criminal process has been crossed. According to Section 10 of the Charter, anyone arrested or detained has the right to be informed promptly of the reason for the arrest or detention and to be told without delay of the right to retain and instruct counsel (and be given the chance to do so). The suspect must be informed of the right to counsel, but it is his or her choice whether to exercise that right or not. A suspect who is interviewed by Canadian police officers in another country must also be informed of the right to counsel (*R. v. Cook*, [1998] 2 S.C.R. 597).

The Charter-based warning read by police officers in independent municipal police services in B.C. is reproduced in Box 6.1. The wording of this communication of Charter rights may vary from police service to police service. In addition to this warning, there are warnings that are to be read by police officers with respect to a demand that the person provide a breath sample for an approved screening device for alcohol, for a demand that the person provide a blood sample, and for a twelve- or twenty-four–hour roadside licence suspension.

Failure to advise a person in a timely manner of the right to counsel upon arrest is an infringement of his or her Charter rights.

Concerns have been expressed about "right to silence" warnings. Research has found that people often do not understand even half the information contained in the "rights" caution, nor do they understand the implications of the caution.[3] The level of comprehension about what the police officer is saying appears to be low. Language barriers, mental disability, and/or impairment from drugs and alcohol may further reduce levels of comprehension of police cautions. The courts are giving attention to this issue. In a 2001 case in Alberta, Crown counsel dropped stayed charges against two teenage boys who were suspected of killing two persons outside Edmonton. The judge had ruled that a statement from one of the boys was inadmissible because the RCMP officer made "confusing and potentially misleading statements" when reading the youth his rights and that "no attempt was made to actually test [the boy's] understanding" of those rights.[4]

Search and Seizure

Section 8 of the Charter protects Canadian citizens against "unreasonable" search or seizure. Evidence obtained during an illegal search may be excluded from trial if, as indicated in Section 24 of the Charter, its use would bring the administration of justice into disrepute. Many of the cases that are decided by the SCC with

Box 6.1

Communicating Charter Rights upon Arrest or Detention

1. Charter of Rights

Sec. 10(a):

"I am arresting/detaining you for:" (State reason for arrest/detention, including the offence and provide known information about the offence, including date and place.)

Sec. 10(b):

"It is my duty to inform you that you have the right to retain and instruct Counsel in private without delay. You may call any lawyer you want."

"There is a 24-hour telephone service available which provides a legal aid duty lawyer who can give you legal advice in private. This advice is given without charge and the lawyer can explain the legal aid plan to you. If you wish to contact a legal aid lawyer I can provide you with a telephone number. Do you understand? Do you want to call a lawyer?"

Supplementary Charter Warning

If an arrested or detained person initially indicated that he or she wished to contact legal counsel and then subsequently indicates that he or she no longer wishes to exercise the right to counsel, read the following additional charter warning.

"You have the right to a reasonable opportunity to contact counsel. I am obliged not to take a statement from you or to ask you to participate in any process which could provide incriminating evidence until you are certain about whether you want to exercise this right. Do you understand? What do you wish to do?"

Secondary Warning

To be used to remove any inducement that may have been made before by other police officers.

"(Name) you are detained with respect to (reason for detainment). If you have spoken to any other police officer (including myself) with respect to this matter, who has offered to you any hope of advantage or suggested any fear of prejudice should you speak or refuse to speak with me (us) at this time, it is my duty to warn you that no such offer or suggestion can be of any effect and must not influence you or make you feel compelled to say anything to me (us) for any reason, but anything you do say may be used in evidence."

2. Official Warning

"You are not obliged to say anything, but anything you do say may be given in evidence."

3. Written Statement Caution

Is to be used when taking a written statement from the accused. The written statement caution should be included in the conversation leading up to the accused making a written statement.

The following written statement caution should be used:

"I have been advised by (Investigating Officer) that I am not obliged to say anything but anything I do say may be given in evidence. I understand the meaning of the foregoing and I choose to make the following statement."

Note: The accused and the investigating officer should sign at the bottom of each page of the statement and at the end of the statement.

Source: Vancouver Police Department, *Regulations and Procedures Manual*, http://vancouver.ca/police/assets/pdf/manuals/vpd-manual-regulations-procedures.pdf

respect to the powers of the police involve search and seizure. Often, the issue is whether the police exceeded their powers and violated the rights of citizens.

The Supreme Court of Canada has held (*R. v. S.A.B.*, 2003, SCC 60) that for a search to be reasonable, (a) it must be authorized by law, (b) the law itself must be reasonable, and (c) the manner in which the search was carried out must be reasonable. The landmark case of *R. v. Mann* is presented in At Issue 6.1 to provide the reader with an opportunity to consider the issues that surround search and seizure cases. Another case of search and seizure is presented in At Issue 6.2.

There is considerable room for interpretation by the courts as to what constitutes an unreasonable search in any particular case and when admission of evidence would bring the administration of justice into disrepute. As a result, conditions and requirements have emerged for prior authorization for a search; this generally involves a **search warrant**. Typically, search warrants are issued by JPs. Before a warrant can be issued, an information must be sworn under oath before a JP to convince him or her that there are reasonable and probable grounds that there is, in a building or place, (1) evidence relating to an act in violation of the Criminal Code or other federal statute, (2) evidence that might exist in relation to such a violation, or (3) evidence intended to be used to commit an offence against a person for which an individual may be arrested without a warrant.

Decisions of the Supreme Court of Canada have established that search warrants are required:

- where there is to be secret recording of conversations by state agents;
- in cases involving video surveillance;
- for perimeter searches of residential premises;
- before the installation of tracking devices to monitor people's movements; *and*
- for searches of automobiles.

The general rule is that a search without a warrant will be considered unreasonable. However, a search can be conducted without a warrant incidental to an arrest in several situations, including when the officer is in fresh pursuit, or when it is necessary to protect life or prevent serious injury, or under the "plain view" doctrine. In the latter instances:

- the object is in plain view of the police, who have a right to be in the position to have the view,
- the discovery of the incriminating evidence is inadvertent, *or*
- it is immediately apparent that the object is evidence of a crime.

Police officers may also search a person and the immediate surroundings for self-protection (i.e., to seize weapons) or to prevent the destruction of evidence (e.g., by stopping the person from swallowing drugs). Also, in an emergency situation where an officer believes that an offence is being committed, or is likely to be committed, or that someone on the premises is in danger of injury, a premise may be entered. In *R. v. Godoy* ([1999] 1 S.C.R. 311), the Supreme Court of Canada held that the forced entry of police officers into a residence from which a disconnected 911 call had been made was justifiable, as was the subsequent arrest of a suspect who had physically abused his wife.

A landmark case that established the right of citizens to be free from unreasonable search and seizure by the police is *R. v. Feeney* [1997] 2 S.C.R. 13 (see Box 6.2).

search warrant
a document that permits the police to search a specific location and take items that might be evidence of a crime

Box 6.2

R. v. Feeney: A Case of Unreasonable Search and Seizure

In investigating a murder, an RCMP officer knocked on the door of Feeney's trailer. Not receiving an answer, the officer entered the trailer (without a search warrant) and found Feeney asleep. After waking him, the officer escorted him into a brighter area of the trailer, where he observed blood on Feeney's shirt. The officer seized the shirt and took Feeney to the local detachment for interrogation. Feeney did not have a lawyer. On the basis of the interrogation, which was conducted without a lawyer being present to represent Feeney, a search warrant was obtained and the trailer was searched. Additional incriminating evidence was found, which was admitted at trial and resulted in Feeney being found guilty of second degree murder. Feeney appealed his conviction, citing violation of his Charter rights, specifically Section 24(2), which states that evidence "obtained in a manner that infringed or denied any rights or freedoms guaranteed by this Charter…should be excluded." On appeal, the central issue was whether Feeney's shirt had been seized by the officer during the initial visit to the trailer (without a warrant). Also at issue was whether there had been violations of Feeney's rights under Charter Section 10 (the right to legal counsel) and Section 8 (the right against unreasonable search and seizure). In a 5–4 decision, the Supreme Court of Canada found that Feeney's Charter rights had been violated. A key factor in the Court's decision was that, before entering the trailer, the investigating officer had no reasonable grounds for making an arrest.

Feeney established parameters on the powers of the police with respect to search and seizure. It is often the courts that decide, ultimately, whether a search warrant was properly obtained and executed or whether a warrantless search was legal. The SCC has also ruled that, in situations where officers may be at risk and/or evidence may be destroyed, the police may abandon the common law "knock and announce" rule (*R. v. Cornell*, 2010, SCC 31).

Entrapment: An Abuse of Police Powers

Entrapment means just what it sounds like: a person ends up committing an offence that he or she would not otherwise have committed, largely because of pressure or cunning on the part of the police, who are most often operating in an undercover role. The following are controversial examples of this practice:

- An expensive car is left with the keys in the ignition, observed by concealed officers waiting to arrest anyone who steals it.
- A police officer poses as a young girl while trolling websites frequented by pedophiles.
- An undercover officer poses as an intoxicated subway passenger, wearing expensive jewellery and a Rolex watch. Anyone who mugs him is arrested.
- An undercover officer poses as a potential client to arrest a prostitute who offers his or her sexual services.

Proactive techniques of this kind can be an effective and cost-efficient use of personnel. There is, however, a line between catching those habitually involved in lawbreaking and creating "situational" criminals. The police are not allowed to create situations where typically law-abiding people would be enticed into criminal activity.

The courts have determined that the line is crossed when a person is persistently harassed into committing an offence that he or she would not have committed had it not been for the actions of the police. People cannot be targeted at random. Rather, there must be a reasonable suspicion that the person is already engaged in criminal activity. For example, in the prostitution example listed previously, the actions of the police do not constitute entrapment because this reasonable suspicion exists.

An SCC case involving the issue of entrapment is presented in Box 6.3.

Box 6.3

The Reluctant Drug Trafficker

The defendant was charged with drug trafficking and, at the close of his defence, brought an application for a stay of proceedings on the basis of entrapment. His testimony indicated that he had persistently refused the approaches of a police informer over the course of six months and that he was only persuaded to sell him drugs because of the informer's persistence, his use of threats, and the inducement of a large amount of money. He also testified that he had previously been addicted to drugs but that he had given up his use of narcotics. The application for a stay of proceedings was refused and he was convicted of drug trafficking. The Court of Appeal dismissed an appeal from that conviction.

The central issue for the Supreme Court of Canada was whether the defendant had been entrapped into committing the offence of drug trafficking. The Court held that the police in this case were not interrupting an ongoing criminal enterprise; the offence was clearly brought about by their conduct and would not have occurred without their involvement. The Court stated that the persistence of the police requests and the equally persistent refusals, and the length of time needed to secure the defendant's participation in the offence, indicate that the police had tried to make the appellant take up his former lifestyle and had gone further than merely providing him with the opportunity.

For the Court, the most important determining factor was that the defendant had been threatened and had been told to get his act together when he did not provide the requested drugs. This conduct was unacceptable and went beyond providing the appellant with an opportunity. The Court found that the average person in the appellant's position might also have committed the offence, if only to finally satisfy this threatening informer and end all further contact. The Court ruled that the trial judge should have entered a stay of proceedings.

Source: *R. v. Mack*, 1988, 2 S.C.R. 903.

Canadian courts have generally not allowed the defence of entrapment, which requires there to have been a clear abuse of process.

THE USE OF FORCE

Police should use physical force only to the extent necessary to ensure compliance with the law or to restore order only after persuasion, advice and warnings are insufficient.

SIR ROBERT PEEL

The authority to use force, including lethal force, is a defining feature of the police role in society.

The Legal Provisions for Use of Force

The use of force, including lethal force, is governed by both law and policy. The legal justification for the use of force is found in the Criminal Code and in case law. Further support is found in provincial laws such as police acts and in firearm regulations. The "justification" sections for the use of force are contained in Sections 25 to 33 of the Criminal Code. These sections, in effect, exempt otherwise criminal actions from criminal liability. Sections 26, 27, and 37 contain equally important provisions pertaining to a police officer's use of force. Court decisions, in both criminal and civil cases, have further shaped the powers and obligations of police officers when utilizing force. In *R. v. Nasogaluak,* 2010, SCC 6, for example, the SCC reiterated that "[w]hile police officers may have to resort to force in order to complete an arrest or to prevent an offender from escaping their custody, the allowable degree of force is constrained by the principles of proportionality, necessity, and reasonableness."

Police Acts and Standards

Besides the Criminal Code, provincial laws such as police acts and standards govern and regulate the use of force by police officers. These provisions generally specify that lethal force can be used only to protect against the loss of life or serious bodily harm. The Ontario Police Standards Relating to Police Use of Force also contain provisions for investigating and preparing a report in every instance in which a police officer discharges his or her weapon, regardless of whether a person was killed or injured by the discharge.

The Force Options Model

The **force options model** for the use of force by police is the foundation of most police training in Canada. It provides police administrators and judicial review personnel with an objective framework for analyzing use-of-force situations. The force options model serves as a guideline, and all police personnel are provided with a working model that clearly outlines the course of action to take in use-of-force situations. It also allows police officers to explain, in an

force options model
provides police officers with a working model that sets out the course of action to be taken in use-of-force situations

accepted format, how and why force was applied at the time of the altercation. The Ontario Use of Force Model (2004), which is based on the National Use of Force Framework, reflects the various components of the process by which police officers assess a situation and determine the proper response in order to protect themselves and the general public. The model is presented in Box 6.4.

Demonstrated Threat

demonstrated threat
the level of potential danger posed by a person confronted by police officers, generally in the form of weapons or levels of resistance

Individuals confronted by the police present various levels of potential danger, often referred to as the **demonstrated threat**. These levels typically correspond to the presence of weapons and levels of resistance. With respect to weapons, both the type of weapon and the manner in which it is carried can influence an officer's perception of potential danger. The dangers associated with levels of resistance can change quickly during any incident, and police officers must be alert to all possibilities.

There are five levels of resistance of individuals and related behaviours:

1. *Cooperative.* There is no resistance. The person responds positively to verbal requests and commands. The person willingly complies.
2. *Non-cooperative.* There is little or no physical resistance. The person does not comply to the officer's request, showing verbal defiance and little or no physical response.
3. *Resistant.* The person demonstrates resistance to control by the police officer through behaviours such as pulling away, pushing away, or running away.
4. *Combative.* The person attempts or threatens to apply force to anyone, for example, by punching, kicking, or clenching fists with the intent to hurt or resist.
5. *Showing the potential to cause grievous bodily harm or death.* The person acts in a manner that the police officer has reason to believe could result in grievous bodily harm or death to the public or to the police—for example, using a knife, a firearm, or a baseball bat.

Levels of Force Intervention

Although police officers often have no control over the types of encounter situations they become involved in, they can achieve a measure of control by exercising an appropriate level of response. These responses include five distinct force options available to police officers:

1. *Officer presence.* The mere presence of a police officer may alter the behaviour of the participants at an altercation, thereby enabling control of the situation.
2. *Dialogue.* Verbal and nonverbal communication skills may resolve the conflict and result in voluntary compliance.
3. *Empty hands.* Physical force is used to gain control.
4. *Compliance tools.* Equipment or weapons are used to gain control.
5. *Lethal force.* The situation requires complete incapacitation of the subject in order to gain control, and lethal force is the only option available to reduce the lethal threat.

Box 6.4

The Ontario Use of Force Model

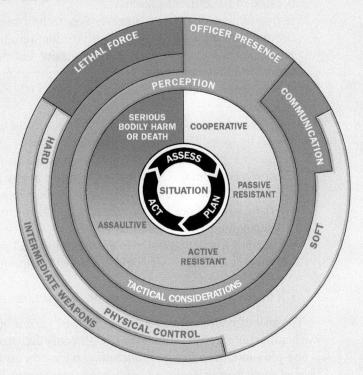

The officer continuously assesses the situation and
selects the most reasonable option relative to those
circumstances as perceived at that point in time.

The Ontario Use of Force Model

There are a number of components in the model, beginning with the inner circle and moving outward:

- The *situation*, which requires the officer to continually assess, plan, and act.
- The *behaviour of the subject*, which can range from cooperative, to passive resistant, to active resistant, to assaultive, to presenting serious bodily harm or death to the officer.
- The officer's *perception* and *tactical considerations*, which are interrelated and which interact with the situation and behaviour of the subject and affect how the officer perceives and assesses the situation.

- The officer's *use of force options*, which range from officer presence, to communication skills, to the use of soft and hard physical compliance techniques, the use of intermediate weapons, and lethal force. The use-of-force model requires that the officer constantly reassess the situation in order to ensure that the appropriate level of force is being used.

Source: © Queen's Printer for Ontario, 2004. Reproduced with permission. The Ontario Use of Force Model (2004) was developed through consultation between the Ministry of Community Safety and Correctional Services and its stakeholders. The Model has been amended and is endorsed by the ministry.

This approach is positive and professional in explaining how and why police use force in their day-to-day activities. Included in the five basic force options are eight progressive use-of-force response levels that are available to police in Canada:

1. *Officer presence.* The officer's presence at a situation may itself affect how it unfolds. It may cause the suspect to cease activity (e.g., stop making noise), or it may provoke a situation (e.g., drunken behaviour may turn violent because of the officer's presence).
2. *Verbal intervention.* Crisis intervention techniques; verbal and nonverbal communication; anger management; conflict resolution.
3. *Empty hand control—soft.* Physical restraint techniques; joint locks; pain compliance; distractions, stuns, creating imbalance; handcuffing.
4. *Aerosol irritants.* Oleoresin capsicum spray (OCS or pepper spray); CS gas (tear gas).
5. *Empty hand control—hard.* Blocks; strikes; carotid control.
6. *Impact weapons.* Use of police extendable baton.
7. *Lethal force.* Use of force that could result in the death of a person; firearms.
8. *Tactical repositioning.* Officers can disengage at any point in the situation:
   - if the likelihood and extent of harm to the public can be reduced by leaving;
   - if there is fear of death or grievous bodily harm, provided it does not expose others to injury or lethal force;
   - if seeking assistance will help ensure public and police safety;
   - if buying time and gaining distance will help ensure public and police safety; *and/or*
   - if the scene has been contained and there is little or no potential for harm.

The goal of police officers is to use the least violent option available that will safely gain control of the situation. The generally accepted use-of-force standard is **one-plus-one**, meaning that police officers have the authority to use one higher level of force than that with which they are confronted. Use of force in excess of what is necessary can leave the officer criminally or civilly liable for assault.

Less Lethal Force Options

A **less lethal force option** (or "lower lethality") is one that is *highly unlikely* to cause death or serious injury to an individual when *properly applied* by a police officer. However, it is possible that death or serious injury may occur, hence the term *less lethal* rather than *less than lethal*. The possibility of serious harm is especially great if the force option is improperly applied by the police officer. In these instances the less lethal options may contribute to or even cause serious injury or death.

Ideally, a less lethal weapon will incapacitate the perceived threat to the officer while inflicting only minor injuries to the attacker. However, situations do arise that result in serious physical harm, or death, to the person who is the target of a less lethal weapon.

The Taser: A Less Than Lethal or Lethal Weapon?

Conducted energy devices (more commonly referred to as Tasers) were adopted by Canadian police services as a force option in the late 1990s. The Taser "gun" fires two metal darts, which are attached to wires and enter the subject's skin,

---

one-plus-one (use of force standard)
the generally accepted use-of-force standard that police officers have the authority to use one higher level of force than that with which they are confronted

less lethal force option (lower lethality)
a control technique that is highly unlikely to cause death or serious injury

generating an electric shock of up to 50,000 volts. The expanded use of the Taser by police services is credited with reducing the number of deaths as a result of the police use of lethal force and, as well, the number of officers injured while carrying out their duties.

Tasers have been the subject of considerable controversy. They have been associated with a number of high-profile incidents, including the death of Robert Dziekanski at Vancouver International Airport in 2008 (see Police File 6.1).

Police File 6.1

The Death of Robert Dziekanski

The most high-profile incident involving the police use of Tasers to date was the death of Robert Dziekanski at the Vancouver International Airport. At 2:50 p.m. on October 13, 2007, Mr. Dziekanski, an immigrant from Poland, arrived at the airport following a long flight from Poland. He was fatigued from the flight and spoke no English. For reasons that have still not been adequately explained, Mr. Dziekanski spent nearly twelve hours wandering around the international arrivals area without securing the assistance that would have led him to his waiting mother. At 1:20 a.m., he became agitated and confused, his situation made more difficult due to his inability to communicate in English. The airport operations centre received calls that a man was acting strangely and security personnel and RCMP officers were called. Four RCMP officers arrived on the scene. Within minutes, Mr. Dziekanski had been restrained on the floor by the officers. Shortly thereafter, he died. An autopsy found no drugs or alcohol in Dziekanski's system.

The encounter had been captured on a cell phone camera by a passenger at the terminal (see YouTube). The RCMP first stated that Dziekanski had been Tasered twice, but the video indicated that he had been Tasered a total of five times. (This is an excellent example of the consequences of the increased visibility of the police.)

The provincial government launched a public inquiry headed by a retired judge, Thomas Braidwood. The inquiry had two phases. The first part focused on the police use of Tasers; the second examined the circumstances surrounding the death of Mr. Dziekanski. On many occasions during the hearing, the four RCMP officers involved in the incident, and their superior officers, provided conflicting testimony. Among the inquiry's findings were that the responding officers had not made any meaningful attempt to de-escalate the situation; that the use of the Taser against Mr. Dziekanski had been premature and inappropriate; and that the four officers involved in the incident had given conflicting testimony to the inquiry that was not credible. The officers were subsequently charged with perjury for lying to the commission. As of mid-2012, there had been no disposition in the cases.

Source: T.R. Braidwood (Commissioner), "WHY? The Robert Dziekanski Tragedy," Braidwood Commission on the Death of Robert Dziekanski (Victoria: Attorney General of British Columbia, 2010), http://www.braidwoodinquiry.ca/report/P2Report.php

A number of issues have surrounded the use of Tasers:

- *The risk of death of a person in a state of excited delirium.* This state can be caused by a number of factors, including mental illness or heavy drug use (often cocaine or crystal meth). A person in this state is often incoherent, violent, and noncompliant. The use of electric shocks on such a person can cause a heart attack.

- *Suspect attributes and CED use.* There are concerns that police may be more likely to use CEDs against visible minorities and poor people (among others). This remains to be explored in Canada. A U.S. research study found that, all things being equal, Hispanic suspects were twice as likely as whites to be Tasered.[5] A few police services prohibit the use of Tasers on children, pregnant women, and the elderly.

- *Children and youth.* There are no age restrictions regarding who can be Tasered. Canadian police officers have Tasered children as young as eleven, as well as elderly persons, one of whom was in a hospital bed.

- *The overuse of CEDs by police officers.* Officers may rely on a CED rather than verbal communication and hands-on applications. This can be related to the "lazy cop syndrome."[6]

- *The use of CEDs may increase injuries to officers and suspects.* Most studies have found that the use of CEDs has reduced injuries to officers. However, the findings are mixed regarding whether CEDs reduce injuries to suspects.[7] A study of the use of force in the Calgary Police Service found that the baton resulted in the most injuries among all force options.[8]

- *The use of CEDs and police legitimacy.* The inappropriate use of CEDs may increase public distrust of the police and reduce public confidence in them.[9] This occurred in the aftermath of the incident at YVR, where a Taser was used and the victim died on scene (see Police File 6.1).

From its examination of the use of Tasers, the Braidwood Commission in British Columbia made a number of recommendations, including these:

- A Taser should be used only in criminal matters and not to enforce municipal bylaws or provincial statutes.
- A Taser should only be used when a subject is causing bodily harm or is about to cause bodily harm.
- A Taser should be used only as a last resort.[10]

These recommendations have been adopted by the RCMP and many other police services. How these policies will affect the use of Tasers by police officers remains to be determined, as does the impact on persons who are Tasered.

ISSUES IN THE POLICE USE OF FORCE

Discussions of the police use of force are hindered by the absence of any national statistics. This makes it difficult to determine the frequency and types of force used in police services. Also, because most civil suits involving alleged misuse of force by police officers are settled out of court, there is no cumulative body of knowledge about the factors that precipitated that use, nor is there about the appropriateness of such force in the circumstances. Research studies and statistical data from the United States indicate that the use of force is rare, as is the improper use of force. Also, the use of force rarely involves weapons and typically occurs at the lower end of the force spectrum, involving grabbing, pushing, or shoving.

Research on the use of force by several Canadian police services found that the police used force in 0.7 percent of encounters with the public.[11] A study conducted by the Calgary Police Service found that the use of force by police was rare, occurring in only 1.5 percent of incidents involving an arrest. Nearly 90 percent of the cases in which force was used involved a person who was under the influence of alcohol and/or drugs.[12]

There has been little research conducted on the use of force by detectives, despite evidence that these officers may use higher levels of force than uniformed patrol officers.[13]

Increased Police Visibility and the Use of Force

The increased visibility of the police is having an impact on the use of force by police officers, who are second-guessing themselves rather than following their training. A patrol sergeant in an urban Canadian police service recalled:

> There was a robbery of a jewellery store in an up-scale mall. Shots were fired by the two perpetrators, both of whom were 17 years of age. One of the robbers ran out of the back of the mall and was confronted by one of my junior police constables. The robber raised his firearm and attempted to fire at the officer, but the gun jammed. The officer pulled out her weapon, but didn't fire. She could have been killed. That hesitation could have cost her life. There seems to be an element of fear in many junior officers to use force. (personal communication)

Police Legitimacy and the Use of Force

The improper use of force by police officers can seriously undermine police legitimacy. This is especially true with high-profile incidents in which the police are perceived as having used excessive force, or in which subsequent investigations have determined that excessive force was used. The increased visibility of the police has also increased the "public view" of use-of-force incidents. Now that cell phone cameras are so pervasive, use-of-force incidents may be posted on network sites such as YouTube within minutes of their occurrence. This explains in part why public approval ratings of the police have fallen from the 80 percent range to 54 percent in 2010. Clear examples of all this were the death of Robert Dziekanski (see Police File 6.1) and the G8 and G20 demonstrations in Toronto in the summer of 2010. Communities that feel that the police use force improperly may have less confidence in the police and may not cooperate with them.[14]

The misuse of force can result in a community protesting against the police (see photo). This occurred in 2010 in Kelowna, B.C., after an incident in which an RCMP officer kicked a suspect who had already followed a command to drop to the ground. A witness captured the incident on video, which made it clear

Community protesters protest a use of force incident.

that the officer kicked the suspect in the face *after* he had dropped to his hands and knees. The officer was subsequently charged with two counts of assault causing bodily harm, in relation to that incident and a previous one.

Police Powers and the Use of Force during Riots and Public Disturbances

The actions of Toronto Police Service officers during the G8 and G20 protests of 2010 highlighted issues related to the police powers and excessive use of force (see Box 6.5).

Correlates of Police Use of Force

A number of factors are associated with the police use of force—including lethal force—in encounter situations. These include the level of crime and violence in a community, the dynamics that develop in the encounter situation (e.g., the actions of the person of interest or suspect), and the attributes of the individual police officer.

Attributes of the police officer. As the average age of police officers increases, their use of force tends to decrease. Younger officers and those with fewer years of police experience are much more likely to use force (including lethal force) in an encounter situation.[15] This finding has particular implications in contemporary police services, because increasing numbers of officers have fewer than five years' experience. There is also some evidence that officers with a university education use force less in encounter situations, perhaps owing to an ability to consider more options to resolve the incident.[16]

It is often assumed that female police officers are unwilling or unable to use coercion during encounters. Yet an American study that examined the use of verbal and physical coercion applied by policewomen in encounters with citizens found that female officers were not reluctant to use coercive force and were similar to their male counterparts in terms of the factors that precipitated the use of various types of coercion.[17] There is also evidence that a

Box 6.5

The G8/G20 Protest in Toronto, 2010

In the summer of 2010, world leaders gathered outside Toronto for the G20 Summit to discuss a variety of global issues. This was immediately followed by a meeting of the G8 leaders in the city itself. These summits ignited large demonstrations that resulted in the Toronto police arresting more than 1,000 people—the largest mass arrest in Canadian history.

After the G8 meeting, the Office of the Independent Police Review Directors (OIPRD) received more than 400 complaints against the police from citizens, including people who had not been involved in the protests but had nevertheless been stopped and searched by police officers. The complaints included allegations of unlawful arrest, unlawful detention, and excessive use of force.

An inquiry into police actions during the protests, conducted by the Ontario Ombudsman, focused on the enactment of a regulation under the Public Works Protection Act that designated a large area not protected by a security fence as "public works"; in effect, this expanded the powers of the police to arbitrarily arrest and detain persons. Many of those who were stopped, questioned, and searched by the police had not been involved in the protests, and like the protestors, they had been unaware of the regulation. Many people were

Protest during the G8/G20 Summit in Toronto.

Richard Lautens/GetStock.com

arrested who were in the vicinity of the security fence. The report concluded that this regulation, which had been designed to control the protestors, infringed on individual freedoms and "was likely unconstitutional."

Source: A. Marin, "Investigation into The Ministry of Community Safety and Correctional Services' Conduct in Relation to Ontario Regulation 233/10 under the Public Works Protection Act: 'Caught in the Act'" (Toronto: Ombudsman of Ontario, 2010), 5.

small number of officers in police services may be disproportionately involved in use-of-force incidents and may be more likely to use excessive force. These "problem officers" are more likely to be younger and to have fewer years on the job.[18]

There is also evidence that the attitudes of officers toward the citizens they police may have a significant impact on the improper use of force. In other words, officers with more negative views may be more likely to use improper force.

The presence of a patrol partner or other officers. The officer's perception of danger may be significantly affected by whether he or she is accompanied by a patrol partner. Shootings are more likely to occur when at least two officers are present. Officers may feel that, had they not acted the way they did, their partner would have suffered grievous bodily harm or death.

The actions, intentions, mental state, and resources of the subject/suspect. When force is used, it is the subject's own actions, such as threats, that most often provoke the officers. Any violence between a police officer and a suspect is often a continuation of the violence the suspect was involved in before the officers arrived on the scene.[19]

Force is more likely to be used on persons who are uncooperative and antagonistic toward the police. There is no evidence, however, that police officers are more likely to use excessive force in situations involving persons with a mental disability.[20]

The lack of research makes it difficult to determine whether Canadian police are more likely to use less lethal and lethal force in encounters with visible minorities and Aboriginal persons. American studies indicate that blacks are shot by the police in numbers that are disproportionately high relative to their numbers in the general population. This has led to the contention that many police services and officers are racist.

Residents in Toronto's black community perceive that the police are more likely to use physical force against them than against other citizens. This perception is supported by a review of cases handled by the SIU which found that blacks and Aboriginals were overrepresented in SIU investigations and in cases in which it was subsequently determined that a civilian death or serious injury had been caused directly by police actions.[21]

The area being policed. There is some evidence that officers who police in high-crime areas are more likely to use force and more willing to accept the unnecessary use of force by fellow officers in that area.[22]

The encounter. Situational factors surrounding the incident are related to the improper use of force, which is more likely in serious offences in which the suspect is antagonistic toward the police.[23]

DEADLY ENCOUNTERS: THE POLICE USE OF LETHAL FORCE

Canadian police rarely use lethal force—only ten times a year, on average. In comparison, around three hundred Americans are shot and killed by the police every year. The circumstances in which American and Canadian officers use lethal force are similar; however, American police are involved more often in situations where the perceived threat to officer safety is high.[24]

Fatal shootings by police fall into three categories: (1) a serious criminal offence is being committed; (2) the shooting was a mistake; and (3) the victim precipitated the shooting. In most police shootings that resulted in fatalities, the deceased had just committed a serious criminal offence.

Sometimes the deceased was already wanted by the police for a serious criminal offence such as murder, attempted murder, robbery, aggravated assault, or drug trafficking. There are also instances, albeit rare, in which the use of lethal force was justified at the time because the police officer feared for his or her life or the lives of others. In hindsight, though, the officer should not have used lethal force. Incidents like these are rare.

Some incidents are **victim-precipitated homicides** (also known as **"suicide by cop"**). These often involve individuals who are mentally ill or heavy substance abusers who proceed to act in a manner calculated to compel police to use lethal force.[25] See Police File 6.2.

> **victim-precipitated homicide ("suicide by cop")**
> an incident in which the victim acts in a manner calculated to provoke the use of deadly force on the part of the police

The Lethal Force Incident

In most cases, the officers involved in a shooting responded to the perceived threat in an automatic manner, based on their training in dealing with life-threatening situations. In most cases as well, the encounter developed into a lethally violent situation within seconds. The Canadian criminologist Rick Parent interviewed police officers and offenders who had been involved in incidents in which suspects had shot at the police. These case studies provide unique insights into the perspectives of each party to the incident. One such case is presented in Police File 6.3.

Police File 6.2

A Suicide by Cop

A male subject, emotionally distraught because of marital difficulties, had talked with his family about dying. The subject then went to a convenience store and purchased a quantity of beer and wine, advising the clerk that it would be his last. The subject then became involved in a lengthy police pursuit, which ended when his vehicle was stopped by the deployment of a spike belt by police. On exiting his vehicle, the subject produced a shotgun and placed it under his chin. He then told police personnel that if they did not kill him he would kill an officer. The subject then turned and pointed his shotgun at two police officers and began to approach them. The officers responded by discharging their weapons, killing the subject. It was later found that the shotgun was unloaded.

Source: R.B. Parent, "Aspects of Police Use of Deadly Force In North America—The Phenomenon of Victim-Precipitated Homicide," PhD diss., School of Criminology, Simon Fraser University, Burnaby, 2004, 233–34. Reprinted by permission of Rick Parent.

Police File 6.3

In Their Own Words: A Police Officer and a Suspect Describe a Police Shooting Incident

Background to the Incident

In a western Canadian city during the summer, at about 8:00 p.m., two uniformed police officers on bike patrol noticed two suspicious individuals near a small shopping area. While the officers were checking the two individuals, one male suddenly ran away. One of the officers immediately began a foot chase. The officer caught up to the fleeing individual, who produced a handgun. Shooting over his shoulder, the subject again began to run from the officer. Firing six rounds as he ran down the street, near a crowded sidewalk, the suspect gained distance from the officer.

The suspect then disappeared around the corner into the courtyard of an apartment complex. Suddenly, the pursuing officer found himself looking down the barrel of a 25-calibre semiautomatic handgun. The suspect, less than three feet away, aimed the gun at the officer's head and pulled the trigger, clicking on an empty chamber. Fortunately, the gun was out of bullets. Unaware of this, the pursuing officer and his partner both discharged their firearms, wounding the suspect.

Police later found two balaclavas and a knife in a nearby vehicle that was being operated by the suspects. It was believed that the two suspects had intended to commit a robbery when they were checked by the bicycle patrol. In explaining how the incident unfolded, the pursuing officer stated:

My partner and myself were on bicycle patrol...The weather was nice, there was a beautiful sunset. We had ridden up to a strip mall where a Mac's Milk was located [in the eastern part of the city]. As we are riding we see these two suspicious guys hanging around the strip mall so we ride up to these two guys. We begin to check them and run their names [to see if there are any outstanding warrants]. I am dealing with this guy's friend and I checked his name. I knew something was off as he didn't have any ID and his information didn't match. I knew he was lying, something wasn't right. So I asked him his zodiac sign and he didn't know it.

We were three to four feet away from them, checking their names, when this guy burst off and ran across the street. I ran after him and caught up with him. I was able to reach out and give him one shot in the side of the face. He then started to reach towards his waist and I saw him grab something. He started yelling "Stay back! Stay back!" while swearing at me. He then started shooting over his shoulder, with his handgun, as he began to run away. I could see all the pedestrians on the street so I decided to hold fire. People are just scattering as this is happening.

I then yelled out to my partner, "Where did he go? Where did he go?" I thought he went inside this apartment complex. I thought he was in the courtyard of the complex. However, as I came around the corner, I could see this peripheral silver object pointed towards my head. I fired a couple of shots and my partner fired a few shots. That's when we then heard him crying "I'm hit! I'm hit!" I think he also got hit from fragments from our rounds.

Then, after he was on the ground, he gave us his real name and said he was an escapee from prison.

The first time I fired my gun was when he was tucked behind the brick wall of the apartment building. Even though it was dry [i.e., there were no bullets in the chamber], he had the gun pointed at my head. To take flight from a police officer is one thing, but to try to kill a police officer is another thing!

When it went to trial he received a fourteen-year sentence. I've never ever talked to him about what happened that night or seen him since the trial.

In reflecting on the incident, the officer stated:

After we fired the rounds, I felt a rush through my body and I started having the shakes. Then I was crying right away. Off and on again I began crying. I called my wife right away and talked to her.

I like what I'm doing now. However, from the time that that incident happened until now I could leave the job…for anything. As a result of this incident, policing is now the fourth or fifth thing in my life. I've prioritized my life, and policing is a lot lower than it was before this incident happened. To have someone dry fire at your head…it's a terrible experience.

I wish it had never happened. Sure I got a Chief Constable's award, and later I was honoured at our Honours night, but…those things really don't mean anything. I wish I had never checked him, I wish that we had just carried on and never seen him. It's just not worth it.

The biggest thing I've learned from this is the priorities in your life. I have a wife and two kids and right after that night, policing dropped right down in my priorities of life. If I could find a comparable job right now that paid the same amount of money I'd be gone.

The Offender's Perspective

During the interview, the inmate spoke calmly and mechanically about the incident. Ten years earlier, he had been convicted of armed robbery in Halifax. The Nova Scotia courts had imposed a lifetime ban on the possession of firearms by the subject. At the time of the police shooting, the subject was considered "unlawfully at large" from a work release program at a minimum-security prison in B.C. He talked about the shooting incident that had resulted in his imprisonment:

I went to the ____ Hotel and bought a .25 calibre handgun. I bought the gun for fifty dollars, a .25 calibre with six rounds. I was flipping it. Bought the gun thirty hours before the incident and I had plans to sell it for three hundred dollars. I wasn't on any cocaine that night, just drinking Coca-Cola at the pub.

I could have shot the f--ker [police officer] in the head but I didn't—I could have killed him. I didn't want to hurt nobody—I never have hurt anyone in my life. What happened is that I was in the area of ____ and ____ when these two guys [police officers] on bikes see buddy and me and decide to check us.

One cop asks for identification and gets him, my buddy, to call a friend, to verify who we are. I'm out on a work release but packing this handgun on my right side. Then this cop says that he is gonna detain me until he finds out who I am. He checked my name and my buddy's name but it didn't come through. While we were waiting, we started a good conversation with the white guy cop, talking about the pussy in the area.

Suddenly, I ran, I took off running. This cop wants to play supercop, he begins chasing me, and I threw a plastic bottle of pop at him to break his stride. However, he caught me and punched me in the right

(Continued)

side of the face. That's when I could have shot him but I didn't.

We both fell down and when I got back up I pulled the gun out...He was about ten feet away. I aimed it over to the right and said "Stay away, I don't want to hurt anyone." I then took off running again. As I was running, I fired my gun over my shoulder [at the police officer]. I also fired the gun from behind a car. I didn't want to hit the cop. I just wanted to scare him so I could get the fuck away.

Once he came around the corner he started firing his gun—"I'm hit, I'm hit!" I went down. When he fired his gun, it went into slow motion—I saw the muzzle face. The whole thing took only ten seconds, max, but it seemed like ten minutes. I was hit, I felt a burning. As I hit the ground I threw my handgun away.

In reflecting on the incident, the inmate stated:

I'm glad I never shot him. I just wanted to scare him. I was hoping he would have hit the ground and waited for cover. Then I could have run off and ditched my gun. Instead he comes after me—who would believe a cop would run after a guy who's shooting at him!

As a result of the incident I got twelve years for attempted murder and two years for possession of a handgun. It was a stupid incident, ten minutes either way and it would never have happened. It was the first time that I'd been shot at or had shot at someone.

Source: R.B. Parent, "Aspects of Police Use of Deadly Force In North America—The Phenomenon of Victim-Precipitated Homicide," PhD diss., School of Criminology, Simon Fraser University, Burnaby, 2004. Reprinted by permission of Rick Parent.

Critical Incident Stress and the Police Shooting

The risks associated with using force are high: for the individual police officer, injury and even death are possible consequences of every confrontation. Besides the physical risks, police who use force may be subject to internal discipline as well as civil or even criminal liability for their actions (or inactions). Add to this the stress and mental anguish that often accompany a physical confrontation.

Police officers involved in a fatal shooting may experience physical and psychological reactions associated with **critical incident stress**. The physical effects include loss of appetite, changes in sleeping patterns, and a marked decrease in sex drive. The psychological effects include depression, guilt, nightmares, flashbacks, fear, and a heightened sense of danger. Police officers involved in shooting incidents that did *not* result in the death of an individual may also experience critical incident stress.

critical incident stress
the physiological, psychological, physical, and emotional reactions that may occur in an individual who has been involved in a traumatic incident, e.g., patrol officers involved in a fatal shooting

Police services have developed debriefing programs for officers involved in shooting incidents and other traumatic events. These programs may involve mental health professionals as well as approaches designed to help the officers address post-traumatic stress reactions. The effectiveness of these interventions has been questioned; some research suggests that in the long term, these programs do little to address post-traumatic stress or physical heath issues. Indeed, for some officers, the debriefings may make the symptoms worse.[26]

Police officers involved in shooting incidents may be more resilient than once thought. One study found that few officers suffered long-term negative effects following a shooting incident. Also, the attitude of the officer after the incident was strongly influenced by his or her personality as well as by the attitudes of family, friends, and police investigators.[27] The level of organizational support received was a major factor in the level of stress experienced.[28] Research on the responses to traumatic events by paramedics and firefighters has also found that individual personality traits play a significant role in how these personnel respond to, and are affected by, critical incidents.[29]

At Issue 6.1

R. v. Mann: A Case of Detainment, Search, and Seizure

As two police officers approached the scene of a reported break and enter, they observed M, who matched the description of the suspect, walking casually along the sidewalk. They stopped him. M identified himself and complied with a pat-down search of his person for concealed weapons. During the search, one officer felt a soft object in M's pocket. He reached into the pocket and found a small plastic bag containing marijuana. He also found a number of small plastic baggies in another pocket. M was arrested and charged with possession of marijuana for the purpose of trafficking.

At trial, the judge found that the search of M's pocket contravened Section 8 of the Canadian Charter of Rights and Freedoms in that, while the police officer was justified in his search of M for security reasons, there was no basis to infer that it was reasonable to look inside M's pocket for security reasons. The evidence was excluded under Section 24(2) of the Charter, as its admission would interfere with the fairness of the trial, and the accused was acquitted. The Court of Appeal, however, set aside the acquittal and ordered a new trial, finding that the detention and the pat-down were authorized by law and were reasonable in the circumstances.

The Supreme Court of Canada subsequently decided that the appeal should be allowed and the acquittal restored. The majority of the Justices found that the police were entitled to detain M for investigative purposes and to conduct a pat-down search to ensure their safety, but that the search of M's pockets was unjustified and that the evidence discovered therein must be excluded. The Court found that the police officers had reasonable grounds to detain M and to conduct a protective search, but no reasonable basis for reaching into M's pocket. This more intrusive part of the search was an unreasonable violation of M's reasonable expectation of privacy in respect of the contents of his pockets.

You Make the Call!

1. Do you agree with the decision of the Supreme Court in this case? Explain.
2. Does this decision place too many restrictions on the powers of the police? Explain.

3. What if the officers had found a handgun rather than marijuana?

Source: *R. v. Mann,* 2004, 3 SCR 59.

At Issue 6.2

The Sniffer Dog and the Backpack

The principal of an Ontario high school issued a standing invitation for the police to bring sniffer dogs into the school to enforce the school's zero tolerance policy for drugs and alcohol. During the search, the drug dog zeroed in on a student's backpack, which was found to contain 10 bags of marijuana, 10 magic mushrooms, and various types of drug paraphernalia. The student, A.M., was charged with criminal offences. However, two Ontario courts subsequently cleared the youth, deciding that his Charter rights had been violated.

The primary issue for the Supreme Court was whether the use of the sniffer dog was an unreasonable invasion of privacy that amounted to unreasonable search and seizure under the Charter. (The Charter states that everyone has the right to be secure against unreasonable search or seizure.) In its decision, the Supreme Court held that the sniffer dog's activities constituted a "search" under the provisions of the Charter and that the dog's search of the backpack as part of a general "sniff search" violated the student's Charter rights not to be subject to unreasonable search and seizure as would such a search in any other public space (e.g., on a ferry).

You Make the Call!

1. Do you agree with the decision of the Supreme Court in this case? Explain.
2. Does this decision place too many restrictions on the powers of the police? Explain.
3. What if the officers had found a handgun rather than drugs?

Source: *R. v. A.M.*, 2008, 1 S.C.R. 569; 2008, SCC 19.

Key Points Review

1. There are tensions between the power and authority of the police and their legal mandate to maintain order, and the values and processes that exist in a democratic society.
2. The Canadian Charter of Rights and Freedoms has had a strong impact on the legal powers of the police.
3. Among the key powers of the police are the ones to arrest and detain, to search and seize, and to use force.
4. The use of force, including lethal force, is governed by both law and policy.
5. The force-options approach is the foundation of most police training in Canada.
6. Five distinct force options are available to police officers.
7. The National Use of Force Framework provides guidelines for the courses of action to be taken in use-of-force situations and the Ontario Use of Force Model illustrates how this framework is put into practice.

8. There are a number of correlates of the police use of force.
9. Incidents in which lethal force is used can result in critical incident stress for the officers involved.

Key Term Questions

1. What role do an *arrest warrant* and the laying of an *information* play in the police powers of arrest?
2. In what situations are *search warrants* required, and in what circumstances can a search be conducted without a search warrant?
3. What is the *force options model*?
4. Discuss what is meant by a *demonstrated threat,* and note the five levels of resistance to the police that may be presented by individuals.
5. What is the *one-plus-one* use-of-force standard in policing?
6. What is a *less lethal force option* (or *lower lethality option*), and what types of less lethal compliance tools are available to police?
7. Define and describe the phenomena of *victim-precipitated homicide ("suicide by cop").*
8. Describe the impacts of *critical incident stress* on police officers.

Notes

1. S. Kari, "Justice's Balancing Act," *National Post,* April 5, 2008, A6.
2. P.F. McKenna, *Police Powers I* (Toronto: Prentice Hall, 2002), 18.
3. J. Eastwood and B. Snook, "Comprehending Canadian Police Cautions: Are the Rights to Silence and Legal Counsel Understandable?" *Behavioral Science and the Law* 28, no. 3 (2001): 366–77.
4. D. Quan, "Police Cautions Not Always Clear to Those Who Are Read Their Rights, Researcher Warns," *Vancouver Sun,* July 15, 2011, http://www .canada.com/news/have+right+remain+baffled+police+cautions+always+ clear/51102
5. J.M. Gau, C. Mosher, and T.C. Pratt, "An Inquiry into the Impact of Suspect Race on Police Use of Tasers," *Police Quarterly* 13, no. 1 (2010): 27–48.
6. M.R. Smith, L.A. Fridell, J. MacDonald, and B. Kabu, "A Multi-Method Evaluation of Police Use of Force Outcomes" (Washington: National Institute of Justice, 2006), http://www.cas.sc.edu/crju/pdfs/taser_summary.pdf
7. G.P. Alpert and R.G. Dunham, "Policy and Training Recommendations Related to Police Use of CEDs: Overview of Findings from a Comprehensive National Study," *Police Quarterly* 13, no. 3 (2010): 235–59; G.P. Alpert, M.R. Smith, R.J. Kaminski, L.A. Fridell, J. MacDonald, and B. Kabu, "Police Use of Force, Tasers, and Other Less Lethal Weapons," *NIJ Research in Brief* (Washington: U.S. Department of Justice, Office of Justice Programs, May 2001), https://www.ncjrs.gov/pdffiles1/nij/232215.pdf; Smith et al., "A Multi-Method Evaluation."
8. C. Butler and C. Hall, "Public–Police Interaction and Its Relation to Arrest and Use of Force by Police and Resulting Injuries to Subjects and Officers: A Description of Risk in One Major Canadian Urban City," (Calgary:

Calgary Police Service, 2008), http://www.icpra.org/sites/default/files/Calgary_Police_Service_Study_Police_Public_Interaction_and_Use_of_Force.pdf

9. W. Terrill and E.A. Paoline, "Conducted Energy Devices (CEDs) and Citizen Injuries: The Shocking Empirical Reality," *Justice Quarterly,* forthcoming in 2012.

10. Braidwood Commission on the Death of Robert Dziekanski, "Restricting the Use of Conducted Energy Weapons in British Columbia," Braidwood Commission on Conducted Energy Weapon Use (Victoria: Attorney General of British Columbia, 2009), http://www.braidwoodinquiry.ca/report/P1Report.php

11. T. Blackwell, "Police vs. the Public," *National Post,* July 16, 2011, A4.

12. Butler and Hall, "Public–Police Interaction."

13. T.D. Bazley, K.M. Lersch, and T. Mieczkowski, "Police Use of Force: Detectives in an Urban Police Department," *Criminal Justice Review* 31, no. 3 (2006): 213–29.

14. C.J. Harris, "Police Use of Improper Force: A Systematic Review of the Evidence," *Victims and Offenders* 4, no. 1 (2009): 25–41.

15. Ibid.

16. J.P. McElvain and A.J. Kposowa, "Police Officer Characteristics the Likelihood of Using Deadly Force," *Criminal Justice and Behavior* 35, no. 4 (2008): 505–21; J. Rydberg and W. Terrill, "The Effect of Higher Education on Police Behavior," *Police Quarterly* 13, no. 1 (2010): 92–120.

17. E.A. Paoline and W. Terrill, "Women Police Officers and the Use of Coercion," *Women and Criminal Justice* 15, nos. 3–4 (2004): 97–119.

18. Harris, "Police Use of Improper Force."

19. National Institute of Justice, *Use of Force by Police: Overview of National and Local Data* (Washington: National Institute of Justice and Bureau of Justice Statistics, U.S. Department of Justice, 1999), http://www.ncjrs.gov/pdffiles1/nij/176330-1.pdf

20. R.R. Johnson, "Suspect Mental Disorder and Police Use of Force," *Criminal Justice and Behavior,* 38, no. 2 (2011): 127–45.

21. S. Wortley, *Police Use of Force in Ontario: An Examination of Data from the Special Investigations Unit* (Toronto: Attorney General of Ontario, 2006), http://www.attorneygeneral.jus.gov.on.ca/inquiries/ipperwash/policy_part/projects/pdf/AfricanCanadianClinicIpperwashProject_SIUStudyby ScotWortley.pdf

22. S.W. Phillips and J.J. Sobol, "Police Attitudes About the Use of Unnecessary Force: An Ecological Examination," *Journal of Police and Criminal Psychology* 26, no. 1 (2011): 47–57; W. Terrill and M.D. Reisig, "Neighborhood Context and Police Use of Force," *Journal of Research in Crime and Delinquency* 40, no. 3 (2003): 291–321.

23. Harris, "Police Use of Improper Force."

24. R.B. Parent, "The Police Use of Deadly Force: International Comparisons," *Police Journal* 79, no. 3 (2006): 230–37 at 235.

25. V.B. Lord and M.W. Sloop, "Suicide by Cop: Police Shooting as a Method of Self-Harming," *Journal of Criminal Justice* 38, no. 5 (2010): 889–95.

26. N. Addis and C. Stephens, "An Evaluation of a Police Debriefing Program: Outcomes for Police Officers Five Years After a Police Shooting," *International Journal of Police Science and Management* 10, no. 4 (2008): 361–73.

27. D. Klinger, *Police Responses to Officer-Involved Shootings* (Washington: National Institute of Justice, 2001), https://www.ncjrs.gov/pdffiles1/nij/grants/192286.pdf

28. P. Hart, A. Wearing, and B. Headey, "Police Stress and Well-Being: Integrating Personality, Coping, and Daily Work Experiences," *Journal of Occupational and Organizational Psychology* 68, (1995): 133–36; C. Regehr, D. Johanis, G. Dimitropolous, C. Bartram, and G. Hope, "The Police Officer and the Public Inquiry: A Qualitative Inquiry into the Aftermath of Workplace Trauma," *Brief Treatment and Crisis Intervention* 3, (2003): 383–96.

29. C. Regehr, J. Hill, G. Goldberg, and J. Hughes, "Postmortem Inquiries and Trauma Responses in Paramedics and Firefighters," *Journal of Interpersonal Violence* 18, no. 6 (2003): 607–22.

Chapter

7

Police Ethics and Professionalism

Learning Objectives

After reading this chapter, you should be able to:

- Discuss the role of the police culture in police misconduct

- Describe what is meant by "rotten apples," "rotten barrels," and "rotten orchards"

- Identify and provide examples of the three general categories of police misconduct

- Describe what is meant by Noble Cause Corruption

- Discuss the issues surrounding the off-duty activities of police officers

- Describe the issues that surround the involvement of police organizations in politics and with private sector sponsors

Key Terms

In Chapter 3, the structures that govern Canadian police services were discussed. In this chapter, we examine the issues surrounding police ethics and professionalism and present case examples of incidents in which complaints were made against police officers. The discussion considers the various types of police misconduct (often referred to as "police deviance" or "police corruption") and the responses to these incidents. Extensive use is made of case studies of police officers involved in various types of misconduct.

The police have a high degree of discretion in carrying out their mandate. This in turn creates the potential that officers will become involved in misconduct and even corruption.[1] Police officers may be held liable for violating the policies and procedures of the police service in which they work. They are also liable, civilly and criminally, for their conduct. Canadian courts have established that police officers are held to a higher standard of conduct than ordinary citizens.

The emphasis on police ethics is intended to reduce the likelihood that police officers will become involved in unprofessional and illegal behaviour. Most jurisdictions have developed **codes of ethics.** These generally contain sections on integrity and ethical decision making. They also require that police officers carry out their duties fairly and impartially; that they uphold the rights and freedoms guaranteed in law; that they uphold the principles of democracy and the rule of law; and that they maintain a high standard of ethics both on and off duty. Note that codes of ethics are directed toward individual officers rather than the police services in which they work. Providing effective oversight of the police organization is much more difficult.

> **code of ethics**
> a policy that establishes standards of behaviour for police officers

WHEN COPS GO BAD: WRONGDOING IN POLICE WORK

The recruitment, selection, and training of police officers has come a long way from the early days of Canadian policing, when officers were often as much a part of the problem as they were a part of the solution (see Chapter 1). Although police services have rigorous admission standards, this does not prevent some police officers from engaging in unprofessional or even illegal conduct while on the job. Police malfeasance can arise during patrol, case investigation, interrogations, court proceedings, or when an officer is off-duty. (The issues surrounding case investigation are discussed in Chapter 10.)

The need for police ethics and professionalism has assumed even greater importance since the Supreme Court of Canada ruling in *R. v. McNeil* (2009, SCC 3), which held that the Crown has a duty to disclose the disciplinary records of officers involved in investigating an accused person. This case arose when it was discovered that the constable investigating a person, who was later charged and convicted of various drug-related offences, had himself been criminally charged with a drug-related offence.

There has been little research on the factors associated with a police officer becoming involved in misconduct. In Chapter 4 the police culture was identified as a major component of the police occupation. That culture has also been identified as contributing to, facilitating, and justifying police misconduct: "The demand for loyalty and solidarity with other police officers serves as a master value that insulates and protects police deviance and makes it difficult to govern officers' behaviour from within but especially from outside the organization."[2] This is often referred to as the "blue wall of silence."

Research studies have found that most police officers will report what they view as serious incidents of misconduct on the part of fellow officers. However, incidents that they view as minor are less likely to be reported. Interestingly, preliminary research has found that civilian police staff are less likely to report police misconduct than sworn officers, especially in situations where the incident is more serious.[3] This is a particularly significant finding, given the increasing role of civilians in police services, for it suggests that the culture of silence may extend to civilian staff.

Rotten Apples, Rotten Barrels, and Rotten Orchards

rotten apples
individual police officer misconduct

rotten barrels
group misconduct by police officers

rotten orchards
misconduct by a police service

Police misconduct may involve individual officers ("**rotten apples**") or groups of officers ("**rotten barrels**"), or it may be engrained in the organizational culture of the police service ("**rotten orchards**").

A "sliding scale" of police deviance has been proposed and is depicted in Figure 7.1. This scale presents a continuum from "Low" to "High" police deviance; it also depicts individual, group, and systemic deviance.

The research suggests that police misconduct in Canada is more of the "rotten apple" and, to a lesser extent, "rotten barrel" variety. One study found no association between level of education and the number of complaints filed against officers alleging misconduct.[4] Younger officers may be involved in more incidents due to their inexperience. Also, there are "problem officers" who involve themselves in misconduct as they move through their career.[5] However, there have been few investigations into systemic police corruption in police services or into the organizational conditions that may foster widespread officer misconduct.[6] For example, in the investigation of the "Starlight Tours," where at least one Aboriginal person was abused at the hands of Saskatoon police officers (see Chapter 11), no attempt was made to address how widespread the practice was in the department, how long officers had been involved in this practice, and whether other Canadian police services have been involved in similar activities past or present.

In the broadest case of police corruption in Canada, several Toronto officers were accused of a variety of wrongdoings relating to the Toronto club scene. However, the case was dismissed by the court six years after the officers were first charged. The presiding judge held that delays in prosecuting the case had breached the defendants' right to a fair trial. The officers had been charged with a variety of offences, including shaking down club owners; accepting payments from club owners relating to liquor licences; and receiving cash and free meals from club owners.

In another case, the misappropriation of pension and insurance funds by several senior officers in the RCMP did much to spur the transformation that is now under way in the force. Investigations by parliamentary committees found that there had been serious violations of the RCMP's core values and code of conduct, as well as of the Criminal Code by some senior officers. One committee report concluded: "The RCMP's normally high ethical standards were

FIGURE 7.1 Sliding Scale of Police Deviance

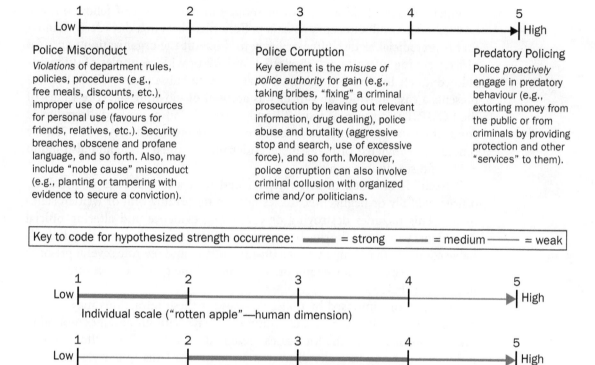

Sliding Scale of Police Deviance

1	2	3	4	5
Low				High

Police Misconduct

Violations of department rules, policies, procedures (e.g., free meals, discounts, etc.), improper use of police resources for personal use (favours for friends, relatives, etc.). Security breaches, obscene and profane language, and so forth. Also, may include "noble cause" misconduct (e.g., planting or tampering with evidence to secure a conviction).

Police Corruption

Key element is the *misuse of police authority* for gain (e.g., taking bribes, "fixing" a criminal prosecution by leaving out relevant information, drug dealing), police abuse and brutality (aggressive stop and search, use of excessive force), and so forth. Moreover, police corruption can also involve criminal collusion with organized crime and/or politicians.

Predatory Policing

Police *proactively* engage in predatory behaviour (e.g., extorting money from the public or from criminals by providing protection and other "services" to them).

Key to code for hypothesized strength occurrence: ▬▬▬ = strong ▬▬ = medium ─── = weak

Individual scale ("rotten apple"—human dimension)

Group scale ("rotten barrel"—police culture dimension)

Systemic scale ("rotten orchard"—organizational dimension)

Source: "Conceptual Framework for Managing Knowledge of Police Deviance," Dean, G., P. Bell, and M. Lauchs, *Policing and Society* 20, no. 2 (Taylor & Francis Ltd.: 2010); Reprinted by permission of the publisher (Taylor & Francis Ltd, http://www.tandf.co.uk/journals).

violated in this case....RCMP senior management allowed an ethical culture to develop which discouraged the disclosure of wrongdoing and did not hold individuals to account for unethical behaviour. This has led to a crisis of confidence amongst the RCMP rank and file."[7]

Generally, police misconduct can be grouped into the following categories: (1) violations of departmental regulations and standards of professional conduct; (2) abuse of discretionary powers and authority; (3) actions, often criminal, that undermine the administration of justice; and (4) the commission of a criminal offence. A single incident of misconduct may involve more than one of these categories—for example, an officer who is charged with the excessive use of force will generally face an internal disciplinary hearing as well. Even if the officer is found not guilty in a court of law, he or she will still face an internal disciplinary hearing, which may result in sanctions, including dismissal from the police service.

Violations of Departmental Regulations and Standards of Professional Conduct

This category encompasses a wide range of behaviours, including discreditable conduct, neglect of duty, insubordination, and harassment of fellow officers. Discreditable conduct occurs when a police officer acts in a disorderly manner that is prejudicial to discipline or likely to discredit the organization (e.g., two officers getting into a brawl). Boxes 7.1 and 7.2 provide examples of discreditable conduct. In Box 7.1, criminal charges were subsequently filed. Box 7.2 presents a case in which an officer was accused of violating the core values of the RCMP. The cases in At Issue 7.1 and At Issue 7.2 also involved discreditable conduct on the part of police officers. In the case presented in At Issue 7.2, the officer was convicted of harassment under the Criminal Code and also found guilty of discreditable conduct.

"Deceit" is included in this category and relates to instances in which an officer, willfully or negligently, makes false or misleading oral or written statements. This includes destroying or concealing evidence and altering official documents without authority. In one case, a constable pleaded guilty to discreditable conduct after he met with an on-duty officer and rewrote several prisoner log sheets to cover up an assault on a prisoner. These types of cases often result in criminal charges.

The sanctions imposed by police services for these infractions may include having the constable work a fixed number of days without pay, a demotion in rank, or dismissal (see the four cases presented in At Issue 7.4). Often, officers resign before being formally dismissed. In some cases, disciplinary action may be delayed to provide the officer with the opportunity to address personal issues that were associated with the misconduct, such as substance abuse, family turmoil, or psychological stress (see At Issue 7.5).

Box 7.1

Incident in the Jail

Four officers, including the Acting Watch Commander with twenty years policing experience, were suspended with pay in the aftermath of an incident during which the officers (along with several civilian jail staff) watched via a video monitor while two women who had been double-bunked in the drunk tank had sex. The women, who were not acquainted, had been arrested separately. The officers and civilians were captured on a jail room surveillance camera. Pending an internal investigation, the supervising officer was suspended with pay, while the other two officers were assigned to administrative duties. The three officers and the jail guard were subsequently charged with "breach of trust by a public official." One of the women later stated that she had been sexually assaulted and filed a civil suit against the police and the federal, provincial, and municipal governments.

Box 7.2

A Case of Breach of RCMP Core Values: Professionalism

A motorcyclist was driving in Alberta when he observed a serious accident involving another motorcyclist. He stopped, ensured that 911 was called, waited for the ambulance, and, because he had been the only witness, waited until the RCMP arrived. When questioned by the attending RCMP officer, he said he did not know whether the victim had been speeding. The member accused him of lying, asked to see the "paperwork" for his motorcycle, and indicated that the motorcyclist's plate validation tag had expired. The member advised the motorcyclist that the expiry carried a $230 fine and that the motorcycle could be ordered towed away, but that he would wait until he saw the complainant's final statement before determining how lenient he would be.

The commission concluded that the complainant was a Good Samaritan going out of his way to help an injured motorist and the RCMP with its investigation. The officer had used the threat of a ticket to get a "suitable" statement. This sort of behaviour tarnishes the reputation of the RCMP and discourages ordinary citizens from voluntarily assisting the RCMP.

Source: Commission for Public Complaints Against the RCMP, "Annual Report 2005–2006," June 2006, http://www.cpc-cpp.gc.ca/af-fr/ar-ra/AR0506_e.pdf, Reproduced with the permission of the MInister of Public Works and Government Services, 2011.

Abuse of Discretionary Power and Authority

Many of the activities in this category are referred to as "corrupt practice." They include an officer (1) failing to account for money or property that has been received, (2) incurring an obligation or debt that may affect his or her duties, and (3) improperly using his or her position for private advantage. Abuse of authority includes arresting or charging someone without cause, using unnecessary force, or being discourteous or uncivil to a member of the general public.

Actions, Often Criminal, That Undermine the Administration of Justice

This category includes activities such as fabricating evidence, backfilling police notebooks, committing perjury in court while under oath (also called "testilying"), and obstructing justice in an attempt to secure a conviction. In 2010 a senior RCMP officer in charge of a wire-tap unit in Ontario admitted that he had drafted a bogus internal memo indicating that the unit was adhering to judicial orders in conducting wire taps. The officer admitted providing the false memo as part of disclosure to defence counsel. The admission resulted in the collapse of a major drug investigation linked to Hells Angels.

Noble Cause Corruption
a view by police officers that the ends justify the means (misconduct)

Many of these actions are referred to as **Noble Cause Corruption,** which is defined as "a mindset of sub-culture which fosters a belief that the ends justify the means." The mission of the police to make communities and their residents safe is seen as justifying the violation of regulations and the law, for a higher good. It means "bending the rules for a greater good." The difficulty with this type of thinking is that it reflects a view that "justice should be dispensed on the street and not in the courtroom." Or, for the more cynical, "Never let the truth stand in the way of justice."[8] The following scenario demonstrates how Noble Cause Corruption may occur:

A subject is walking down the street when he turns and takes flight because he observes a police car coming in his direction. While engaging in a foot pursuit, the officer observes the subject discard an unknown item into the bushes. After capturing the suspect, the officer discovers that he is a convicted felon on probation. The officer retrieves a firearm from the bushes; but he never actually saw what the item was that the subject discarded. If the officer testifies truthfully, the subject may survive his probation violation hearing. If the officer lies at the hearing and testifies that he saw the subject discard a firearm, his probation will be definitely violated and a dangerous criminal will be off the streets.[9]

This is the type of dilemma that a police officer may face. It involves a temptation to exaggerate the truth. Overzealous officers may rationalize their decisions:

Several teens are driving around in a stolen motor vehicle, and the officers stop them. The young men jump out and run away. The officers chase them but succeed in arresting only two passengers. Unfortunately for the officers, neither was driving the vehicle. The officers file a report identifying one of the teens as driving the vehicle and the other as possessing contraband found on the floorboard. The officers chalk up felony arrests and call it a productive night.[10]

Following is an actual case in which a Canadian police constable manipulated evidence and lied about it:

A constable with expertise in forensics was called to assist in the investigation of a double homicide. Following the investigation, the constable provided the senior investigator on the case with her field notes, which indicated that the rifle that was the murder weapon was found at the scene, unloaded. The exhibit custodian found that the rifle had ammunition in it. A week later, the constable provided field notes from a second notebook which indicated that she had found ammunition in the rifle during her initial investigation. When questioned by her supervising officer as to the discrepancy between the two sets of field notes, the constable lied and stated that her first set of field notes had been contaminated with blood at the murder scene. The first notebook was then turned over to the exhibit custodian. It had been smeared with red paint, which she later admitted was intended to look like dried blood.[11]

Another example of police officers not telling the truth is the testimony given under oath by the four RCMP officers involved in the death of Robert Dziekanski at Vancouver International Airport (see Police File 6.1, p. 151). From his inquiry into the incident, retired Justice Thomas Braidwood concluded that the four officers had made "deliberate misrepresentations" to the inquiry regarding the events that culminated in Mr. Dziekanski's death.[12] More specifically, Justice Braidwood stated:

- "The initial claims by all four officers that they wrestled Mr. Dziekanski to the ground were untrue. In my view, they were deliberate misrepresentations, made for the purpose of justifying their actions."[13]
- One of the constables "consistently and deliberately misrepresented and overstated Mr. Dziekanski's behaviours and actions in a manner prejudicial to Mr. Dziekanski, and chose self-serving language for the purpose of justifying his actions."[14]
- "This tragic case is, at its heart, the story of shameful conduct by a few officers."[15]

After the release of the Braidwood Report, the B.C. government appointed a special prosecutor to review the evidence in the case to determine what, if any, charges should be laid against the officers. In his report, released in May 2010, the special prosecutor recommended that charges of perjury be laid against the four officers involved in the incident.

Another practice that undermines the administration of justice is "backfilling." Officers have sometimes been caught making additional entries subsequent to those made at the time of the incident or shortly afterwards. This practice may be revealed during the examination of an officer's notes by defence counsel during a trial, at which time entries in addition to those that have been disclosed to the defence are discovered.

The practice of backfilling seriously undermines the evidence given at a trial and may preclude the officer from continuing to refer to the notes during the trial. It may also result in a stay of proceedings on the grounds that there was nondisclosure of evidence to defence counsel by the prosecution. The Canadian courts regard a police officer's notes as a reflection of the professionalism and credibility of the police officer. Loss of credibility seriously limits the ability of that officer to bring cases to court. In addition, notes that have been backfilled are unreliable as an investigative tool.

Commission of a Criminal Offence

Police officers may become involved in the commission of criminal offences in conjunction with their policing duties or while off duty. These offences may range in severity from petty crimes, such as disturbing the peace, to more serious offences, such as domestic violence, drug trafficking, and, in extreme cases, murder.

Recent cases involving police officers who have been convicted of criminal offences include the following:

- Three off-duty police officers (from different police services in the Greater Vancouver Region) were convicted in 2010 of assaulting a newspaper deliveryman following a long night of bar-hopping (see At Issue 7.1).
- A Peel Regional Police officer was sentenced to five years and eight months in federal prison for stealing what he thought were kilos of cocaine involved in an RCMP sting operation.
- Two Saskatoon Police Department officers were convicted of unlawful confinement of an Aboriginal man and sentenced to eight months in prison (see Chapter 11 on the "Starlight Tours").

Rotten Orchards: The New Orleans Police Department

In rare instances, an entire police service may be infected with corruption and criminal activity. The New Orleans Police Department (NOPD) has a long history of documented malfeasance, but the depth of the department's problems received national recognition following Hurricane Katrina in 2005. The storm, which destroyed much of the city, created chaos on a broad scale. The NOPD often added to the struggles faced by residents trying to survive the storm's aftermath. On many occasions, police officers were found to have used excessive force. In one incident, the police shot a person in the back seven times and then attempted to destroy the evidence of the killing. Officers testified that they had been given orders to "shoot looters" and to "take back the city," but the origins of that order were never identified. Several officers were subsequently convicted for their role in the shooting deaths of several African Americans. All received lengthy prison terms (one of twenty-five years). The actions of the NOPD in the aftermath of the storm are captured in a film titled *Law and Disorder*, available for viewing on the website of *Frontline* (www.pbs.org).

This incident and others prompted the U.S. Department of Justice to investigate the department. The final report, released in March 2011, concluded that the department's problems were structural: "For far too long, the Department has been largely indifferent to widespread violations of law and policy by its officers. NOPD does not have in place the basic system known to improve public safety, ensure constitutional practices, and promote public confidence."[16] Specific findings of the investigation included these:

- Numerous instances in which NOPD officers used deadly force, contrary to department policy and law.
- A pattern of unreasonable use of less lethal force, including the unjustified use of force against mentally ill persons.
- Few meaningful controls over the officers' misuse of force, and inadequate investigations into use-of-force incidents.
- A pattern of stops, searches, and arrests that violated constitutional rights and that evidenced discrimination against African Americans and lesbian/gay/bisexual/transgender persons.
- Poor case investigation and systemic problems in handling domestic violence cases and those involving sexual assault.

New Orleans police on patrol in the aftermath of Hurricane Katrina, 2005.

The Department of Justice report identified a number of steps that needed to be taken in order to reform the department. These included developing policies to ensure constitutional practices and to hold supervisors and officers accountable; improving recruitment and training guidelines; enhancing front line supervision; developing effective policies for evaluating and promoting officers; and developing effective relationships with the community.[17]

Activities in the Grey Area of Police Work

Some activities fall into what is often called the *grey area of police work,* and individual police officers are required to exercise good judgment in ensuring that their behaviour is not improper. It is often difficult to determine the point where discretion crosses the line and becomes discriminatory or illegal. An example involves officers accepting gifts and gratuities (such as free or discounted restaurant meals) or favourable treatment from the general public or the business community (often referred to as graft). These may be viewed as gestures of goodwill and appreciation rather than as efforts to compromise the integrity of the officer or police service.

Off-Duty Activities and Misconduct

One grey area in police ethics and professionalism relates to the off-duty conduct of police officers. To what extent should officers be held accountable for their actions and decisions when not in uniform and not on duty? Canadian courts have ruled that police officers are held to a higher standard of conduct than ordinary citizens; but it is also recognized that officers have the right to a measure of freedom when they are off duty. The challenge is to maintain a balance between the interests of the police service and the privacy rights of officers (see At Issue 7.6).[18]

Most police services require officers to swear an oath that they will conduct their private and professional lives in an exemplary manner. Many provincial police acts and individual police services have provisions that address off-duty conduct. In British Columbia, the Police Act contains a Code of Professional Conduct Regulations which state that "a police officer commits the disciplinary default of improper off-duty conduct if (a) the police officer, while off duty, asserts or purports to assert authority as a police officer and does an act that would constitute a disciplinary default if done while the police officer is on duty, or (b) the police officer, while off duty, acts in a manner that is likely to discredit the reputation of the municipal police department with which the police officer is employed."[19]

Off-duty officers are required to exercise diligence and attentiveness when away from the workplace. Also, they must conduct their personal lives in a manner that does not jeopardize the integrity of the police service that employs them. Every officer has an obligation to maintain a healthy and balanced lifestyle to ensure that he or she is both mentally and physically able to work effectively while on duty.

Most police services have policies regulating "extra-duty" and "off-duty" employment. Extra-duty employment is when the police service, for a fee, hires out officers who would otherwise be off shift to provide security for events (e.g., sporting events and film shoots). Off-duty employment includes activities in the private sector that are entirely separate from the police service. Most police services either restrict or prohibit off-duty employment.[20]

Police work requires officers to exercise enforcement authority 24 hours a day, 365 days a year. It would be unprofessional and unethical for a police officer to ignore this obligation even on days off. For example, an off-duty officer who observes an impaired driver or a shoplifter has a professional obligation to intervene. The level of intervention will vary with the circumstances and the gravity of the offence.

At a minimum, the off-duty officer has an obligation to report the incident to the nearest police service. The off-duty officer may sometimes feel that direct intervention is required, which may include arresting the offender. This is provided for, both in Section 494 of the Criminal Code, which authorizes anyone to make an arrest under certain circumstances, as well as in Section 495, which relates more specifically to the powers of arrest of those who identify themselves as police officers.

Off-duty police officers who intervene where a crime or other situation is taking place over which they would have authority had they been on duty are generally considered to have the authority to arrest someone as if they were on duty. However, an officer who abuses his or her authority while off duty may face departmental sanctions. This occurred in the following case:

> An officer who was on his way home from work in his own car, was "cut off" on the highway by another vehicle. He began to flash his headlights at the other vehicle in front of him, indicating that the driver should pull over. When she did not, he followed her until she pulled into the driveway of her home. He pulled into the driveway behind her, and proceeded to write out a traffic ticket for her alleged driving infraction. During this encounter he used very abusive and insulting language. As a result of the other driver's complaint, the officer was disciplined for disreputable conduct.[21]

In this situation, the officer had the authority to intervene in an offence that he observed, and in so doing put himself back on duty. But after that, he engaged in disreputable conduct.

The provisions regarding off-duty activities are necessarily vague, and incidents are considered on a case-by-case basis. Illegal behaviour by officers who are off duty is unethical, but not all unethical behaviour by off-duty officers is illegal. Generally, an officer will be sanctioned by the police service for off-duty behaviour only when the officer's actions were connected to his or her position as a police officer.

Citizens may file a complaint against a police officer for off-duty conduct, but a connection must be established between the conduct and the job. The Cornwall (Ont.) Community Police Service website states: "A complaint may be filed about the conduct of an off-duty officer; however, there must be a connection between the conduct and either the duties of a police officer or the reputation of the Police Service."

Officers who are accused of off-duty criminal behaviour may be subject to both the criminal court process and the police service's own disciplinary process.

The Role of Police Leadership in Police Ethics and Professionalism

Effective police leadership is required to ensure that a police service carries out its activities in an ethical and professional manner. When police officers engage in misconduct, be it individually or in groups, it is often a result of weak leadership and an organizational environment that does not have in place clear lines of accountability and effective supervision.

A research study conducted on the Philadelphia Police Department found that police officers who perceived the department as fair and just in its managerial practices were less likely to follow a "code of silence" or to believe that Noble Cause Corruption was justified. Also, there were lower levels of misconduct among those officers who felt that the police service was organizationally "just"—in other words, that supervisors treated officers fairly, that promotions were based on merit, and that discipline was meted out fairly.[22]

Police leaders can imprint a strong sense of ethics and professionalism in their police services, but this requires ongoing vigilance and constant organizational improvement. Unfortunately, most police services do not provide in-service ethics training, nor do they require officers to complete ethics programs and courses in order to advance. As one scholar has noted: "Law enforcement agencies often view ethics instruction as a single training block, when it should be continually re-enforced....One lone course is unlikely to develop values or to change behaviors."[23]

Senior police officials, too, may become involved in ethical dilemmas. Two examples are the involvement of Canadian police associations and organizations in political lobbying efforts for specific legislation; and the relationship between the Canadian Association of Chiefs of Police and private company sponsors (see At Issue 7.7 and 7.8). There is little doubt that ethics requires far more attention from police services and police scholars, given the importance of this issue for police work in Canada (see At Issue 7.9).

At Issue 7.1

An Assault on a Newspaper Delivery Man

In the early morning hours of January 21, 2009, three off-duty police constables from three separate municipalities around Vancouver committed an unprovoked assault on a newspaper deliveryman in downtown Vancouver. The three had been out for an evening of binge drinking and were extremely intoxicated. The incident was witnessed by a taxi driver who called the police. Patrol officers from the VPD responded to the call and the three officers were arrested for alleged robbery (taking a cell phone from the victim) and assault. (One of the VPD arresting officers had been taught use of force by one of the accused at the police academy.) Charges of assault were subsequently laid against two of the officers, Const. Gillan of the West Vancouver Police Department and Const. Klassen of the New Westminster Police Department. The third officer, from the Delta Police Department, was not charged. The victim incurred soft-tissue injuries from the assault. There were no visible cuts or visible injuries to his head or hands.

Const. Gillan

Const. Gillan had been a police officer for one year and admitted that he had up to twenty-five drinks during the evening. Following the incident, he was suspended without pay, which resulted in a gross wage loss of $120,0000. Gillan pleaded guilty to Assault. At sentencing, the prosecutor asked that the provincial court judge impose a sentence of four to six months in jail, followed by probation. The judge imposed a twenty-one–day conditional sentence (which required him to be home from 10 p.m. to 6 a.m. every night) and six months' probation, including the condition that he attend anger management and alcohol counselling. In court, Gillan apologized to the victim, to the

West Vancouver Police Department, and to the Vancouver Police Department and accepted responsibility for his actions. Letters of support from police supervisors and friends stated that his behaviour that night was out of character.

A subsequent internal disciplinary investigation conducted by the department, presided over by the Chief Constable of another municipal police service, found Gillan guilty of two breaches of conduct under the Police Act: improper off-duty conduct and conduct constituting an offence. It was recommended that Gillan be allowed to keep his job but that he be demoted to probationary constable, receive a suspension of ten days without pay, and take alcohol counselling. An internal West Vancouver Police Department professional standards investigation recommended that Gillan be dismissed. In August 2011, a police complaints adjudicator accepted a joint proposal from Gillan's lawyer and the public hearing officer and imposed a thirty-day suspension and a one-year demotion in rank.

Gillan's case generated considerable online comment, most of it negative, including the following comments:

"How do you expect a community to have trust in their law enforcers when they themselves break the law and get away with it so easily—with pay and a little punishment?"

"Are the police subject to the same laws as the rest of us or aren't they? It's just that simple."

"Gotta love a system where someone with the job of upholding the law gets to keep their job after participating in a violent crime."

"If it were the other way around and the delivery man had assaulted the officer, what would have been the outcome?"

"Sure Gillan is an idiot when he's drunk but so are many people."

You Make the Call!

Based on the information provided on the case of Gillan:

1. Do you agree with the sentence imposed by the provincial court judge? If not, what sentence would you have imposed had you been the judge?
2. Do you agree with the recommendations of the internal disciplinary hearing? If not, what recommendations would you have made had you been the hearing officer?
3. In your view, should Gillan have been allowed to keep his job as a police officer?
4. Should the fact that Gillan was a "rookie" police officer have made a difference in the decisions that were made in this case? Did it affect your view? If yes, how so?

Const. Klassen

Const. Klassen was an experienced officer who had taught use of force at the Justice Institute of British Columbia Police Academy. At trial, Klassen testified that he had consumed approximately eleven beers during the evening prior to the attack on the delivery man, although, in his view, he was not drunk. The presiding judge did not accept this. He was found guilty of assault in provincial court. The prosecutor asked the court to sentence Klassen to thirty to sixty days in jail, arguing that "a discharge would send the wrong message to Klassen and other officers." Klassen's defence lawyer countered that an absolute discharge (which means that Klassen would not have a criminal record) was appropriate, as the assault was out of character and he had believed that his friend, Gillan, was being attacked by the victim. The defence lawyer also argued that Klassen had lost income and received adverse publicity. Also, that he had apologized to the victim. The presiding judge imposed a conditional discharge, one year's probation, and 100 hours of community service. A conditional discharge meant that Klassen had been found guilty of the offence but was deemed not to have been convicted. The record would be kept for three years and then be purged. If Klassen failed to fulfill the conditions of the sentence, he might be returned to court, where the discharge would be cancelled and there would be a conviction and sentence on the original offence. If Klassen met the conditions of his sentence, then an absolute discharge would be entered and the case would be over. Klassen was suspended without pay while he awaited a disciplinary hearing.

You Make the Call!

1. Do you agree with the sentence imposed by the provincial court judge? If not, what sentence would you have imposed had you been the judge?
2. Do you agree with the recommendations of the internal disciplinary hearing? If not, what recommendations would you have made had you been the hearing officer?
3. In your view, should Klassen have been allowed to keep his job as a police officer?
4. Should the fact that Klassen was an experienced officer and a former instructor at the police academy have made a difference in the decisions that were made in this case? Did it affect your view? If yes, how so?

Sources: S. Lazaruk, 2011, "Prosecutor Pushes for Jail Sentence for Cop Convicted of Assaulting Delivery Driver," *The Province*, May 10, 2010, http://www.theprovince.com; N. Hall, "Officer Avoids Jail Time for Assault," *Vancouver Sun*, June 11, 2011, A10, http://www.vancouversun.com

At Issue 7.2

A Drive-By Response to a 911 Call: A Case of Discreditable Conduct

On the night of September 18, 2008, Lisa Dudley and her partner, Gutherie McKay, were shot by an assailant in their home in Mission, B.C. At 10:42 p.m., a neighbour called 911 to report that six shots had been fired on the street. Two internal investigations by the RCMP, an investigation conducted by the Alberta Serious Incident Response Team (ASIRT, a civilian investigative team; see Chapter 3), and a review of the case by the Commission for Public Complaints Against the RCMP documented the events that unfolded after the dispatcher received the 911 call and dispatched Constable Mike White to the scene. (Note that the two internal RCMP investigations did not discover the 911 transcript. It was discovered by the ASIRT in its investigation.)

> *Dispatcher*: Radio, Theresa.
> *White*: Hello.
> *Dispatcher*: Hi.
> *White*: Six gun shots in a row and a crash.
> *Dispatcher*: Yeah.
> *White*: [sound of chuckling]
> *Dispatcher*: Yeah, exactly.
> *White*: [sound of chuckling]
> *Dispatcher*: Don't ya love this?
> *White*: Yeah, I'll head out. [call disconnected]

White drove to the street and was joined by another constable, who had an auxiliary member in her vehicle. The officers drove around the subdivision. At no time did the officers exit their patrol cars or contact the 911 caller, although they drove past his residence. The records indicate that White was in the area for thirteen minutes before leaving the area to attend another call. The file was closed as "unfounded."

Four days later, Dudley and McKay were found in their residence, both victims of a shooting. McKay was deceased. Dudley was still alive when discovered by police but died en route to hospital. The victim's home was across the street from that of the 911 caller.

Dudley's parents were dissatisfied with the RCMP internal investigation and filed a complaint with the Commission for Public Complaints Against the Police. In its final report, the commission concluded: "Corporal White's dismissive comments and tone serve to further demonstrate that he had predetermined that there was no validity to the complaint of shots fired. This explains his lack of investigation and the results that followed" (3).

The RCMP conducted two internal investigations, and yet another inquiry was conducted by the Alberta Serious Incident Response Team. An RCMP Board of Adjudication found the constable guilty of "disgraceful conduct" and imposed a reprimand and one day's loss of pay.

At a subsequent Internal Code of Conduct hearing, Corporal White (who had been promoted from constable during the investigation) was reprimanded for "disgraceful conduct" and docked one day's wages. Three suspects in the killings were arrested and charged with murder in 2011. The mother of Lisa Dudley filed a civil suit against the RCMP in 2011.

Source: Commission for Public Complaints Against the RCMP, "Chair's Final Report After Commissioner's Notice," http://www.images.ctv.ca/ctvlocal/britishcolumbia/pdfs/Dudley_CPC_Final_Report_CTVBC.pdf

You Make the Call!

1. The parents of Lisa Dudley expressed disappointment with the decision of the RCMP Adjudication Board. In your view, was the reprimand and loss of one day's wages a sufficient sanction in this case? If not, what in your view would have been a more appropriate sanction for the officer? The maximum penalty that the adjudication committee could have imposed was dismissal from the RCMP.
2. Recalling the role that police dispatchers played in the Winnipeg 911 murders (see

Police File 5.1, p. 113), do you think that sanctions should have been imposed on the dispatcher in this case?
3. Is the fact that the two internal RCMP investigations did not discover the existence of the 911 transcript a cause for concern?
4. Are there any "lessons learned" as to the issues surrounding police investigating police, as discussed in Chapter 3?

At Issue 7.3

A Case of Criminal Harassment: Ottawa Police Services Board, Hearing Officer Decision, February 24, 2011

Following is the decision of a Hearing Officer in a disciplinary hearing in a case involving an officer of the Ottawa Police Service.

**Appearance: February 3, 2011. Const. Percival. Hearing Officer: Knowlton Roberts, Supt. (retired), Ottawa Police Service
Prosecutor: C___H___, Legal Services, Ottawa Police Service
Counsel: G___B___, Ottawa Police Association
Guilty Plea Entered by Const. Percival that:**

On October 2, 2011, Const. Percival pled guilty to a criminal offence of Harassing Telephone Calls contrary to Section 372(3) of the Criminal Code of Canada, before Judge Kirkland, Ontario Provincial Court, thereby constituting an offence against discipline, Discreditable Conduct as prescribed in Section 2(1)(a)(ix) of the Code of Conduct, Ontario Regulation 268/10 as amended.

An agreed Statement of Facts (Exhibit #8) was submitted by the Prosecutor with agreement from Counsel for the accused officer. In summary, Const. Percival and the complainant met as coworkers of the Ottawa Police. They entered into a romantic relationship in February 2009. The complainant ended the relationship in September 2009.

Const. Percival struggled with the ending of the relationship and attended the complainant's residence on a few occasions. On one occasion he set up a giant card to profess his love and on another occasion he set up a giant bed sheet on which he wrote a coded message to the complainant to profess his love in an attempt to resume their relationship. These gestures made the complainant uncomfortable. Const. Percival repeatedly telephoned the complainant to the point of making the complainant fearful and increasingly uncomfortable with the situation.

(*Continued*)

The complainant advised Const. Percival as did some coworkers and members of the Ottawa Police Services, to leave the complainant alone. Const. Percival did not listen to the requests and continued to repeatedly telephone the complainant. Const. Percival's behaviour escalated and he began sending the complainant text messages demanding the claimant return his telephone calls.

The final incident occurred on _____. Const. Percival was assigned to the _____ and the complainant was assigned to police _____ located at _____. On _____, Const. Percival, while off-duty attended in full uniform [at the] report room where the complainant was working and they became involved in a verbal confrontation. This incident was witnessed by the complainant's coworkers. The complainant lodged a formal complaint into Const. Percival's behaviour.

On February 5, 2010, Const. Percival was arrested and charged with three (3) counts of criminal harassment (s. 264(2)(b)) of the Criminal Code of Canada. Const. Percival was also charged with one count of breaching the Section 810 peace bond conditions he entered into on January 29, 2009, to keep the peace and be on good behaviour on a domestic matter unrelated.

On October 25, 2010, Const. Percival pled guilty to having made harassing telephone calls contrary to Section 372(3) of the Criminal Code of Canada. The criminal harassment charges and breach of peace bond charges were withdrawn by the Crown. At the time of sentencing, the Crown's position was one of a suspended sentence, along with a period of probation. After hearing sentencing submission by the Defence, Justice Kirkland ordered a conditional discharge after the successful completion of six (6) months probation.

As a result of his being charged with and pleading guilty to a Criminal Code Offence, Const. Percival was charged under the Police Service Act for Discreditable Conduct.

The hearing was presented with a joint submission on penalty, (Exhibit #9) recommending:

forfeiture of 48 hours in accordance with Section 68(1) of the Police Services Act.

There is no documentation provided by the prosecution of any previous discipline or documentation of poor performance. There were no submissions for consideration from counsel to Const. Percival as to his performance or character.

Seriousness of the Charge

In the agreed statement of facts by way of pleading guilty, Const. Percival has taken responsibility for his actions. The criminal offence was serious and the officer has been dealt with in the courts. Threats against others must be treated seriously because of the potential for harm and damages to the complainant. Complainants must be satisfied that their safety is treated respectfully in their work environment. The threats and actions of Const. Percival caused the complainant enough concern to file an official complaint.

Specific and General Deterrence

The behaviour of the officer clearly and convincingly demonstrated discreditable conduct prescribed in Section 2(1)(a)(ix) of the prescribed Code of Conduct, Ontario regulation 268/10 as amended.

The punishment proposed would have to deter the officer from further offences of this nature and demonstrate to officers of the Ottawa Police Service that this behaviour is unacceptable to the Ottawa Police Service and the community.

In considering the officer's response, Const. Percival has taken responsibility for his actions by pleading guilty at the Criminal Court proceedings and at this hearing. His demeanour at this hearing has demonstrated his appreciation for the seriousness of the charges. I also considered that Const. Percival did not make any threats or resort to violence and that with the passage of time since the offence, Const. Percival has ceased his inappropriate behaviour.

Conclusion

Const. Percival appeared in court, pled guilty at the first opportunity and was given a conditional discharge after the successful completion of six (6) months probation. This is an appropriate punishment considering his profession and the implications of a Criminal Record.

Const. Percival has taken responsibility for his actions and ceased his behaviour. I accepted his plea of guilty.

In considering the joint submission on penalty, I have considered the seriousness of the offence and adequate deterrence. The penalty proposed will also act as a general deterrent. The penalty is also consistent with case law, considering the seriousness of the offence.

Const. Percival will be relinquishing 48 hours of time. This will serve as an adequate admonition to Const. Percival that he erred and will be held responsible and accountable for his actions by the Ottawa Police Service.

Disposition

I accept the joint submission of penalty.

_____

(Knowlton Roberts)   Feb. 24, 2011

Superintendent (retired)

Ottawa Police Service

You Make the Call!

1. Do you agree with the judgment of the hearing officer and the reasons for the judgment?
2. What arguments might be made in support of the position that the penalty imposed by the hearing officer was not sufficient, given the severity of the offence?
3. What arguments might be made in support of imposing a more severe sentence?
4. If a more severe penalty were to be imposed, what would it be?
5. What arguments might be made in support of the judgment made by the hearing officer?
6. If you had been the hearing officer, would you have imposed a more severe penalty, a less severe penalty, or the same penalty?
7. What are your views with respect to the hearing officer being a retired Superintendent of the Ottawa Police Service?

Source: Ottawa Police Service, 2011, "Police Services Act Hearing" (2010), http://www.ottawapolice.ca/Files/Vetted%20Decision%20Cst%20Percival.pdf

At Issue 7.4

Officer Misconduct and Discipline: Case Studies

Following are several cases involving misconduct by police officers and the discipline that was imposed.

Case 1: The Smackdown

While off duty in a small northern community, a police constable drove around in his police

(Continued)

cruiser looking for an eleven-year-old boy who had allegedly assaulted the officer's nine-year-old stepson. The constable was accompanied by his wife, his stepson, and their baby. When the boy was located, the constable's wife exited from the cruiser and invited her son to punch the eleven-year-old. The son hit the eleven-year-old several times, leaving the boy bloodied. The constable then drove away without offering any assistance to the boy. The constable's wife subsequently pled guilty to assault. The constable was not charged with assault, but an adjudication board imposed a sanction of loss of four days' wages. He was allowed to continue on active duty.

Case 2: Incident at McDonald's

An off-duty constable entered the drive-through lane at a McDonald's and became involved in a confrontation with three youths who were on foot and placing an order in front of him. The constable left his vehicle, grabbed a young woman, and punched her in the face. Bleeding profusely and with fractured teeth, she fell to the ground. The constable left the scene. He was charged with common assault, pled guilty, and received a suspended sentence and one year's probation. The police adjudication board docked him ten days' pay and he returned to active duty.

Case 3: The Case of the Wrong-Way Officer

After having a few beers with a colleague while off duty, the police inspector drove his car into a lane reserved for transit buses. He was stopped by a municipal transit officer, at which point he flashed his badge and told the transit officer he was on duty. The transit officer allowed the police officer to drive away but pulled him over again when he noted that the officer's vehicle was swerving. The local municipal police were called and, following a Breathalyzer test, the police inspector received a twelve-hour roadside suspension. The adjudication board subsequently imposed a sanction of loss of five days' wages and he returned to active duty. This same officer had seven previous incidents of disgraceful conduct, related to inappropriate sexual relations with a female officer who was taking one of his courses. After attempting to disrupt the investigation, he had been suspended for fifty-five days, docked twenty-five days' pay, and prohibited from teaching courses.

Case 4: The Constable, His Wife, and the Hells Angels

While crossing the border from Manitoba into the United States, an RCMP constable's wife was stopped and questioned by U.S. border authorities. During the interview, she told the agents she had former business dealings with a member of Hells Angels and continued to visit him in prison. The U.S. authorities contacted the RCMP, which conducted an internal investigation. This revealed that the constable had viewed 185 documents relating to his wife and the Hells Angel in the RCMP's national data bank over a period of several months. When interviewed by RCMP investigators, the constable admitted he made the data checks but denied sharing the information with Hells Angels, although he did admit to sharing some of the information with his wife. The investigation resulted in the constable being docked eight days' pay.

You Make the Call!

For each case, consider the following:

1. Whether the discipline imposed was appropriate.
2. What discipline you would have imposed had you been a member of the adjudication board.

Sources: B. Hutchinson, "What Does the Force Do with a Wayward Mountie?" *National Post*, December 12, 2009, A9; G. Dimmock, "Mountie Disciplined for Sharing Crime Data," *Vancouver Sun*, May 30, 2011, B3.

At Issue 7.5

Second Chance for a Constable

While off duty, an officer was found in an intoxicated state in the company of four prostitutes on a public street. He was also consuming alcohol in his personal vehicle at the time. He was charged with discreditable conduct and found guilty. The penalty imposed was that he resign within seven days or be dismissed. On his appeal to the municipal police board, an agreed settlement of the matter was reached between the constable, the police chief, and the board, under which the original penalty was replaced by the following:

1. Const. [X] will be reinstated on the [ABC] Police Department effective [date].
2. Const. [X] will not receive any pay or allowance from the date of his dismissal until [the date of his reinstatement].
3. For a period of one year commencing [on the date of his reinstatement], Const. [X] will be on probation with the [ABC] Police Department, the conditions of which are:

   (a) That he not drink alcoholic beverages
   (b) That he continue to the satisfaction of the Chief with his present course of rehabilitation, including his attendance at A.A. and his ongoing participation in the Department's Employee Assistance Program
   (c) That he properly perform his duties as a constable in the Department.

4. At the conclusion of one year, the Chief shall report to the Commission and if the terms of the probation have been met to the satisfaction of the Commission, Const. [X] will revert to normal status.
5. If Const. [X] should breach any term of its probation, his dismissal from the Department will be confirmed by the Commission.

In its report, the board stated: "The Commission was convinced on the evidence that Const. [X] is an alcoholic, that his behaviour on the evening in question was related to his alcoholism, and that since then he has taken steps to rehabilitate himself. This agreement was proposed by the Commission to give Const. [X] a chance to continue with that rehabilitation and to turn himself into a strong link and competent performer in the [ABC] Police Department."

You Make the Call!

Do you agree with the decision of the Commission?

Source: Royal Canadian Mounted Police External Review Committee, Discussion Paper 7. Off-Duty Conduct, http://www.erc-cee.gc.ca/publications/discussion/dp7-eng .aspx#a7, R.J. Marin, 2010. Reproduced with the permission of the Minister of Public Works and Government Services Canada, 2012.

At Issue 7.6

The Case of the Off-Duty Date

Two patrol constables in an urban police service are called to the scene of a domestic dispute. On arrival, they determine that the woman has been physically assaulted by her boyfriend, who is subsequently arrested and charged under the Criminal Code. Several days after the incident, one of the officers involved in the incident, who is on his day off, sees the other officer, who is also on his day off, in a city park with the female victim of the assault. The officer and the female victim are walking hand in hand. In the view of the other officer, they are obviously on a "date." A month later, the boyfriend appears in court and the two officers are called to give evidence under oath about the incident.

You Make the Call!

1. Is there anything wrong with the officer dating the crime victim?
2. What action, if any, should be taken by the officer who observed his colleague with the woman in the park?
3. Should either or both of the officers be precluded from giving evidence in the court case? Explain.

At Issue 7.7

Should Police Associations and Unions Be Involved in Lobbying?

A key principle in policing in a democratic society is that the police should be independent of political control. However, the discussion in Chapter 2 suggested that it is impossible for the police to escape political influences. In some instances, police services proactively involve themselves in the political process. Across the country, police associations and unions are actively involved in supporting legislation, advocating for legislation, and other initiatives. The Canadian Professional Police Association (CPPA) represents the interests of the police across the country and lobbies MPs on specific issues, which have included an increased voice for the victims of crime and proposed legislation to alter sentencing options in the Criminal Code. Among the resolutions adopted by the Ontario Association of Chiefs of Police in 2009 was a position against offenders being awarded double credit for time served in pre-sentence custody (a practice since abolished by the federal government).

Supporters of police involvement in the political process argue that:

- the police are in the best position to provide legislators with information on issues related to crime and social disorder; *and*
- the primary interest of the police is public safety, and the police are advocating on behalf of the general public.

Opponents of the police being involved in the political process counter that:

- a key principle of policing in a democratic society is that the police are independent of politics; *and*
- the police place themselves in a conflict-of-interest position when they take sides in debates over legislation.

You Make the Call!

In your view, what ethical issues are raised when Canadian police unions and organizations involve themselves in lobbying efforts for specific legislation?

At Issue 7.8

The Canadian Association of Chiefs of Police, Long Guns, and Tasers

The Canadian Association of Chiefs of Police (CACP; http://www.cacp.ca) is a national organization "dedicated to the support and promotion of efficient law enforcement and to the protection and security of the people of Canada." The CACP Mission Statement is: "The Canadian Association of Chiefs of Police is leading progressive change in policing." Despite the prominent role of the CACP in Canadian policing, questions have been raised about the ethics of the organization, centring on potential conflicts of interest involving the long gun registry as well as CACP's relationship with Taser International, manufacturer of the Taser.

The Chiefs and the Long Gun Registry

The long gun registry was designed to provide a master database for police officers to query when responding to calls for service and conducting investigations. From its inception, the registry has been surrounded by controversy, with critics arguing that it had been a multibillion-dollar boondoggle that had not reduced violent crime, does not protect police officers, and penalized law-abiding citizens who had a legitimate use for long guns (criminals don't register their guns). Debates in Parliament over the long gun registry pitted cop against cop, with one retired police officer stating, "Never have I attended a killing when a registry of any kind of weapon would have prevented that killing from occurring." Criticism has also been forthcoming from scholars, one stating, "It is difficult to understand why the chiefs of police support the long gun registry. It has so many errors that relying on it puts the lives of rank-and-file police members at risk. Millions of entries are incorrect or missing." Critics of the CACP's support for the long gun registry also pointed out that in 2009, the association accepted $115,000 from CGI Group, a Bell

(Continued)

Mobility affiliate that is the software contractor for the gun registry. According to media reports, "the CGI donation was used to send CACP conference delegates to a Celine Dion concert."

In 2011, the federal government introduced legislation to abolish the long gun registry. The long gun registry was abolished by the federal Conservative government in 2011.

The Chiefs and Taser International

The CACP's relationship with Taser International, the manufacturer of the Taser (see Chapter 6), has been surrounded by controversy in recent years. In 2009, Taser International paid a $25,000 fee to be a "Platinum sponsor" for the annual CACP conference. This provided the company with access to the conference sessions as well as space for promoting the Taser.

Taser International is one of dozens of sponsors of the annual CACP conference. The CACP conference website describes "sponsorship opportunities": "In addition to prominent recognition during the conference, you will have an unmatched opportunity to reach out to conference delegates from the outset of the conference and inform them of your commitment to CACP." Companies can purchase a Platinum membership for $25,000+, which includes the following: "your company name and logo on a banner and signs prominently displayed at the conference"; an "option to provide one promotional option to be included in the delegates' registration kit"; complimentary conference registrations and attendance at conference sessions for three company staff members; and reserved seating at the Gala Awards Banquet

(http://cacpconference.ca/page/sponsorship/17). Concerns about the CACP's actions prompted a highly respected member of the organization's ethics committee to resign and to state: "What makes it unethical for me is that first step that puts you in debt to those corporations." In defence of its practices, the CACP has stated:

> Sponsorship is a well-accepted strategy for not-for-profit organizations, as a means of increasing their financial resources and securing in-kind assistance. This is a normal practice for many professional associations and organizations, including those related to the health, legal, information technology and education professions, other national associations with mandates and interests in policing and community safety, and many others. The CACP accepts sponsorships from corporations, governments, and their departments and agencies for two reasons. The first is in order to finance ongoing operations and professional activities of the Association and its multiple business lines. The second is that corporations, in particular, undertake research and development in response to policing needs and produce tools and technology that contribute to the safety and security of our communities.…The CACP will continue to enter into agreements with responsible, reputable companies from a variety of businesses and public sector agencies that choose to support the mandate, objectives, and beliefs of the CACP through sponsorship funds.[a]

You Make the Call!

1. What is your opinion on the CACP actively lobbying for retention of the long gun registry?

2. What is your opinion on the CACP accepting sponsors for its annual conference?

3. Consider the arguments put forth against and in support of corporate sponsorship. Which do you find most convincing?

4. If you were drafting a new policy for the CACP relating to sponsorship, what would it look like?

---

[a]Sources: L. Whitmore, "Ethics Expert Says Police Chiefs' Association has a Track Record of 'Dodgy Behaviour,'" *Canadian Shooting Sports Association*, August 24, 2010, 2; S. Chabot, "Sponsorship Position of CACP," June 5, 2009, http://www.cacp.ca/media/news/download/736/SponsorEng.pdf; Canadian Association of Chiefs of Police.

At Issue 7.9

Ethics in Police Work

In a discussion of ethics in police work, one scholar has stated: "Ethics in policing bears directly on issues of reform, control, and the legitimacy of law enforcement institutions in a democratic society."[24]

You Make the Call!

Based on the materials presented in this chapter, explain what the police scholar means by this statement.

Key Points Review

1. The fact that the police have a high degree of discretion in carrying out their mandate creates the potential that officers will become involved in misconduct and even corruption.

2. The police culture may contribute to, facilitate, and justify police misconduct.

3. Misconduct by the police may involve individual officers or groups of officers, or it may be engrained in the organizational culture of the police service.

4. Research studies suggest that in Canada, police misconduct is more of the rotten apple rather than the rotten barrel or rotten orchard variety.

5. Generally, police misconduct can be grouped into these categories: violations of departmental regulations and standards of professional conduct; abuse of discretionary powers and authority; actions, often criminal, that undermine the administration of justice; and commission of a criminal offence.

6. Police officers may be charged with violating the policies of the police service and/or with Criminal Code offences.

7. Even if an officer is found not guilty in a court of law, the officer may still be sanctioned by the police service.

8. A challenging area in the study of police ethics and professionalism is the activities and conduct of police officers who are off duty.

9. Police leadership plays a significant role in ensuring ethics and professionalism in the police service.

10. Issues of ethics are not limited to patrol officers; they may also surround police unions and associations.

Key Term Questions

1. What are **codes of ethics** and what role do they play in the discussion of police ethics and professionalism?
2. What is meant by **rotten apples**, **rotten barrels**, and **rotten orchards**?
3. What is **Noble Cause Corruption** and how does it occur?

Notes

1. G. Dean, P. Bell, and M. Lauchs, "Conceptual Framework for Managing Knowledge of Police Deviance," *Policing and Society* 20, no. 2 (2010): 204–22.
2. C. Murphy and P.F. McKenna, "Rethinking Police Governance, Culture, and Management: A Summary Review of the Literature" (Ottawa: Task Force on Governance and Cultural Change in the RCMP, Public Safety Canada, 2007), 7, http://www.publicsafety.gc.ca/rcmp-grc/_fl/eng/rthnk-plc-eng.pdf
3. B. Wright, "Civilianising the 'Blue Code'? An Examination of Attitudes to Misconduct in the Extended Police Family," *International Journal of Police Science and Management* 12, no. 3 (2008): 339–56.
4. J. Manis, C.A. Archbold, and K.D. Hassell, "Exploring the Impact of Police Officer Education Level on Allegations of Police Misconduct," *International Journal of Police Science and Management* 10, no. 4 (2008): 509–23.
5. C.J. Harris, "Problem Officers? Analyzing Problem Behavior Patterns from a Large Cohort," *Journal of Criminal Justice* 38, no. 2 (2010): 216–25.
6. Dean, Bell, and Lauchs, "Conceptual Framework."
7. Canada, House of Commons, "Restoring the Honor of the RCMP: Addressing Problems in the Administration of the RCMP's Pension and Insurance Plans," Report of the Standing Committee on Public Accounts, Ottawa, 2007, 3, http://www.parl.gc.ca/HousePublications/Publication.aspx?DocId=3188528&Language=E&Mode=1&Parl=39&Ses=2
8. S. Rothlein, "Noble Cause Corruption," *PATC Newsletter* (2008), http://www.srassociatesinc.org/files/noble-cause-corruption.pdf
9. Ibid., 2.
10. T.J. Martinelli, "Unconstitutional Policing: The Ethical Challenges in Dealing with Noble Cause Corruption," *The Police Chief* 73, no. 10 (2006): 16–22.
11. B. Hutchinson, "What Does the Force Do with a Wayward Mountie?" *National Post*, December 12, 2009, A9.
12. Mr. Justice T.R. Braidwood (Commissioner), "WHY? The Robert Dziekanski Tragedy" (Victoria: Attorney General of British Columbia, 2010), http://www.braidwoodinquiry.ca/report/P2Report.php
13. Ibid., 12.
14. Ibid., 13.
15. Ibid., 14.
16. U.S. Department of Justice, "Investigation of the New Orleans Police Department" (Washington: Civil Rights Division, 2011), 1, http://www.justice.gov/crt/about/spl/nopd_report.pdf

17. Ibid.

18. T.J. Martinelli, "Minimizing Risk by Defining Off-Duty Police Misconduct," *The Police Chief* 74, no. 6 (2007): 40–45.

19. British Columbia, *Police Act,* "Code of Professional Conduct Regulation," B.C. Reg. 205/98, Section 16, 1998, http://www.qp.gov.bc.ca/police/r205_98.htm

20. R.J. Marin (Chair), "Discussion Paper 7: Off-Duty Conduct" (Ottawa: RCMP External Review Committee, 2010), http://www.erc-cee.gc.ca/publications/discussion/dp7-eng.aspx

21. Ibid., 9.

22. S.E. Wolfe and A.R. Piquero, "Organizational Justice and Police Misconduct," *Criminal Justice and Behavior* 38, no. 4 (2011): 332–53.

23. J.M. Pollock and H.E. Williams, 2012, "Using Ethical Dilemmas in Police Training," in *Justice, Crime, and Ethics,* ed. M.C. Braswell, B.R. McCarthy, and B.J. McCarthy (Cincinnati: Anderson, 2012), 91–109 at 93.

24. S.J. Ellwanger, "How Police Officers Learn Ethics," in *Justice, Crime, and Ethics*, ed. M.C. Braswell, B.R. McCarthy, and B.J. McCarthy (Cincinnati: Anderson, 2012), 45–69 at 45.

Chapter

8

Models of Police Work

Learning Objectives

After reading this chapter, you should be able to:

- Discuss the principles and effectiveness of the professional model of police work

- Define and discuss the principles of community policing

- Compare and contrast the professional model of police work and community policing

- Discuss what is meant by the organizational, external, and tactical elements of community policing

- Describe public attitudes, images, and expectations of the police

- Discuss the role of volunteers in community policing

- Describe the challenges in involving the community in policing

- Discuss the effectiveness of community policing

Key Terms

clearance rate   194

community engagement   199

community policing   197

external elements
(of community
policing)   203

organizational elements
(of community
policing)   200

police legitimacy   206

professional model of police
work   193

three P's of community
policing   197

three R's of professional
police work   193

zone (team or turf)
policing   203

THE PROFESSIONAL MODEL OF POLICE WORK

In the discussion of the history of police work in Chapter 1, it was noted that the **professional model of police work** emerged during the mid-twentieth century. This model (also referred to as the military model) was driven by the development of mobile patrol and radio communication systems as well as by the growth and centralization of police services.

The professional model of police work is based on **three R's:** *random patrol, rapid response,* and *reactive investigation.* The central premise of random patrol—also known as the *watch system*—is that the mere presence and visibility of patrol cars serves as a deterrent to crime and at the same time makes citizens feel safer. During a typical shift, patrol officers respond to calls and spend the rest of the time patrolling randomly, waiting for the next call for service. In this model of policing, any information gathered by the police is limited to specific situations and does not include analysis of the problems that precipitate crime and disorder. Little attention is paid to proactive police interventions that might prevent crime and address the underlying causes of crime in communities. Patrol operations are based on a hierarchical military model that is highly centralized; command-and-control principles are emphasized; and the range of police response options is narrow. Little effort is made to consider the needs of specific neighbourhoods or to involve community residents in identifying and addressing crime and social disorder.[1] This approach to police work is:

- *incident oriented*—the focus is on responding to specific incidents, calls, cases, or events;
- *response oriented*—police leaders and operations are mobilized and oriented to respond to events as they arise; response capacity and capability are emphasized; little time and few resources are devoted to proactive intervention or prevention activities; *and*
- *lacking in analysis*—rapid response with available resources becomes the priority; as a result, information gathering is limited to specific situations and analyses do not focus on the problems that precipitate events.

> **professional model of police work**
> a model of police work that emerged during the mid-twentieth century that was based on the three R's

> **three R's of professional police work**
> random patrol, rapid response, and reactive investigation, which are the basis of the professional model of police work

The Effectiveness of the Professional Model of Police Work

It is difficult to assess the professional model of police work. Little information is available on how patrol officers conducting random patrols spend their time, on the amount of time officers spend responding to calls for service (reactive or "allocated" patrol time), and on how much "unallocated" time patrol officers have for proactive police work. Without this sort of information, it is difficult to determine how effective the deployment of officers is, whether additional police resources are required, and what alternative strategies for resource allocation and officer deployment might be available.

This model of patrol deployment enables close supervision of patrol officers. However, it has a number of serious deficiencies. There is little consideration of community needs. Also, patrol officers are not assigned to specific areas for defined periods of time, which makes it hard for them to become familiar with the issues in the community. This in turn hinders the development of police–community partnerships and stifles creativity among patrol officers. In the words of one retired senior officer: "Traditional police work becomes an unknown police officer patrolling familiar buildings and unfamiliar faces" (personal communication with author).

In the early 1970s, questions were being raised about the effectiveness of random mobile patrol in preventing and reducing crime. In a landmark study known as the Kansas City Preventive Patrol Experiment, fifteen areas of that city were divided into three groups: (1) reactive beats, in which police did not engage in preventative patrol and officers were instructed to respond only to calls for service; (2) control beats, in which routine preventative patrol was maintained at the usual level of one car per beat; and (3) proactive beats, in which routine preventative patrol was intensified to two or three times the usual levels.[2]

The results of the experiment suggested that neither doubling patrol coverage nor eliminating it has any significant impact on reported crime, actual victimizations, fear of crime, or citizen satisfaction with the police. As well, random, preventative patrol does not help reduce crime and disorder, nor does it facilitate the development of partnerships with the community.

This lack of impact is due, in part, to the fact that many of the incidents to which the police respond are only symptoms of broader problems in the community. When the police respond *only* when they are called and deal *only* with the incident at hand, the reasons *why* the incident occurred in the first place remain unaddressed, which increases the likelihood of similar incidents happening again. One observer commented this way on the results from Kansas City: "It makes about as much sense to have police patrol routinely in cars to fight crime as it does to have firemen patrol routinely in fire trucks to fight fires."[3] Furthermore, this model of patrol may contribute to low officer morale and high levels of dissatisfaction with policing as a career.

A persistent measure of police performance that is grounded in the professional model of police work is the "catch" or **clearance rate.** This rate is, in effect, the percentage of cases in which an offence has been committed and a suspect identified, regardless of whether the suspect is ultimately convicted of a crime.

Even with the emergence of community policing (discussed below), most police services continue to assess performance by crime rates and, more specifically, by percentage increases or decreases in levels of specific types of crime. Clearance rates are generally quite low for nonviolent offences and are not an especially good indicator of the effectiveness of police work. More specifically:

1. *Police officers do not spend most of their time chasing criminals.* In fact, they spend most of it on nonenforcement activities such as maintaining order, providing services, and preventing crime.
2. *Not all police officers work in the same types of communities.* Some officers are assigned to remote and rural areas; others work in suburban and urban areas. The levels and types of crime in these areas vary, which means that police officers are confronted with different types of problems and situations.
3. *Not all police officers engage in the same type of police work.* This makes it unfair to use only one measure of police effectiveness.
4. *The use of clearance rates precludes any assessment of the attitudes and expectations of community residents or any determination of community involvement in the prevention of or response to crime.*

> **clearance rate**
>
> the percentage of cases in which an offence has been committed and a suspect identified, regardless of whether the suspect is ultimately convicted of a crime

Another measure often used to assess the effectiveness of the police is crime rates. These are problematic as well. Rising crime rates can reflect either good or poor police performance: when official crime rates go down, the police are generally credited with doing a good job; when official crime rates go up, the police are seen as doing a poor job. Yet increases in the official crime rate can also indicate *good* police performance, since they may reflect an increase in the number of criminals apprehended and an increase in the number of calls received from a supportive public. For these reasons, police performance should not be judged solely on crime control types of measures. Relying solely on official crime statistics fails to capture the multifaceted role of the police; it also ignores the fact that crime rates are a function of a variety of social, economic, political, and individual offender factors. Developing appropriate measures of police performance for police work is one of the major challenges facing Canadian police services.

Research File 8.1 sets out some key findings with respect to the effectiveness of the professional model of police work.

Research File 8.1

The Effectiveness of the Professional Model of Police Work

Question: Does an increase in random police patrols have an impact on crime levels?
Answer: Probably not. While studies attempting to assess this dimension of police crime prevention have many methodological problems, research generally has recorded no appreciable impact from an increase in random patrol.

Question: Are police response times related to reduced crime levels?
Answer: Not likely. Reduced response times seem to have little impact on crime rates. However, it is possible that quick police response to serious crimes and emergencies can increase the likelihood that the offender will be apprehended, that crime scene evidence will be preserved, and that information will be gathered from witnesses and complainants. Rapid response may also protect lives and reduce the risk of serious injury to crime victims. Police services whose response times to serious incidents approach the best practice benchmark of seven minutes may also enjoy higher levels of legitimacy (see below, and Chapter 5).

Question: Is there a relationship between the number of arrests the police make and the crime rate? In other words, do reactive arrests serve as a general deterrent to crime?
Answer: No. Reactive police arrests do not serve as a general deterrent to criminal activity. The exception may be in communities of fewer than 10,000 residents, but even here the research findings are inconsistent.

Question: Does any relationship exist between the reactive arrest of specific individuals and the crime rate? In other words, are reactive arrests a specific deterrent to crime?
Answer: Generally not, with a few possible exceptions, e.g., chronic offenders. For many individuals, arrest increases subsequent reoffending. Unemployed people who are arrested tend to reoffend, whereas for employed people, arrest seems to act as a deterrent.

Source: "Preventing Crime: What Works, What Doesn't, What's Promising." Published by the National Institute of Justice, US Department of Justice, 1997.

COMMUNITY POLICING IN THE TWENTY-FIRST CENTURY

In Chapter 1 you learned that in Canada, the concept of community policing re-emerged during the 1980s. This development was precipitated in part by evidence that the professional model of police work generally was doing little to prevent and respond to crime and disorder in communities. However, the adoption of the principles and practices of community policing across Canada has been uneven. There has often been a considerable gap between the rhetoric and the reality of community policing. Part of this gap is a result of vagueness regarding what community policing actually is. Part of it reflects the fact that methods for assessing whether a police service is a "community policing service" are still being developed. Yet another factor hindering the adoption of community policing has been resistance to this model from the police themselves; their view, which often prevails, is that enforcement and public security is their priority and that they don't have enough time to do community policing. That priority has been strengthened even more since the 9/11 attacks on New York City and Washington.

What *Is* Community Policing?

Hundreds of books, articles, and reports have been written about community policing, yet it remains poorly defined and is the subject of considerable debate—and confusion—among scholars, politicians, and the police. As of this writing, police services vary greatly in the extent to which they have adopted the principles and practices of community policing. Trendy terms are applied to traditional practices, and new policing programs are developed in the absence of a new framework for delivering them.

Over the past two decades, the term has come to refer to both a philosophy of police work and the mechanics of police operations. Any definition of community policing needs to acknowledge that this model of police work incorporates many elements of traditional policing; at the same time, though, it expands the role, activities, and objectives of police services and patrol officers. As a concept, community policing has the following features:

1. *It is an organizational strategy and philosophy.* Community policing is based on the idea that the police and the community must work together as equal partners in order to identify, prioritize, and solve problems such as crime, drugs, fear of crime, social and physical disorder, and neighbourhood decay. The goal is to improve the overall quality of life in the area.
2. *It requires a department-wide commitment.* Community policing requires all personnel in the police service—both civilians and sworn members—to balance the need to maintain an effective police response to incidents of crime with the goal of exploring proactive initiatives aimed at solving problems before they arise or escalate.
3. *It rests on decentralizing and personalizing police services.* Decentralization gives line officers the opportunity, freedom, and mandate to focus on community building as well as community-based problem solving, so that each and every neighbourhood can become a better place in which to live and work.[4]

Community policing involves much more than introducing new programs to a community: it requires substantial changes in how police services are organized and delivered, as well as an expansion of the roles and responsibilities of officers. The implementation of a community policing model has significant implications for a police service—for its mission, structure, leadership, and personnel—as well as for the community.

Community policing can thus be defined as a philosophy, a management style, and an organizational strategy centred on police–community partnerships and problem solving to address the conditions that contribute to crime, social disorder, and fear of crime in communities.

The differences between community policing and the professional model of police work with respect to relationships with the community are outlined in Figure 8.1.

community policing
a philosophy of policing centred on police–community partnerships and problem solving

The Principles of Community Policing

Community policing is based on the **three P's:** *prevention, problem solving,* and *partnership* (with the community). The basic idea is that the police and the community constitute a partnership that brings together the resources and talents of each to identify and solve problems. The key principles of community policing include the following:

three P's of community policing
prevention, problem solving, and partnership

- Citizens are responsible for becoming actively involved in identifying and responding to problems in their neighbourhoods and communities.
- The community is a source of operational information and crime control knowledge for the police.
- Police are more directly accountable to the community.
- Police have a proactive and preventative role in the community that goes beyond traditional law enforcement.
- The cultural and gender mix of a police agency should reflect the community it serves.
- The operational structure of the police agency should facilitate broad consultation on strategic and policing issues.
- To gain the confidence and trust of the community, the police must establish and maintain their legitimacy through proactive initiatives and the fair treatment of residents.[5]

Although the activities of community policing have expanded considerably since the 1980s (see below), police observers have pointed out that community policing is *not:*

- a panacea for solving all of a community's problems of crime and disorder;
- a generic, "one size fits all" policing model that can be applied without adaptation to the specific needs of communities across the country;
- a program or series of initiatives that can be imposed on a traditional, hierarchical police organizational structure; *or*

FIGURE 8.1   Police–Community Relations, Community Partnership versus Justice Process

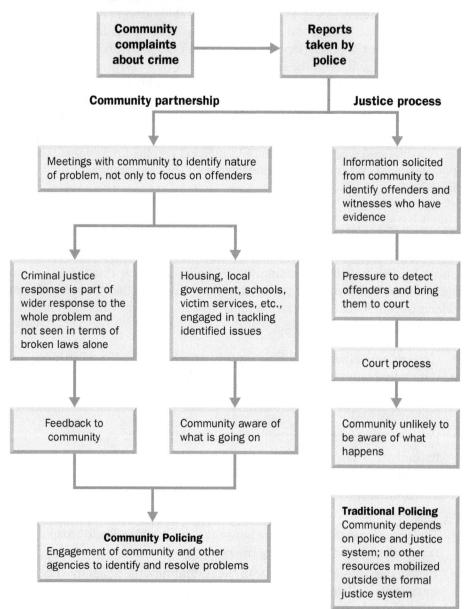

Source: C.G. Nicholl, "Community Policing, Community Justice, and Restorative Justice: Exploring the Links for the Delivery of a Balanced Approach to Public Safety" (Washington: Office of Community Oriented Policing Services, U.S. Department of Justice, 1999), 50, http://www .cops.usdoj/gov/files/ric/Publications/e09990014_web.pdf

- a substitute for having the capability in a police service to fight more sophisticated types of criminal activity (although even these strategies may be more effective if there are police links with agencies and community residents).

Community policing addresses crime and social disorder through traditional law enforcement measures but also through prevention, problem solving,

community engagement, and partnerships. The community policing model balances reactive responses to calls for service with proactive problem solving centred on the causes of crime and disorder. Table 8.1 compares the professional and community-based models of police work.

The most current version of community policing incorporates a number of proactive, enforcement-oriented approaches to strategic partnerships with the community as well as the use of analysis to identify crime trends and "hot spots." Note that in both models of police work, patrol officers are often reactive; that is, they respond to calls from citizens. A major difference is how the officers approach the calls to which they have been dispatched: an officer with a community policing orientation is likely to take a broader view of the situation and, if necessary, access additional resources from the community and/or other agencies to address the problem.

A number of police observers have asked whether the founding principles of community policing are being compromised as a result of the increasing emphasis on security. The Canadian police scholar Chris Murphy, for example, has argued that there has been a "securitization" of community policing, in the sense that community policing is increasingly being used as a security strategy. Under this approach, the community is viewed as "a strategic resource, a source of security information and intelligence."[6]

In Murphy's view this trend is undermining the local origins of community policing and is posing challenges for police and communities. Specifically, how are police to "balance the tensions between state security and local policing needs, between individual and collective rights, and community collaboration and the problematic nature of 'community' in a security context"?[7] American studies have found that most police chiefs think it is possible to balance

> **community engagement**
> police strategies that facilitate the involvement of citizens and communities in initiatives to address crime and social disorder

TABLE 8.1	Comparison of the Professional and Community-Based Strategic Models of Police Work	
	Professional Model	**Community Policing Model**
Administrative approach (locus of control)	Centralized/hierarchical	Decentralized with strong management and organizational support
Authority	Statute	Community/statute
Community role	Report violations of the law; passive	Strategic partnerships, formalized by protocols and agreements, which integrate into police operations
Operational focus	Crime and disorder	Crime and disorder; national security; quality of life; fear of crime and disorder
Operational strategies	Random patrol; reactive investigation; rapid response	Targeted/directed patrol focused on "hot spots"; strategic partnerships; integrated service delivery; intelligence-led policing; ongoing evaluation; problem-based deployment of personnel

community policing with close attention to security threats.[8] A cynic might argue that security concerns are "where the money is"—that is, a source of new funding in times of fiscal restraint—and thus will only increase the focus on crime control. This further highlights the tensions surrounding policing in a democratic society (see Chapter 2). To date, no studies have been conducted that might tell us how effective the more security-oriented initiatives of police services are in countering threats to public safety.

The emerging trend toward security issues has been accompanied by an increase in the number of specialty units operated by police services. Most community policing programs are staffed by uniformed patrol officers; in contrast, most specialty units are composed of plainclothes officers, who typically work in a manner that is less visible (if not invisible) to the general public. The effectiveness of these units has been little examined. Pertinent questions are these: Has increasing the number of plainclothes officers reduced the capacity of police services to deploy uniformed officers in marked patrol vehicles? And has it weakened community policing initiatives?

For purposes of discussion in this chapter and in Chapter 9, we will be using the term "community policing." Be mindful throughout, though, of the increasing focus on crime attack strategies and the trend toward specialization. These factors may be contributing to an increasing centralization of police services—a centralization that runs counter to the principle of community policing that emphasizes decentralized service delivery. We can expect the community policing model to continue to evolve in the coming years.

The Core Elements of Community Policing

Perhaps the best way to capture the wide range of organizational, operational, and community partnership activities that are now included under the rubric of community policing is to identify the model's core elements. Those core elements can be grouped under three headings: organizational, external, and tactical.[9] This chapter considers the organizational and external elements of community policing; the tactical elements are examined in Chapter 9.

Table 8.2 lists the core elements of community policing, some of the attributes of each, and examples of the police strategies associated with each.

ORGANIZATIONAL ELEMENTS OF COMMUNITY POLICING

organizational elements (of community policing)
how a police service is structured to implement community policing

The **organizational elements of community policing** centre on how the police service itself is structured. A police service crafts a mission/vision statement; identifies core values that reflect the principles of community policing; alters its command and control structures to provide line-level officers with greater autonomy; changes how it deploys patrol officers in response to demands for service; encourages police–community partnerships and problem solving; and develops capacities to analyze information, which it can then use to increase its effectiveness and efficiency.

TABLE 8.2   The Core Elements, Attributes, and Strategies of Community Policing

Core element	Attributes	Strategies
Organizational	Community policing philosophy adopted organization-wide and reflected in mission/vision/core value statements, policies, procedures, and operations Decentralized decision making; patrol officers given the discretion to solve problems and to make operational decisions Fixed geographic accountability; the majority of staffing, command, deployment, and tactical decisions are geographically based; personnel are assigned to fixed geographic areas for extended periods of time Use of volunteers and active encouragement for citizens to become involved in police-sponsored initiatives and activities Use of technology and analytical capacities to facilitate information generation and effective allocation of departmental resources	Community police stations and storefronts Zone/turf/team policing Evidence-based policing Recruitment and deployment of volunteers Organizational reform
External	Public involvement and community partnerships Partnerships with governments and other agencies	Police partnerships with key community stakeholders Private sector initiatives
Tactical	Enforcement of law Proactive crime prevention Problem-solving	Crime prevention Problem-oriented policing Intelligence-led policing/Compstat Zero tolerance policing Quality-of-life policing Integrated service teams Neighbourhood service teams Crime attack strategies Community service approaches

Source: U.S. Department of Justice, "Community Policing Defined" (Washington: Office of Community Oriented Policing Services [COPS], 2005), http://www.cops.usdoj.gov/default.asp?Item=36

Mission Statements, Vision Statements, and Core Values

Mission statements (or vision statements) generally refer to the key elements of community policing, which include crime prevention and police–community partnerships. They also emphasize both public safety and the accountability of the police. That said, one should not necessarily assume that the actual practices of a police service reflect its mission/vision statement (see At Issue 8.2).

Redesigning the Organizational Structure

Community policing presents police leaders with a formidable management challenge. The transitions required for community policing include the following:

From	To
bureaucratic management	strategic management
administrative management	people management
maintenance management	change management

An organizational environment must be created in which the ideas and requirements of line-level officers can be incorporated into decision making. This in turn requires a decentralization of decision making. Also, line-level officers must be given more autonomy to work collaboratively with community residents. In addition, bureaucracy of the sort that often hinders officer initiative must be reduced; this means reducing the levels of management and supervision in ways that continue to hold patrol officers accountable.

Community policing requires police leaders to abandon traditional command-and-control practices and to decentralize power in order to create a more participatory organizational environment. The focus shifts away from achieving the goals set by senior managers toward building communities and solving problems. The task of senior police managers is to provide leadership and support for the patrol officers who are implementing the principles of community policing every day. Put another way, implementing community policing requires police services to "invert the pyramid" (see Figure 8.2).

FIGURE 8.2   Inverting the Police Pyramid

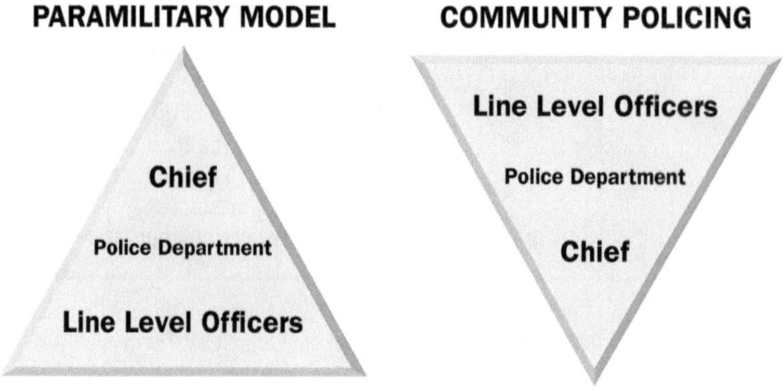

PARAMILITARY MODEL

Chief

Police Department

Line Level Officers

COMMUNITY POLICING

Line Level Officers

Police Department

Chief

Source: This model was published in *Community Policing: How to Get Started* by R. Trojanowicz and B. Bucqueroux, pp. 83–84. Copyright Elsevier (1998).

Zone Policing

A community policing model also requires a police service to alter the ways in which patrol officers are deployed. Many police services use **zone** (or **team,** or **turf**) **policing** to ensure the geographic stability of patrol; this entails assigning permanent teams of police to small neighbourhood areas. This can maximize the collaboration of patrol officers as well as improve police–community relationships. Many patrol supervisors encourage their officers to be proactive and to develop projects that target specific problems in their areas, including problem premises (addresses that receive repeated police attention) and chronic offenders (e.g., offenders who are committing property crimes). In the words of one staff sergeant: "I expect my patrol teams to develop and implement projects on an ongoing basis" (personal communication).

> **zone (team or turf) policing**
> a deployment strategy designed to enhance community policing

THE EXTERNAL ELEMENTS OF COMMUNITY POLICING

The ability of the police to perform their duties depends upon public approval of their actions.

SIR ROBERT PEEL

The police can be effective only to the extent that they establish and sustain partnerships with the community. A key feature of community policing is networking with community groups and organizations as well as with the private sector and with other government agencies at the municipal, provincial, and federal levels. These are the **external elements of community policing.** The police must also develop strategies to involve more marginalized community residents on a permanent basis. Otherwise, these residents may feel that police interventions are targeting them and, as a result, develop a sense that the police are intruding on their neighbourhoods. In many provinces there are policing standards that mandate police services to consult with communities.

> **external elements (of community policing)**
> police–community partnerships and initiatives that enhance community policing and increase police legitimacy, visibility, and accessibility

Police–community partnerships may have more general objectives, such as improving the quality of life in the community; or they may be directed toward specific issues in specific neighbourhoods, such as problem premises, street-level drug trafficking, or traffic problems.

Police services must also find ways to determine community priorities and to solicit feedback from community residents (including complainants and victims) regarding their experiences with and satisfaction with the police.

Police–Community Partnerships

A review of individual police service websites reveals a myriad of partnerships designed to strengthen police–community relations, enhance efforts to address problems of crime and disorder, and improve the overall quality of life in communities. The Ottawa Police Service, for example, is involved in a variety of community partnerships throughout the city, including the following:

- *Somali Youth Basketball League (SYBL).* This is a volunteer, not-for-profit basketball league intended to provide a safe environment for Somali youth, where they can develop life and leadership skills and benefit from positive role models.

- *Police Youth Centre.* This centre provides a wide range of counselling services, sports and recreation programs, and leadership programs for children and youth between ages six and nineteen. As well, the centre works with parents and parents' groups to address the challenges faced by youth in the community.
- *Street Ambassador Program.* In this program, volunteers, who wear shirts and name tags identifying themselves as ambassadors, serve as a front line resource for tourists in the ByWard Market area and work with community organizations (http://www.ottawapolice.ca).

Other programs involving the police and the community are discussed in Chapter 9.

Canadian police services operate a variety of facilities designed to increase police visibility in the community as well as to provide access to the general public. These include community police centres and storefronts, which are staffed largely by civilian employees and volunteers. These sites serve as places for community residents to file complaints and information about individual and community problems; they also serve as information and referral sources. Several police services also operate fully functional "mini"–police stations staffed by sworn and civilian personnel. The officers assigned to a community police station are responsible for a defined territory and conduct patrol and investigative operations from these stations.

Few studies have been conducted about the impact of community police centres, and the ones that have been done have not been encouraging. There is no evidence that these centres help reduce levels of crime and social disorder. Nor is there any indication that these centres have been a catalyst for sustainable police–community partnerships. It may be more productive for police to focus on specific activities such as problem solving; and to explore alternative strategies for developing police–community partnerships.

Police services have tried various other approaches to connecting with community organizations and residents. The Edmonton Police Service, for example, has neighbourhood empowerment teams (NETs), which operate in at-risk neighbourhoods. The NETs focus on two things: developing community partnerships and community capacities to prevent and respond to crime and social disorder; and improving social development in communities. NETs operate storefront offices to provide a police presence in their communities. There is strong support for the program among community residents, and the program has resulted in improved attitudes toward the police, especially among minority groups. The impact on crime rates is less conclusive, although the NET program does appear to have improved the quality of life in the communities in which it operates.[10]

In addition, police services and officers across the country involve themselves in a wide range of charitable events. These raise money for important causes; they also allow officers to contribute to the community and to meet community residents in a non–law enforcement capacity. Among the more high-profile initiatives are Cops for Cancer, which encompasses a range of fundraising activities. For example, officers allow their heads to be shaved for donations; and they participate in multiday cycling events, during which officers stop in communities to raise funds for cancer research.

Police officers on a Cops for Cancer bike ride.

Community Consultation

For community policing to succeed, the residents must be involved in identifying problems of crime and disorder and in generating solutions to those problems. When solutions are developed by police and imposed on the community, they generally fail. The most effective strategies are likely to be the ones that are aimed at increasing community engagement. Successful strategies include conducting foot patrols, which enable the police to develop relationships with residents and businesses; responding to requests for service in a professional manner; and communicating information on police initiatives in effective ways.[11]

The idea is for citizens to network within their communities and to assume ownership of problem-solving strategies. This requires an understanding of the factors that affect public perceptions of the police, as well as strategies for developing and sustaining police–community partnerships.

Community consultation can take a number of forms. Police–community meetings provide a forum where the problems and concerns of community residents can be identified and where strategies can be developed for addressing them. However, community meetings are generally not effective when the goal is to mobilize residents and to strengthen confidence in the police. These meetings are often attended by only a few community members, including those who are representing specific interests. At-risk groups and visible minorities are less likely to attend.

Community consultation committees (often called community–police liaison committees) are another strategy for police services to develop partnerships with the community. The Toronto Police Service has a liaison committee for every police division in the city. These committees include community residents and police representatives, who work together to identify and prioritize local issues and to develop solutions. They play an especially important role in fostering positive relationships with diverse groups in the community, including visible minorities and the G/L/B/T communities (see Chapter 11).

The RCMP uses the Annual Performance Plan (APP) as a way to secure community input into policing plans and priorities at the individual detachment level. An APP is developed every year by the detachment commander and includes information on (1) the detachment, (2) community consultation and infrastructure, (3) risk and protective factors, (4) community issues, and (5) the detachment work plan. The effectiveness of the APP in facilitating community consultation, however, has not been studied. A major challenge for all police services is to develop effective strategies for community consultation, which can be time-consuming and resource-intensive.

THE COMMUNITY AND COMMUNITY POLICING

Though many police services have adopted community policing, the presence of police officers on the street is still most often associated with a troublesome incident. When we see a police car parked by the road or police officers talking to someone on the sidewalk, our initial thought is "What's the trouble?" "Who's in trouble?" "What did he/she do?" The general public has become so conditioned to the idea that police officers spend most of their time responding to crime and chasing criminals that their presence is likely to be taken as a sign that a criminal act has occurred. The possibility that there is nothing wrong—that the police officers are having a normal conversation with people who are not suspects, and that the police presence is a normal part of community life—may not even be considered.

The routine work of police officers is less visible. That work includes police officers in high schools working to build relationships with teenagers; or in community police stations helping homeless people access social services; or in the Canadian North participating in sentencing circles and helping residents revitalize their communities.

A common theme in the community policing literature is **police legitimacy.** This has to do with the collective actions taken by the police to strengthen citizens' trust and confidence in them. Community policing initiatives enjoy much greater success when the community trusts and has confidence in the police. Police legitimacy, however, is fragile, and it can be undermined by high-profile incidents, including those that involve the misuse of force and police corruption.

> **police legitimacy**
> the collective actions taken by the police to enhance the levels of trust and confidence that citizens have in the police

What Does the Public Think about the Police?

This is a simple question to ask but a difficult one to answer. The most accurate response to it is: it depends. Canadians generally express low levels of confidence in the criminal justice system, yet they have traditionally given the police high approval ratings. However, public trust in the police has declined in recent years; one national poll found that between 2003 and 2011, police officers' ratings on the trust survey had declined from 73 percent to 57 percent.[12] It is likely that a number of high-profile incidents, including the death of Robert

Dziekanski at the Vancouver International Airport in 2007 and the events surrounding the G8/G20 Summit in Toronto in 2010, have contributed to this decline. As one officer stated, "When a critical incident like YVR happens, we all wear it" (personal communication). As well, there is evidence of perennial distrust of the police in many visible minority and Aboriginal communities (see Chapter 11).[13]

Caution should be exercised in accepting the results of public opinion surveys about the police. There are significant problems with how the data are gathered. Surveys about attitudes toward the police often ask people who have little or no personal contact with them and tend to underrepresent youth (including at-risk youth), persons in conflict with the law, and visible minorities.

Focus groups are a much better strategy for gathering information from community residents. These sessions involve small groups representing various segments of the community (e.g., youth, the elderly, visible minorities, Aboriginal persons). The sessions provide an opportunity for these people to discuss their experiences and attitudes toward the police as well as to suggest how police–community relations can be improved. These sessions can include segments of the community who are at risk of involvement in the legal system and/or who distrust the police, whatever their reasons.

Participants in focus group sessions held as part of an environmental scan conducted by the Toronto Police Service found that most of those who had contact with the police felt they had been treated fairly and with respect. The most common concerns expressed related to the perception that the officer(s) did not take the situation seriously and/or had a bad attitude. Troubling, however, was that relative to previous scans, there had been a decline in the number of participants who perceived that the police were trustworthy. One finding of concern was that only 57 percent of high school students felt comfortable speaking with the police: for others, interacting with the police made them nervous that they would be viewed as a snitch.[14]

Community Expectations of the Police

Less positive views of the police may be due, in part, to unrealistic expectations on the part of the public. The increasing demands on police services, combined with fiscal challenges, have contributed to the demise of full-service policing. Citizens in communities that are disordered tend to express lower levels of confidence in the police, reflecting the perception that the police are least partly responsible for the disorder and crime.[15] Of all of the agencies in the criminal justice system, community residents tend to hold the police most responsible for neighbourhood disorder.[16]

The reduced ability of the police to respond to all of the demands of a community or neighbourhood may lead to frustration and to residents "taking the law into their own hands." This happened in a case involving a grocer in Toronto who apprehended a thief who had repeatedly victimized his and other businesses in the neighbourhood (see At Issue 8.2).

On the flipside, the inability of the police alone to address issues in the community can also be a catalyst for police–community partnerships, when community residents become more involved in addressing issues relating to crime prevention and neighbourhood quality of life, instead of relying solely on the police.

Involving the Community: The Role of Volunteers

Citizen volunteers serve in a wide range of capacities—for example, they staff store-fronts, victim services units, and community policing committees; they participate in special police–community projects; they conduct citizen patrols, thus serving as extra "eyes and ears" for the police; and they serve as police auxiliary constables. Volunteers help the police develop partnerships with the community and are a means for the community to take ownership of problems. They are a continual source of new energy and fresh ideas; and, finally, they help reduce the workload on patrol officers. Police services generally offer a range of training programs for volunteers and have developed strategies for recruiting and retaining volunteers.

The Waterloo Regional Police Service, for example, provides a number of opportunities for volunteers, including the Children's Safety Village/Fire Prevention Centre, as well as programs like Neighbourhood Watch, Block Citizen Advisory Committee, and victim services. The Citizen Advisory Committee is made up of concerned citizens who offer input and support to the police service. Volunteers also serve as interpreters. The Children's Safety Village is a kid-sized replica of a community, complete with streets, traffic control devices, a railway crossing, and storefronts. Kids drive minicars through the village to learn about traffic safety (see photograph below).

The "Community" in Community Policing

Most discussions and research studies on community policing have focused on only one part of the police–community equation: the police. Little attention has been paid to the role and responsibilities of community residents in developing and implementing community policing. This lack of attention raises a number of problems, especially in terms of the *community* part of community policing.

Schoolchildren learn about traffic and safety in the Children's Safety Village, adjacent to the Waterloo Regional Police Headquarters.

First, it is one thing to declare that communities are actively responsible for policing themselves and quite another thing to bring this about. Who is responsible for ensuring that communities become involved? The police? The community? Municipal and provincial governments?

Second, while the term *community* arises quite often, the *who* and *what* of the community are rarely specified. Too often it is assumed that all of the community's residents have a common interest and live in the same neighbourhood. Little consideration is given to the opportunities and obstacles that arise in culturally and economically diverse communities in which there are many different neighbourhoods. The boundaries of policing zones have long been established by the police alone rather than by the police in consultation with community residents. Often these boundaries are arbitrary and are drawn to meet organizational rather than community needs. Needless to say, community residents may define the boundaries of their neighbourhoods quite differently from the way the police organization does.

Third, it is important to consider both the *level* of participation in a community and the *distribution* of that participation. In any community policing initiative, some parts of the community may be underrepresented; at the same time, members of certain community interest groups—for example, business owners—may be overrepresented relative to those of lower socioeconomic status. Little is understood about the factors that affect community involvement in policing. Ironically, the residents who are most likely to be policed are the same ones who are the least likely to have access to the police, to affect police policy and practice, and to participate in police–community initiatives.[17]

A fourth question to consider: What is the community supposed to do? Community residents may not understand clearly the principles of community policing and may, like police officers, equate it with crime prevention. Where community committees do exist, their roles and responsibilities are often not clearly defined, or they may focus on only one issue.

Finally, a key question, and one that has generally remained unaddressed in discussions of community policing, is this: Does the community *want* to become involved in police–community partnerships? Community residents may reject involvement in such partnerships for various reasons: apathy; fear of retaliation from the criminal element; hostility toward and distrust of the police; a lack of understanding as to what their role in these initiatives would be; and the diversity of needs among community residents. Furthermore, there is considerable variability among neighbourhoods in terms of their "amenability" to forming partnerships with the police and in terms of the resources the area can bring to efforts to address crime and disorder.

Once they understand that there are different types of neighbourhoods, with different capacities and levels of interest among the residents, police services can tailor their approaches to developing police–community partnerships according to neighbourhood conditions. Unfortunately, there is in Canada a paucity of best-practice materials on this topic.

A major challenge in all this is community representation. Most often, community participants are heavily middle class. The research on citizen involvement in neighbourhood crime prevention efforts indicates that volunteers tend to have higher incomes and more education; they also tend to own their own homes and to have lived in the area for a longer time.[18] Communities that are plagued with high rates of crime and social disorder may have less capacity to mobilize and sustain involvement in crime prevention initiatives with the police. This may be particularly difficult in rural and remote communities where the available pool of interested persons may be small.

IMPLEMENTING COMMUNITY POLICING: RHETORIC VERSUS REALITY

Despite the emergence of community policing in the mid-1980s, field research studies indicate that the professional model of police work is "alive and well" in many police services. The focus in these police services is on law enforcement and the generation of arrest statistics, and officers are provided with little incentive, or time to involve themselves in proactive, problem-solving initiatives.[19]

Police services still focus much of their attention and resources on enforcement, and performance measures for police services tend to centre on enforcement: crime rates, clearance rates, and annual percentage reductions in specific types of crime. This is due to a number of factors, including growing concerns with public safety and security as well as pressure from the community for aggressive law enforcement approaches to crime and criminal organizations, such as drug traffickers.

Police organizations can face a number of obstacles in implementing community policing:

- *The failure of senior police leaders to "walk the talk."* Senior officers may be unwilling to relinquish control, and may perceive that community policing is "soft on crime."

- *Resistance among line-level officers.* Some police officers simply do not believe in a community policing approach. Even when officers do subscribe to its principles, often they are not provided with organizational support for community policing initiatives. This can hinder the quality of service delivery.[20] Some police officers are much more oriented toward community policing than others. Many police officers feel that community policing is nothing new and that it has always been standard police practice. This is often suggested by officers who work in smaller communities, where they have always pursued a no-call-too-small policy.

Some officers remain committed to reactive, enforcement-oriented policing, even in the face of mounting evidence that this approach doesn't work. Other officers find themselves trapped in an endless cycle of calls for service from the public, which limits the time they can spend on proactive initiatives. In police services that have designated officers to pursue community policing initiatives, there may be resentment on the part of other officers who are required to pick up the slack with respect to responding to calls for service.[21] There may also be differences between the community and the police with respect to the importance given to community-oriented policing programs. Research studies suggest that residents often assign a higher priority to these types of programs than do officers.[22]

Officers may struggle to carry out the priorities and plans developed by senior supervisors. In the absence of a clear framework for implementation, officers may view community policing as merely adding to their workloads. While officers may contend that they don't have time to do community policing, recall from Chapter 5 that most calls for service are for order maintenance and service rather than for law enforcement.[23] In the absence of "time and task" studies that examine how patrol officers spend their time, it is difficult to determine what officers are busy "doing."

And even when the principles of community policing have been incorporated into mission and value statements as well as community development programs, the criteria for assessing officer performance may remain firmly grounded in the professional model of policing. Finally, in the absence of specific skill sets, officers may find it difficult to work directly with community residents in identifying and resolving problems, especially if they have been trained to do reactive, incident-driven police work.

- *Lack of participation by communities and neighbourhoods.* This may be a result of poor police–community relations, as characterized by mutual suspicion and distrust. The likelihood of residents participating in police–community partnerships seems to increase with levels of confidence in the police and with police legitimacy in the community.[24]

- *Lack of planning and analytical capacities in the police service.* Many police services still have not developed the capacity to plan, analyze, and evaluate their policies and practices on an ongoing basis. This makes it difficult for them to assess the outcomes of specific strategies and programs.

- *Failure to develop sustainable police–community partnerships.* This may be owing to a lack of police strategies to engage the community and to provide community residents and organizations with a substantive role in preventing and responding to crime and disorder.

- *Failure to identify the roles and responsibilities of communities and neighbourhoods.* It is largely unexplored just how communities and neighbourhoods can become involved in police–community partnerships, how community participation can be built and sustained, and how community performance can be assessed with regard to identifying and responding to crime and disorder. It should not be assumed that the same interventions will work in every area and in every situation: "The best practice for any community is one that fits their needs and conditions and is compatible with available resources."[25] Soliciting and sustaining the interest and participation of residents in community policing initiatives can be a time-consuming and resource-intensive enterprise. Generating and sustaining the interest and participation of residents in community policing initiatives can be a time-consuming and resource-intensive enterprise.

- *Organizational features of police services.* The organizational features of specific police services can hinder the development and implementation of community policing strategies. Provisions in collective bargaining agreements (e.g., the requirement for two-officer patrol cars) may limit senior managers' options when it comes to deploying officers. Also, recall from Chapter 2 the transfer policy of the RCMP, which results in officers being moved to new detachments on a regular basis. This practice has always been at odds with the requirements of community policing, for patrol officers, supervisors, and senior officers may not remain in any one detachment long enough to develop an intimate knowledge of the communities and neighbourhoods they are policing and to create sustainable police–community partnerships.

THE EFFECTIVENESS OF COMMUNITY POLICING

A review of the extensive research in the United States (there are few Canadian studies) tells us that it is possible for police services to adopt the principles of community policing; that community policing strategies may increase the legitimacy of the police in the community; and that such strategies may help the police and the community identify and target specific issues relating to crime and disorder.[26] Selected findings from studies that have examined the impact of community policing are presented in Research File 8.2.

Among police scholars, there are skeptics who contend that for many police services, community policing is still an "add-on"—that there has not been a significant shift in the culture of policing, nor has there been a change in how most

Research File 8.2

The Impact of Community Policing

Public-opinion surveys and field research studies have found the following:

- *Public attitudes toward community policing.* People like community policing. Community residents express greater satisfaction (often more than do police officers) with the community policing model than with the traditional model.

- *Programs and services.* Only a small number (generally less than 10%) of crime victims access programs and services for victims and community residents rarely use the services offered by community police stations.

- *Public complaints against the police.* There is no evidence that community policing reduces the number of complaints against the police.

- *Public confidence in the police.* Community policing increases public confidence and trust in the police. It also increases police legitimacy.

- *Fear of crime.* Community policing seems to have the potential to reduce fear of crime in communities. In particular, it seems to reduce the fear of crime when it is accompanied by higher levels of police–citizen interaction, such as foot patrols.

- *Reduction in levels of crime.* There is little evidence that community policing reduces crime, although some crime response strategies (discussed in Chapter 9) have been found to be effective. Community policing initiatives may lead residents to perceive that crime levels have fallen—a significant finding that may have a number of positive implications (e.g., increased community awareness and solidarity).

- *Community residents' perceptions of their neighbourhood.* There is some evidence that community policing leads residents to develop more positive perceptions of their neighbourhood and community as well as more positive attitudes toward the police.

- *The attitudes of police officers.* Researchers have found that community policing can increase the job satisfaction of police officers, as well as their productivity and their commitment to the organization. It can also improve relations with co-workers. In addition, officers develop more positive attitudes toward community residents and become more knowledgeable about the communities they police.

police resources are deployed. In the words of one police observer: "The vast majority of departments still expend most of their energies tracking traditional crime and enforcement statistics, rather than developing performance systems that track neighbourhood quality of life and problem-solving."[27]

Various means to measure the performance of Canadian police services in a community policing model have been developed in recent years, including the following:

- Levels of community and victim satisfaction with the police and feelings of safety, as measured by surveys.
- The success of a police service in achieving its stated goals and objectives and fulfilling its mission statement.
- The success of the police in achieving specific performance objectives, including a reduction in response times for 911 calls and effective target hardening and problem solving with respect to specific types of crime.
- The extent to which the police are involved in developing innovative programs to address issues relating to diversity, including G/L/B/T/communities, visible-minority communities, and Aboriginal communities.
- The degree to which the police are involved in interagency partnerships with social service agencies, nongovernmental organizations, and community groups.
- The nature and extent of involvement of community volunteers in various police programs and services.

Parting Thoughts on Community Policing

The causes of crime and disorder in any community are varied and complex. It is unrealistic to expect that the police alone—or even the police acting in concert with dedicated community residents—can reduce or eliminate all of society's problems. This requires that police services partner with the community and other agencies and organizations rather than going it alone, as was the case under the professional model of police work.

Community policing re-emerged in the 1980s in Canada and since then has undergone a significant transformation. Many police services have thoroughly restructured themselves. While working to develop and strengthen partnerships with the community, police services are also implementing a number of strategic approaches for targeting crime and disorder and for improving the quality of life in communities. These proactive strategies encompass a range of enforcement, order maintenance, and service-oriented activities that have often produced positive outcomes.

In many police services the long-standing discrepancy between how police services are organized and the actual demands made on those services has been reduced. As a model of police work, community policing holds considerable promise as a way to increase the effectiveness of the police, to involve the community in significant ways in identifying and responding to problems of crime and disorder, and to maximize police and community resources in times of increasing fiscal restraint. The extent to which concerns with safety and security will affect (and possibly undermine) the emphasis on localized policing remains to be seen and is certainly worth watching in the coming years.

The strategies a police service develops to implement community policing vary among communities as a function of the demands made on the police and the community's interest in and capacity for involvement. The strategies a community employs to become an equal partner in preventing and responding to crime and disorder depend on the personal and fiscal resources it can commit to the endeavour, as well as on the levels of interest that exist among different segments of the community. How to implement community policing, how to measure whether it is succeeding, and how to determine which initiatives the police and the community must take, are all questions that have yet to be answered. But we know that those answers must be arrived at on a community-by-community basis and that they must reflect the needs of the community in question and the outcomes of the dialogue between the police and community residents.

The increasing sophistication and globalization of crime means that police organizations must have access to the latest technologies as well as the officers who are technology-literate. The strategies for combating wire fraud, for example, are considerably different from those required to implement community policing at the neighbourhood level. This difference suggests that over the next decade, urban police services may be required to develop at least two separate divisions: one directed toward community policing, the other focused on sophisticated criminal activities.

At Issue 8.1

Of Vision and Mission Statements

Police services generally have Vision and Mission Statements that are prominently featured on their websites and print materials and even on patrol cars. These statements often include terms such as "community," "partnerships," and other community-policing related terms. Following are examples:

Halifax Regional Police

"Our Mission: Leading and Partnering in our Community to Serve and Protect"[a]

"Our Vision: Safety, Peace and Order in our Community"

http://www.halifax.ca/police

Winnipeg Police Service

"Vision: A safer community built on strong, trusting relationships."[b]

http://www.wps.ca

Nishnawbe-Aski Police Service (Ontario)

Mission Statement: "The mission of the Nishnawbe-Aski Police Service is to provide a unique, effective, efficient and culturally appropriate service to all people of the Nishnawbe-Aski area that will promote harmonious and healthy communities."[c]

http://www.naps.ca

RCMP

"Mission: The RCMP is Canada's national police service. Proud of our traditions and confident in meeting future challenges, we commit to preserve the peace, uphold the law and provide quality service in partnership with our communities."[d]

http://www.rcmp-grc.gc.ca

You Make the Call!

In discussing the implementation of community policing by police services, the police scholar Stephen Mastrofski has cautioned:

> Mission statements by themselves tell us little about the goals that the organizational really enacts. We learn more about the organization's commitment to the community-oriented missions by examining such things as how the organization routinely evaluates itself, how it evaluates and rewards its officers, and how it prepares them to answer the demands of community policing.[e]

Assume that you have been retained to analyze whether these police services have succeeded in achieving the objectives set out in their Mission/Vision Statements. What indicators of success would you use? What challenges would you encounter in developing measures of success?

Source: [a]Courtesy Halifax Regional Police Service
[b]"Vision: A safer community built on strong, trusting relationships."
[c]Courtesy Nishnawbe-Aski Police Services
[d]Reproduced with the permission of the RCMP.
[e]S. Mastrofski, "Community Policing: A Skeptical View," in *Police Innovation: Contrasting Perspectives,* ed. D.P. Rosenbaum and A.A. Braga (Cambridge: Cambridge University Press, 2006), 44–73 at 47.

At Issue 8.2

The Grocer and the Thief

In 2009, Toronto grocer David Chen and two of his employees at the Lucky Moose Food Mart in Toronto's Chinatown apprehended and detained Anthony Bennett, a career thief (forty-three convictions over thirty-three years). Earlier in the day, Bennett had stolen $60 worth of plants from the store. This had been captured on an in-store video camera, which Chen reviewed. Inexplicably, Bennett returned to the Lucky Moose store later in the day, at which point Chen and two store employees chased Bennett out of the store, caught him, tied him up, and put him in the back of a delivery van until police arrived.

Responding to 911 calls by bystanders who had witnessed the incident, the police arrested the three grocers and took them to the police station, where they were searched and held overnight until being granted bail. Bennett was charged with petty theft. Chen and his employees were charged with assault, forcible confinement, and carrying a concealed weapon. (Chen had a box cutter in his pocket for opening

(Continued)

cases of produce.) The latter two charges were dropped, and the Crown proceeded to trial on the assault charge. To secure his testimony at trial against Chen, Crown prosecutors struck a deal with Bennett, getting his sentence reduced by two-thirds.

Evidence introduced at trial indicated that the Toronto police often take hours to respond to calls of minor shoplifting. One day prior to the theft, Chen had phoned the police about another theft and it had taken five hours for the police to respond.

At trial, the Crown argued that Chen had violated the law and that, since Bennett had not committed a crime when he returned to the store, the citizen's arrest and the detention were unlawful. The trial judge acquitted the three men on the basis of reasonable doubt as to the events that occurred that day. In his ruling, the judge stated, "David Chen tried to fill a void where the justice system failed." Critics argued that the Crown should have never charged Chen in the first place.

While, legally, the case turned on whether Chen had the right to arrest Bennett, the larger issue is to what lengths a private citizen, in this case the owner of a grocery store, can go to protect his or her property. And what happens when a shopowner gets tired of being victimized and perceives that the justice system (the police in this case) are not available? A Toronto Police Service spokesperson stated that the police take theft seriously, but acknowledged that it was not a high priority.

You Make the Call!

1. In your view, should the police have charged Chen?
2. Do you think the Crown was correct in reaching a plea bargain with Bennett in exchange for his testimony?
3. Was the decision of the judge the correct one? If not, why not?

Key Points Review

1. The professional model of police work, centred on random patrol, rapid response, and reactive investigation, is not effective in preventing and responding to crime and disorder in communities.
2. Community policing can be defined as a philosophy, management style, and organizational strategy centred on police–community partnerships and problem solving to address problems of crime and disorder in communities.
3. The core elements of community policing are organizational, external, and tactical.
4. The organizational elements of community policing are centred on how the police service itself is structured and the requirements of a community policing police service.
5. The external elements of community policing involve the police service developing partnerships with the community and undertaking initiatives that increase police legitimacy, visibility, and accessibility.

6. Public trust in the police has eroded in recent years and public confidence in the police is necessary for police–community partnerships.
7. There are a number of potential obstacles to the community becoming involved in partnerships with the police, including public apathy and disinterest and variations in neighbourhood capacities.
8. There are a number of potential obstacles to implementing community policing relating to the police service and the community.

Key Term Questions

1. Describe the key features of the *professional model of police work,* including the *three R's.*
2. What is the *clearance rate,* and why are clearance rates not an especially good indicator of the effectiveness of police work?
3. Identify and discuss the philosophy and key principles of *community policing,* including the *three P's.*
4. What is *community engagement* and what role does it play in community policing?
5. Two core elements of community policing are *organizational* and *external.*
6. What is *team* (or *zone,* or *turf*) *policing,* and what role does it play in community policing?
7. What is meant by the term *police legitimacy* and why is it important in any discussion of community policing?

Notes

1. G.L. Kelling and M.H. Moore, "From Political to Reform to Community: The Evolving Strategy of Policing," in *Community Policing: Rhetoric or Reality?* ed. J.R. Greene and S.D. Mastrofski (New York: Praeger, 1988), 3–25.
2. G.L. Kelling, T. Pate, D. Dieckman, and C.E. Brown, *Kansas City Preventive Patrol Experiment* (Washington: Police Foundation, 1974).
3. C.B. Klockars, *Thinking About Police: Contemporary Readings* (New York: McGraw-Hill, 1983).
4. R. Trojanowicz and B. Bucqueroux, *Community Policing: How to Get Started,* 2nd ed. (Cincinnati: Anderson, 1998).
5. U.S. Department of Justice, "Community Policing Defined" (Washington: Office of Community Oriented Policing Services [COPS], 2005), http://www.cops.usdoj.gov/default.asp?Item=36
6. C. Murphy, "Securitizing Community Policing: Towards a Canadian Public Policing Model," *Canadian Review of Policing Research* 2, (2005): 25–31 at 25, 27.
7. Ibid., 29.
8. C. Jones and S.B. Supinski, "Policing and Community Relations in the Homeland Security Era," *Journal of Homeland Security and Emergency Management* 7, no. 1 (2010): 1–14.

9. U.S. Department of Justice, "Community Policing Defined."

10. M. Pauls, "An Evaluation of the Neighbourhood Empowerment Team (NET): Edmonton Police Service," *Canadian Review of Policing Research* 2, (2005): 19–23.

11. A. Rix, F. Joshua, M. Maguire, and S. Morton, "Improving Public Confidence in the Police: A Review of the Evidence." "Research Report 28" (London: Research, Development, and Statistics Directorate, Home Office, 2009), http://www.homeoffice.gov.uk/publications/science-research-statistics/research-statistics/police-research/horr28/horr50-report?view=Binary

12. Ipsos Reid, "A Matter of Trust," January 11, 2011, http://www.ipsos-na.com/news/client/act_dsp_internal_pdf.cfm?pdf=5100.pdf

13. C.D. O'Connor, "Citizen Attitudes Toward the Police in Canada," *Policing: An International Journal of Police Strategies and Management* 31, no. 4 (2008): 578–95.

14. Toronto Police Service, "2009 Update to the Environmental Scan," 2009, 99, http://www.torontopolice.on.ca/publications/files/reports/2009envscan.pdf

15. L. Cao, "Visible Minorities and Confidence in the Police," *Canadian Journal of Criminology and Criminal Justice* 53, no. 1 (2011), 1–26.

16. J. Sprott and A.N. Doob, "The Effect of Urban Neighborhood Disorder on Evaluations of the Police and Courts," *Crime and Delinquency* 55, no. 3 (2009): 339–62.

17. L. Ren, J.S. Zhao, N.P. Lovrich, and M. Gaffney, "Participation in Community Crime Prevention: Who Volunteers for Police Work?" *Policing: An International Journal of Police Strategies and Management* 29, no. 3 (2006): 464–81.

18. W.G. Skogan, *Community Policing: Can It Work?* (Belmont: Wadsworth/Thomson, 2004), 62.

19. W. Wells, "Problem Solving," in *Implementing Community Policing: Lessons from 12 Agencies,* ed. E.R. Maguire and W. Wells. Washington: U.S. Department of Justice, Office of Community Oriented Policing Programs, 2009), 31, http://www.cops.usdoj.gov/files/RIC/Publications/e080925236-ImpCP-Lessons.pdf

20. Rix et al., "Improving Public Confidence in the Police," 1.

21. E. Maguire and M. Gantley, "Specialist and Generalist Models," in *Implementing Community Policing: Lessons from 12 Agencies,* ed. E.R. Maguire and W. Wells (Washington: Office of Community Oriented Policing Services, 2009), 45–55, http://www.cops.usdoj.gov/files/RIC/Publications/e080925236-ImpCP-Lessons.pdf

22. J. Liederbach, E.J. Fritsch, D.L. Carter, and A. Bannister, "Exploring the Limits of Collaboration in Community Policing: A Direct Comparison of Police and Citizen Views," *Policing: An International Journal of Police Strategies and Management* 31, no. 2 (2008): 271–91.

23. E. Maguire and W. Wells, "The Future of Community Policing," in *Implementing Community Policing: Lessons from 12 Agencies,* ed. E.R. Maguire and W. Wells Washington: Office of Community Oriented Policing Services, 2009), 173–83, http://www.cops.usdoj.gov/files/RIC/Publications/e080925236-ImpCP-Lessons.pdf

24. M.M. Wehrman and J. DeAngelis, "Citizen Willingness to Participate in Police–Community Partnerships: Exploring the Influence of Race and Neighborhood Context," *Police Quarterly* 14, no. 1 (2011): 25–47.
25. Rix et al., "Improving Public Confidence in the Police," 1.
26. Skogan, *Community Policing*.
27. S. Mastrofski, "Community Policing: A Skeptical View," in *Police Innovation: Contrasting Perspectives*, ed. D.P. Rosenbaum and A.A. Braga (Cambridge: Cambridge University Press, 2006), 44–73 at 47.

Chapter
9

Crime Prevention and Crime Response Strategies

Learning Objectives

After reading this chapter, you should be able to:

- Identify and discuss primary, secondary, and tertiary crime prevention programs

- Discuss the effectiveness of crime prevention programs and the factors that may hinder program success

- Identify and discuss the various crime response strategies used by the police, including problem-solving policing and zero-tolerance policing

- Identify and discuss the various crime attack strategies used by the police, including tactical/directed patrol and specific initiatives designed to target high-risk offenders

- Discuss the use and impact of foot patrols and bicycle patrols in crime response and crime prevention strategies

- Describe restorative justice and how the police are involved in the various restorative justice approaches

- Discuss the effectiveness of police crime response strategies

Key Terms

Recall from Chapter 8 that there are three elements in the current incarnation of community policing: organizational, external, and tactical. That chapter considered the organizational features of a police service that uses a community policing model and the types of relationships it can establish with the community. This chapter examines the tactical elements of community policing, with a focus on crime prevention and crime response strategies.

The tactical elements of community policing include crime prevention programs, community service programs, problem-solving policing, zero-tolerance policing, quality-of-life policing, and a variety of crime attack strategies. Police–community partnerships can be a key feature of the tactical element of community policing.

CRIME PREVENTION

The basic mission of the police is to prevent crime and disorder.
SIR ROBERT PEEL

Crime prevention programs are generally aimed at reducing crime, fostering community involvement in addressing crime, and strengthening citizens' perceptions of safety. Crime prevention initiatives can be categorized as (1) primary prevention programs, (2) secondary prevention programs, or (3) tertiary prevention programs. Police departments are most extensively involved in primary programs, though they participate in secondary and (to a lesser extent) tertiary prevention as well.

Primary Crime Prevention Programs

Primary crime prevention programs are the most common type and are designed to alter the conditions that provide opportunities for criminal offences. Police services are involved in a wide variety of these programs (see Research File 9.1). Note that in Research Files 9.1, 9.2, and 9.3, for many of the strategies, the comments on effectiveness either begin with "can" or include phrases such as "has the potential to" or "in some jurisdictions." This reflects the paucity of the research that has been conducted to date, particularly in Canada.

CCTVs are perhaps the most controversial of the primary crime prevention programs. Although CCTV has been used extensively in Britain and the

primary crime prevention programs
prevention programs designed to alter the conditions that provide opportunities for criminal offences

Research File 9.1

Selected Primary Crime Prevention Programs

Program	Strategy	Effectiveness
Crime Prevention Through Environmental Design (CTPED)	Altering the physical environment of structures and places to reduce criminal opportunities, e.g., improved lighting.	In some jurisdictions, altering the designs of buildings and pedestrian routes has helped reduce levels of robberies, assaults, and residential break-and-enters.
Closed circuit television (CCTV)	Placing cameras in business and/or residential areas to provide live images 24/7.	Pilot projects in Calgary and Toronto and cities in the U.S. and the U.K. found that CCTVs are most effective when targeted at specific locales (e.g., drug-dealing spots, parking garages) and can assist in investigations. May be most effective in apprehending perpetrators after a crime has been committed.[a]
Operation Identification/ Operation Provident	Citizens and businesses mark their property with ID numbers to make it difficult to fence stolen goods and to assist in recovery by the police.	Impact on property crimes uncertain. Do increase police–public interaction and citizens' awareness of police crime prevention activities. May displace crime.
Neighbourhood Watch	Organizes residents to make them aware of strangers and criminal activities in their neighbourhood.	Is effective in reducing crime in some communities, although little is known about the factors that influence its effectiveness. Implementation most successful in low crime, middle-class neighbourhoods.[b]
Citizen patrols	Citizen foot and vehicle patrols under the supervision of the police.	American and European studies have found some reduction in crime levels and in citizens' fear of crime. Increases community participation.
Media-based programs	Educate the public about crime and solicit public assistance in locating offenders (e.g., tip lines, Crime Stoppers), often for a monetary reward.	Can increase arrest rates although little impact on the overall crime rate. Does stimulate community involvement.[c]

[a]M. Barkley, "CCTV Pilot Project Evaluation Report" (Toronto: Toronto Police Service, 2009), http://geeksandglobaljustice .com/wp-content/TPS-CCTV-report.pdf; City of Calgary, "Wireless Pubic Video Surveillance Pilot Evaluation and Final Report" (Calgary: 2011); B.C. Welsh and D.P. Farrington, "Public Area CCTV and Crime Prevention: An Updated Systematic Review and Meta-Analysis," *Justice Quarterly* 26, no. 4 (2009): 716–45; J.H. Ratcliffe, T. Taniguchi, and R.B. Taylor, "The Crime Reduction Effects of Public CCTV Cameras: A Multi-Method Spatial Approach," *Justice Quarterly* 26, no. 3 (2009): 746–70.

[b]T. Bennett, K. Holloway, and D.P. Farrington, "Does Neighborhood Watch Reduce Crime? A Systematic Review and Meta-Analysis," *Journal of Experimental Criminology* 2, no. 4 (2006): 437–58.

[c]D. Challinger, "Crime Stoppers Victoria: An Evaluation" (Canberra: Australian Institute of Criminology, 2004), http://www .popcenter.org/library/scp/pdf/198-Challinger.pdf

United States for many years, only recently cameras have been installed in some Canadian municipalities, and even these have often been temporary, for specific events such as the Vancouver Olympics (after which they were removed). While concerns over privacy have been expressed, Canadian society is well on the way to becoming a "surveillance" society. The movements and behaviours of citizens are recorded tens or perhaps hundreds of times per day as they move around the community. There are cameras on buses and taxis and in most private businesses, not to mention on every smartphone.

Secondary Crime Prevention Programs

Secondary crime prevention programs target areas that produce crime and other types of disorder. Some initiatives focus on identifying high-risk offenders and analyzing high-crime areas. Others are designed to assist at-risk youth and to help vulnerable groups avoid becoming crime victims (see Research File 9.2).

> **secondary crime prevention programs**
> programs that focus on areas that produce crime and disorder

Examples of police-sponsored secondary crime prevention programs targeting at-risk youth include the following:

Camp Little Buffalo, Grand Prairie, Alberta RCMP Detachment. This five-day leadership camp for at-risk youth between the ages of eleven and thirteen is a collaborative effort of the RCMP, municipal agencies, not-for-profit groups, and private businesses. Fiscal and goods-and-services donations are contributed by a wide range of businesses in Grand Prairie, including Costco and Safeway. The camp program, which is available free to the youth participants, focuses on the development of skills in the areas of assertiveness, communication, decision making, consequences, goal setting, and problem solving. As well, there are a number of sports and outdoor activities, including canoeing, hiking, and crafts. RCMP members serve as mentors for the campers. The overall goal is to foster positive interaction between youth and the police (www.cityofgp.com/citygov/dept/rcmp/programs/camplittlebuffalo.htm).

Ecotrip, York Regional Police. This year-long program is directed toward at-risk youth between the ages of fourteen and seventeen. These youth are mentored by police officers during the program, which includes a number of pre-trip training sessions as well as a four-day, three-night wilderness trip. Among the goals of Ecotrip are the development of youth life and leadership skills and the development of positive police–youth relationships (ecotrip@yrp.ca).

Community Cadet Corps Program. The program is directed toward at-risk youth up to the age of eighteen. It focuses on goal setting and the development of self-esteem, discipline, and leadership skills. Program activities include military-style drill and marching, sports and recreational activities, and cultural events. Originally developed by the RCMP in the rural First Nations community of Hobemma, Alberta, it has expanded across Canada to other First Nations communities and to urban centres, including Regina and Winnipeg.

Tertiary Crime Prevention Programs

Tertiary crime prevention programs focus on adults and youths who have already committed a crime. A key objective of these programs is to prevent future reoffending. Many tertiary programs are directed toward first-time, less

> **tertiary crime prevention programs**
> programs designed to prevent adults and youths from reoffending

Research File 9.2

Selected Secondary Crime Prevention Programs

Program	Strategy	Effectiveness
Drug Abuse Resistance Education (DARE) for youth	School-based program that provides information to youth about the perils of drug use.	While there are generally high levels of support for the program among educators, parents, and youth, the program has no impact on student attitudes and beliefs about drugs or drug use.[a]
Crime Prevention Through Social Development (CPSD)	Collaborative efforts to reduce the risks faced by individuals, families, and communities (e.g., early intervention programs, programs to strengthen families and to increase community capacities to prevent crime).	Effectiveness unknown. Few Canadian evaluations. Requires collaboration among the police, social agencies, and community groups.[b]
Positive Youth Development	A holistic strategy based on CPSD, designed to build capacity in communities and in youth, in order to improve the quality of life and decision making among youth and to facilitate the development of positive attitudes and behaviour. Multi-agency (including the police) initiatives may be directed toward individual youth, families, and communities.	Has the potential to significantly impact youth with low levels of competencies and to improve community capacities to assist at-risk youth.[c]
Programs for at-risk youth (e.g., summer camps, wilderness experience programs)	Developing leadership and life skills in at-risk youth and increasing positive police–youth interactions.	Few evaluations. Programs may have a positive impact on youth attitudes and behaviour, but follow-up is required or results fade over time.
Police school liaison officer programs	Police officers are assigned to schools on a residential (full-time, in-school) or non-residential (periodic officer visits) basis. Officers make class presentations and participate in school activities. Objectives are primary and secondary crime prevention.	Few evaluations. May increase the legitimacy of the police with students and have indirect benefits (e.g., identifying at-risk youth, providing intelligence to patrol and investigative units).
Crime reduction	A holistic, multiagency approach designed to prevent and deter crime; to apprehend/prosecute/treat offenders; and to address citizens' fear of crime.	Effective in facilitating the development of police/community/agency partnerships. Absence of evaluations makes it difficult to determine program success and the factors that contribute to positive and sustainable outcomes.

[a]D.P. Rosenbaum, "Just Say No to D.A.R.E," *Criminology and Public Policy* 6, no. 4 (2007): 815–24.

[b]L. MacRae, J.J. Paetsch, L.D. Bertrand, and J.P. Hornick, 2005, "National Police Leadership Survey on Crime Prevention Through Social Development" (Ottawa: 2005), http://www.publicsafety.gc.ca/res/cp/res/_fl/police-survey-cpsd-eng.pdf

[c]S.A. Anderson, R.M. Sabatelli, and J. Trachtenberg, "Community Police and Youth Programs for Positive Youth Development," *Police Quarterly* 10, no. 1 (2007): 23–40.

serious offenders and have a strong record of success. The challenges are greater for programs that target repeat offenders, which generally involve close supervision and surveillance. Tertiary prevention programs are often collaborative efforts of justice and social service agencies and community groups.

Crime Reduction

A trend in the early twenty-first century is the development of comprehensive, integrated approaches designed to address crime and disorder and to build sustainable relationships with the community. In the past, the police, other agencies, nongovernmental organizations (NGOs), and community groups worked at cross-purposes, which limited the effectiveness of interventions and programs. **Crime reduction** models were pioneered in Britain and have since been adapted by several Canadian jurisdictions. Crime reduction focuses on the people, places, and situations where criminal activity occurs. This is a holistic approach to crime, one that involves the community, government agencies (including the police), and NGOs.

crime reduction
a holistic approach to crime that focuses on the people, places, and situations where criminal activity occurs

Surrey, B.C., has developed what is perhaps the most comprehensive crime reduction strategy (CRS) in Canada. The primary objectives of that city's CRS are to (1) reduce crime and increase community safety, (2) increase public involvement in reducing crime, (3) increase integration among all stakeholders involved in crime reduction, and (4) improve public awareness about the reality of crime.

To accomplish these goals, a four-strand strategy was developed: (1) prevent and deter crime, (2) apprehend and prosecute offenders, (3) rehabilitate and reintegrate offenders, and (4) inform the public about the reality of crime. Subcommittees were convened to develop specific strategies; represented on these were the city, NGOs, schools, health authorities, and local universities. With respect to the first objective—to prevent and deter crime—a number of strategic actions were planned, including Crime Prevention Through Environmental Design (CPTED), which involved identifying areas for improved lighting, applying CPTED to new developments, and requiring property managers to receive training in CPTED principles (http://www.surrey.ca).

The Surrey CRS is an ambitious attempt to bring a comprehensive approach to crime and social disorder and to develop cooperative networks in the community to address issues. A key element in the success of this initiative, however, will be sustaining the involvement of all stakeholders. It remains to be seen whether the program will be sustainable in the long term. In the absence of any evaluations, it is difficult to determine whether the CRS has succeeded in achieving its objectives.

OBSTACLES TO EFFECTIVE CRIME PREVENTION PROGRAMS

Crime prevention programs have been proliferating, yet evidence that they work is sketchy and often inconclusive. It *can* be said that these initiatives have suffered from poor planning, poor implementation, lack of support from police services, and an absence of community involvement.

Many crime prevention initiatives have been introduced without any analysis and also without clear and measurable objectives. There is often a failure to consider best-practice crime prevention programs and the lessons learned from past efforts. With respect to program implementation, an important issue is *where* crime prevention initiatives are implemented: "All too often, programs are initiated in neighbourhoods that really don't need them, while less organized neighbourhoods with higher crime rates are not served by programs because local residents have not taken the initiative or do not have the capacity to start them and because programs are much more difficult to implement in high-needs communities."[1]

Also, police services vary greatly regarding the extent to which they integrate crime prevention into their operations and resource their crime prevention initiatives. In some police services, crime prevention is an ancillary function; in others, it is a core objective. When budgets are tight, crime prevention programs may be vulnerable to resource cuts. Also, participation in crime prevention initiatives requires that patrol officers have the time to engage in proactive policing.

Hindering community involvement in crime prevention initiatives are these factors: residents' apathy toward and lack of participation in crime prevention programs; the absence of a clearly defined role for the community; community distrust of and hostility toward the police; and the fact that communities afflicted by high rates of crime and disorder are often the same ones where it is most difficult to interest residents.

Remember, though, that a reduced crime rate is only one indicator of success for crime prevention programs. Other important markers are stronger police–community relationships, a reduced fear of crime, more positive experiences of crime victims, and stronger community participation in the long term.

Comprehensive crime prevention strategies hold the most promise. Two types of comprehensive initiatives are those which focus on the needs of an entire community or on high-crime neighbourhoods in the community, and those which are designed to address a particular problem, such as domestic violence or vehicle theft, on a broad scale.[2]

Police Legitimacy and Crime Prevention

Police sometimes continue to champion programs that evaluative studies have determined to be ineffective. An excellent example of this phenomenon is D.A.R.E. (Drug Abuse Resistance Education), a drug prevention program offered by police services in many high schools across the country. More than two decades' worth of studies have found that, while there is strong support for the program among parents, educators, the police, and youth, the program has had very little impact on student attitudes and beliefs about drugs or on drug use. The extent to which the program is effective in the other areas it addresses has not been examined. D.A.R.E. is a good example of a widely used program whose effectiveness is more often assumed than demonstrated and that many police services continue to promote because it increases their legitimacy in the community.[3]

Sustaining Community Involvement in Crime Prevention Initiatives

In the discussion of community policing in Chapter 8, it was noted that generating and sustaining community involvement in policing is a challenge. These challenges also exist when it comes to mobilizing community residents to participate in crime prevention initiatives.

FIGURE 9.1   Key Elements in Sustaining Crime Prevention Initiatives

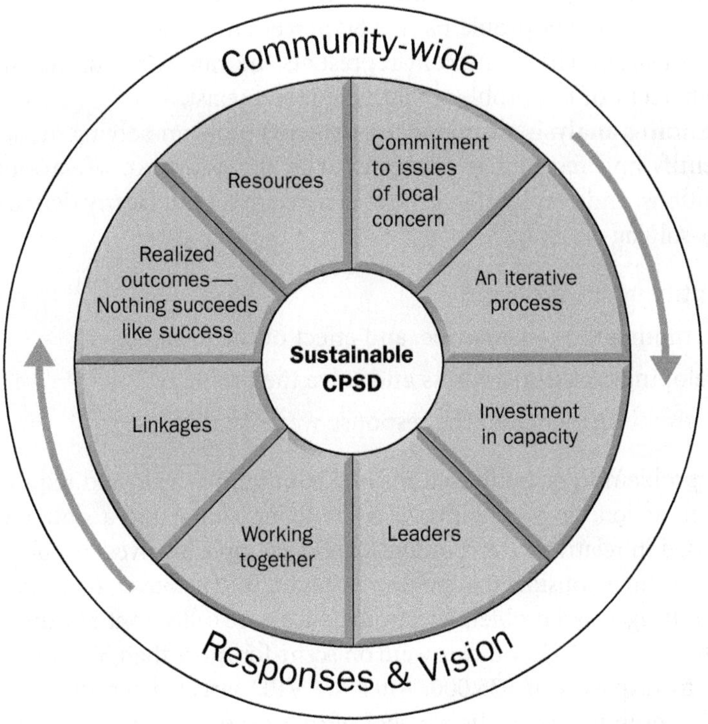

Source: T. Caputo, K. Kelly, W. Jamieson, and L. Hart, "A Portrait of Sustainable Crime Prevention in Selected Canadian Communities, Vol. 1, Main Report," p. iii, 2004, Carleton University.

A key question is this: "How can community involvement in crime prevention initiatives be sustained?" Both the police and the community must anticipate and address obstacles to community involvement. A review of crime prevention through social development initiatives in six Canadian communities has identified several factors that contribute to sustainability. These are depicted in Figure 9.1. Basically, successful programs are relevant to and "owned" by the community and reflect a community vision.

CRIME RESPONSE

The crime response strategies used in community-focused strategic policing include a range of tactical initiatives. Several of the more common ones are discussed below.

Problem-Oriented Policing (POP)

An important community policing strategy is **problem-oriented policing (POP)**, which is based on the idea that policing should pinpoint the root causes of crime and disorder and then fashion solutions to those problems, often in

problem-oriented policing (POP)
a tactical strategy based on the idea that the police should address the causes of recurrent crime and disorder

iceberg (or 80/20) rule
the view that crime is only a visible symptom of much larger problems

collaboration with community residents. A central tenet of POP is the **iceberg (or 80/20) rule,** which posits that crime (the visible 20 percent of the iceberg) is only a symptom of much larger problems (the 80 percent of the iceberg that lies below the water's surface). The 80 percent represents the causes or conditions that allow the 20 percent of the problem that is visible to exist.

The **SARA (scanning, analysis, response, assessment)** problem-solving model helps officers identify and respond to problems with the assistance of various agencies, organizations, and community groups. There are several clearly defined stages to problem-solving policing:

SARA (scanning, analysis, response, assessment)
a problem-solving model for police

- *scanning*—identifying the problem
- *analysis*—determining the cause, scope, and effect of the problem
- *response*—developing a plan to address and solve the problem
- *assessment*—determining whether the response was effective

The particular problem to be addressed may be community-wide and require a long-term plan of action, or it may involve a single individual and a situation that can be addressed in relatively short order. A good example involves "problem premises," which consume considerable police resources. In Vancouver, one small rooming house was flagged as a problem location: police were called to it 259 times in eighteen months. A total of 413 officers were on scene for more than 320 hours, at an overall cost to taxpayers of $25,000. After the VPD targeted specific individuals living in the rooming house, the number of calls for service was reduced.[4]

Problem solving is a key component of the RCMP's CAPRA model. CAPRA involves focusing on **C**lients, **A**cquiring and **A**nalyzing information, developing and maintaining **P**artnerships, generating an appropriate **R**esponse, and **A**ssessing the intervention. This model emphasizes identifying and responding to problems of crime and social disorder in the community by applying a problem-solving approach. It highlights the importance of consultation and collaboration with community partners.

The Broken Windows Approach

broken windows approach
the view that if minor crimes are left unaddressed an environment for more serious crime will be created

The **broken windows approach** emerged in New York City in the 1980s. The term is a metaphor for neighbourhood deterioration. It is rooted in the observation of patrol officers that if a window in a building is broken and is not replaced, in very short order all the windows in that building will be broken. According to this approach, a broken window that no one fixes amounts to a statement that no one cares enough about the neighbourhood to bother fixing the little things that go wrong. A broken window is a small thing, yet it may trigger further neglect and cause the entire neighbourhood to deteriorate.

The central thesis of the "broken windows theory," then, is that "the existence of unchecked and uncontrolled minor incivilities in a neighborhood—for example, panhandling, public drunkenness, vandalism, and graffiti—produces an atmosphere conducive to more serious crime."[5]

This model of policing emphasizes rapid deployment of officers and relentless follow-up. It was associated with a significant reduction in crime in New York City and has since been adopted by many police services in Canada and the United States.

Zero-Tolerance Policing and Quality-of-Life Policing

A policing strategy that has gained popularity in the past decade or so is zero-tolerance policing, also referred to as "confident policing," "proactive policing," or "community policing with the gloves off." The key principle here is that a strict order maintenance approach by the police in a specific area, coupled with high police visibility and presence, with a focus on disorder and minor infractions, will reduce more serious criminal activity.

Increased police visibility is a core component of quality-of-life policing, which involves efforts to improve conditions in an area by targeting annoying behaviour such as panhandling, loitering, and public drug and alcohol use. A highly visible police presence may deter and alter criminal behaviour, increase residents' sense of security, and increase the legitimacy of the police. These strategies are often applied in conjunction with police crackdowns, which are designed to instill in the criminal population the perception that they are more likely to be apprehended or intervened against.

Crime Attack Strategies

Crime attack strategies target and apprehend criminal offenders, especially those deemed likely to reoffend. Components of this strategy include increased patrol visibility, proactive policing, and rapid response.

> **crime attack strategies**
> proactive operations by the police to target and apprehend criminal offenders

One widely used strategy is tactical/directed patrol, which involves saturating high-crime areas (often referred to as "hotspots") with police officers, or targeting individuals engaged in specific types of criminal activity. A multitude of crimes can be addressed in this way: gun crimes, auto thefts, assaults (including sexual assaults); or, more prosaically, public drunkenness, vandalism, and unwanted noise. Hotspots are often identified through intelligence-led policing and are plotted on crime maps. Directed patrols are usually aimed at either locations

Vancouver Police Department Beat Enforcement Team members in the troubled Downtown Eastside area of the city.

or persons. Tactical patrol strategies give police managers greater control over their most valuable resource—the time and activities of patrol officers. Foot and bicycle patrols may also be used in hotspot areas. The Vancouver Police Department deploys dedicated foot patrol officers on beat enforcement teams in the troubled Downtown East Side.

Many police services have developed initiatives designed to target high-risk offenders:

Calgary Police Service Serious Habitual Offender Program (SHOP) and Multi-Disciplinary Resource Team (MDRT). SHOP is a multiagency (police, probation, Crown, social services agencies, corrections) information and case management program for youths and adults designated as serious habitual offenders. SHOP monitors the activities of offenders both during custody and upon their release in an attempt to reduce serious crime. The MDRT initiative is designed for early intervention and support for high-risk youths.

Repeat Offender Program Enforcement Squad (ROPE). The ROPE squad, with officers from the Toronto Police Service and the York Regional Police, locates and apprehends criminal offenders who are unlawfully at large because they have violated the conditions of their release from custody, have failed to return to custody, or have escaped from correctional authorities.

The Integrated Police-Parole Initiative (IPPI). This program places police officers in the parole offices of the Correctional Service of Canada (CSC). These officers work alongside parole officers to monitor the activities of high-risk offenders released into the community. A preliminary evaluation of the program found a reduction in technical violations of conditional release by offenders in those CSC offices participating in the IPPI program, which suggests that this approach may help reintegrate offenders.[6]

Many initiatives have both a prevention component and a response component. One example is the Toronto Police Service's Anti-Violence Intervention Strategy (TAVIS). This initiative is intended to reduce gun violence in high-crime

Police tactical team in action.

neighbourhoods in Toronto. Its strategies include intervention, prevention, and community support and mobilization. The components of TAVIS include community meetings, high-profile police patrols, and the identification of crime hotspots and individuals involved in gun violence (www.torontopolice.on.ca/tavis).

Another proactive strategy that many Canadian police services use to manage high-risk offenders is community notification. This involves advising the media, crime victims, and the public when certain offenders are released (generally from federal correctional facilities). The decision to issue a community notification is generally made by a committee composed of justice personnel, including the police. Photographs and descriptions of these offenders are often placed on police service websites. This practice has not been without controversy and raises the issue of public safety and security versus individual rights. There is no evidence that community notification is effective in ensuring community safety or reducing reoffending.[7]

Targeting Specific Types of Crime

Police services may develop strategies to address specific types of crime. Car thieves and gang members are two groups that have received considerable police attention.

Auto theft is a high-profile crime that has long been associated with high-speed police pursuits, which often have tragic consequences for the offender and innocent persons. In 2002 the Vancouver Police Department launched the first Bait Car program in Canada, patterned on a similar initiative in Minneapolis, Minnesota. The program has since spread across the country (see photo, next page).

The program involves rigging police-owned vehicles with GPS and audio and visual equipment, as well as with technology that allows the vehicle to be stopped remotely. The bait car program has resulted in significant decreases in the rates of auto theft in jurisdictions where it is used. During the six years between 2003 and 2009, auto theft incidents decreased 61 percent in the Greater Vancouver Region.

Police services have also been highly proactive in their efforts to suppress gang activity and its associated violence. This has included targeted investigations and the development of integrated gang task forces. In an attempt to reduce gang violence, the Vancouver Police Department, in collaboration with a number of downtown nightclubs, created the Bar Watch program. Bars that are approved by the police install metal detectors and identification scanners and agree to allow the police to enter the bar and remove patrons without permission. The program operates in conjunction with a number of other proactive initiatives designed to reduce gang violence in the city. The police point to a reduction in the number of "shots fired incidents" from 2007 (72) to 2010 (28), as well as a reduction in the number of gang-related homicides in the city from 2007 (13) to 2010 (3), as evidence that the Bar Watch program has succeeded. The program, however, has not been without controversy, which centres on issues related to civil liberties and personal privacy. This highlights, again, the tensions that exist in a democratic society between safety and security and individual rights (a common theme in studies of police work; see At Issue 9.1 and At Issue 9.2).

Restorative Justice Approaches

Restorative justice is based on the principle that criminal behaviour injures not only the victim but also the community and the offender and that any effort to resolve the problems created by criminal behaviour should involve all parties. Among the

restorative justice
an approach based on the principle that criminal behaviour injures the victim, the community, and the offender

A police bait car poster.

more common restorative justice initiatives are victim–offender mediation, circle sentencing, community holistic healing programs, and family group conferences. These programs vary in terms of the types of offences and offenders processed; the procedures for hearing cases, reaching dispositions, and imposing sanctions; and the extent to which justice system professionals, including police officers, are involved. Box 9.1 compares retributive justice and restorative justice principles.

A feature shared by all restorative justice approaches is that the response to criminal behaviour addresses not only the offender and the offence but also the crime victims and their families, the offender's family, community residents, and justice personnel, including police officers. Together, those who have been affected formulate a sanction that addresses everyone's needs.

Among the better known restorative justice programs in which police officers play a key role are circle sentencing and community and family group conferencing. Circle sentencing was first used in Yukon; family group conferencing originated in New Zealand and has since been exported to Australia, Canada, and the United States.

In circle sentencing, all the participants—including judge, defence lawyer, prosecutor, police officer, victim and family, offender and family, and community residents—sit facing one another in a circle. The discussions within the

Box 9.1

Comparison of Retributive and Restorative Justice Principles

Retributive justice	Restorative justice
Crime violates the state and its laws	Crime violates people and relationships
Justice focuses on establishing guilt so that doses of pain can be meted out	Justice aims to identify needs and obligations so that things can be made right
Justice is sought through conflict between adversaries in which the offender is pitted against the state	Justice encourages dialogue and mutual agreement and gives victims and offenders central roles
Rules and intentions outweigh outcomes; one side wins and the other loses	The outcome is judged by the extent to which responsibilities are assumed, needs are met, and healing (of individuals and relationships) is encouraged

Source: Zehr, H., *Changing Lenses: A New Focus for Crime and Justice,* © 1990, Herald Press. Reprinted by permission of the publisher.

circle are intended to reach a consensus about the best way to dispose of the case, taking into account the need to protect the community as well as the punishment and rehabilitation of the offender. Circle sentencing is generally available only to offenders who plead guilty. Offenders who have their cases heard in a sentencing circle may be sent for a period of incarceration; however, many other sanctions are available, including house arrest or community service.

Police officers apply community conferencing in a variety of settings. For example, school liaison officers (SLOs) often use conferencing to address conflicts between students, or groups of students, that arise in school settings.

The Effectiveness of Crime Response Strategies

The absence of evaluation studies, especially in Canada, makes it difficult to determine the extent to which police crime response strategies reduce the levels of crime and disorder in communities and improve the quality of life for community residents. Studies conducted so far (primarily in the United States and Britain) have produced mixed findings.

The many differences in how individual police services plan and implement crime response strategies, variations in the extent to which police services have established productive collaborations with other agencies and with community groups, and the specific challenges confronting individual neighbourhoods, combine to make it difficult to reach definitive conclusions about the effectiveness of police crime response strategies. It does appear that many of the strategies succeed in increasing police legitimacy—something that is vital to effective community policing. The effectiveness of selected crime response and crime attack strategies and restorative justice approaches strategies is presented in Research File 9.3.

Research File 9.3

The Effectiveness of Selected Crime Response, Crime Attack Strategies, and Restorative Justice Approaches

Strategy	Technique	Effectiveness
1. Crime Response		
Problem-oriented policing (POP)	Police attempt to address the root causes of crime and disorder and fashion solutions to those problems in collaboration with community residents. The use of SARA.	Has the potential to reduce crime and disorder and to reduce the fear of crime. Can improve police–community relations and develop skills in patrol officers.[a]
"Broken windows"	The existence of unchecked and uncontrolled minor infractions/incivilities in a neighbourhood produces an environment conducive to serious crime.[b]	Studies on the impact of broken windows have produced mixed results. Some studies have found no impact on crime rates; others have found a reduction in property crime rates.[c] It is likely that the broken windows approach may work in some types of neighborhoods and that its impact may be increased if it is combined with community policing initiatives. A concern is that, in adopting the broken windows approach, the increased police activity may result in elevated levels of fear in the community. The legitimacy of the police may be compromised if certain segments of the community perceive they are being targeted.[d]
Zero-tolerance/quality-of-life policing	Influenced by broken windows. Strict order maintenance approach in a specific area, including high police visibility and a focus on disorder and minor infractions. Often involves police crackdowns on specific criminal activities, such as drug dealing.	Police presence may alter offender's behaviour. Increased police visibility increases citizens' sense of security, may deter criminal behaviour, and increases police legitimacy.[e] As with broken windows, may undermine police legitimacy with certain groups.

[a]J.E. Eck, "Why Don't Problems Get Solved?" in *Community Policing: Can It Work?* ed. W.G. Skogan (Belmont: Wadsworth/Thomson, 2004), 185–206.

[b]R.H. Burke, "The Socio-political Context of Zero Tolerance Policing Strategies," *Policing* 21, no. 4 (1998): 666–82.

[c]B.E. Harcourt and J. Ludwig, "Broken Windows: New Evidence from New York City and a Five-City Social Experiment," *University of Chicago Law Review* 73, no. 1 (2006): 271–320; J. Hyunseok, L.T. Hoover, and B.A. Lawton, "Effect of Broken Windows Enforcement on Crime Rates," *Journal of Criminal Justice* 36, no. 6 (2008): 529–38.

[d]J.C. Hinkle and D. Weisburd, "The Irony of Broken Windows Policing: A Micro-Place Study of the Relationship Between Disorder, Focused Police Crackdowns, and Fear of Crime," *Journal of Criminal Justice* 36, no. 6 (2008): 503–12.

[e]M.S. Scott, "The Benefits and Consequences of Police Crackdowns" (Washington: Office of Community Oriented Policing Services, U.S. Department of Justice, 2003), http://www.policyalmanac.org/crime/archives/police-crackdowns.pdf

2. Crime Attack		
Tactical/directed patrol	Proactive, aggressive patrol in high-crime areas. Patrol officers use unallocated time to engage in purposeful activities directed by analysis of crime data. May be location-focused or person (offender)-oriented. Often applied in conjunction with crackdowns, focusing on specific types of criminal activities (e.g., drug dealing).	Increasing the number of uniformed police officers in patrol cars in hotspots and during hot times (crime peaks) may significantly reduce levels of criminal activity. Proactive police arrests, including zero-tolerance arrest policies that focus on high-risk people and offences, can reduce the levels of serious violent crime. The impact of crackdowns may depend on the community. Initiatives are resource-intensive and difficult to sustain over the long term. May undermine the legitimacy of the police, particularly among young men and other groups who are more likely to be the targets of police attention.[a]
"Hotspots" policing	Police focus on areas that have a high concentration of crime and/or disorder and a high risk of criminal victimization.[b]	Can reduce crime and disorder without displacing crime to surrounding areas; long-term effectiveness is enhanced by the use of POP.
Focusing on high-risk offenders	Special police units monitor chronic and violent offenders. Often involves collaboration of multiple police services and other agencies.	Can result in high levels of arrest and incarceration and reduction in violent crime incidents.
Bike patrols	Officers on bikes often deployed to areas of high crime and disorder. Provide excellent mobility in the urban environment.	Can be an effective component of community policing. Bike patrol officers can have much more personal contact with citizens than patrol car officers.[c]
Foot patrols	Officers walk a "beat" in a neighbourhood or district. Some police services have dedicated foot patrols; others encourage officers to park their patrol cars and walk when they have the opportunity.	Do not directly affect levels of crime. Reduce citizens' fear of crime and calls for service. Improve officers' familiarity with neighbourhoods. To be effective, must be deployed as part of a comprehensive community policing strategy rather than as an add-on.
Community notification	Advising the media, crime victims, and the general public when certain offenders are released from confinement. Used most often with sex offenders.	No evidence that it reduces reoffending. May increase citizens' fear of crime and further marginalize offenders released from confinement. Raises issues of public security versus individual privacy.

[a] J.M. Gau and R.K. Brunson, "Procedural Justice and Order Maintenance Policing: A Study of Inner-City Young Men's Perceptions of Police Legitimacy," *Justice Quarterly* 27, no. 2 (2010): 255–79.

[b] J.E. Eck, "Why Don't Problems Get Solved?" in *Community Policing: Can It Work?* ed. W.G. Skogan (Belmont: Wadsworth/Thomson, 2004), 185–206.

[c] C. Menton, "Bicycle Patrols: An Underutilized Resource," *Policing: An International Journal of Police Strategies and Management* 31, no. 1 (2008): 93–108.

(Continued)

3. Restorative Justice		
Family and community conferencing	Uses problem-solving and may involve officers as participants or facilitators. Most often used for less serious criminal offences or for school-based disputes between students or groups of students.	Provides an opportunity for police officers to develop an important problem-solving skill sets as well as to develop partnerships with agencies and organizations in the community. Restorative justice face-to-face meetings mediated by police officers can improve perceptions of the criminal justice system, positive views of the police, high levels of victim satisfaction, and perceptions of fairness among offenders. Programs may also function to increase police legitimacy.[a] Police can be as effective as facilitators as civilians.[b]

[a]P. McCold, "Police-Facilitated Restorative Conferencing: What the Data Show," Paper presented to the Second Annual International Conference on Restorative Justice for Juveniles, Florida Atlantic University, November 7–9, 1998, http://fp.enter.net/restorativepractices/policeconferencing.pdf; A. Rix, F. Joshua, M. Maguire, and S. Morton, "Improving Public Confidence in the Police: A Review of the Evidence. Research Report 28" (London: Research, Development, and Statistics Directorate, Home Office, 2009), http://webarchive.nationalarchives.gov.uk/20110218135832/http://rds.homeoffice.gov.uk/rds/pdfs09/horr28c.pdf

[b]N.K. Hipple and E.F. McGarrell, "Comparing Police- and Civilian-Run Family Group Conferences," *Policing: An International Journal of Police Strategies and Management* 31, no. 4 (2008): 553–77.

The Issue of Crime Displacement

crime displacement
the relocation of crime from one place, time, target, offence, or tactic to another due to effective crime prevention and crime response strategies

In any attempts to determine the effectiveness of crime prevention programs, there is the slippery issue of **crime displacement**—"the relocation of crime from one place, time, target, offense, or tactic to another as a result of some form of crime initiative."[8] Crime displacement can take a number of forms: (1) *geographic*, which involves offenders moving their criminal activity to another area; (2) *temporal*, in which criminals alter the times they commit offences; (3) *tactical*, in which offenders develop different strategies to commit crimes; (4) *target*, in which offenders select different places to commit crimes or different people to victimize; and (5) *functional*, in which changes in technology reduce criminal opportunities in some areas but open them up in others (e.g., bank robberies are declining as we move toward a cashless society, whereas wire fraud is growing as a new criminal opportunity).[9]

In B.C., for example, the proactive efforts of the Vancouver Police Department to reduce gang violence have resulted in some gang activity shifting to the northern community of Prince George and to the suburban community of Abbotsford, east of Vancouver (which in 2008 and 2009 was the murder capital of Canada). There has also been an increased gang presence in the resort community of Whistler, north of Vancouver. Police services in these areas may not have the resources to effectively respond to these developments.

STRATEGIES TO IMPROVE THE EFFECTIVENESS OF CRIME PREVENTION AND CRIME RESPONSE

Police services are making increasing use of strategies for improving the effectiveness of crime prevention and crime response. These include strategic planning, crime analysis/criminal intelligence analysis, intelligence-led policing, and Compstat.

Strategic Planning

A key feature of contemporary police services is **strategic planning,** which involves identifying priorities for allocating existing police resources and then setting annual and/or multiyear goals. Besides producing an annual report, many police organizations have a multiyear strategic plan in place that sets out priorities and objectives for the organization and the specific initiatives that will be undertaken to achieve them. The requirement that police services engage in strategic planning has been enshrined in policing standards in many jurisdictions.

There is often a considerable gap between strategic plans and the resulting outcomes. Police services, along with other public sector institutions such as schools and social service agencies, have been slow to develop means for analyzing the extent to which the goals and objectives of strategic plans have been achieved.

> **strategic planning**
> the identification of police priorities and objectives and associated resource requirements

Crime Analysis

Crime analysis helps police services deploy their resources effectively; it also assists in case investigations. Police use the information it provides to deploy resources effectively and efficiently. Crime analysts, many of them civilians, use sophisticated statistical tools to "mine" data gathered by the police service and to improve decision making and strategic planning.[10] There are several types of crime analysis:

- *Tactical* analyses focus on the "when, where, and how" of crimes.
- *Strategic* analyses examine long-term crime patterns and trends, including seasonal variations in crime.
- *Administrative* analyses provide information to police managers, including comparative figures for police services.
- *Investigative* analyses profile suspects (and crime victims for police investigators), including chronic offenders and specific types of offenders (e.g., car thieves).
- *Intelligence* analyses focus on linkages between offenders and between crime groups, identifying patterns.
- *Operational* analyses focus on how the police service is utilizing its resources—including its patrol units, its specialty units, and so on.[11]

> **crime analysis**
> a systematic approach to crime prevention and crime response based on the analysis of statistical and other data

A key component of crime analysis, including Compstat policing (discussed on the next page), is *crime maps.* These are computer-generated maps that depict the incidence and patterns of specific types of criminal activity in specific geographic areas. This information is used to identify crime hotspots, to which patrol and investigative units can then be deployed. Statistical programs are also used to depict links among various crime elements. Crime maps are created using geographic information systems (GISs).

Intelligence-Led Policing

Intelligence-led policing (ILP) involves applying criminal intelligence analyses in order to reduce and prevent crime. ILP is one example of how police services use technology to generate information and deploy resources.

A number of police observers have cautioned that translating the concept of ILP into actual practice will encounter a number of challenges.[12] Concerns have been expressed that ILP represents a move away from community-focused policing back toward the crime control orientation. Also, there is often a disconnect between analyses and police operations. However, the ILP model does enable problem identification and problem solving as well as consultation with communities. ILP also enables police to assess the impact of specific strategic interventions.

Compstat

Compstat, short for "computer statistics," is a strategy for increasing the effectiveness and efficiency of police services while at the same time holding police personnel and the police service accountable for achieving objectives in crime reduction. Compstat has been a key part of the movement of police services toward results-oriented police management. It is based on four general principles:

1. *Timely and accurate intelligence.* District commanders, supervisors, and patrol officers are provided with information regarding where crimes are occurring, how crimes are being committed, and who is committing the crimes.
2. *Effective tactics.* Based on a careful analysis of crime data, tactical options are considered. These tactics focus not only on the apprehension of criminal offenders, but also on the social and environmental contexts in which crime is occurring.
3. *Rapid deployment.* A proactive response to crime is developed, which involves a coordinated effort of patrol officers, investigative units, and support personnel.
4. *Relentless follow-up and assessment.* The effectiveness of tactical strategies in preventing and reducing crime is evaluated on an ongoing basis. This entails a constant stream of information from patrol officers and supervisors to senior management regarding the outcomes of specific strategies and tactics.[13]

The effective implementation of Compstat requires that a police service assess on a regular basis the results from the strategies and tactics being deployed. The point of this is to understand why specific strategies are effective, or not. This is a process of continuous learning for the police service and can be incorporated into the development of specific interventions.[14]

Compstat meetings, attended by district commanders, supervisors, and selected support personnel, may be held weekly or monthly. The focus is on ascertaining crime trends and patterns in different areas and on developing specific strategies and tactics. It is expected that district commanders will have specific knowledge of crime and crime trends committed in their districts as well as tactical solutions for dealing with crimes committed in their districts, informed where appropriate by best practices. District commanders must put forward plans for utilizing resources in their districts to respond to and prevent crime. Compstat provides the police with a mechanism for implementing effective initiatives to address problems of crime and disorder; at the same time, it keeps the focus on the key elements of community policing.[15]

Versions of Compstat are being used in several Canadian police services, including the Toronto Police Service, the Ontario Provincial Police, the Vancouver Police Department, the Saskatoon police, and in a number of RCMP detachments. In many police services, patrol deployments and initiatives are Compstat-driven. One staff sergeant noted: "Whether it's giving an area special attention, deploying undercover surveillance teams, or having teams develop their own projects, it's almost always driven by Compstat" (personal communication).

There is considerable debate about Compstat, centred on how effective it is at reducing levels of crime and how well it interfaces with community policing. The debate over Compstat highlights the often "uneasy fit" between tactical strategies and the community policing model. This is illustrated by the comparison of community policing with Compstat in Table 9.1.

TABLE 9.1 A Comparison of the Doctrine of Compstat and Community Policing

Reform element	Community policing	Compstat
Mission clarification	Broadening of police mission to include wide range of objectives	Focusing core mission on reducing crime
Internal accountability	Peripheral or nonexistent	Highest priority
Decentralization of decision making	To lowest level in the organization (patrol officers)	To middle managers (district commanders)
Organizational flexibility	Capacity to accommodate innovation and differing needs within communities	Capacity to reallocate resources for effective accomplishment of crime control objectives
Data-driven problem identification and assessment	Empirical analysis is expected and valued	Empirical analysis is essential
Innovative problem solving	Innovation is expected and valued	Innovation is expected and valued
External accountability	Police consult with community on objectives and progress toward them	Police publicize traditional crime statistics as measures of agency accomplishments

Source: Willis, Mastrofski, and Kochel, 2010: 970. (Willis, J.J., S.D. Mastrofski, and T. Kochel. 2010. "The Co-Implementation of Compstat and Community Policing," *Journal of Criminal Justice,* 38(5), 969–80.)

Note: The darkest cells represent elements where the two reform doctrines show the greatest difference. The medium shaded cells are where there are some differences, but they are not great. The lightest cells are those where there are no appreciable differences.

There is concern that Compstat places too strong an emphasis on crime fighting and that it generally does not include measures of other strategies within the community policing model.[16] Field research has also found that there is often a disconnect between the managerial level in the police service and line-level officers with respect to Compstat objectives. This is reflected in the following exchange between a researcher and a foot patrol officer:

Officer: Everybody feels the pressure to make bodies, to lock people up.
Researcher: Is that because you feel like you are evaluated at the end of the week?
Officer: Yup.[17]

District commanders are often under considerable pressure to show decreases in crime levels. This could lead officers to make "statistical adjustments" in crime reports.[18]

For Compstat to be effective, there must be "buy in" from police leaders, middle managers, and line-level officers. Note also that Compstat was developed in a major urban police service (the New York Police Department) and has been adopted by police services in large Canadian municipalities. The extent to which Compstat could be modified for use by police services that provide services to rural and remote communities in Canada remains unexplored.

Final Thoughts on Effective Crime Prevention and Crime Response Strategies

To be effective, and to achieve the objectives of specific projects, tactical patrol strategies must be implemented on the basis of careful analyses and evaluations of crime data. And since aggressive patrol may involve zero-tolerance enforcement, car stops, identity checks, and other crackdowns, officers must ensure that their actions do not violate the rights of citizens as guaranteed by the Charter of Rights and Freedoms. In addition, patrol officers must have sufficient unallocated time to engage in proactive policing activities. Finally, strategies that combine tactical patrol with longer term problem-solving approaches may ultimately be more effective and have more impact over time.

It is important to note that these various strategies have the *potential* to prevent crime and reduce levels of crime and disorder in communities. The extent to which these objectives are actually *achieved* depends in large measure on how specific interventions are designed and implemented and on the quality of the relationship between the police and the community.

Merely adopting a community policing model is not an effective crime prevention and crime response approach. Police services must make efforts to "personalize" community policing through strategies that strengthen their legitimacy, increase personal contacts with community residents, and ensure that police–citizen interactions are positive and respectful. Police are more effective when they combine enforcement with a variety of other approaches, such as problem-oriented policing, intensive enforcement, and hotspot patrols.

There is consistent evidence that "service-oriented" models of policing—models that include procedural fairness in encounters with citizens, high visibility patrols, a problem-solving approach, and engagement with the community—contribute to higher levels of public confidence in the police.[19] Furthermore, two critical ingredients for success appear to be (1) utilizing a diversity of approaches, and (2) applying strategies that focus on specific crime and disorder problems. The least effective interventions use neither of these: "If diverse approaches are used without focus, it is difficult to apply the appropriate approach to the places and people who most require it. If the police are focused on hot spots, but only enforce the law, they limit their effectiveness. A fully effective police service must take advantage of the details of crime situations to reduce crime opportunities."[20]

It should not be assumed that the same interventions will work in every area and in every situation: "The best practice for any community is one that fits their needs and conditions and is compatible with available resources."[21]

At Issue 9.1

Bar Watch: Protecting Patrons or Violating Their Civil Liberties?

In an attempt to reduce the presence of gangs and associated gang violence in bars and restaurants, the Vancouver Police Department collaborated with establishments to develop Bar Watch and Restaurant Watch. Participation in the program is voluntary. Bars and restaurants operate the program through an association to which the police do not belong. This program has been been adopted by a number of cities in British Columbia and Alberta and in Halifax, Nova Scotia.

Common components of the programs include these: (1) participating establishments are required to install a CCTV and metal scanners at the entrance; (2) signs are posted, advising patrons that they are entering a premise that is participating in the Bar Watch program; (3) patrons are advised that the tapes from the CCTV may be turned over to police; (4) patrons are required to "swipe" their driver's licence into a scanner that collects personal information, which is retained in a master database; and (5) this information can be shared with other establishments and the police. "Undesirable persons" (persons who are gang-affiliated and/or who

have a criminal record) can be refused entry or removed from the premises by staff or the police.

The program has not been without controversy. Privacy Commissioners in B.C. and Alberta have expressed concerns about violations of civil liberties—specifically, about the gathering of personal data from patrons and how those data are stored and accessed. Patrons have also expressed concerns, as reflected in the comments on Internet discussion forums regarding the adoption of the Bar Watch program in Calgary:

"I think Bar Watch is a good idea, to keep everyone safe of course, but...I don't think it's necessary for police to be walking around removing patrons from a local establishment when there are plenty more crimes going on just in the streets. This is what our taxpayers money is going to?"

"Calgarians are contributing taxes to run this city, why do the police have the right to harass and defame citizens, when these citizens are NOT breaking any laws? They are merely just out trying to have fun?"

(Continued)

Supporters of the Bar Watch/Restaurant Watch counter that it increases the safety of law-abiding citizens and that the program is not coercive:

"The last time I checked, it wasn't your RIGHT to go into a bar/lounge...places like that are private establishments & the owners/operators have the RIGHT not to service (or not to serve) or admit (or not to admit) whoever they choose to."

"Entertainment spots are supposed to be placed where you can go and have a good time. The last thing someone wants to worry about is getting caught in the middle of a violent incident."

You Make the Call!

1. Have you ever been to a Bar Watch or Restaurant Watch premise?
2. If yes, what did you think about having to scan your driver's licence and the fact that this information is stored in a database?
3. What are your views on the issues that surround the Bar Watch/Restaurant Watch program?
4. Would you be in support of, or opposed to, the adoption of a Bar Watch/Restaurant Watch program in your community?
5. Would you patronize a bar or restaurant that participated in the program?

At Issue 9.2

CCTVs in the Neighbourhood?

Many municipalities across Canada are debating whether to install police-monitored CCTVs. Concerns have been raised about privacy issues and the location of the cameras (e.g., whether CCTVs should be limited to specific high-crime areas and business centres or located throughout the municipality). An issue that is likely to emerge in the coming years is whether facial recognition technology should be incorporated into the cameras, allowing monitoring personnel to identify persons in the video images.

You Make the Call!

Assume that you are a member of a subcommittee of the municipal council that is considering installing police-monitored CCTVs.

1. Should the municipality install police-monitored CCTVs?
2. If yes, should the CCTVs be installed (a) only in specific high-crime areas? (b) only in the business centre of the municipality? (c) throughout the municipality, including in residential neighbourhoods?
3. If yes, should facial recognition technology be incorporated into the CCTVs?
4. As a community resident, would you support the installation of CCTVs in your neighbourhood?

Key Points Review

1. The tactical element of community policing encompasses crime prevention and crime response strategies.
2. The police are involved in primary, secondary, and tertiary crime prevention programs.
3. The evidence regarding the effectiveness of police-sponsored crime prevention initiatives is sketchy and inconclusive.
4. The causes of crime and social disorder in any community are varied and complex, and it is unrealistic to expect that the police can reduce or eliminate all of society's problems.
5. Problem-oriented policing is based on the idea that policing should address the root causes of recurring problems of crime and disorder and then fashion solutions to those problems.
6. Zero-tolerance policing is premised on increased police visibility and a strict order maintenance approach.
7. Crime attack strategies are proactive police operations designed to target and apprehend criminal offenders.
8. Police officers are involved in a variety of restorative justice programs, including circle sentencing and family group conferencing.
9. The absence of evaluation studies in Canada makes it difficult to determine the extent to which the various police crime response strategies are effective in reducing levels of crime and disorder in communities and improving the quality of life for residents.
10. Effective police work requires a diversity of approaches and strategies that focus on specific crime and disorder problems.

Key Term Questions

1. Identify the objectives of **primary crime prevention programs, secondary crime prevention programs,** and **tertiary crime prevention programs** and provide examples of each.
2. Describe what is meant by **crime reduction** and provide an example of a crime reduction plan for one Canadian municipality.
3. Describe **problem-oriented policing (POP),** and discuss how the **iceberg (80/20) rule** and **SARA** are related to this crime response strategy.
4. What is the **broken windows approach** to crime and disorder?
5. Discuss the focus of **crime attack strategies** and how patrol officers are deployed under this approach.
6. What is **crime displacement,** and what forms can this phenomenon take?
7. Describe the basic principles of **restorative justice** and contrast them with the principles of the adversarial system.
8. Describe and discuss the role that **strategic planning, crime analysis, intelligence-led policing (ILP),** and **Compstat** play in policing.

Notes

1. R. Linden and R. Chaturvedi, "The Need for Comprehensive Crime Prevention Planning: The Case of Motor Vehicle Theft," *Canadian Journal of Criminology and Criminal Justice* 47, no. 2 (2005): 251–70 at 252.

2. Ibid.

3. D.P. Rosenbaum, "Just Say No to D.A.R.E.," *Criminology and Public Policy* 6, no. 4 (2007): 815–24.

4. J. Keating, "City Rooming House Costs a Whopping $25,000 for Police," *The Province,* July 20, 2010, A4.

5. R.H. Burke, "The Socio-Political Context of Zero Tolerance Policing Strategies," *Policing* 21, no. 4 (1998): 666–82 at 667.

6. M. Axford and R. Ruddell, "Police–Parole Partnerships in Canada: A Review of a Promising Program," *International Journal of Police Science and Management* 12, no. 2 (2010): 274–86.

7. C.T. Griffiths, *Canadian Corrections,* 3rd ed. (Toronto: Nelson, 2010).

8. R.T. Guerette, "Analyzing Crime Displacement and Diffusion" (Washington: U.S. Department of Justice, Office of Community Oriented Policing Services, 2009), http://www.popcenter.org/tools/pdfs/displacement.pdf

9. D.K. Rossmo, "Strategic Crime Patterning: Problem-Oriented Policing and Displacement," in *Crime Analysis Through Computer Mapping* (Washington: Police Executive Research Forum, 1995), 1–14 at 5–6.

10. D. Osborne and S. Wernicke, *Introduction to Crime Analysis: Basic Resources for Criminal Justice Practice* (New York: Haworth, 2003), 5, http://www.crim.umontreal.ca/cours/cri3013/osborne.pdf

11. Ibid.

12. N. Cope, "Intelligence Led Policing or Policing Led Intelligence? Integrating Volume Crime Analysis into Policing," *British Journal of Criminology* 44, no. 2 (2004): 188–203; J.H. Ratcliffe, "Intelligence-Led Policing and the Problems of Turning Rhetoric into Practice," *Policing and Society* 12, no. 1 (2002): 53–66.

13. P. Parshall-McDonald, *Managing Police Operations—Implementing the New York Crime Control Model—CompStat* (Belmont: Wadsworth/Thomson, 2002).

14. Vancouver Police Department, "COMPSTAT (2006)," internal document.

15. J.J. Willis, S.D. Mastrofski, and T. Kochel, "The Co-implementation of Compstat and Community Policing," *Journal of Criminal Justice* 38, no. 5 (2010): 969–80.

16. Ibid.

17. D. Dabney, "Observations Regarding Key Operational Realities in a Compstat Model of Policing," *Justice Quarterly* 27, no. 1 (2009): 28–51.

18. J.A. Etero and E.B. Silverman, "The NYPDs Compstat: Compare Statistics or Compose Statistics?" *International Journal of Police Science and Management* 12, no. 3 (2010): 426–49.

19. A. Myhill and P. Quinton, "What Is Trust and Confidence in the Police?" *Policing* 4, no. 3 (2010): 241–48.

20. R.V. Clarke and J.E. Eck, "Crime Analysis for Problem Solvers in 60 Small Steps" (Washington: U.S. Department of Justice, Office of Community Oriented Policing Services, 2005), http://www.popcenter.org/library/reading/PDFs/60steps.pdf

21. A. Rix, F. Joshua, M. Maguire, and S. Morton, "Improving Public Confidence in the Police: A Review of the Evidence." "Research Report 28" (London: Research, Development, and Statistics Directorate, Home Office, 2009), 1, http://webarchive.nationalarchives.gov.uk/20110218135832/http://rds.homeoffice.gov.uk/rds/pdfs09/horr28c.pdf

Chapter

10

Case Investigation

Learning Objectives

After reading this chapter, you should be able to:

- Discuss the role of patrol officers and specialty units in case investigations

- Discuss the role of police informants and the issues that surround their use in case investigation

- Describe the fundamentals of case investigation, including the role of detectives, the crime scene search, police note-taking, and the various types of evidence

- Discuss the issues that surround the use of eye-witnesses in case investigation

- Describe the use of the Mr. Big strategy in case investigation and why the technique is surrounded by controversy

- Identify the various analytical tools that are used by the police in case investigations

- Discuss the use of DNA in case investigations

- Discuss the issues that surround the interrogation of crime suspects and, particularly, false confessions

Key Terms

The investigation of criminal offences is an important yet understudied aspect of Canadian police work. Depending on the circumstances of the case, investigations may involve patrol officers, detectives, undercover officers, informants, and surveillance teams, as well as special techniques such as wiretaps.

Various commissions of inquiry and review committees have identified police investigations as a major contributor to wrongful convictions.[1] Among the factors that have contributed to innocent persons being found guilty are false confessions, improperly conducted photo line-ups, erroneous information provided by informants, and "tunnel vision"—that is, investigators becoming so focused on certain pieces of evidence and/or suspects that critical evidentiary clues and other potential perpetrators are overlooked.

PATROL OFFICERS: THE FIRST RESPONDERS

Most case investigations are conducted by patrol officers, who learn the fundamentals of case investigation during their initial years working the street. In later years, when they become part of specialized investigative units, they will apply these skills in more complex investigations.

Toronto Sun/Dave Thomas

Patrol officers search for evidence.

In their daily activities, front line patrol officers gather a considerable amount of raw criminal intelligence. For example, an officer may stop a vehicle for speeding and, while issuing a summons to the driver, obtain the identity of three other individuals in the car. This information is important because it establishes a relationship among all four parties. Investigators from the major crimes section can use this information to help them identify suspects in a criminal conspiracy. This information may also be vital for obtaining judicial authorization to install a wiretap or listening device in a dwelling.

The patrol officers who are the first to arrive at a crime scene usually have little information, or conflicting information, about what has occurred. The most important duties of first responders include ensuring that emergency medical personnel have access to and from the scene; securing and protecting the crime scene; and establishing the continuity of the scene and the evidence. Patrol officers must also attend to the needs of victims, which includes mobilizing victim services personnel.

SPECIALTY UNITS

There has been exponential growth in the number of specialized investigative units. There are two general types of special units in police services: **problem-oriented special units** and **method-oriented special units.**

problem-oriented special units
investigative units that focus on specific types of offenders or criminal activities

Problem-oriented special units focus on specific types of offenders or criminal activities and include outlaw motorcycle gang units, financial crime units, and sex offence units. Problem-oriented specialty units are created to address a particular problem that is perceived to be beyond the capacity of patrol officers or general investigators. Method-oriented special units are distinguished by specialized equipment and tactics. These include emergency response teams (ERTs), strike force units, and bomb squads.

method-oriented special units
police units that are distinguished by specialized equipment and tactics

Detectives staff the various specialty units in a police service. The work of police detectives is mainly reactive. They arrive on the scene once it has been secured, having been called by patrol supervisors already in attendance. Once the detectives have been briefed by patrol officers and have had an opportunity to gather information from witnesses (if any), they assign investigative follow-up roles or conduct further inquiries themselves. For serious crimes, Identification Section officers come to collect evidence at the scene. The Criminal Code and provincial laws give police officers the authority to freeze or hold a crime scene for a prescribed length of time.

Recent years have a seen a rapid proliferation of problem-oriented special units, many of which bring together officers from a number of police services and, in some instances, personnel from other criminal justice agencies such as corrections. Examples of integrated units are Integrated Market Enforcement Teams (IMETs), which operate in urban financial centres and focus on capital markets fraud and market-related crimes; and Combined Forces Special Enforcement Units (CFSEUs), which operate in Toronto, Montreal, and Quebec City as well as in British Columbia. In Ontario the unit is composed of the Toronto Police Service, Ontario Provincial Police, York Regional Police, Peel Regional Police, Royal Canadian Mounted Police,

Citizenship and Immigration Canada, and Criminal Intelligence Service Ontario.

On paper, integrated specialty units would appear to be an excellent strategy for responding to specific types of criminal activity. However, there have been few published evaluations of the effectiveness of this police strategy. This is unfortunate, for these units are costly and require participating police services to second experienced investigators. Integrated units may also be created by provincial governments in response to public pressure following a critical event or series of events (e.g., gangland shootings). It is important to determine whether a specialty unit has been created to make the police service more effective or, conversely, for "ceremonial" purposes (i.e., to give the appearance of accomplishment and to preserve the legitimacy of the police service).[2]

One police observer has noted that specialty units provide the police with legitimacy in the community, "providing the appearance of, if not an effective response to, the special or intense problems in the community."[3] A good example of appearance's sake are media "photo-ops" where the police display their prize seizures, most often drugs and weapons. While these events are quite photogenic, one might well ask: "So what?" That is, "What impact do these seizures have on the flow of illicit weapons and drugs and on the crime rate?" Furthermore, "Was the investigation that led to the seizures an effective use of police resources?" "Was the evidence gathered (and the manner in which it was gathered) sufficient to secure a conviction in court?" These questions are rarely if ever asked by the media and the general public and remain largely unexplored by researchers.

A police seizure.

FUNDAMENTALS OF MAJOR CASE INVESTIGATION

A case (or criminal) investigation is intended to develop reasonable grounds to make an arrest, or at least identify suspects. This relatively simple objective can be highly complex and time-consuming. Recall from Chapter 1 that legislation, case law, public policy, and the increasing sophistication of criminal activity have led to significant increases in police workloads. Contrary to the images presented on television and in movies, many criminal investigations do not result in the arrest of suspects. Both time and the odds favour the criminal offender, especially in nonviolent offences, where clearance (catch) rates may be quite low. Case investigations can be costly and require the commitment of significant resources. Investigators must often prioritize cases on the basis of "solvability."

Investigators of serious crimes in Canada are guided by the **major case management model**, which sets out a protocol for conducting investigations. (See Figure 10.1.) The model is designed to facilitate the collection, management, retrieval, and analysis of large volumes of data that are gathered in major crime investigations. The failure to follow this model may affect the quality of a police investigation and reduce the likelihood that the offender will be apprehended.

Police officers involved in case investigations must be aware of changes in the Criminal Code, provincial statutes, court decisions, and changes in internal police policies and procedures, among other things. In Canada, evidence obtained in a manner that breaches the Charter of Rights and Freedoms is not automatically excluded.

Case investigators face pressure to gather evidence that will withstand scrutiny and challenges in the courts. There is some evidence that a *"CSI effect"*

> **major case management model**
> the protocol for conducting investigations

FIGURE 10.1 The Major Case Management Model

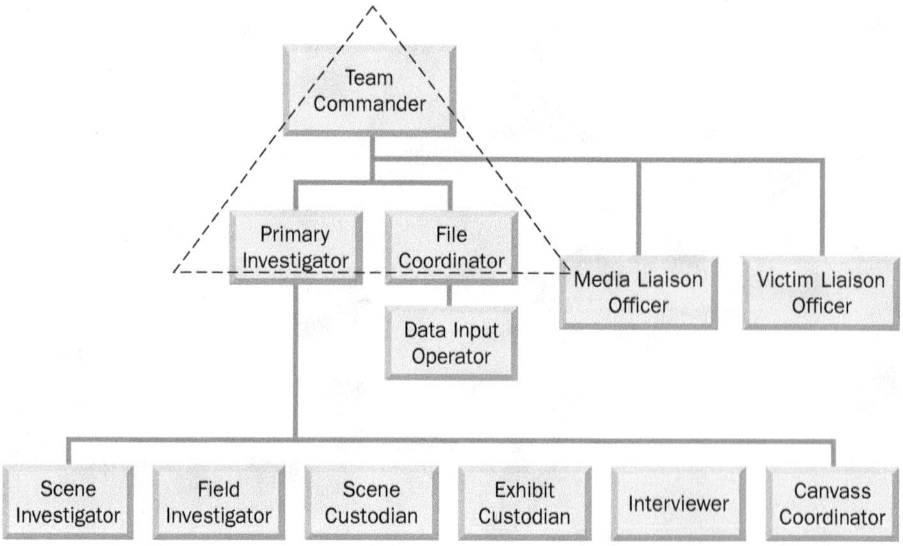

Source: Campbell and LePard (2007), 20. Reprinted by permission of Doug LePard.

(named after the popular TV show *Crime Scene Investigation*) may exist among jurors, who expect the prosecutor to present them with clear and unequivocal scientific evidence.[4] In one American case, jurors asked the judge whether a cigarette butt had been tested for a DNA match with the defendant. It had been, but the defence lawyer, quite inexplicably, had failed to introduce the test results as evidence. The DNA results were introduced and the defendant was acquitted.[5] A Canadian study, based on interviews with police detectives, found that most officers felt that programs such as *CSI* were leading the public to engage in "Monday morning quarterbacking," with citizens questioning how an investigation was being conducted. The officers also expressed concern that the general public would lose confidence in the police once they noticed the discrepancy between well-resourced TV-based investigators and under-resourced investigative units in the real world.[6]

A number of factors affect case investigations, including the ingenuity, skills, and motivation levels of the investigator(s); the priorities of the police service; the sophistication of the crime; and the willingness of Crown counsel to proceed with the case. Police services make extensive use of the Internet in their attempts to solve crimes. Many police websites have "Most Wanted" pages, as well as pages for unsolved crimes, missing persons, and unidentified bodies/remains (for examples, visit the OPP website at http://www.opp.ca).

Investigations must be both strategic (as in determining when to execute search warrants, interview suspects, and make arrests) and tactical (as in deciding on approaches to establishing reasonable grounds). There are two types of investigations, one at each end of the spectrum. In **smoking gun investigations**, either the accused is found at the scene of a crime or circumstantial evidence clearly points to the accused (e.g., the accused leaves his driver's licence at the crime scene). In **whodunit investigations**, the suspect is unknown, and investigations require considerable time and usually rely heavily on circumstantial and forensic evidence gathered at the scene. These latter investigations are resource intensive, may take several years to conduct, and may never result in an arrest.

Notwithstanding the development of high technology as part of the investigator's tool kit, the fundamental role of investigators is encapsulated in the acronym GOYAKOD (Get Off Your Ass—Knock On Doors). Solving crimes still depends on that basic technique, which highlights the importance of community assistance. This may be a challenge in a multicultural society, for language barriers and mistrust of the police may hinder police investigations.

smoking gun investigations
cases in which the perpetrator is readily identifiable

whodunit investigations
cases in which the suspect is unknown and extensive investigation is required

The Use of Informants in Case Investigation

Informants are an important resource for police investigators. They inhabit a grey and understudied region of Canadian police work. Police officers are trained to remember that all the offenders with whom they have contact are potential informants.[7] The policies and procedures for managing informants reside largely within individual police services. There are no national standards or protocols for recruiting and managing informants. In Quebec, committees composed of representatives from police services and the public prosecutor's office supervise the use of informants.[8]

Investigators of major cases, as well as patrol officers, may use informants at the street level. Remuneration for informants ranges from nothing at all to millions of dollars. Typically, for higher amounts, a formal contract is signed between the police service and the informant. In one investigation into Hells Angels, the RCMP paid an informant, who had connections with that gang in Vancouver, $1 million to wear a "wire" and gather incriminating evidence. During the months he was on the payroll, the informant was a big-time spender on women and in the clubs. The informant's testimony in several court cases resulted in several Hells Angels being convicted. He was subsequently relocated to an undisclosed location under an assumed name.

Police informants played a critical role in a 2006 case that foiled what would have been the largest ever terrorist attack on Canadian soil. In a case that came to be known as the "Toronto 18," the RCMP paid out more than $4 million to two informants, who infiltrated a group that intended to carry out a series of attacks, including storming Parliament Hill in Ottawa, beheading politicians, and bombing the Toronto Stock Exchange and other prominent buildings. Their goal was to force the Canadian government to withdraw from the conflict in Afghanistan. Several individuals were subsequently convicted of a variety of offences under the Anti-Terrorism Act and received lengthy prison terms.

Critics argue that the effectiveness of this practice has not been documented and that paying persons who are often themselves associated with criminal activities compromises the principles of justice.[9] Section 25 of the Criminal Code contains a controversial provision that allows undercover officers and informants to commit acts that are criminal (except violence), including drug dealing. Two other concerns relate to the motives of informants—whether they are in it for the money or for a higher moral purpose—and to the quality and validity of the information gathered. There are also instances of "rogue" informants, who, while working for the police, continue to be involved in criminal behaviour or do not follow the instructions of their police handlers. Much more research remains to be conducted on the role of informants in police work.

Informants have become integral to police work. However, a recent decision of the Supreme Court of Canada held that the right of the police to protect the identify of an informer was not absolute. Provided the method was lawful, the defence could make every effort to identify the informant and "make full answer and defence." (*R. v. Barros*, 2011, SCC 51).

The Crime Scene Search

A crime scene search is conducted in order to gather evidence that will:

- determine the facts of the crime committed;
- establish the methods used to commit the crime; *and*
- identify the perpetrator(s) of the crime.

Two basic approaches are used to search a crime scene: a *cautious search* of visible areas, taking steps to avoid evidence loss or contamination; followed by a *vigorous search* for hidden/concealed areas. Case investigators may also gather photographic evidence that can be presented in court in the place of actual evidence. Photographs are often taken of physical evidence that is too large to move or store, or in situations in which the owner of the evidence would experience hardship by losing possession of it. Witnesses may be able to help the investigator locate evidence.

Police Note Taking

The notes made by officers at the scene are an important source of evidence and may help identify suspects who might otherwise go undetected. They may also establish patterns connecting seemingly unrelated criminal events; link suspects who might otherwise not be linked; and provide a source of recall for the officer, who may be required to testify months or even years after an incident. Yet police notes are often incomplete and insufficiently detailed.

Officers who attend court are often asked to refer to their notes. Both the prosecution and the defence ask whether the officer recorded the notes at the time of the incident or as soon as practical thereafter. If the answer is yes, and no challenges are made, the officer is free to refer to the notes. Generally, a police officer's notes remain in the possession of the investigating officer, although copies of them accompany all arrest reports and are routinely disclosed to defence counsel. There have been cases where officers "backfilled" their notebooks in order to cover for mistakes in an investigation (see Chapter 7).

Types of Evidence

At a crime scene, investigators look for several general types of evidence:

- *Oral (or testimonial) evidence* provided by witnesses, suspects, and victims. These may be provided in written form or verbally. Oral evidence includes confessions by suspects as well as sworn statements.
- *Real evidence,* which includes physical objects such as weapons, paint chips, and broken glass.
- *Documentary evidence,* such as written materials and records, including letters, invoices, bank records, and accounting ledgers.
- *Social media evidence,* including Facebook and images on smartphones.

The "crime scene" may not be a physical place. It may be located on the Internet (cybercrime), a computer, a smartphone, or other electronic device. Social media, including Facebook, are playing a greater role as a source of evidence for police investigations. See Police File 10.1.

Crime scene investigators also distinguish between direct and circumstantial evidence. **Direct evidence** is information detected through at least one of the five senses: sight, touch, hearing, smell, and taste. Eyewitness accounts are a form of direct evidence. **Circumstantial evidence** is not directly observed; even so, it links the victim to the accused by inference. In *R. v. John,* 1971, S.C.R. 781, the trial judge explained the distinction between direct and circumstantial evidence:

> If a witness gives evidence that he saw A stab B with a knife, that is direct evidence that A stabbed B. If a witness gives evidence that he found a dagger with an unusually long blade in the possession of A and another witness testified that such a dagger could have caused B's wounds, that is circumstantial evidence tending to prove that A did in fact stab B.

direct evidence
evidence in criminal investigations that is detected through one of the five senses

circumstantial evidence
evidence not directly observed but that can implicate an offender

Police File 10.1

The Role of Social Media in Case Investigation: The Vancouver Hockey Riot, 2011

Following the Vancouver Canucks' loss to Boston in Game 7 of the Stanley Cup playoffs in June 2011, a riot ensued that resulted in millions of dollars in property damage. The riot erupted after as many as 150,000 people crowded into the downtown area, many of whom watched the game on giant screens that had been erected. Fights broke out, cars (including two police cruisers) were set ablaze, and stores were looted. It took police more than three hours to restore order. During the melee, thousands of photographs and videos were taken on cell phones and TV cameras. The Vancouver police put out a general call for the public to send in their images of perpetrators. There were so many responses that the VPD computer server crashed. Images were posted on Facebook, and many of the rioters who looted and caused damage were "outed" by friends and associates. The images were used by investigators to identify and arrest persons who had committed criminal offences (see At Issue 10.1 at the end of the chapter).

Observers have commented that these events indicate that society may be entering a new arena of "citizen surveillance." Concerns have been raised that this may, ironically, undermine any sense of community rather than solidify it.

The riot in Vancouver after the final Stanley Cup game, 2011.

Jason Payne/Postmedia News Service

"It's so hard to choose just one—can't I pick two?"

Eyewitnesses: An Unreliable Source of Evidence

Information gathered from individuals who have witnessed events surrounding the commission of a crime is often used in forming reasonable grounds in case investigations, especially in the absence of physical evidence. This evidence, however, is notoriously unreliable and must be used with caution (see Research File 10.1).

It has been found that mistaken eyewitness identification accounts for more convictions of innocent people than all other errors combined.[10] The ability of an eyewitness to accurately describe an offender may be hindered by a number of factors, including light conditions, weather conditions, the chaos surrounding the incident, the speed with which an offence occurred, and attributes of the eyewitness, including age (young children and the elderly are, generally, less reliable eyewitnesses than are young adults).[11] Also, surprise or distraction may interfere with an eyewitness's ability to notice important information such as the offender's height, weight, and clothing; the colour, make, and licence plate of a vehicle; and even the number of suspects involved. For a powerful and moving story of a man who was wrongfully convicted based on faulty eyewitness testimony by the victim of the crime, read *Picking Cotton: A Memoir of Injustice and Redemption* (2009). The book was co-authored by Jennifer Thompson-Cannino, the victim, and Ronald Cotton, the man who was wrongfully convicted and spent eleven years behind bars before being exonerated by a DNA test.

Specific criticisms have been directed toward police line-ups, which involve placing the suspect (or a photo of the suspect) among other individuals (or photos of other individuals), then presenting the array to eyewitnesses to see

Research File 10.1

The Unreliability of Eyewitness Testimony

Many experimental studies have illustrated the unreliability of eyewitness evidence. This should alert criminal investigators to the need to search for physical evidence whenever possible. In one field study, two researchers went to various convenience stores posing as customers. They stayed in each store for three to four minutes, drawing attention to themselves intentionally by displaying certain behaviours, such as paying for the entire amount of their purchase in pennies and making lengthy searches for money. The researchers also asked for directions that required lengthy explanations by the clerks. Two hours after the researchers left, two individuals entered the store posing as police officers searching for the two customers. A photo lineup consisting of six mug shots was presented to each store employee. Only 32 percent of the witnesses accurately identified either customer.

Source: J.C. Brigham, A. Maass, L.D. Snyder, and K. Spaulding, "Accuracy of Eyewitness Identifications in a Field Setting," *Journal of Personality and Social Psychology* 42, no. 4 (1982): 673–81.

whether they select the suspect.[12] For a test of your eyewitness capacities, keyword "Gary Wells Eyewitness Test," prepared by one of the leading experts in eyewitness testimony.

CCTVs are electronic eyewitnesses and can provide a more accurate record of events than human eyewitnesses. The Supreme Court of Canada has ruled that videotape evidence can be used in criminal trials, although any electronic image—including videos and photographs taken by cell phones—can be misleading. The lighting and camera angle may present an inaccurate picture of the incident, and the images often do not capture the entire incident.

Police Interviews with Victims and Witnesses

A critical component of all case investigations is the interviews with victims and witnesses. Interviewing skills are a key component of police recruit training and in-service training. The police interviewer must take particular care with vulnerable groups, including children, to ensure that "leading" questions are not posed and that the information gathered in the interview is accurate. It is also important to ensure that the victim is not traumatized ("revictimized") by the interview.

The consequences of poor interviewing techniques can be profound. In one case it resulted in two wrongful convictions in a high-profile trial. Irreparable damage was done to the reputations of the defendants, several of whom were police officers. Read about the "Martensville Nightmare" ritual abuse case in Box 10.1.

Linkage in Criminal Investigations

A primary objective in case investigations is to link the various facets of the crime scene, the victim, the physical evidence, and the suspect. Each of these

Box 10.1

The "Martensville Nightmare"

Ron and Linda Sterling, along with their twenty-five-year-old son Travis, ran a baby-sitting service in the small bedroom community of Martensville, just north of Saskatoon. One of their clients, a nurse, noticed that her two-year-old had chafing and redness around her genitals. When questioned, the little girl stated "a stranger poked my bum with a pink rope." This set in motion a police investigation that resulted in the Sterlings, an unidentified female minor, and five other men being charged in 1992 with 190 counts of physical and sexual abuse against two dozen children who had attended the baby-sitting service. Several of those charged were local police officers, who were implicated by the children.

The case was assigned to the newest member of the Martensville police department, a female constable who had little training or experience in conducting child interviews. The constable, who had herself been abused as a child, used repeated, direct questioning, which has been shown to produce false accusations in children.

Among the statements the children made were that they had been taken to a "Devil Church" in the country. There, they had been physically abused and forced to drink urine and eat feces, threatened with guns, and forced to perform oral sex. One child stated that another child's nipple had been cut off and eaten by one of the abusers. At the time, there was a widespread belief—even among the police—that Satanic rituals were being held in the community. But there was no other evidence against the accused except the children's testimony, and experts who reviewed the taped interviews that the constable and her colleague had conducted determined that the interviews were rife with leading questions. It was noted, for example, that the children were praised when a "right" answer was provided.

The trials of the accused began in 1993. In the end, only Travis Sterling and the unnamed female minor were found guilty, though their convictions were later overturned. Ron and Linda Sterling were found not guilty, and charges against the remaining defendants—all police officers—were later dismissed. In 2002 the Saskatchewan government reached an out-of-court settlement with several of the defendants, including the Sterlings, that reached into the millions of dollars.

This case highlights how important it is for police officers to be trained in conducting investigative interviews, especially with children and other vulnerable groups.

Sources: "The 'Martensville Nightmare' Ritual Abuse Case," *ReligiousTolerance.org* (1998), http://www.religioustolerance.org/ra_marte.htm; CBC News, *Fifth Estate*, "Hell to Pay" (2003), http://www.cbc.ca/fifth/martin

components must be connected to the others if the case is to be resolved successfully. The basis for conducting this four-way linkage rests on the **principle of transfer and exchange**.

Perhaps the most fundamental of all assumptions made by investigators is that physical evidence is transferred during the commission of a criminal offence. The offender may well have *left* something at the scene and may well have *taken* something from the scene. The key is to find or recognize the

principle of transfer and exchange
the assumption that physical evidence is transferred during the commission of a criminal offence

evidence. For example, a residential break and enter may involve the transfer of physical evidence:

- *from the offender to the crime scene* (fingerprints, footprints, palm prints, treadmarks from footwear or tires, blood, saliva, hair, dirt from footwear); *and*

- *from the crime scene to the offender* (carpet fibre, victim's blood, hair, or saliva, drywall dust, glass).

> **linkage blindness**
> the investigative failure to recognize a pattern linking one crime with one or more others

Linkage blindness is the investigative failure to recognize a pattern linking one crime with one or more others. For example, investigators may fail to notice similar crimes in other jurisdictions, or the offender's signature or modus operandi.[13] Linkage blindness is a major cause of police failures to solve major serial crimes in a timely manner. The absence of interoperability (i.e., the failure to share information) among police services may also hinder police investigations. The lack of interoperability was a key feature in two high-profile cases: the terrorist bombing of Air India Flight 182 (see Police File 10.2) and the case of Robert Pickton, who was ultimately convicted of killing a number of women in the Vancouver area (see Police File 10.3). A central objective of the major case management model is to ensure that investigators make the proper linkages in case investigations.

Police File 10.2

The Bombing of Air India Flight 182

On June 23, 1985, Air India Flight 182 exploded and crashed into the Atlantic Ocean off the coast of Ireland while on a flight from Montreal to London. All 329 passengers on board, most of whom were Canadian citizens, were killed. It was the worst terrorist incident in Canadian history, and the worst aviation disaster in the world until the 9/11 attacks of 2001 on New York and Washington.

The investigation into the bombing centred on individuals in B.C.'s Sikh community, which was involved in a struggle for an independent Khalistan in India. An Air India Task Force, led by the RCMP working in collaboration with police agencies in Europe, India, the United States, and Asia, spent fifteen years investigating the case. More than three hundred RCMP officers worked on the case for over twenty years; there were more than a million documents of evidence; more than one thousand witnesses and

experts were interviewed, some of them multiple times. A $1 million reward was offered for evidence that would help convict the perpetrators.

In 2000, two B.C. residents were charged with multiple offences under the Criminal Code relating to the deaths of the passengers and crew on Air India 182. The charges included first degree murder, conspiracy to commit murder, and attempted murder. In 2001 a third defendant was charged with the same offences; two years later he pleaded guilty to manslaughter for his part in the bombing and received a sentence of five years.

The Crown proceeded by direct indictment against the remaining two defendants. The trial began in April 2003 and continued for nineteen months. In March 2005 the presiding judge found the two defendants not guilty of all charges, stating that "despite what appears to have been the best and most earnest efforts by the police and the Crown, the evidence has fallen markedly short." The judge also commented on what he found to be "unacceptable negligence" on the part of Canada's spy agency, the Canadian Security Intelligence Service (CSIS).

Responding to considerable pressure from the families of the victims, the federal government appointed retired Supreme Court Justice John Major to conduct a judicial inquiry into a number of outstanding questions, including whether problems in information sharing among the RCMP, CSIS, and other agencies hindered the investigation. Among the findings of the Major report, issued in 2010, were these:

- CSIS failed to disclose to the RCMP in a timely manner important information from its investigation.

- CSIS destroyed valuable evidence, including taped conversations that might have incriminated the defendants, under the guise that CSIS does not have as part of its organizational mandate the collection of evidence.

- The RCMP failed to follow up on intelligence leads that did not conform to its theory as to who was involved in the bombing ("tunnel vision").

- The RCMP did not recognize the serious threat posed by Sikh extremism and did not adequately protect informants and witnesses.

- There was intra-organizational strife in the RCMP within the E Division investigative team and between E Division and RCMP Headquarters in Ottawa.

In this case, the lack of interoperability between CSIS and the RCMP, internal difficulties in the RCMP, and "tunnel vision" on the part of case investigators, among others, seriously compromised the investigation.

Source: J.C. Major (Commissioner), "Air India Flight 182: A Canadian Tragedy" (Ottawa: Minister of Public Works and Government Services, 2010), http://epe.lac-bcp/100/206/301/pco-bcp/commissions/air_india/2010-07-23/www.major-comm.ca/en/reports/finalreport/default.htm

Police File 10.3

The Missing Women Case

During the mid to late 1990s, a number of sex trade workers from Vancouver's Downtown Eastside began to go missing. These women, many of who were addicted to drugs, disappeared and did not make contact with family or friends. In 1998, a Vancouver Police Department (VPD) Detective Constable was assigned to the case and received tips suggesting that Robert "Willie" Pickton could be responsible for the missing women. Pickton was a pig farmer whose property was in the rapidly

developing suburban municipality of Coquitlam, a few kilometres from Vancouver. Coquitlam is policed under contract by the RCMP.

During the next several years, women continued to disappear. Finally, in 2002, during an investigation unrelated to the missing women (suspicion that Pickton had an unregistered firearm), the IDs and a number of personal effects belonging to several of the missing women were found on his property. The search for evidence on Pickton's property

(Continued)

over the next several years, which became the largest police investigation in Canadian history, cost an estimated $124 million and at its peak involved hundreds of police officers and civilians (including over 102 anthropologists), who searched for DNA evidence on the property. Over the two-year period, 235,000 pieces of DNA evidence were gathered and the remains of thirty women were identified.

It is estimated that Pickton killed sixty-five women on his farm over a fifteen-year period. In 2007, he was convicted of the second degree murder of six women and given a life sentence with no possibility of parole for twenty-five years.

Following Pickton's arrest, the Vancouver Police Department conducted a detailed examination of how the case had been investigated. The study, prepared by a Deputy Chief Constable in the department, involved interviewing hundreds of officers and reviewing thousands of pages of documents. A number of internal organizational and operational factors were identified that had hindered the investigation. As well, the report documented ongoing difficulties experienced by the VPD in securing the RCMP's involvement in aggressively pursuing the investigation. Following the release of this report (perhaps the most exhaustive of its type), the VPD issued a public apology to the families of the victims (38, 39, 40). The RCMP subsequently apologized and released limited documentation on how the case had been investigated.

In 2010, under pressure from the victims' families and various Aboriginal groups, the provincial government established a commission of inquiry to examine the investigative activities of the VPD and the RCMP in the missing women's cases.

As part of its inquiry, the commission retained the services of a Deputy Chief of Peel Regional Police who produced a report that examined a number of issues related to the investigations conducted by the VPD and the RCMP. The findings of this report, which closely mirrored those of the VPD study, included the following:

- Senior management in both services failed to recognize the seriousness of the case, to take ownership of the case, and to provide sufficient resources for the investigation.
- There was a failure to recognize that a serial killer was at work.
- There were systemic problems in communication and cooperation between the VPD and the RCMP which contributed to linkage blindness.
- The lack of a standardized Major Case Management approach by the VPD and the RCMP hindered the investigation.
- An effective multi-jurisdictional investigation was made more difficult by the absence of a regional police service (see Chapter 2).

The commission, which was still in session as of early 2012, heard from current and former police officers, as a well as a number of other persons associated with the investigation. The final report of the commission is scheduled for release in late spring of 2012 (http://www.missingwomeninquiry.ca).

Source: D. LePard, "Missing Women Investigation Review," ©2010 Vancouver Police Department. Reprinted by permission; J. Evans, "Missing Women. Commission of Inquiry, British Columbia," 2012 http://beta.images.theglobeandmail .com/archive/01344/Evans_Report_-Par_134418a.pdf

ANALYTICAL TOOLS

To assist in case investigations, police services use sophisticated analytical techniques. Some systems combine behavioural science research with computer analysis to generate profiles of crime scenes and perpetrators; others apply forensic science to evidence gathered during the investigation. Some of the more commonly used analytical tools are described as follows.

Criminal Profiling

Criminal profiling has been described as "the practice of predicting a criminal's personality, behavioral and demographic characteristics based on crime scene evidence." The typical profile involves preparing a biographical sketch based on information taken from the crime scene as well as victim-related materials.

The objective of criminal profiling is to provide the investigation with a personality composite of the unknown suspect(s). The profiler studies a crime scene from a psychological standpoint, interpreting the evidence there for clues to the personality of the individual who committed the crime. The profiler is able to analyze the scene in terms of emotions such as rage, hate, love, fear, and irrationality.

A criminal profile attempts to determine the attributes of the offender, which may include age, gender, ethnicity, marital status/adjustment, intelligence, education level, lifestyle, the environment in which the person was raised, social adjustment, personality style/characteristics, demeanour, appearance and grooming, emotional adjustment, evidence of mental decomposition, pathological behavioural characteristics, employment/occupational history and adjustment, work habits, residency in relation to the crime scene, socioeconomic status, sexual adjustment, type of sexual perversion or disturbance (if applicable), and motive.

Concerns have been raised about the validity and effectiveness of criminal profiling. Police scholars have argued that the approach lacks a scientific basis and that there is no evidence it works.[14] Evaluative research is required to test the assumptions on which criminal profiling is premised, as well as to address the concerns that have been expressed about its use.

> **criminal profiling**
> a strategy to identify suspects by constructing biographical and psychological sketches based on crime scene evidence

ViCLAS (Violent Crime Linkage Analysis System)

Canadian police services collaborated in the development of a system to track serial killers and violent offenders and link their crimes. Known as the **ViCLAS** (Violent Crime Linkage Analysis System), this system combines current findings from behavioural research with sophisticated computer technology.

ViCLAS is designed to capture information on all homicides that are sexual or predatory in nature and/or that are apparently random, motiveless, or suspected of being part of a series; as well as all sexual assaults or attempted assaults of a predatory nature, including stranger-to-stranger assaults, date rapes, and pedophilia crimes. It also captures information on missing persons when the circumstances indicate a strong possibility of foul play and when the victim is still missing; on unidentified bodies when the manner of death is unknown or suspected to be a homicide; and on all nonparental abductions and attempts at abduction. The premise of ViCLAS is that repeat offenders follow similar patterns and that homicidal and sexual offenders have identifiable and often predictable characteristics and motives.

> **ViCLAS**
> Violent Crime Linkage Analysis System; a system used by investigators that includes information on predatory and sexual crimes of violence

Geographic Profiling

Geographic profiling is related to the broader investigative strategy of criminal or psychological profiling. Essentially, geographic profiling involves analyzing behavioural patterns that relate to space or geography and incorporating the findings as they relate to the journey to crime, or to the crime trip distance.

> **geographic profiling**
> the analysis of behaviour patterns that relate to space or geography, with particular reference to the journey to crime

This is the distance offenders travel from their residence or place of work to commit crimes.

Geographic profiling is based on a number of key findings with respect to patterns of criminal offending, including that most crimes occur in relatively close proximity to the offender's place of residence or work, often referred to as the offender's "comfort zone." Also, the number of crimes committed by an offender decreases as the distance from the offender's residence increases, and the distance an offender travels often increases as his or her criminal career develops. For example, the first murder committed by a serial killer is likely to be the one closest to the offender's home.[15]

Geographic profilers often apply computer technology to create geographic information systems. These systems can be used to plan patrol and investigative strategies. The sources of information required to conduct geographic profiling include data on the crimes, the locations where the crimes were committed, data on the victims, a criminal profile, and data on the suspect.[16]

Through spatial analysis, high-volume crimes often associated with career criminals (e.g., break and enters, auto theft, armed robbery) can be charted, and three-dimensional computer maps can be generated that indicate the areas most likely to be associated with the residence, worksite, social venue, and travel routes of offenders.

Criminal Intelligence Analysis

Case investigation is often assisted by criminal intelligence analysis, which utilizes sophisticated computer programs to analyze information gathered on suspected criminal activity. These analyses attempt to identify relationships between criminal groups and among individuals and are utilized by case investigators on an operational level. Criminal intelligence analysis can also be used to inform strategic decision making in a police service regarding potential threats and emerging criminal issues.

THE ANALYSIS OF SPECIFIC TYPES OF EVIDENCE

Evidence gathered at a crime scene must be analyzed to determine its usefulness in solving the crime and identifying suspects. In forensic analysis, trained personnel and laboratory technicians examine this evidence. They play a critical role in case investigations by providing laboratory analyses and examinations of physical evidence. They also prepare reports and arrange expert court testimony on the results of their analyses. Forensic scientists and technologists can be civilians or sworn police officers.

Specific types of evidence are regularly subjected to forensic analysis as part of case investigations. Fingerprints are useful in placing an individual at a crime scene, although they cannot be lifted from all surfaces. Once fingerprints are lifted, the investigators may access the national Automated Fingerprint Identification System (AFIS). AFIS is a system of fingerprint workstations and databases across Canada, many of which are networked together and to the RCMP national system in Ottawa. Evidence can also be gathered from firearms, bullets, and casings. Hair can be used in DNA analysis, and fibres found at a crime scene can be positively compared to fibres found on the suspect or in the suspect's car or home.

© Christopher J. Morris/Corbis

A police investigator retrieves evidence at a crime scene.

DNA: The Genetic Fingerprint

DNA is the abbreviation for deoxyribonucleic acid, which is often referred to as the blueprint of the body and the basic building blocks of life. Human bodies have trillions of cells. Each cell contains a nucleus, within which are forty-six chromosomes divided into twenty-three pairs. These chromosomes are inherited from both parents. Chromosomes consist of two long, twisted strands of DNA, called a double helix. Human DNA is divided into about 100,000 clusters called genes. Genes determine human characteristics such as height, eye colour, and hair colour. Each gene is composed of molecules called nucleotides, which occur in four different shapes—adenine, cytosine, guanine, and thymine—and which are arranged in pairs along the strands of DNA.

The DNA of every person is unique (except in the case of identical twins, who receive the same genetic material from both parents). DNA analysis, or genetic fingerprinting, involves various molecular biological techniques and allows perpetrators to be identified through direct analysis of specific sites on the DNA molecule (see Figure 10.2).

DNA testing has been accepted by Canadian courts since 1988 and the use of DNA evidence by investigators has increased significantly, especially since 1995, when the Criminal Code was amended, allowing police to obtain warrants for bodily substances that enable DNA analysis. Acting under the authority of a search warrant, police can obtain either blood (by a simple finger lancet) or saliva (by swabbing the inside of the mouth). Box 10.2 presents some of the many types of DNA evidence, the possible locations of DNA on the evidence, and the sources of the DNA. The Supreme Court of Canada

DNA
genetic information that can be used in case investigations

Box 10.2

Identifying DNA Evidence: Selected Examples

Evidence	Possible location of DNA on the evidence	Source of DNA
Bandanna, hat, mask	Anywhere (inside or outside)	Dandruff, hair, saliva, sweat
Bite mark	Clothing, skin	Saliva
Blanket, pillow, sheet	Surface area	Blood, hair, saliva, semen, sweat, urine
Bottle, can, glass	Mouthpiece, rim, sides	Saliva, sweat
Fingernail, partial fingernail	Scrapings	Blood, sweat, tissue
Used cigarette	Cigarette butt	Saliva
Used condom	Inside/outside surface	Rectal or vaginal cells, semen

Source: http://www.dna.gov/basics/evidence_collection/identifying

held in *R. v. Stillman*, 1997, 1 S.C.R. 607, that the police can use DNA evidence collected from discarded items, such as chewing gum, drink containers, and cigarettes and that gathering such evidence does not violate a person's privacy rights, nor does it breach a person's Charter rights.[17]

Under Section 487.04 of the Criminal Code, the police can obtain DNA warrants only for certain offences. These include murder, manslaughter, assault, sexual assault, and sexual exploitation, as well as a number of other specifically identified crimes.

DNA testing has been accepted by Canadian courts since 1988. DNA analysis is most commonly used to identify suspects by analyzing biological samples (e.g., semen, saliva, hair, blood) found at crime scenes. DNA analysis serves a number of other important functions in case investigations. For example, it can:

- establish the association between the victim and the suspect in a murder, a sexual assault, or another violent crime;
- identify the weapon used;
- identify where the crime took place;
- determine whether a series of murders or sexual assaults has been committed by the same person or whether a copycat offender is involved;
- exonerate the wrongly accused; *and*
- identify the remains of victims.

FIGURE 10.2 How DNA Fingerprinting Works

How DNA Fingerprinting Works

The process for analyzing DNA—deoxyribonucleic acid, the genetic blueprint found in every cell of the human body—to determine whether two samples "match" is enormously complicated. It involves intricate laboratory work and sophisticated application of mathematical formulas.

1. Forensic experts begin by taking blood, saliva, semen, skin, or hair from the crime scene and a suspect.

2. The genetic material is extracted and mixed with enzymes, which cut the material into fragments.

3. Sometimes fragments are replicated by a technique known as polymerase chain reaction (PCR).

4. After being placed in a special gel, an electrical current is applied to sort the fragments by size.

5. Lasers light up fluorescent tags and the fragment lengths are measured.

6. The resulting patterns, which resemble a supermarket bar code, can be photographed and examined.

Crime evidence   Suspect 1   Suspect 2

No Match   Match

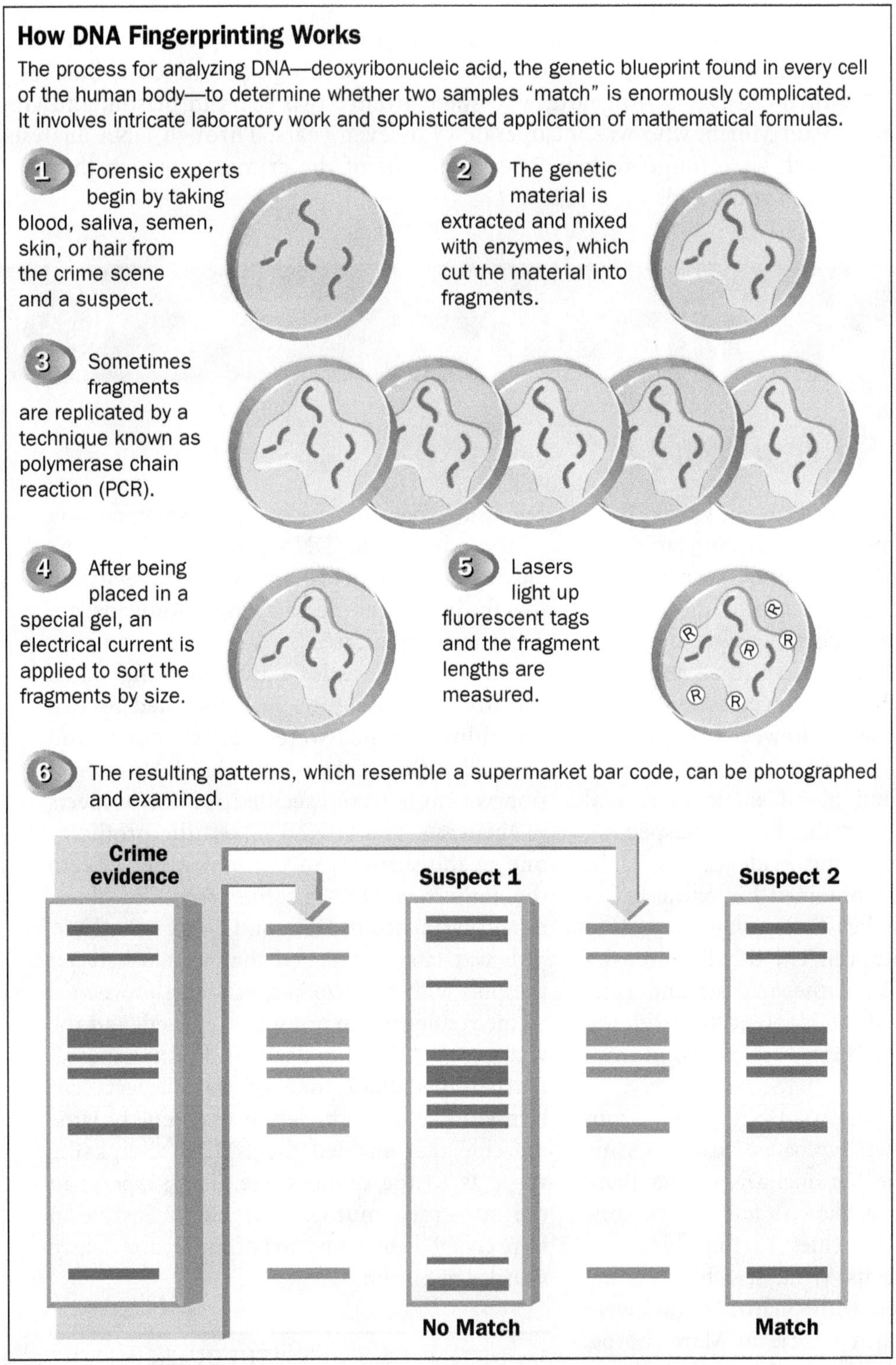

Source: S. Strauss, "Fingerprints Leaving Fingerprints of Their Own," *Globe and Mail*, June 19, 1997, A1, A3. Created from material by Cellmark Diagnostics, Lifecodes Corp., and Cetus Corp.

DNA enables crime investigators to solve crimes that would in many cases go unsolved. See Police File 10.4.

DNA analysis can also be used to exonerate people who have been wrongfully convicted. Two of the more recent high-profile Canadian cases involved David Milgaard, who spent twenty-two years in prison, and Guy Paul Morin, who was incarcerated for seven years. Through DNA analysis, both were found to have been innocent of the crimes of which they had been convicted.

Police File 10.4

DNA Helps Solve a Murder

On April 23, 2002, in Dawson Creek, B.C., Shawn's family reported him missing. Police determined that the twenty-nine-year-old had last been seen nine days earlier at a local pub with two unknown men. The two men were tentatively identified and associated to a nearby residence. When police arrived at the residence, however, they found it abandoned.

The police found blood stains in several locations throughout the home. Suspecting foul play, they sent the evidence for DNA analysis. They also obtained biological reference samples from the missing man's parents to help with identification. The RCMP Forensics Laboratory completed the analysis and confirmed that some of the blood at the residence matched to Shawn. There was also blood from another person.

The unknown person's DNA profile from the crime scene was uploaded to the Crime Scene Index at the National DNA Data Bank (NDDB). Unsure of Shawn's fate, police continued to follow all clues to find him and his assumed assailants. While searching for the two men last seen with Shawn, police were led to an abandoned vehicle in Mayerthorpe, Alberta. Several blood-soaked household items were found in the vehicle, along with Shawn's knapsack. These items were sent to the RCMP

Forensic Laboratory for analysis. A comparison of the crime scene DNA profiles and Shawn's yielded a match. This supported the evidence that the police were dealing with a homicide, not a missing person case.

Shortly afterwards, a man walking down the street in Saskatoon was assaulted by two individuals, who were apprehended and charged with attempted murder. DNA collection warrants were executed for the suspects in this case. The NDDB linked the profile of one of the suspects in the Saskatoon case to the unknown DNA profile from the abandoned residence in Dawson Creek.

It was later confirmed that Shawn had left the pub with the two suspects and proceeded to the residence. An argument ensued, and the victim was stabbed to death and dismembered. During the attack, one of the suspects cut himself. The blood he left at the scene became the clue that enabled the NDDB to link the suspects to the crime scene. The suspects in the attempted murder charged in Saskatoon were charged and convicted of the second degree murder of Shawn.

Source: © 2010 HER MAJESTY THE QUEEN IN RIGHT OF CANADA as represented by the Royal Canadian Mounted Police (RCMP). Reproduced with the permission of the RCMP.

However, contaminated or improperly collected DNA has also led to *wrongful* convictions. When confronted with DNA evidence, defence lawyers have generally counselled their clients to accept a plea bargain. Concerns have centred on cross-contamination and mislabelling of DNA samples, a lack of quality control in testing procedures, and, in some instances, DNA analysts who falsify test results. Gregory Turner, convicted of killing an elderly woman in Newfoundland, spent twenty-seven months in prison before it was determined that the technician who analyzed the DNA sample in the laboratory had contaminated the evidence.[18]

Advances in DNA technology will soon allow the identification of a suspect's ancestors, and this has raised concerns about genetic profiling. In the United States and Britain, familial DNA matches have been used to identify suspects. See At Issue 10.3. Police in Los Angeles had the DNA of the suspect in the "Grim Reaper" serial killer case but could not find a match on any DNA database. They did, however, find a near match in the DNA databank from a young man recently convicted of a weapons charge. The investigators followed his father and lifted a DNA sample from a discarded slice of pizza. His father turned out to be the Grim Reaper.[19] The use of familial DNA is controversial; as of 2011, it remains to be seen whether the legal provisions will be put in place for this practice to be used by Canadian police services.

The National DNA Data Bank

The National DNA Data Bank was established under the DNA Identification Act (1998, c. 37) (http://www.nddb-bndg.org) and a legislative amendment (Bill C-13). This legislation sets out the procedures for collecting, storing, using, and destroying DNA samples taken from criminal offenders as well as for identifying those offenders who are required to submit a DNA sample. The bank, which is managed by the RCMP, holds the genetic profiles of more than three thousand offenders. Its objective is to link unsolved crimes and to determine whether DNA from a person matches DNA found at these crime scenes. The bank also contains DNA evidence from the scenes of unsolved crimes.

The DNA samples are taken from people who have been convicted of certain serious crimes, including murder and sexual assault. These samples are matched with samples of blood, hair, bone, or semen taken from crime scenes or from the bodies of crime victims. With the approval of a judge, DNA samples can be taken from convicted offenders without their consent.

INVESTIGATIVE STRATEGIES AND TECHNIQUES

Cold Case Squads

Many urban police services have created **cold case squads**, which focus exclusively on unsolved serious crimes. Sophisticated techniques for gathering and analyzing DNA specimens, and computer-based systems such as ViCLAS, now allow police investigators to revisit—and often solve—crimes that are years or even decades old. A cold case that was solved through the use of DNA is presented in Police File 10.5.

cold case squads
specialized units that focus on unsolved serious crimes

Police File 10.5

DNA Closes a Cold Case

On July 17, 1984, Denise Morelle, a popular performer in a children's theatre in Montreal, was found strangled in a vacant apartment in Montreal. The actress had gone to the apartment during a search for new accommodation. The owner had indicated it was unlocked and that she could visit it anytime. Her body, with small burn marks, was found the next day. Initially, investigators believed she had surprised vagrants who were in the apartment. However, the case went cold and remained unsolved for twenty-three years.

In 2006, Montreal police announced that they had arrested forty-nine-year-old Gaetan Bissonnette and charged him with first degree murder. Bissonnette had been convicted of break and enter in 2006 and was required to submit a DNA sample to the National DNA Data Bank. His DNA matched that found on Denise Morelle years earlier. Bissonnette was subsequently convicted of second degree murder with no possibility of parole for twenty years.

Source: Royal Canadian Mounted Police, "The National DNA Data Bank of Canada: Annual Report 2009–2010" (Ottawa: 2010), 9, http://www.nddb-bndg.org/ train/ docs/Annual_2009-2010_e.pdf

Forensic Specialists

A number of other forensic specialists may be called on to assist in criminal investigations. These include forensic anthropologists, who help identify bones and skeletal remains. These specialists focus on identifying the deceased person (gender, race, age) and determining the cause of death as well as the circumstances surrounding the death. Forensic entomology is the study of insects associated with a human body. It is used in death investigations to determine time of death, but it can also be used to determine other factors, such as whether the body was moved or disturbed after death, the position of the body at death, and the presence of wounds (see Police File 10.6).

Catching Offenders with the Mr. Big Technique

Mr. Big technique
a controversial investigative strategy designed to secure confessions from crime suspects

A highly controversial investigative technique used by Canadian police is the **Mr. Big technique.** This is referred to as a "noncustodial" interrogation strategy and is prohibited in the United States as well as in Europe, where it is seen as entrapment and as contributing to false confessions. The technique involves undercover officers befriending crime suspects, who are subsequently introduced to "Mr. Big," a purported organized crime boss. The target(s) are then invited to join the crime group, but only if they admit to having committed a major crime.[20]

Police services point out that the Mr. Big technique has a 75 percent confession rate and a 95 percent conviction rate, but this has not silenced critics. There are concerns that Mr. Big stings are actually dirty tricks that lead to false

Police File 10.6

The Use of Forensic Entomology to Solve a Crime

On June 4, 1984, the partly clad body of a young female was found alongside a rural highway in the northwestern United States. An autopsy revealed that she died of multiple head and neck wounds inflicted by a heavy, sharp object. She was later identified as a fourteen-year-old prostitute. Her brother had reported her as missing around four days before her corpse was discovered.

She was last seen alive on the morning of May 31 in the company of a thirty-year-old army sergeant, the primary suspect. While strong circumstantial evidence supported the theory that the sergeant had murdered her, an accurate estimation of time of death was crucial to establishing a possible link between the suspect and the victim at the time the death occurred.

Several estimates of PMI (postmortem interval: the time elapsed since a person died) were offered by medical examiners and investigators. These were based largely on the physical appearance of the body and on the extent to which decompositional changes had occurred in various organs. They were not based on any quantitative scientific methodology.

Numerous fly larvae (maggots), adult flies, and other insects were observed and collected in and around the victim's wounds. Some were placed alive in small containers and later reared to produce adult flies. Others were placed immediately in a liquid preservative. Additional specimens collected at the autopsy were processed in a similar manner. Numerous photographs were taken of the crime scene, the surrounding vegetation and terrain, and the corpse. These photographs included enlargements illustrating the adult flies and maggots present at the time the body was discovered.

Reports describing the condition of the body when found and detailing autopsy procedures and results were reviewed. Climatological data, including maximum and minimum temperatures, incidence of rainfall, cloud cover, wind speed and direction, and relative humidity, were obtained from a government weather station a short distance from where the victim was found. These data indicated the environmental conditions to which the remains and its insect associates had been exposed.

Based on this array of evidence, entomologists determined that the first insects to colonize the remains had arrived on May 31. The insect evidence indicated a PMI. Based on this evidence, the army sergeant with whom the victim had last been seen alive was arrested and charged with first degree murder. On questioning, he admitted to having murdered the girl by striking her six to eight times with a small hatchet sometime around noon on May 31. Subsequently, he pled guilty to the murder charge and was sentenced to life in prison without parole.

Source: http://dc387.4shared.com/doc/HMnqRkQG/preview.html

confessions and the conviction of innocent persons. Critics argue that the practice raises legal, moral, and ethical issues.[21] Suspects who are questioned about crimes in a Mr. Big scenario enjoy none of the legal safeguards of those who are interrogated in a "custodial" setting. And there is little documentation regarding what happens when the strategy fails and what the consequences are of such failures (e.g., false confessions and wrongful convictions) (see At Issue 10.2).

For a case in which a suspect who confessed to police in a Mr. Big operation was later exonerated by DNA evidence, see Police File 10.7.

Police File 10.7

Mr. Big and a False Confession

On June 24, 1990, the body of sixteen-year-old Brigitte Grenier was found on the grounds of a ski resort in Roseisle, Manitoba. She had been strangled and her body mutilated. One of two suspects in the killing was nineteen-year-old Kyle Unger, who had been seen with Grenier at a rock concert near where the body was located. Unger and his friend were charged and arrested for first degree murder. The Crown entered a stay of proceedings. However, while being held in custody awaiting bail, Unger made statements to his cellmate (a jailhouse informant) that implicated him in the murder.

Based on this, the RCMP developed a Mr. Big scenario in order to gather more evidence from Unger. Two undercover agents pretended to have their vehicle break down near a farm where Unger was working. The two officers befriended Unger and led him to believe they were part of a criminal organization. Unger was invited to join the group but was told he would have to be truthful about his past criminal activities in order to become part of the gang. Unger stated that he had killed Brigitte Grenier. At trial, Unger recanted his confession, stating that during what turned out to be a Mr. Big scenario, he had been offered employment, the potential to earn a lot of money, and membership in the gang. He indicated that, although he initially denied having killed the victim, he subsequently confessed to the crime for financial gain. He was convicted on the basis of his Mr. Big confession and two pieces

of corroborative evidence: hair consistent with his found on the victim's sweater, and comments he had made to the jailhouse informant.

Mr. Unger appealed his conviction to the Manitoba Court of Appeal on the grounds that the Mr. Big sting involved entrapment. This appeal was rejected and leave to appeal to the Supreme Court of Canada was also denied. He then spent fourteen years in prison. In 2004, the hair comparison evidence used at trial was called into question by a forensic review committee. DNA testing found no trace of Unger on any of the exhibits used at trial and did not link him to the crime scene.

He was released on bail in 2005 pending a ministerial review of his case. In 2009 the Crown dropped murder charges against him, admitting there was insufficient evidence for a retrial.

When asked by a reporter following his acquittal why he would have confessed to a crime he had not committed, Unger replied: "When you're young, naive, and desperate for money, they hold a lot of promises to you, so you say and do what you have to do to survive."

Sources: T.E. Moore, "Eliciting Wrongful Convictions by Mr. Big Lies—the Unger Case," *LEAP Blog*, November 21, 2009, 1–2, http://windsorlaw-leap.blogspot.com/2009/11/eliciting-wrongful-convictions-by-mr.html; K. Puddister and T. Riddell, "The RCMP's Use of Mr. Big: An Independence and Accountability Media Case Study" (Guelph: University of Guelph, 2010), http://www.cpsa-acsp.ca/papers-2010/Puddister-Riddell.pdf

Interrogation of Crime Suspects

The tools and techniques discussed so far in this chapter are intended to identify an individual (or individuals) who may have committed the crime. Once
this has been done, the police interrogate the suspect in an attempt to confirm
the results of their analysis of the evidence. Despite the importance of this
phase of the investigation, the interrogation of crime suspects is one of the least
studied features of police work.

Interrogations are usually conducted with four objectives: (1) to obtain a
confession or at least a partial admission of guilt; (2) to eliminate innocent
people from the investigation; (3) to identify the guilty party (even if a confession is not obtained, the interrogator may become aware of the guilty party
and follow up with other investigative options such as surveillance, undercover
operatives, or wiretaps); and (4) to gather information regarding other crimes
and/or suspects. A considerable amount of skill is involved in conducting
interviews, and investigating officers use various techniques to obtain information from suspects, witnesses, and victims.

Officers rely mainly on psychological persuasion to obtain confessions. In
an era of Charter rights, extreme interview tactics are seldom used. However,
the Supreme Court of Canada has ruled that the Charter does not confer
a right of suspects to have a lawyer present during interrogation (see *R. v.
Sinclair*, 2010, SCC 35; *R. v. McCrimmon*, 2010, SCC 36; and *R. v. Willier*, 2010,
SCC 37).

An experienced police investigator will attempt to "bond" with the suspect
and to gain his or her trust and confidence. There are even instances in which
the suspect has re-enacted the crime for the interrogator.

For an inside look at a police interrogation in a high-profile case involving
heinous crimes, see the police interviews with Colonel Russell Williams, a
Commanding Officer in the Canadian Air Force who was subsequently convicted of a series of brutal sexual assaults and murders (See *The Confession:
Inside the Interrogation of Russell Williams*. http://www.cbc.ca/2010-2011/
theconfession/). The eighteen-hour interview with Williams was conducted
by an OPP Detective Sergeant, a specialist in that police service's Behavioural
Sciences and Analysis Services unit, which works on violent and sexual crimes.
Williams subsequently pled guilty to a total of eighty-eight crimes: two counts
of first degree murder, two counts of sexual assault, two counts of forcible confinement, and eighty-two counts of break and enter and attempted break and
enter. He received two life sentences, with no eligibility for parole for twenty-
five years.

The Rights of Suspects to Remain Silent

Under Canadian law, police officers have no formal powers to compel crime
suspects to answer their questions. Suspects have a right to remain silent, and
police officers must inform them of that right. They must also inform suspects
that any statements they do make may be used against them in a criminal trial.
(In reality, remaining silent may only make things worse for the suspect: when

a person refuses to answer some general questions asked by the officer, this may raise suspicions and result in an arrest.) The right to remain silent does not extend to situations where a citizen would thereby be able to obstruct a police officer from carrying out his or her duties. Suspects who have low levels of intelligence or other impairment may not understand their right to silence and its implications.

The courts have also taken a dim view of the use of trickery by police to obtain confessions. The classic case involves placing an undercover police officer in a cell with a suspect; the officer then encourages the suspect to make incriminating statements. The Supreme Court of Canada has established strict limits on the extent to which police can use this tactic to obtain a confession from a suspect who has refused to make a formal statement to the police. However, voluntary statements made by a suspect to a cellmate (who may be an undercover police officer) may not violate the suspect's right to remain silent and may be admissible at trial if the admission does not bring the administration of justice into disrepute.

Interrogation and False Confessions

While false confessions are rare, investigating officers must always carefully assess the reliability of a suspect's statement or confession against all other known facts. Actual innocence may not protect individuals from being wrongfully convicted. Innocent people often waive their right to legal assistance, and certain interview techniques can elicit false confessions. It has been stated that "innocence puts innocents at risk."[22] Officers must be cognizant that the ways in which questions are asked may induce a suspect to falsely confess. Criticism has been directed toward the "Reid technique," a widely used interrogation strategy which an Alberta judge once labelled a "huge brainwashing exercise." In the words of a man who (along with two others) falsely confessed to the rape and murder of a fourteen-year-old girl in Regina (and was later exonerated when DNA evidence convicted another man): "I'm not even sure how to explain it because I'm not sure how it happened to me.... All I know is for hours on end I said 'No, I had nothing to do with it.' Next thing you know I'm sitting there going 'Sure, why not. I did it.' More or less it's like they kill your spirit or something."[23]

There seem to be a number of reasons why, during police interrogations, innocent people confess to crimes they did not commit. These include a desire to escape the psychological pressures of the interview room; sleep deprivation; an attempt to cover for another suspect; a desire to please the police; mental impairment; and, drug or alcohol addiction or withdrawal.[24]

For an excellent case study of false confessions, see the documentary film "The Confessions," produced for the program *Frontline* by PBS (http://www .pbs.org/wgbh/pages/frontline/the-confessions). The film tells the story of the false confessions of four U.S. Navy sailors to a crime they did not commit. The same website provides links to research on interrogation and false confessions.

At Issue 10.1

The Vancouver Hockey Riot, 2011: The "Name and Shame" Phenomenon

In the days following the Stanley Cup riot in Vancouver, a campaign emerged of "name and shame"—that is, posting images and names of rioters on the Web, or images asking for identification. The posting of images taken by smartphones resulted in many of the rioters losing their jobs. In one instance the family of a youth who was photographed lighting a police car on fire was forced to flee after their home address was posted on the Internet. Significantly, much of the name and shame was carried out by younger persons, and this process raced ahead of the police investigation.

Concerns were raised about "vigilante" justice and about the violation of civil liberties. Many of the persons identified issued apologies and admitted their criminal actions in online postings or in public statements to the media.

You Make the Call!

1. If you had been at the riot and taken photographs of persons involved in the riot—for example, looters or arsonists—would you have submitted them to the police?

2. Would you have submitted the digital image and/or identity of a
   a. family member?
   b. close friend?
   c. neighbour?
   d. fellow employee?

At Issue 10.2

Should the "Mr. Big" Technique Be Discontinued in Canada?

Following is a case in which the Mr. Big strategy was used to secure a conviction.

On March 22, 1992, in Sydney, Nova Scotia, convenience store clerk Marie Dupe was stabbed to death during a robbery. The assailant fled the store with cash and cartons of cigarettes and then disappeared into a snowstorm that prevented police dogs from picking up his trail. Left behind at the scene were several pieces of evidence, including a coffee cup and several cigarette butts. Owing to the state of forensic science at the time, the items could not be

(Continued)

analyzed for DNA, so instead they were put into an evidence storage locker. The crime remained unsolved for a decade. In 2001, advances in forensic technology made it possible to conduct a DNA analysis on the evidence. Using the National DNA Databank, the police scored a hit on Gordon Strowbridge, who had provided DNA after being convicted of an assault. The DNA matched that found on one of the cigarette butts outside the convenience store where Marie Dupe had been killed. This placed him at the scene but did not prove he had committed the crime.

While being processed for an outstanding warrant, Strowbridge was befriended by an undercover police officer, who, while posing as a criminal, offered him a job. Over the following months, Strowbridge was involved in a number of car thefts that had been set up by the police. He was then offered a chance to meet "Mr. Big" and to move higher in the criminal organization. During the interview with Mr. Big, he admitted to killing Marie Dupe. This was recorded on a hidden camera and led to Strowbridge pleading guilty and being sent to prison.

You Make the Call!

Does this case example raise any concerns for you about the use of the Mr. Big technique?

Source: S.M. Smith, V. Stinson, and M.W. Patry, "Using the 'Mr. Big' Technique to Elicit Confessions: Successful Innovation or Dangerous Development in the Canadian Legal System?" *Psychology, Public Policy, and Law* 15, no. 3 (2009): 168–93.

At Issue 10.3

Should Police Be Able to Cast a Wide DNA "Net" in Case Investigations?

In August 2010, a nurse in Orangeville, Ontario, was murdered. The police investigation revealed that prior to her death, she had visited a number of online dating sites, where she exchanged photographs and personal information with a number of men. Investigators believed there was a high likelihood that one of the men was responsible for the murder. In their investigation into her death, the police recovered what they believed to be DNA from a source they believed to be the killer.

In 2011 the police asked a select group of men who had had contact with the victim to provide DNA samples. The position of the police was that men with nothing to hide would agree to provide samples and that doing so would expedite the investigation and the eventual identification of the killer. The police provided assurances that these DNA samples and all documentation related to the sampled men (who were not identified as suspects) would be destroyed. An OPP spokesperson stated that individuals had the right to refuse the request (DNA samples can only be obtained involuntarily by a court order) but that the refusal, including why the person refused, would become part of the investigative process.

This technique was also used by the RCMP in its Highway of Tears investigation of missing women along Highway 16 in northern B.C. Over the past forty years, more than twenty-four women have gone missing along that highway. In 2010, more than one hundred taxi drivers in Prince George were asked to provide DNA samples (all agreed). No arrests followed, and as of mid-2012, the cases remain unsolved.

Supporters of the practice, including the police, contend that it expedites investigations and allows resources to be utilized more effectively. As well, it is argued that "if you haven't done anything wrong, you don't have anything to worry about." Some equate it with the police asking a person for an alibi.

As one person stated on an Internet forum: "There's nothing illegal or wrong about police asking for a voluntary sample, just like there's nothing illegal or wrong about people voluntarily providing information to the police. Many crimes would not be solved were it not for this exchange of information."

Critics of this practice, including the civil liberties association and a number of defence lawyers, argue that the process is inherently coercive and that the police should be required to seek the permission of the courts before gathering the DNA. This is reflected in one comment posted on the Internet: "Dude, this isn't like 'No problem officer, I'll pop the trunk for you to check.'"

You Make the Call!

1. Which arguments that are presented in support of casting a wide DNA sample net or in opposition to this practice do you find most persuasive?

2. If you were asked to provide a DNA sample as part of a police investigation, would you do so? What would be your reasoning for agreeing or declining to participate?

Key Points Review

1. While most case investigations are conducted by patrol officers, more serious crimes and criminal incidents require the involvement of specially trained police officers.
2. There has been exponential growth in the number of specialty investigative units in police services, although the effectiveness and efficiency of these units has rarely been studied.
3. A case (or criminal) investigation is intended to form reasonable grounds so that an arrest can be made, or at least suspects identified.
4. A case investigator attempts to gather as much evidence as possible that can be analyzed to link the crime scene, the victim, and the offender.
5. Eyewitnesses are an unreliable source of evidence.
6. Police investigators use a variety of analytical tools, including behavioural science research, computer analysis, and forensic science methods.
7. Investigators' use of DNA has increased significantly over the past decade, although there are concerns with wrongful convictions based on DNA evidence.

8. The Mr. Big strategy is surrounded by controversy and may lead to false confessions.
9. Interrogation of suspects is an important component of case investigation.
10. Police investigators must ensure that interrogation techniques do not result in false confessions.

Key Term Questions

1. Distinguish between **problem-oriented special units** and **method-oriented special units** in police services.
2. Compare and contrast **smoking gun investigations** and **whodunit investigations**.
3. What is the **major case management model**?
4. Compare and contrast **direct evidence** and **circumstantial evidence**.
5. What is the **principle of transfer and exchange**?
6. What is meant by **linkage blindness** in case investigations?
7. What is **criminal profiling** and how is it used in case investigations?
8. What is the **ViCLAS** system, and how does it assist criminal investigation?
9. Describe the investigative strategy of **geographic profiling** and the principles on which it is based, and then note how geographic information systems are used to assist in geographic profiling.
10. Describe **DNA**, provide examples of the types of DNA evidence that may be gathered by case investigators, and discuss how DNA has been used to solve crimes.
11. Describe the work of **cold case squads**.
12. Describe the **Mr. Big technique** and the issues that surround its use in case investigation.

Notes

1. E. Campbell and D. LePard, "How Police Departments Can Reduce the Risk of Wrongful Convictions," in *Wrongful Convictions in Canada*, ed. R. Bajer et al. (Vancouver: International Society for the Reform of the Criminal Law, 2007), http://www.isrcl.org/Papers/2007/YMC.pdf
2. L.R. Rubenser, "Special Units in Policing: Functionality or Legitimacy Maintenance," in *Policing and Special Units,* ed. P.W. Phillips (Upper Saddle River: Prentice-Hall, 2005), 24–53.
3. Ibid., 26.
4. D.E. Shelton, "The 'CSI Effect': Does It Really Exist?" *NIJ Journal* 259, (2008): 1–6.
5. *The Economist*, April 24, 2010, 78.
6. L. Huey, "'I've Seen this on CSI': Criminal Investigators' Perceptions About the Management of Public Expectations in the Field," *Crime, Media, Culture: An International Journal* 6, no. 1 (2010): 49–68.
7. M. Turcotte, "Shifts in Police–Informant Negotiations," *Global Crime* 9, no. 4 (2008): 291–305.
8. Ibid.
9. Ibid.
10. J. Thompson-Cannino, R. Cotton, and E. Torneo, *Picking Cotton: Our Memoir of Injustice and Redemption* (New York: St. Martin's, 2009); G.L. Wells, A. Memon, and S.D. Penrod, "Eyewitness Evidence: Improving Its Probative Value," *Psychological Science in the Public Interest* 7, no. 2 (2006): 45–75.

11. G.L. Wells and E.A. Olson, "Eyewitness Testimony," *Annual Review of Psychology* 54, (2003): 277–95, http://www.psychology.iastate.edu/~glwells/Wells_articles_pdf/Eyewitness_Testimony_Ann_Rev.pdf

12. Ibid.

13. V.J. Geberth, *Practical Homicide Investigation: Tactics, Procedures, and Forensic Techniques,* 3rd ed. (New York: Elsevier, 1996).

14. B. Snook, R.M. Cullen, C. Bennell, P.J. Taylor, and P. Gendreau, "The Criminal Profiling Illusion: What's Behind the Smoke and Mirrors?" *Criminal Justice and Behavior* 35, no. 10 (2008): 1257–76.

15. D.K. Rossmo, *Geographic Profiling* (Boca Raton: CRC, 1999).

16. F. Wang, *Geographic Information Systems and Crime Analysis* (Hershey: Idea Group, 2005).

17. J. Burchill, "Mr. Stillman, DNA, and Discarded Evidence in Criminal Cases," *Manitoba Law Journal* 32, no. 2 (2008): 5–33.

18. K. Makin, "The Dark Side of DNA," *Globe and Mail,* March 13, 2010, A4; W.C. Thompson, "Tarnish on the 'Gold Standard': Recent Problems in Forensic DNA Testing," *Champion: National Association of Criminal Defense Lawyers,* January–February 2006, http://www.nacdl.org

19. D. Quan, "U.S. Using Familial DNA in Policing," *Vancouver Sun,* May 21, 2011, B2.

20. Royal Canadian Mounted Police, *The National DNA Data Bank of Canada: Annual Report 2009–2010* (Ottawa: 2010), http://www.nddb-bndg.org/train/docs/Annual_2009-2010_e.pdf

21. K.T. Keenan and J. Brockman, *Mr. Big: Exposing Undercover Investigations in Canada* (Halifax and Winnipeg: Fernwood, 2011), 9.

22. S.M. Kassin, "On the Psychology of Confessions: Does Innocence Put Innocents at Risk?" *American Psychologist* 60, no. 3 (2005): 215–28.

23. CBC News, "Widely Used Police Interrogation Technique Can Result in False Confession: Disclosure" (2003), http://www.cbc.ca/news/canada/story/2003/01/27/interrogation030127.htm

24. S.M. Kassin, S.A. Drizin, T. Grisso, G.H. Gudjosson, R.A. Leo, and A.D. Redlich, "Police-Induced Confessions: Risk Factors and Recommendations," *Law and Human Behavior* 34, no. 1 (2010): 3–38.

Chapter

11

Police Work in a Diverse Society

Learning Objectives

After reading this chapter, you should be able to:

- Identify the types of diversity that exist in Canada
- Describe the importance of the Charter of Rights and Freedoms and the Canadian Human Rights Act for policing
- Briefly discuss relations between the police and the gay/lesbian/bisexual/transgender (GLBT) communities
- Define and discuss bias-free policing and racial profiling
- Identify the difference between racial profiling and criminal profiling
- Discuss the perceptions that visible minorities have of the police
- Define and discuss overpolicing and pretext policing
- Describe a case in which a police officer was found to have racially discriminated against a person, and a case where racial profiling occurred
- Describe a case in which a police organization was found to have discriminated against a person
- Describe the relations between the police and Aboriginal peoples
- Discuss the challenges of policing in northern communities

Key Terms

DIVERSITY IN CANADA

A key feature of Canada is diversity. Besides being geographically diverse, this country is home to visible minorities, indigenous peoples, a multitude of religious beliefs and sexual orientations, and so on. In this chapter we examine the challenges that diversity of all kinds presents to Canadian police services in terms of recruitment and training, police–community relations, and encounters between police and citizens.[1] The discussion here makes extensive use of case studies to illustrate the various dimensions of police work in a diverse society.

About 13 percent of Canadians are visible minorities. Among the provinces, British Columbia has the highest percentage of visible minorities (21.6), followed by Ontario (19.1) and Alberta (11.2). In terms of raw numbers, 54 percent of all of Canada's visible minorities live in Ontario. Toronto is the most diverse urban community in the country—about 37 percent of its residents belong to a visible minority. The residents may speak little or no English (or French) or speak English as a second language.

This diversity is expected to increase: estimates are that by 2031, visible minorities will comprise 63 percent of Toronto's population, 59 percent of Vancouver's, and 31 percent of Montreal's. It is also projected that between now and 2031, the foreign-born population will increase four times faster than the Canadian-born. Also by 2031, nearly half of Canadians aged fifteen and over will be foreign-born or have at least one parent who was. Changes in Canada's religious composition are also forecast. It is estimated that by 2031, 14 percent of the population will be non-Christian, up from 8 percent in 2010. About half of these non-Christians will be Muslims.[2]

Policing a Multicultural Society

Canada's diversity has significant implications for police work (and for other criminal justice agencies). Section 15(1) of the Charter of Rights and Freedoms guarantees equality rights: "Every individual is equal before and under the law and has the right to the equal protection and equal benefit of the law without discrimination and, in particular, without discrimination based on race, national or ethnic origin, colour, religion, sex, age or mental or physical disability." Section 3(e) of the Canadian Multicultural Act (R.S. 1985, c. 24 (4th Supp.)) states that it is the policy of the Government of Canada to "ensure that all individuals receive equal treatment and equal protection under the law, while respecting and valuing their diversity."

The Canadian Human Rights Act prohibits discrimination on the grounds of "race, national or ethnic origin, colour, religion, age, sex, sexual orientation, marital status, family status, disability and conviction for which a pardon has been granted."[3] Many provinces, including Ontario, B.C., Alberta, and Manitoba, have human rights codes that mirror the federal human rights code and contain sections proclaiming the right of residents to be free from discrimination and creating human rights tribunals.

Many new immigrants have arrived from countries where the criminal justice system and the police are to be feared. It is understandable that these people are reluctant to call the police for help or to provide eyewitness information.

It has been found that the experiences people had with the justice system in their country of origin influence their perceptions of the police in Canada—for example, Chinese immigrants who held positive attitudes toward the police in China tended to have positive perceptions of the police in New York and Toronto.[4] In the absence of research findings, however, it is difficult to determine just how reluctant immigrants to Canada are to report crimes to the police. The problem is especially acute in rural areas, where there are few resources and programs (e.g., multilingual services). These issues remain to be explored by police scholars and police services in Canada.

In the absence of adequate training and initiatives for improving police–community relations, the potential is strong for misunderstanding—and mutual suspicion and distrust—between police officers and residents. The inability of police officers to speak a second language can hinder the development of police–community partnerships and contribute to misunderstandings that can have serious consequences.

Most urban police services have diversity advisory committees, composed of community representatives, that advise senior police management and work to develop positive police–minority relationships. The Toronto Police Service, for example, has established Community Consultative Committees (CCCs) with the city's Aboriginal, black, Asian, French, gendered, Muslim, and South and West Asian communities (http://www.torontopolice.on.ca/communitymobilization/ccc.php).

Also, police services are focusing more on hate crimes, which are defined as "criminal offence[s] committed against a person or property where the motivation is bias prejudice or hate, based on the victim's race, national or ethnic origin, language, colour, religion, sex, age, mental or physical disability, sexual orientation, or any other similar factor" (see Criminal Code, ss. 318 and 319 and 718.2(a)(i)). The Toronto Police Service has a Hate Crime Unit, with coordinators in each police division who are responsible for investigating such crimes.

The Police and the Gay/Lesbian/Bisexual/Transgender (GLBT) Communities

In the past, relations between the police and GLBT communities were characterized by conflict and mistrust. Police officers were generally drawn from the working class and held conservative, inflexible attitudes toward nonheterosexual persons—views that were reinforced by a "macho" police culture. Police services were charged with enforcing laws that prohibited consensual homosexual conduct; this meant conducting raids on gay clubs, cinemas, and bathhouses.[5] In the early 1980s the Toronto police were involved in a series of high-profile raids on gay bathhouses, which prompted legal action and the beginning of a change in police attitudes and behaviour.

Officers were often unsympathetic to gay victims, and police services were slow to respond to crimes motivated by hate. People in these communities were often reluctant to report victimization. Their experiences with the police were typically negative, and there was often the perception that police services were unaware of the issues facing GLBT communities.[6]

Poster against homophobic violence, sponsored by the Toronto Police Service and a community coalition.

Canadian police services have made efforts to improve their relations with GLBT communities and to increase their officers' awareness of those communities through training programs. The Windsor Police Service, in collaboration with the advocacy group Equality for Gays and Lesbians Everywhere (EGALE), has implemented a mandatory training program (the first of its kind in Canada) for its officers and staff. It is designed to build awareness of homophobic violence and to develop positive relationships with GLBT communities. The Ottawa Police Service has a liaison committee that facilitates contact between the OPS and GLBT communities and advocates for issues of mutual interest (http://glbt.ottawapolice.ca).

Police services in other Western counties have launched similar programs. The New South Wales Police Force has developed a Policy on Sexuality and

Gender Diversity that sets out a number of initiatives with the GLBT communities.[7] One of these is a Gay and Lesbian Liaison Officer program; another is a campaign to encourage GLBT persons to report violence.

DISCRIMINATORY POLICING

Biased Policing and Racial Profiling

Two issues have been flashpoints between the police and visible minority communities: **bias-free policing** and **racial profiling.** Bias-free policing requires police officers to make decisions "based on reasonable suspicion or probable grounds rather than stereotypes about race, religion, ethnicity, gender or other prohibited grounds."[8] Bias-free policing requires that *all* people be treated the same. Since the 9/11 terrorist attacks, there have been concerns that people who appear to be Muslims and/or of Middle Eastern origin may be singled out for discriminatory treatment by security personnel at airports, by customs officers, and by the police.

Racial profiling is most commonly associated with visible minorities and Aboriginal people and has been defined in a number of ways. The definition used significantly affects the focus of research studies as well as how the findings of those studies are interpreted; it also affects determinations regarding whether a police service engages in racial profiling. In the United States, Fridell and colleagues contend that racial profiling occurs "when law enforcement inappropriately considers race or ethnicity in deciding with whom and how to intervene in an enforcement capacity."[9] This definition leaves open the possibility that police officers may at times "appropriately" consider race or ethnicity when deciding whether to intervene in situations. In *R. v. Brown* [2003] O.J. No. 1251, the Ontario Court of Appeal defined racial profiling as involving "the targeting of individual members of a particular racial group, on the basis of the supposed criminal propensity of the entire group."

Profiling may lead to racial discrimination, which can be overt, subconscious, or systemic. Canadians often hold stereotypical views of visible minorities that are not conscious. One issue is whether police actions with respect to minorities are based on *racial* profiling or *criminal* profiling (see At Issue 11.1).

Two police practices that are associated with racial profiling are **overpolicing** and **pretext policing.** Overpolicing occurs when the police focus disproportionately on a racialized population or neighbourhood. In pretext policing, officers "ostensibly detain or investigate an individual for one reason when, in reality, there is a secondary purpose or ulterior reason to the interaction."[10] Pretext policing is most commonly associated with police stops or searches and may occur for a minor reason, such as a traffic violation, which then leads to a more intrusive intervention (e.g., a vehicle search). Overpolicing often results in visible minority or Aboriginal persons having disproportionate contact with the police. Besides leading to distrust of the police, it fosters the belief among officers that the particular group is prone to criminality.[11]

bias-free policing
the requirement that police officers make decisions on the basis of reasonable suspicion and probable grounds rather than stereotypes

racial profiling
police targeting of members of a particular racial group, on the basis of the supposed criminal propensity of the entire group

overpolicing
a disproportionate police focus on a racialized population or neighbourhood

pretext policing
police stops or searches for a minor reason that are used for more intrusive intervention

Michael Conrad.

Male. Age 28.

Trafficking.

Armed Robbery.

Assault and Battery.

Extortion.

Rape.

Murder.

Apprehended

January 1994 by

Police Lieutenant

Joseph Cruthers,

shown here.

Urban Alliance
on Race Relations

Breaking down racial stereotypes.

"You look like this sketch of someone who's thinking about committing a crime."

The debate over racial profiling in Canada has been complicated by vague definitions as well as by a lack of solid research into police decision making and police–minority relations.[12] This makes it difficult to determine the extent to which the police discriminate against visible minorities. Regardless, Canadian police services are giving increasing attention to the issue of racial profiling. In 2011, the Ottawa Police Service developed a "Racial Profiling Policy" that sets out the definitions of racism and racial profiling and the expected standards of behaviour for police officers.[13]

Minority Perceptions of Treatment by the Police

There is evidence that many visible minorities perceive that they are treated differently by the police. A research project that conducted focus groups with youth, Chinese, and blacks in Toronto found a perception among visible minorities that the police were not approachable, that they made little or no effort to get to know community residents, and that they did not work *with* the community but rather in opposition to it. The same project found a widespread perception that the police were not treating visible minorities fairly; in particular, black participants felt that they were likely to be subjected to racial profiling. High school students in the focus groups were less likely than other community residents to feel that the police were doing a good job and more likely to believe that police officers targeted visible minorities in their enforcement activities.[14]

A 2003 report from the Ontario Human Rights Commission found a widespread perception among cultural and visible minorities that the police engage in racial profiling. A number of police services have acknowledged that racial profiling does occur and have taken measures to address it, including upgrading training for officers, identifying officers at risk of engaging in racial profiling, and improving community relations.

Discrimination by Individual Police Officers

Courts and human rights tribunals have determined in some cases that the behaviour of individual police officers was racist and discriminatory (see Box 11.1 and At Issue 11.2 and 11.3).

The following two cases were heard by the Quebec Police Ethics Committee in 2010. That committee is an independent administrative tribunal created under the Quebec Police Act to hear cases brought by the Police Ethics Commissioner against police officers whose conduct is alleged to have violated the Quebec Code of Police Ethics. Those cases in which the committee imposes a sanction are automatically appealed to the provincial court.

Allegation of Racial Profiling and Abusive Fine in Downtown Montreal

Two black brothers drove downtown in a Mercedes on a Saturday afternoon in the fall of 2007 and were tailed by a police vehicle for several blocks.

Box 11.1

Racial Profiling in a Case Investigation

In February 2003, a Peel Regional Police officer was dispatched to investigate a possible shoplifting incident at a large department store in Mississauga. The alleged shoplifter, a black woman, had been apprehended for stealing a low-priced item. She denied the allegation. Upon arrival, the police officer conducted what the Ontario Human Rights Commission determined was a discriminatory investigation that included the following:

- Stereotypically assuming that a black suspect might not speak English.

- Assuming that the white security guard was telling the truth and that the black suspect was not, without properly looking at all of the evidence, including a videotape of the alleged theft, which exonerated her.

- Adopting an "assumption of guilt" approach to the investigation by immediately demanding that the suspect produce the missing item.

- Unnecessarily arranging for a second body search after the first one had demonstrated that she did not have the alleged stolen item.

- Continuing the investigation, rather than releasing the suspect, even after the second body search confirmed that she did not have the stolen item.

- Spending up to one hour pursuing an allegation of theft, in the face of fragile evidence, for an item worth less than $10.

The commission further found that during the investigation, the officer referred to the suspect as a "f---ing foreigner." The tribunal ordered the Peel Regional Police to pay the exonerated suspect $20,000 in damages and to increase training for officers in the service to raise awareness about racial profiling.

Source: Ontario Human Rights Commission News Release, May 17, 2007. © Queen's Printer for Ontario, 2007. Reproduced with permission.

When they parked their car to go shopping, the police car parallel parked next to them. When the brothers came over to inquire if something was wrong, they were each fined $37 for walking on the street. The Police Ethics Commissioner ruled that the officers had abused their powers. One of the officers was already the subject of a police ethics sanction, this one dating back to 2005, when he stopped and violently detained a black Concordia University student in a barbershop in the St-Laurent neighbourhood. This same officer was, at the time of the incident, also the subject of a third civil rights complaint for racial profiling and the abusive detention of another young black man, who had been driving downtown with his white girlfriend in broad daylight.[15]

Abusive Arrest, Use of Force, and Negligent Use of Firearm

In February 2009 a young black male health care worker was driving on the freeway near Quebec City in broad daylight when he was stopped by a police officer and ordered at gunpoint to come out of his car and lie down on the road. The case turned out to be one of mistaken identity. The police had been looking for a black male suspect whose physical description was vague. The Police Ethics Commissioner ruled that the officer had abused his power to arrest the driver and had used his weapon without due care.[16]

This second case raises the issue of police dispatchers sending out vague subject descriptions that include only gender and colour (i.e., "black male"). This may result in police officers stopping, detaining, and/or arresting (sometimes at gunpoint) innocent persons. Critics of this practice have called on police services to ensure that suspect descriptions are more specific in terms of both physical description (e.g., height, weight, clothing) and location.

Discrimination by a Police Service

Racial discrimination is not limited to encounters between police officers and persons on the street; it can also occur in the other activities of a police service. In Box 11.2, a police service was found by the Canadian Human Rights Tribunal to have discriminated against a cadet during recruit training.

THE POLICE AND ABORIGINAL PEOPLE

Nearly 4 percent of Canadians are Aboriginal people. This figure includes Status and non-Status people, Métis, and Inuit. Aboriginal people are unevenly distributed across the country: figures range from 60 percent in the Northwest Territories to 20 percent in Yukon, 6 percent in Saskatchewan and Manitoba, and 3 percent in Alberta and B.C.

Aboriginal cultures and communities are highly diverse. Also, while most First Nations people live in rural and remote areas, there are significant numbers in urban areas such as Vancouver, Winnipeg, Toronto, and Montreal. Recent studies indicate that the urban Aboriginal population is now nearly as large as the one on reserves. It is estimated that 70,000 Aboriginal people live in Metropolitan Toronto.

Box 11.2

The Case of the Muslim Cadet

In pursuit of a career in the RCMP, Mr. Ali Tahmourpour, a Muslim Canadian born in Iran, applied to the RCMP and, following acceptance, was sent to the RCMP Training Academy in Regina. He entered the training program in July 1999, but on October 20, 1999, his training contract was terminated and he was dismissed from the program and prohibited from re-enrolling at a future date. Mr. Tahmourpour filed a complaint with the Canadian Human Rights Commission (CHRC) alleging discrimination by the RCMP under the Canadian Human Rights Act. Discriminatory practice under the act is defined as harassment of an individual in employment-related matters; harassment is broadly defined as "repetitive and unwelcome conduct related to one of the prohibited grounds of discrimination that detrimentally affects the work environment or leads to adverse job-related consequences for the victims."

Mr. Tahmourpour's contention was that his termination occurred following months of harassment and discrimination by training officers "due to his race, religion and ethnic, or national origin" (2008, 1). The complaint alleged that "the negative treatment he received was a manifestation of systemic discrimination against visible minorities at Depot" (ibid., 2). In one alleged incident, the firearms instructor yelled to him that he was a "coward," "f---ing useless," and "incompetent" (ibid., 7).

The commission held that the complaint was substantiated and directed the RCMP to offer Mr. Tahmourpour an opportunity to re-enroll in the RCMP training program and to pay him additional monetary compensation based on the salary he would have earned had he completed training and been on the job. In her final report, the tribunal member concluded that Mr. Tahmourpour had been the victim of systemic discrimination at the training academy. The RCMP was directed to address the organizational factors that contributed to a training environment in which women and members of visible minorities felt harassed. This included creating a mandatory program for cadets and training personnel focusing on diversity and cultural sensitivity (2008, 24).

The RCMP filed an appeal of this decision, and the Federal Court of Canada directed that the issue of compensation to be paid to Mr. Tahmourpour be reconsidered. The amount of compensation was subsequently reduced, although the findings of the original hearing officer in 2008 that Mr. Tahmourpour had been the victim of racial and religious discrimination were reconfirmed by another commission hearing officer (2010). Mr. Tahmourpour subsequently indicated his intent to re-enroll in the RCMP training program.

Source: Canadian Human Rights Tribunal, *Tahmourpour v. Royal Canadian Mounted Police* (Ottawa: 2008), http://www.chrt-tcdp.gc.ca/search/files/t1151_3306ed16april08.pdf; *Tahmourpour v. Royal Canadian Mounted Police*, 2010 CHRT 34 (Ottawa: 2010), http://www.chrt-tcdp.gc.ca/aspinc/search/vhtml-eng.asp?doid=1040&lg=_e&isruling=0

Aboriginal people have high rates of contact with the police and the criminal justice system. One in five inmates in federal prison is Aboriginal. For provincial institutions, this figure is much higher; in many jurisdictions, up to 90 percent of inmates are Aboriginal. Despite efforts over the past three decades to reduce the involvement of Aboriginal people in the criminal justice system, Aboriginal overrepresentation rose nearly 20 percent between 1998 and 2008; this included a staggering 131 percent increase in the number of Aboriginal women confined in federal correctional institutions.[17] In addition to that, Aboriginal people are much more likely than non-Aboriginals to be crime victims and to be victims of violent offences.[18]

A consistent finding by many research studies and commissions of inquiry is that relations between police and Aboriginal persons have often been characterized by distrust, mutual hostility, and in some instances racial discrimination.[19] These findings have prompted many police services to improve the training and cultural sensitivity of police officers, to establish better lines of communication with First Nations communities, and to support First Nations police forces. The RCMP, for example, has printed a Native Spirituality Guide, the intent of which is to provide a general overview of some of the sacred ceremonies practised by First Nations peoples as well as some of the sacred items that Native people may be carrying. The guide has a section titled "Treatment of Medicine Bundles by Law Enforcement Officials" that highlights the spiritual significance of the Medicine Bundle and describes how to conduct a search of a person who is carrying a bundle:

> The spirituality of the bundle is only violated if it is touched or opened without the carrier's permission. It is therefore important that police officers be aware that spiritual items of religious significance should be treated with the proper respect and not be touched by anyone except the Elder/ Custodian. Female police officers should, whenever possible, have a male officer conduct this search."[20]

Whether in the remote and rural regions of the country or in the urban centres of the south, Aboriginal communities present police with many challenges, and the expectations placed on officers are high.

Many police officers encounter problems policing First Nations persons and communities owing to a lack of knowledge of Aboriginal culture, the community being policed, and its residents. In carrying out their duties, they often focus on crime control instead of improving police–community relations through the strategy of community policing. This is especially true in communities that are afflicted with high rates of crime and social disorder. Moreover, many Aboriginal people lack information about the criminal justice system, the role of the police in it, and their legal rights as citizens, including their right to file complaints.

The high rates of Aboriginal arrests in many parts of the country have led observers to wonder whether police officers discriminate against Aboriginal people. A number of incidents have been determined to have been the result of discriminatory actions by police.

Police Officer Attitudes, Decisions, and Tragic Outcomes

In a number of high-profile incidents, decisions made by police officers have resulted in the deaths of Aboriginal persons and allegations of racism. See Boxes 11.3, 11.4, and 11.5. Although the incidents described occurred in different regions of the country, each conveys a sense that the officers involved

Box 11.3

A Death in Ipperwash Provincial Park: The Shooting of Dudley George

In 1995, Dudley George, an unarmed Aboriginal protester, was shot and killed by an OPP officer during a standoff at Ipperwash Provincial Park. The park had been occupied by members of the Kettle and Stony Point First Nation over a land claims dispute with the provincial and federal governments. An OPP officer was later convicted of criminal negligence causing death and sentenced to two years of community service. A commission of inquiry into the circumstances surrounding George's death (completed twelve years later) concluded that the death occurred as a result of actions of the federal and provincial governments and of the police. The report criticized the OPP for failing to develop proper communications and intelligence during the incident and found that "cultural insensitivity and racism on the part of some of the OPP officers involved, were evident both before and after Dudley George's death. They created a barrier to understanding and thus made a timely, peaceful resolution of the occupation more difficult." Among the recommendations of the inquiry were that the OPP develop better strategies for policing First Nations protests and work to enhance relationships with Aboriginal peoples and communities.

Source: The Hon. S.B. Linden (Commissioner), "Report of the Ipperwash Inquiry" (Toronto: Attorney General of Ontario, 2007), 683, http://www.attorneygeneral.jus.on.ca/inquiries/ipperwash/report/index.html

Box 11.4

"Starlight Tours" in Saskatchewan

In January 2000, two Saskatoon police officers picked up an Aboriginal man, Darrell Night, drove him to an industrial park on the outskirts of the city, and abandoned him in extreme winter weather. Luckily, Night was assisted by a security guard and made his way back to the city, where he filed a complaint against the police. On the basis of his testimony, two city police officers were convicted at trial of unlawful confinement, removed from their positions, and sentenced to eight months in jail. The court rejected a request by the two officers that they be sentenced by an Aboriginal sentencing circle. In 2003 the Saskatchewan Court of Appeal upheld the convictions and the officers began serving their sentences.

This case raised suspicions that the Saskatoon police had for years been transporting and

(Continued)

dumping Aboriginal people outside the city, some of whom had frozen to death. Similar incidents: the frozen body of Rodney Naistus was discovered on January 29, 2000 (one day after Night had been dumped), in the same industrial area; and Lawrence Wegner had been found frozen to death on February 3, 2000, in a field outside the city. Naistus was naked from the waist up; Wegner was not wearing shoes and had no jacket, even though it was winter. Later investigations by the RCMP failed to determine the circumstances surrounding the deaths of the two men.

These cases focused attention on the death of an Aboriginal teenager, Neil Stonechild, whose frozen body had been found in a field on the outskirts of Saskatoon ten years earlier, on November 29, 1990. Stonechild had last been seen alive by his friend Jason Roy; at the time, he had been struggling with two Saskatoon police officers, who forced him into the back of their cruiser. On the night Stonechild disappeared, the temperature was −28 degrees Celsius. In February 2003, the Saskatchewan Justice Minister announced an inquiry into Stonechild's death.

In its final report, the commissioner, the Honorable Mr. Justice D.H. Wright, found that Stonechild had been in the custody of two Saskatoon police officers on the night he disappeared and that the injuries on his body had been caused by handcuffs. But there was no evidence that the two police constables had actually dropped him off outside the city, and therefore, the circumstances surrounding his death could not be determined. Even so, the inquiry's report was severely critical of the initial investigation conducted by the Saskatoon police. Furthermore, Wright rejected the version of events offered by the police. The absence of evidence, however, precluded criminal charges being laid against the officers who had been seen with Stonechild. These cases heightened tensions between Aboriginal people (especially Aboriginal youth) and the police; they also seriously undermined earlier efforts by the Saskatoon police to improve police–Aboriginal relations. Significantly, none of the investigations considered how long the "starlight tours" had been taking place in the Saskatoon Police Department, nor was any attempt made to examine the attitudes and behaviour of other members of the department toward Aboriginal people.

For an account of the Stonechild case, see the book *Starlight Tour: The Last, Lonely Night of Neil Stonechild.*

Sources: Hon. Mr. Justice D.H. Wright, "Commission of Inquiry into Matters Relating to the Death of Neil Stonechild" (Regina, Department of Justice, 2004), http://www.justice.gov.sk.ca/stonechild; S. Reber and R. Renaud, *Starlight Tour: The Last, Lonely Night of Neil Stonechild* (Toronto: Random House Canada, 2005).

held attitudes toward Aboriginal peoples that were tinged by racism. Box 11.4 discusses the "Starlight Tours" in Saskatoon, during which police officers transported Aboriginal persons outside the city and dumped them off in inclement weather, often with tragic consequences. Box 11.5 presents a high-profile incident that was the catalyst for major reforms in policing in one jurisdiction.

The Police and Aboriginal Peoples in Urban Centres

Research studies indicate that in urban areas, a disproportionate number of Aboriginal persons reside in low-income neighbourhoods. In addition, Aboriginal families are likely to be single-parent, and urban Aboriginals are more likely to experience domestic violence than urban non-Aboriginals. Residing in disadvantaged neighbourhoods with high crime rates may contribute to increased encounters with the police and arrest rates.[21]

Box 11.5

A Death in Custody: The Case of Arnold Silverfox

An RCMP police constable picked up Arnold Silverfox at the Salvation Army shelter in Whitehorse in the early morning hours and transported him to the Whitehorse RCMP detachment. There, Silverfox was placed in the drunk tank, where, over the next sixteen hours, he continually vomited (at least twenty-three times) and soiled himself, until he died. At one point during this time, when Silverfox asked for a mat to sleep on, a constable stated, "Yeah, and you need a pizza too. Is there anything else I can get you?" Contrary to jail policy, only six personal checks were made on Silverfox during the time he was in the drunk tank. The required number was around thirty. Nor was his cell cleaned at any point, which was also contrary to jail policy. No calls were made to emergency medical personnel until it was too late.

The death of Arnold Silverfox prompted a review of the RCMP in Yukon, which included extensive consultations with communities and agencies. The review, directed by a Steering Committee composed of the Deputy Minster of Justice, a representative from the Council of Yukon First Nations, and the Officer in Command of M Division RCMP, culminated in a report setting out a number of recommendations. These included the creation of a Yukon Police Act, Police Council, and police complaints process, as well as a variety of initiatives for improving police–community relations and community trust in the police and for increasing the skill sets of RCMP members posted to Yukon communities.

Source: S. Arnold, P. Clark, and D. Cooley, "Sharing Common Ground: Review of Yukon's Police Force" (Whitehorse: Government of Yukon, 2011), http://www .justice.gov.yk.ca/pdf/Sharing_Common_Ground_Final_ Report.pdf

In a survey of Aboriginal people, Métis, and Inuit living off-reserve, most of them stated that they had directly experienced racism and discrimination from businesses, employers, and the police, among others.[22] A study that interviewed a large sample of urban Aboriginal persons in cities across the country found that up to three-quarters of the respondents believed that non-Aboriginals held negative stereotypes of them (e.g., they were lazy, poor, and drug-addicted). Over half the respondents had little confidence in the criminal justice system.[23]

To address the unique needs of this population, the Toronto Police Service has established an Aboriginal Peacekeeping Unit composed of Aboriginal police officers. The unit is involved in a variety of activities designed to foster trust and understanding between the police and the Aboriginal community. This program includes an Aboriginal Youth Mentoring Program in which officers serve as role models for youth, liaise with Aboriginal social services and organizations in the city, and help with efforts to increase the numbers of Aboriginal police officers in the TPS (http://www.torontopolice.on.ca/communitymobilization/ aboriginal.php).

Policing in the Canadian North

A little studied and less visible aspect of Canadian police work is policing in remote and northern communities. Policing in Yukon, Nunavut, the Northwest Territories, and the northern regions of the provinces presents officers with a multitude of challenges. Indeed, those challenges are often what attracts police officers to northern postings.

The Challenges of Policing in the North

Northern jurisdictions consistently report the highest rates of crime, violence, and victimization in Canada—rates that exceed those of high-crime cities in the United States. Crime data from Statistics Canada indicate that in 2007, the homicide rate in Whitehorse, Yukon, was 355 percent higher than the Canadian average; the rate of aggravated assault in Yellowknife, NWT, was more than 350 percent higher; and the rate of sexual assault in Iqaluit, Nunavut, was 1033 percent higher.[24] The homicide rate in Nunavut is one thousand times higher than the Canadian average. If Nunavut were an independent country, its crime statistics would place it in the same league as Mexico and South Africa.[25] One-third of the residents in the territories report having been victimized in the previous twelve months.[26] Also, the rate of homicides against police officers is highest in Nunavut (54.3) and the Northwest Territories (15.6); compare this with the Canadian average of 5.6.[27]

In 2010 the four members of the RCMP detachment in Cape Dorset were removed from the community and placed on stress leave (termed an "advanced health intervention" by their commander) after a month that saw two homicides (in the community of 1,200) and a shooting spree by two teenagers that resulted in bullets lodging in an RCMP residence and a wound to one of the young men.[28] The settlement of Cape Dorset is internationally renowned

RCMP officer in Whale Cove, Nunavut.

for its artists and stone carvers, but it is also highly troubled. A number of shooting deaths of RCMP members in Arctic communities resulted in the implementation of a policy that requires every RCMP detachment to have at least three officers.

Given the small size of northern communities, the role of the police is even more significant than in urban areas. Policing in the North is **high visibility/ high consequence policing:** high visibility in the sense that members are operating in small detachments in communities that generally have fewer than five hundred residents, and high consequence in the sense that the dynamics that develop between officers and the community have a strong impact on everyone concerned: the officer, his or her family, community residents, crime victims, and offenders.

> **high visibility/high consequence policing** police work in northern communities that places officers under constant scrutiny; also, the high impact of their decisions

The challenges encountered by police officers in northern communities only highlight a fundamental principle of community policing, which calls for the destructuring of centralized "command and control" and the empowerment of line-level officers to work with communities to address problems of crime and disorder and to establish and sustain trust. Police work in northern communities tests officers' resourcefulness, resilience, and mental and physical stamina as well as their policing skills. They often experience high stress owing to the geographic isolation, the lack of infrastructure support, and the high levels of crime and violence.

In northern communities, police officers may be the only permanent representatives of the criminal justice system and the support structures and services found in larger communities are often absent. One RCMP constable commented on the difference between being one of many officers in a large detachment and being part of a small detachment in Nunavut. He pointed out that in remote communities, officers are on call twenty-four hours a day:

> When I was in Coquitlam [a detachment near Vancouver with around 120 officers], I was only a police officer when I was on shift. Here, you only have one life, one identity. There is never a hanging up of the hat.[29]

Officers in northern communities perform a much more multifaceted role than their counterparts in the southern, more urban regions of the country. One officer posted to Nunavut commented:

> Our mandate is to do just about anything that needs doing in the town and that includes everybody else's job. I've done everything—filling out income tax returns, being involved in funerals or hunting with the elders, or fixing the hamlet truck or doing plumbing repairs at the teachers' houses. It's part-time policeman, part-time maintenance man.[30]

Officers, most of whom are not Aboriginal or Inuit, must develop trusting and cooperative relations with the people and must be sensitive to a host of factors that would be less relevant in more densely populated areas of the country. One officer recalled how policing had to adapt to the community environment:

> You had to be a diplomat first before you were a policeman. The books are there, but you had to put your own interpretation to those

books and those laws. If a community as a whole saw no need to wear life jackets or the community saw no need to wear helmets on four-wheelers, then you left it at that. I'm not saying you bent the rules, but you adapted them to the community and for the betterment of the community.[31]

The individual officer's personality and style of police work will have a much greater impact in a northern community than in larger police services in southern communities. Residents in northern communities can often recall by name those officers who had a positive impact on the community during their tour—and, as well, officers who experienced difficulties with the community. The constant turnover of officers, however, makes it difficult to sustain police–community partnerships.

There is also the issue of "mandate creep"—officers in the communities are often required to "cover" for other agencies after hours and on weekends and holidays. Officers often find themselves working days without rest. Only 25 percent of the RCMP officers surveyed in G Division (NWT) felt that they could complete their assigned workload during regular working hours—a figure much higher than for the national sample of officers surveyed.[32]

Those who have policed in the North have identified a number of traits that officers must have if they are to deliver policing services effectively. These include maturity, common sense, and self-reliance. As one officer stated, "You have got to be easy going. You can't let things bother you. You have to be capable of working alone and dealing with a certain amount of stress."[33] Officers also need to have self-confidence and an ability to make decisions, most often without the support and input of fellow members. An RCMP member in Yukon commented: "You need to be able to talk with people and to have the confidence to work by yourself" (personal communication with author).

Officers also identified the importance of a stable family life. Policing in northern communities places stress on the police officer's family, which may be affected by the isolation and by officers going for days, or months, without a day off.

Improving Police–Aboriginal Relations

A number of initiatives have been undertaken by police services in recent years to improve police–Aboriginal relations. Examples include the RCMP's Aboriginal Cadet Development Program, (see Chapter 4) and the First Nations Community Police Service (FNCPS). This program provides First Nations communities with the opportunity to have police services delivered by a contingent of First Nations RCMP officers or to develop their own police service.

An evaluation of the FNCPS in B.C. found that the program had improved the relationship between First Nations communities and the police, owing to an increased presence and visibility of officers and their active involvement in the community. These positive relationships, however, were undermined by the constant turnover of officers as a result of the transfer policy. A particular challenge is finding ways to generate and sustain the interest of residents in participating in community consultation groups.[34]

At Issue 11.1

Racial Profiling versus Criminal Profiling

Part of the difficulty in determining whether a police service and its officers engage in racial profiling is distinguishing between racial profiling and criminal profiling. As discussed in Chapter 4, a defining attribute of the police culture is suspiciousness of people and circumstances. While critics of the police argue that racial profiling is endemic to police work, police officers contend that they profile criminals, with particular attention to "signals and unusual fits." This is the process of *typification* discussed in Chapter 5.

Officers in the Hamilton Police Service offered the following perspectives on racial profiling, criminal profiling, and the importance of the context in which a person is identified for a police stop. In speaking of one particularly high-crime area with a large black population, an officer stated:

> If that's where the crime is, I'm going to be pulling over people who do crime. It's like going fishing. You go where the fish are if you're going to catch fish. If you're going to catch criminals, you end up having to do that. (2009, 209)

A visible minority police officer offered an additional perspective:

> When we're out on the street, we rely on our instincts. We are trained investigators in the sense that we need to do profiling. And what kind of profiling is that? Criminal profiling. It has nothing to do with racial profiling. ...We profile criminals. (210)

The importance of placing profiling in the larger context of police work was noted by another minority police officer:

> It's a very difficult job and the nature of the job forces you to stereotype and discriminate. When I'm driving my cruiser at two o'clock in the morning, and I see [one of the interviewers] in a shirt and tie driving a Mercedes, I think nothing of it. But if I was to see a black twenty-year-old, guess what? He's getting pulled over. (210)

You Make the Call!

1. What is your reaction to the perspectives of the officers interviewed in the Hamilton Police Service?
2. What methods would you use to determine whether or not a police officer, or a police service, was engaged in racial profiling?

Source: V. Satzewich and W. Shaffir, "Racism versus Professionalism: Claims and Counter-Claims About Racial Profiling," *Canadian Journal of Criminology and Criminal Justice* 51, no. 2 (2009): 199–226.

At Issue 11.2

The Police Officer, the Aboriginal Men, and the Bike: Human Rights Tribunal of Ontario, Decision, March 17, 2011

This case was brought before the Human Rights Tribunal of Ontario. The complainant, Gary McKay, alleged that he was subjected to racially biased policing by Const. Christopher Fitkin of the Toronto Police Service.

McKay, an Aboriginal from Manitoba, was walking with his friend Morris Mack, also an Aboriginal, in a laneway in Toronto in the early morning hours of July 9, 2003. McKay had worked for several years delivering flyers for a pizza shop and was showing Mack his delivery route so that Mack could cover the route while McKay recovered from an operation. The two were walking through a laneway on the way to a coffee shop prior to beginning the delivery route. McKay was walking a blue Kona mountain bike that he had purchased the previous year and that he intended to ride home after showing Mack the delivery route.

Fitkin, a three-year member of the Toronto Police Service, was on patrol with Const. Chad Ramsay, who had been with the TPS for seven months. The patrol officers spotted McKay and Mack heading into the laneway. Viewing the two men as suspicious, given the time of day, the officers stopped and questioned the two men separately.

Fitkin asked McKay to provide ID and why he was in the laneway. McKay provided his name, date of birth, and address, but did not have any identification on him. Fitkin stated that he recognized that McKay was Aboriginal. Both men agreed that throughout the encounter, Fitkin was polite and McKay was fully cooperative. Fitkin stated that he asked McKay why the two men were in the laneway and that McKay stated they were delivering flyers. McKay had no response to Fitkin's question as to why the two men would be delivering flyers in a laneway.

Fitkins stated that this led him to have the "feeling" that McKay was lying and to become "very suspicious." Fitkin later testified that he believed McKay's flyer delivery explanation was a "good cover story." Fitkin also stated that McKay and Mack were wearing "dirty clothes" and were "dishevelled" and that this was incongruous with McKay possessing an expensive bike.

Fitkin then questioned McKay about the bike and McKay indicated that it belonged to him. Fitkin then asked McKay for the receipt. McKay indicated the name and location of the store where the bike was purchased and that he could retrieve a receipt if given time. Fitkin refused the suggestion. Given the circumstances, Fitkin later stated that he became "very suspicious" of McKay. Fitkin asked for the serial number of the bike and two sets of numbers were discovered on the bike frame. Fitkin contacted dispatch, which indicated that one set of numbers matched those of a red bike previously stolen in Winnipeg. Although the bike in McKay's possession was blue, Fitkin placed McKay under arrest for bike theft. McKay was handcuffed, frisked, and detained in the patrol car for nearly twenty minutes. Following a discussion with Ramsay, Fitkin released McKay, who rode away on his bike. McKay alleges that Fitkin threatened to re-arrest him if he did not produce a receipt for the bike. McKay subsequently faxed the bike receipt to the police station, to the attention of Fitkin. Following the release of McKay, a total of thirteen criminal record searches were conducted of McKay and the bike: four by dispatch and nine by the officers.

The Ontario Human Rights Tribunal found that Fitkin's detention, arrest, and subsequent release of McKay "were shaped by negative stereotypes of Aboriginal people being untrustworthy and involved in criminal activity" and that "the interactions between Fitkin and McKay were permeated by racial bias and stereotyping" (2011, 24). The tribunal accepted McKay's perception that he "was subjected to unfair treatment and unduly scrutinized" (24). It also accepted the complainant's allegation that he had been treated differently than a non-Aboriginal person would have been treated in the same circumstances, that race was a factor in his arrest, and that Fitkin's treatment of McKay "was influenced by an underlying racial bias, which shifted the encounter from a routine patrol stop to an incident of racial discrimination" (30).

You Make the Call!

1. Do you agree with the findings of the Human Rights Tribunal of Ontario?
2. In your view, does this case raise the issue of the thin line between good police work and racial discrimination? If yes, how so? In your view, was there a point in the encounter where the line was crossed between a legitimate investigation and racial discrimination?

Source: Ontario Human Rights Tribunal (2011). http://www.lexisnexis.com

At Issue 11.3

The Case of the African Canadian Letter Carrier:
Phipps v. Toronto Police Services Board, Case Resolution Conference Decision, June 18, 2009

In this case, a Toronto police officer was found to be in violation of the Ontario Human Rights Code. This decision followed an investigation of an encounter between two Toronto Police Service officers and an African Canadian male letter carrier.

On March 9, 2005, Mr. Phipps, in his capacity as a relief letter carrier employed by Canada Post, was delivering mail in the area of the Bridle Path, a highly affluent neighbourhood in Toronto. It was his second day delivering mail on that route and he was wearing a Canada Post coat. He was observed by the police not stopping at every house to deliver the mail.

That day, Michael Shaw, a police constable who had served in the area for several years, was training a new constable, Diane Noto. At the start of their shift, the two officers were given a directed patrol assignment recommending that they patrol the area where the applicant was delivering mail between 12 p.m. and 4 p.m. The assignment details were that phone lines had been cut in the area by suspects described as male, white, and eastern European who were using a vehicle.

(Continued)

Shaw decided to patrol the identified area that morning, in accordance with the directed patrol assignment. From a distance, the two officers saw Phipps. As the applicant approached, they discerned that he was an African Canadian male wearing a Canada Post jacket and carrying material in his hand. Having worked in the area for a number of years, Shaw realized that Phipps was not the usual letter carrier and that he was not stopping to deliver mail at every house.

Noto drove the police car at a slow pace and followed the applicant. They observed him go up to a house, knock on the door, and speak to the woman who answered. They did not see him deliver anything, which they thought unusual. Shaw instructed Noto to inquire of the resident why the applicant had knocked. Noto spoke to the resident, who advised that the applicant had stopped to advise her that he had delivered something in error. Noto advised Shaw of this information. Shaw found this suspicious and decided to investigate Phipps. They asked for his identification, and after further investigation, the two officers let Phipps continue on his route.

Shortly after this, they encountered another male letter carrier (Finlay) at a relay box. Shaw recognized him as a carrier on a nearby route. Shaw made inquiries of Finlay regarding the letter carriers in the area. Finlay related that there was a temporary carrier, a "black man," in the area. The police drove on. The applicant subsequently hailed the police officers to inquire why they had stopped him. A conversation ensued, the contents of which are disputed.

Issue

Was Phipps's skin colour a factor in Shaw's surveillance, his decision to stop him, and his subsequent inquiry?

The relevant principles that apply in cases where an allegation of racial discrimination has been raised have been usefully summarized as follows:

(a) The prohibited ground or grounds of discrimination need not be the sole or the major factor leading to the discriminatory conduct; it is sufficient if they are a factor.

(b) There is no need to establish an intention or motivation to discriminate; the focus of the inquiry is on the effect of the respondent's action on the complainant.

(c) The prohibited ground or grounds need not be the cause of the respondent's conduct; it is sufficient if they are a factor or operative element.

(d) There need be no direct evidence of discrimination; discrimination will more often be proved by circumstantial evidence and inference.

(e) Racial stereotyping will usually be the result of subtle unconscious beliefs, biases, and prejudices.

Arguments

Shaw argued that the applicant's skin colour was not a factor in his actions or his patrol partner's and was not discussed between them. He stated that he stopped the applicant as a result of a number of unusual circumstances, including these: Phipps was not the usual letter carrier, he was crossing back and forth along the street, he did not stop at every house, and he was observed knocking on the door of a house but not delivering any mail. However, a white male delivering water in the neighbourhood was not stopped or questioned by the officers.

Decision

It was determined that the applicant's colour was a factor in Shaw's actions, thus breaching the code. The chair found that it was not unusual for letter carriers to change, nor was it for a letter carrier not to stop at every house. The chair also observed that Shaw pointed out the applicant as a person of note immediately upon turning onto the street. As well, the chair did not accept Shaw's evidence that the applicant was crossing the street back and forth in an unusual manner. Finally, the chair concluded that Shaw would not have noticed that the applicant knocked on a door but did not deliver mail had his suspicions not already been improperly heightened. The chair accepted the applicant's evidence that he was intimidated and treated disrespectfully by Shaw.

The Chief of the Toronto Police Service and the Toronto Police Services Board were found to be liable for the discriminatory actions of Shaw. The applicant was granted $10,000 for his losses arising out of the infringement of the code and post-judgment interest.

You Make the Call!

1. Do you agree with the decision of the hearing officer? Why or why not?
2. What challenges do the "principles" set out by the hearing officer pose for investigations of cases where discrimination is alleged?
3. In the debate over racial profiling, some police observers have argued that profiling is "just good police work." In this case, the patrol constables determined that a person was "out of place" in the neighbourhood. What would be your response to this assertion?

Source: Ian B. Johnstone B.Sc., LL.B., LL.M., Johnstone Daniels & Cowling LLP.

Key Points Review

1. Canada is a diverse country, which has significant implications for police work.
2. In recent years, efforts have been made by Canadian police services to address the needs of the gay/lesbian/bisexual/transgender communities.
3. Two issues that have been flashpoints between the police and visible minority communities are bias-free policing and racial profiling.
4. Racial profiling can lead to racial discrimination, which may manifest itself overtly, subconsciously, or systemically.
5. Two police practices that are associated with racial profiling are over-policing and pretext policing.
6. Historically, police–Aboriginal relations have been characterized by hostility and mutual distrust.
7. The "Starlight Tours" in Saskatoon revealed that at least two members of the department held racist attitudes toward Aboriginal people.
8. Aboriginal people residing in urban centres face challenges that may result in high levels of contact with the police.
9. Policing in the Canadian North presents police officers with unique challenges.

Key Term Questions

1. Define **bias-free policing**.
2. Define **racial profiling** and note why this is an important consideration in any study of the police and visible minorities.
3. How are the concepts of **overpolicing** and **pretext policing** related to racial profiling?
4. Why is police work in northern communities described as **high visibility/ high consequence policing**?

Notes

1. G. Ben-Porat, "Policing Multi-Cultural States: Lessons from the Canadian Model," *Policing and Society* 18, no. 4 (2008): 411–25.

2. Statistics Canada, "Study: Projections of the Diversity of the Canadian Population" (Ottawa: 2010), http://www.statcan.gc.ca/daily-quotidien/100309/dq100309a-eng.htm

3. Canada, Department of Justice, "Canadian Human Rights Act" (1985), 1, http://laws-lois.justice.gc.ca/eng/acts/h-6

4. D.C. Chu and J. H.-C. Song, "A Comparison of Chinese Immigrants' Perceptions of the Police in New York City and Toronto," *Crime and Delinquency*, forthcoming.

5. A. Cherney, "Gay and Lesbian Issues in Policing," *Current Issues in Criminal Justice* 11, no. 1 (1999): 35–52.

6. K. Radford, J. Betts, and M. Ostermeyer, *Policing, Accountability, and the Lesbian, Gay, and Bisexual Community in Northern Ireland* (Belfast: Institute for Conflict Research, 2006), http://www.nipolicingboard.org.uk/lgb_book1-2.pdf; K.R. Wolff and C.L. Cokely, "'To Protect and to Serve?' An Exploration of Police Conduct in Relation to the Gay, Lesbian, Bisexual, and Transgender Community," *Sexuality and Culture* 11, no. 2 (2007): 1–23.

7. New South Wales Police Force, "Policy on Sexuality and Gender Diversity, 2011–2014: Working with Gay, Lesbian, Bisexual, Transgender, and Intersex People" (Parramatta: 2011), http://www.police.nsw.gov.au/_data/assets/pdf_file/0007/195154/Sexuality_and_Gender_Policy_Doc_LRES.pdf

8. Canadian Association of Chiefs of Police, "Bias-Free Policing," (2004), 7, http://www.cacp.ca/media.resolutions/efiles/38/Resolution2004Eng.pdf

9. L. Fridell, R. Lunney, D. Diamond, and B. Kubu, "Racially Biased Policing: A Principled Response" (Washington: Police Executive Research Forum, 2001), 5, http://www.cops.usdoj.gov/files/RIC/Publications/raciallybiasedpolicing.pdf

10. Human Rights Tribunal of Ontario, *McKay v. Toronto Police Services Board*, 2011 HRTO 499, 15, (Toronto: 2011), http://www.canlii.org/en/on/onhrt/doc/2011/2011hrto499/2011hrto499.html

11. Rubin, in ibid., 16.

12. T.I. Gabor, "Inflammatory Rhetoric on Racial Profiling Can Undermine Police Services," *Canadian Journal of Criminology and Criminal Justice* 46, no. 4 (2004): 457–66.

13. D. M. Tanovich, *The Colour of Justice: Policing Race in Canada* (Toronto: Irwin Law, 2006), http://www.ottawapolice.ca

14. Toronto Police Service, "2009 Update to the Environmental Scan" (Toronto: 2009), http://www.torontopolice.on.ca/publications/files/reports/2009envscan.pdf

15. Centre for Research–Action on Race Relations, "Quebec Police Ethics Tribunal to Hear CRARR-Assisted Cases of Police Misconduct Filed by Black Montrealers" (2010), http://www.crarr.org/?q=node/403

16. Ibid.

17. Ontario Provincial Police, "Environmental Scan 2010" (Orillia: 2010), 61, http://www.policecouncil.ca/reports.OPP_Env_Scan_2010.pdf

18. S. Perreault, "Violent Victimization of Aboriginal People in the Canadian Provinces, 2009" (Ottawa: Statistics Canada, 2011), http://www.statcan.gc.ca/pub/85-002-x/20101001/article/11415-eng.pdf

19. Mr. Justice R.A. Cawsey (Chair), "Justice on Trial: Report of the Task Force on the Criminal Justice System and Its Impact on the Indian and Metis People of Alberta," vol. 1: Main Report (Edmonton: Attorney General and Solicitor General of Alberta, 1991); Commission on First Nations and Metis Peoples and Justice Reform, "Legacy of Hope: An Agenda for Change," vol. 1: Final Report (Regina: Department of Justice, 2004); Associate Chief Justice A.C. Hamilton and Associate Chief Judge C.M. Sinclair, "Report of the Aboriginal Justice Inquiry of Manitoba: The Justice System and Aboriginal People," vol. 1 (Winnipeg: Queen's Printer, 1991).

20. RCMP, "Native Spirituality Guide" (Ottawa: 2010), 10, http://www.rcmp-grc.gc.ca/pubs/abo-aut/spirit-spiridualite-eng.htm

21. R.T. Fitzgerald and P.J. Carrington, "The Neighbourhood Context of Urban Aboriginal Crime," *Canadian Journal of Criminology and Criminal Justice* 50, no. 5 (2008): 523–57.

22. Ekos Research Associates and Anishinabek Consultants, Inc., "Survey of First Nations People Living Off-Reserve, Métis and Inuit" (Ottawa: Indian and Northern Affairs Canada, 2006), http://knet.ca/documents/OFF_RESERVE_SURVEY_E1.pdf

23. Environics Institute, "Urban Aboriginal Peoples Study" (Toronto: 2010), http://uaps.ca/wp-content/uploads/2010/04/UAPS-FULL-REPORT.pdf

24. N. Macdonald, "Northern Blight: Canada's Real Violent-Crime Hot Spot Is Three Tiny Cities in the North," *Macleans* (March 26, 2009), http://ww2.macleans.ca/2009/03/26/northern-blight/.

25. S. Dunn, "Police Officers Murdered in the Line of Duty, 1961 to 2009" (Ottawa: Statistics Canada, 2010), http://www.statcan.gc.ca/pub/85-002-x/2010003/article/11354-eng.htm

26. S. Perrault and T.H. Mahony, "Criminal Victimization in the Territories, 2009," *Juristat* (Ottawa: Minister of Industry, 2012), http://www.statcan.gc.ca/pub/85-002-x/2012001/article/11614-eng.pdf

27. P. White, "The Trials of Nunavut: Lament for an Arctic Nation," *Globe and Mail*, April 3, 2011.

28. G. Galloway, "Mounties Pulled from Cape Dorset After Rash of Gunplay," *Globe and Mail*, October 16, 2010, A10.

29. C.T. Griffiths, G. Saville, D.S. Wood, and E. Zellerer, *Crime, Law and Justice Among Inuit in the Baffin Region, N.W.T, Canada* (Burnaby: Criminology Research Centre, Simon Fraser University, 1995).

30. Ibid., 50–51.

31. Ibid.

32. RCMP, "Results—RCMP Employee Opinion Survey" (Ottawa: 2009), http://www.rcmp-grc.gc.ca/surveys-sondages/2009/emp/empl2009_result-eng.htm

33. Ibid., 30.

34. S. Watt, "RCMP FNCPS Review" (Ottawa: Royal Canadian Mounted Police, 2008), http://www.pssg.gov.bc.ca/police_services/publications/other/fncpsreview.pdf

Glossary

allocated patrol time the amount of time that patrol officers spend responding to calls from the general public (p. 116)

arrest warrant a document that permits a police officer to arrest a specific person for a specific reason (p. 140)

basic qualifications the minimum requirements for candidates applying for employment in policing (p. 81)

best practices organizational, administrative, and operational strategies that are effective in preventing and responding to crime (p. 21)

bias-free policing the requirement that police officers make decisions on the basis of reasonable suspicion and probable grounds rather than stereotypes (p. 282)

blue-light syndrome an attitudinal set that emphasizes the high-risk/action component of police work (p. 95)

broken windows approach the view that if minor crimes are left unaddressed an environment for more serious crime will be created (p. 228)

call shedding a strategy to discard or divert calls for service to match available police resources (p. 114)

call stacking prioritizing calls for service (p. 114)

Canadian Charter of Rights and Freedoms a component of the Constitution Act that guarantees basic rights and freedoms (p. 32)

Canadian Police Information Centre (CPIC) the centralized, computer-based information system used by police services (p. 112)

careerism individual police officers putting their professional interests above those of the police service (p. 100)

circumstantial evidence evidence not directly observed but that can implicate an offender (p. 253)

clearance rate the percentage of cases in which an offence has been committed and a suspect identified, regardless of whether the suspect is ultimately convicted of a crime (p. 194)

code of ethics a policy that establishes standards of behaviour for police officers (p. 167)

code of silence officers protecting one another from outside scrutiny and criticism (p. 94)

cold case squads specialized units that focus on unsolved serious crimes (p. 267)

collaborative policing the cooperation between public and private police (p. 23)

Commission for Public Complaints Against the RCMP (CPC) an independent civilian body that receives complaints made by citizens against sworn and civilian members of the RCMP (p. 60)

community engagement police strategies that facilitate the involvement of citizens and communities in initiatives to address crime and social disorder (p. 199)

community policing a philosophy of policing centred on police–community partnerships and problem solving (p. 197)

competency-based training recruit training that focuses on the acquisition of specific skills and knowledge (p. 89)

Compstat a strategy designed to increase the effectiveness and efficiency of police services while holding police personnel accountable for achieving crime reduction objectives (p. 238)

Constitution Act, 1867 legislation that includes provisions that define the responsibilities of the federal and provincial governments in the area of criminal justice (p. 32)

contract policing an arrangement whereby the RCMP and the Ontario Provincial Police provide provincial and municipal policing services (p. 40)

crime analysis a systematic approach to crime prevention and crime response based on the analysis of statistical and other data (p. 237)

crime attack strategies proactive operations by the police to target and apprehend criminal offenders (p. 229)

crime displacement relocation of crime from one place, time, target, offence, or tactic to another due to effective crime prevention and crime response initiatives. (p. 236)

crime reduction a holistic approach to crime that focuses on the people, places, and situations where criminal activity occurs (p. 225)

Criminal Code federal legislation that sets out criminal law, procedures for prosecuting federal offences, and sentences and procedures for the administration of justice (p. 33)

criminal profiling a strategy to identify suspects by constructing biographical and psychological sketches based on crime scene evidence (p. 261)

critical incident stress the physiological, psychological, physical, and emotional reactions that may occur in an individual who has been involved in a traumatic incident, e.g., patrol officers involved in a fatal shooting (p. 160)

DNA genetic information that can be used in case investigations (p. 263)

dark figure of crime the difference between how much crime occurs and how much crime is reported to or discovered by the police (p. 49)

demonstrated threat the level of potential danger posed by a person confronted by police officers, generally in the form of weapons or levels of resistance (p. 148)

dependent model (of investigation) the practice of police investigating themselves (p. 63)

differential police response (DPR) categorizing calls for service based on the response required; e.g., patrol car/no patrol car (p. 115)

direct evidence evidence in criminal investigations that is detected through one of the five senses (p. 253)

discretion the freedom to choose among different options when confronted with the need to make a decision (p. 34)

environmental scan a study designed to identify trends that may impact demands on the police (p. 21)

external elements (of community policing) police-community partnerships that enhance community policing and increase police legitimacy, visibility, and accessibility. (p. 203)

First Nations Policing Policy a framework that allows First Nations to negotiate a policing arrangement suitable to their needs (p. 44)

force options model provides police officers with a working model that sets out the course of action to be taken in use-of-force situations (p. 147)

frankpledge system a system of maintaining order in early England (p. 4)

geographic profiling the analysis of behaviour patterns that relate to space or geography, with particular reference to the journey to crime (p. 261)

high visibility/high consequence policing police work in northern communities that places officers under constant scrutiny; also, the high impact of their decisions (p. 293)

hue and cry in early England, the requirement that able-bodied men assist the police (p. 3)

hypervigilance elevated alertness about potential dangers in the environment (p. 95)

iceberg (80/20) rule the view that crime is only a visible symptom of much larger problems (p. 228)

independent model (of investigation) a complaint procedure in which civilians conduct all phases of the investigation (p. 68)

information a written statement sworn by a police officer alleging that a person has committed a specific criminal offence (p. 140)

in-service training training courses for serving police officers (p. 92)

intelligence-led policing (ILP) the application of criminal intelligence analysis to facilitate crime reduction and prevention (p. 238)

interdependent model (of investigation) a procedure for complaint investigation with varying degrees of civilian involvement (p. 67)

interoperability the sharing of case file and database information among police services and criminal justice agencies (p. 50)

Justice of the Peace Act (1361) centralized peacekeeping duties under justices of the peace (p. 5)

less lethal force option (lower lethality) a control technique that is highly unlikely to cause death or serious injury (p. 150)

linkage blindness the investigative failure to recognize a pattern linking one crime with one or more others (p. 258)

major case management model the protocol for conducting investigations (p. 250)

method-oriented special units police units that are distinguished by specialized equipment and tactics (p. 248)

Metropolitan Police Act (1829) established a full-time, unarmed police force in London (p. 6)

Mr. Big technique a controversial investigative strategy designed to secure confessions from crime suspects (p. 268)

Noble Cause Corruption a view by police officers that the ends justify the means (misconduct) (p. 172)

Office of the Independent Police Review Director (OIPRD) a civilian agency in Ontario responsible for receiving complaints about the police (p. 61)

one-plus-one (use of force standard) the generally accepted use-of-force standard that police officers have the authority to use one higher level of force than that with which they are confronted (p. 150)

Ontario Civilian Police Commission (OCPC) oversees police services in Ontario and hears appeals of officers who have been disciplined (p. 61)

operational field training instructing the recruit in how to apply principles from the training academy in the community (p. 93)

organizational elements (of community policing) how a police service is structured to implement community policing (p. 200)

overpolicing a disproportionate police focus on a racialized population or neighbourhood (p. 282)

parapolice unarmed officers who generally have special constable status (p. 44)

pluralization of policing the expansion of policing beyond the public police to include parapolice and private security (p. 23)

police acts the legislative framework for police services (p. 59)

police boards (*also* police commissions) bodies that provide oversight of police (p. 59)

police legitimacy the collective actions taken by the police to enhance the levels of trust and confidence that citizens have in the police (p. 206)

policing standards provisions that set out how police services are to be maintained and delivered (p. 59)

preferred qualifications requirements that increase the competitiveness of applicants seeking employment in policing (p. 81)

pretext policing police stops or searches for a minor reason that are used for more intrusive intervention (p. 282)

previously experienced officers (PEOs) in-service police officers who are interested in leaving their current police service (p. 92)

primary crime prevention programs prevention programs designed to alter the conditions that provide opportunities for criminal offences (p. 221)

principle of transfer and exchange the assumption that physical evidence is transferred during the commission of a criminal offence (p. 257)

problem-oriented policing (POP) a tactical strategy based on the idea that the police should address the causes of recurrent crime and disorder (p. 227)

problem-oriented special units investigative units that focus on specific types of offenders or criminal activities (p. 248)

professional model of police work a model of police work that emerged during the mid-twentieth century that was based on random patrol, rapid response, and reactive investigation (p. 193)

racial profiling police targeting of members of a particular racial group, on the basis of the supposed criminal propensity of the entire group (p. 282)

RCMP External Review Committee an oversight body of the RCMP that hears appeals from RCMP officers who have been disciplined (p. 60)

recipes for action the actions taken and decisions made by patrol officers in various types of encounter situations (p. 122)

restorative justice an approach based on the principle that criminal behaviour injures the victim, the community, and the offender (p. 231)

rotten apples individual police officer misconduct (p. 168)

rotten barrels group misconduct by police officers (p. 168)

rotten orchards misconduct by a police service (p. 168)

Royal Canadian Mounted Police Act federal legislation that provides the framework for the operations of the RCMP (p. 33)

SARA (scanning, analysis, response, assessment) a problem-solving model for police (p. 228)

search warrant a document that permits the police to search a specific location and take items that might be evidence of a crime (p. 144)

secondary crime prevention programs programs that focus on areas that produce crime and disorder (p. 223)

selective (or situational) enforcement discretionary enforcement due to the inability of police officers to enforce all of the laws at all times (p. 121)

Sir Robert Peel founded the first organized police service (p. 6)

smoking gun investigations cases in which the perpetrator is readily identifiable (p. 251)

soft skills (of police work) patrol officer skills sets centred on information collection, communication, and conflict resolution (p. 119)

Special Investigations Unit (SIU) a civilian agency that investigates serious police incidents in Ontario (p. 61)

Staff Relations Representative Program in lieu of a union, a program that provides RCMP officers with a way to express their concerns to management (p. 42)

Statute of Winchester (1285) a statute that made policing a community responsibility (p. 5)

strategic planning the identification of police priorities and objectives and associated resource requirements (p. 237)

symbolic assailants individuals encountered by patrol officers who display mannerisms and behaviours that suggest the potential for violence (p. 123)

task (or policing] environment the organizational context and the community or areas in which patrol officers carry out their activities (p. 124)

tertiary crime prevention programs programs designed to prevent adults and youths from reoffending (p. 223)

three P's of community policing prevention, problem solving, and partnership (p. 197)

three R's of professional police work random patrol, rapid response, reactive investigation, which are the basis of the professional model of police work (p. 193)

tired cop syndrome a jet-lag state of police officers, primarily due to shift work (p. 101)

typifications how patrol officers depict or categorize the people and situations they encounter (p. 122)

unallocated patrol time the amount of time that patrol officers have that is not committed to responding to calls for service (p. 117)

ViCLAS Violent Crime Linkage Analysis System; a system used by investigators that includes information on predatory and sexual crimes of violence (p. 261)

victim-precipitated homicide ("suicide by cop") an incident in which the victim acts in a manner calculated to provoke the use of deadly force on the part of the police (p. 157)

"W" system the approach used by police dispatchers to determine key facts about a call (p. 112)

whodunit investigations cases in which the suspect is unknown and extensive investigation is required (p. 251)

working personality of police officers a set of attitudinal and behavioural attributes of police officers (p. 94)

zone (team or turf) policing a deployment strategy designed to enhance community policing (p. 203)

Index

NOTE: Page numbers followed by *f* and *t* denotes figures and tables, respectively. Page numbers italicized denote photos/illustrations.